CRIMINAL LAW REFORM NOW

If you could change one part of the criminal law, what would it be?

The editors put this question to nine leading academics and practitioners. The first nine chapters of the collection present their responses in the form of legal reform proposals, with topics ranging across criminal law, criminal justice and evidence – including confiscation, control orders, criminal attempts, homicide, assisted dying, the special status of children, time restrictions on prosecution, the right of silence, and special measures in court. Each chapter is followed by a comment from a different author, providing an additional expert view on each reform proposal. Finally, the last two chapters broaden the debate to discuss criminal law reform in general, examining various reform bodies and mechanisms across England, Wales and Scotland. *Criminal Law Reform Now* highlights and explores the current reform debates that matter most to legal experts, with each chapter making a case for positive change.

Criminal Law Reform Now

Proposals and Critique

Edited by
J J Child
and
R A Duff

•HART•
OXFORD • LONDON • NEW YORK • NEW DELHI • SYDNEY

HART PUBLISHING

Bloomsbury Publishing Plc

Kemp House, Chawley Park, Cumnor Hill, Oxford, OX2 9PH, UK

1385 Broadway, New York, NY 10018, USA

HART PUBLISHING, the Hart/Stag logo, BLOOMSBURY and the Diana logo are trademarks of Bloomsbury Publishing Plc

First published in Great Britain 2019

Reprinted 2020

A catalogue record for this book is available from the British Library.

Library of Congress Cataloging-in-Publication data

Names: Criminal Law Reform Now (2016 : University of Sussex) | Child, John (John J.). editor. | Duff, Antony, editor.

Title: Criminal law reform now : proposals and critique / edited by J J Child and R A Duff.

Description: Oxford, UK : Hart Publishing, 2019. | Includes index. | Includes papers from "a three-day conference at the University of Sussex in September 2016 … entitled Criminal Law Reform Now"—ECIP introduction.

Identifiers: LCCN 2018028442 (print) | LCCN 2018030721 (ebook) | ISBN 9781509916795 (Epub) | ISBN 9781509916771 (hardback : alk. paper)

Subjects: LCSH: Criminal law—Great Britain—Congresses. | Law reform—Great Britain—Congresses. | Great Britain. Law Commission—Congresses. | Scottish Law Commission—Congresses. | LCGFT: Conference papers and proceedings.

Classification: LCC KD7869.A2 (ebook) | LCC KD7869.A2 C75 2016 (print) | DDC 345.41—dc23

LC record available at https://lccn.loc.gov/2018028442

ISBN: HB: 978-1-50991-677-1
ePDF: 978-1-50991-678-8
ePub: 978-1-50991-679-5

Typeset by Compuscript Ltd, Shannon
Printed and bound in Great Britain by TJ International Ltd, Padstow, Cornwall

To find out more about our authors and books visit www.hartpublishing.co.uk. Here you will find extracts, author information, details of forthcoming events and the option to sign up for our newsletters.

CONTENTS

List of Contributors vii
Introduction ix

1. *Reflections on Proceeds of Crime: A New Code for Confiscation?* 1
   Michael Levi
   Comment from Colin King 25
2. *Rationalising Civil Preventive Orders: Opportunities for Reform* 37
   Stephen Shute
   Comment from Zachary Hoskins 67
3. *Reforming the Law of Criminal Attempt: Take Two* 75
   Shachar Eldar
   Comment from JJ Child 92
4. *Done to Death? Reform of Homicide Law* 101
   Sally Kyd
   Comment from Simon McKay 124
5. *The CPS, Policy-Making and Assisted Dying: Towards a 'Freedom' Approach* 133
   Andrew Sanders
   Comment from RA Duff 155
6. *How Should the Criminal Law Respond to the 'Special Status' of Children?* 165
   Heather Keating
   Comment from Gideon Yaffe 184
7. *The Time Limit on Prosecutions for Underage Sexual Intercourse in the Sexual Offences Act 1956: A Continuing Problem* 193
   Jonathan Rogers
   Comment from Hannah Quirk 214
8. *Safe and Effective Courtroom Participation for Domestic Violence Complainant-Witnesses* 223
   Charlotte Bishop
   Comment from Vanessa Munro 243

9. *The Case for Restoring the Right of Silence* ... 253
Hannah Quirk

Comment from Abenaa Owusu-Bempah ... 270

10A. *'Lawyers' Law' and the Limitations and Flaws of the Role of Reform Bodies in Criminal Law* ... 279
Peter Alldridge

10B. *Criminal Law Reform: A View from Across the Border* ... 293
Pamela R. Ferguson

Index ... 307

LIST OF CONTRIBUTORS

Peter Alldridge, Drapers' Professor of Law, Queen Mary, University of London, UK

Charlotte Bishop, Lecturer in Law, University of Exeter, UK

JJ Child, Senior Lecturer in Law, University of Birmingham, UK & Co-Director of the Criminal Law Reform Now Network

RA Duff, Professor Emeritus in Philosophy at the University of Stirling, UK

Shachar Eldar, Professor of Law, Ono Academic College, Israel

Pamela R Ferguson, Professor of Scots Law, University of Dundee, UK

Zachary Hoskins, Assistant Professor, Philosophy, University of Nottingham, UK

Heather Keating, Professor of Criminal Law & Criminal Responsibility, University of Sussex, UK

Colin King, Reader in Law, University of Sussex, UK

Sally Kyd, Professor, Leicester Law School, University of Leicester, UK

Michael Levi, Professor, School of Social Sciences, Cardiff University, UK

Simon McKay, Barrister, UK

Vanessa Munro, Professor, Law School, University of Warwick, UK

Abenaa Owusu-Bempah, Assistant Professor of Law, London School of Economics, UK

Hannah Quirk, Reader in Criminal Law, King's College London, UK

Jonathan Rogers, Lecturer in Criminal Justice, University of Cambridge, UK & Co-Director of the Criminal Law Reform Now Network

Andrew Sanders, Professor of Criminal Law & Criminology, University of Sussex, UK

Stephen Shute, Professor of Criminal Law and Criminal Justice, Pro-Vice-Chancellor, University of Sussex, UK

Gideon Yaffe, Professor of Law, Philosophy and Psychology, Yale University, USA

INTRODUCTION

JJ CHILD & RA DUFF

There is plenty about our systems of criminal law, in England and Wales and in Scotland, that needs reform; there are plenty of groups working to reform particular aspects of our criminal law. There are also two Law Commissions, for England and Wales and for Scotland, whose responsibilities cover law reform more generally – although they are not of course concerned only with criminal law. Each Law Commission develops regular 'Programmes of Reform' to guide its work over a number of years: the Law Commission for England and Wales published its 13th Programme in December 2017; the Scottish Law Commission produced its Tenth Programme in January 2018; in both cases, the Programme was based on a process of wide consultation. Law Commissions, both here and abroad, perform essential work in improving the quality of law reform, and provide an invaluable link between legal experts and the reform process. What is missing, however, is any systematic inquiry into the possibilities of, and needs for, *criminal* law reform – an inquiry that would engage practitioners, policy makers, academics, and citizens in the discussion of criminal law reform, and whose results could then help the Law Commissions (and other reform-oriented agencies) in developing concrete reform proposals. This book marks the first stage of a new project (described further below), which is intended to promote this kind of inquiry.

Criminal Law Reform Now brings together a set of legal experts to debate contemporary proposals for change within the criminal law. The first nine chapters of this volume outline and defend these proposals, with topics ranging across criminal law, criminal justice and evidence – including confiscation, control orders, criminal attempts, homicide, assisted dying, the special status of children, time restrictions on prosecution, the right of silence, and special measures in court. Each chapter is followed by a comment, providing an additional expert view on each reform proposal. Finally, the last two chapters broaden the debate to discuss criminal law reform in general, examining various reform bodies and mechanisms across England, Wales and Scotland.

The reform proposals in this volume were first discussed at a three-day conference at the University of Sussex in September 2016. The conference, also entitled *Criminal Law Reform Now*, provided the forum for a host of reform ideas to be presented, and then debated in round-table workshops. The conference was designed to coincide with the consultation on the 13th Programme for the Law Commission of England and Wales, and short papers from the conference were delivered to the Commission as consultation responses. We were very happy to engage with the Commission's work during the conference, and grateful for the presence of Professor David Ormerod QC (Criminal Law Commissioner) who gave some further insights into the Commission's working priorities. The conference was generously supported by funding from the University of Sussex, the Sussex Crime Research Centre, and the ESRC; and was ably assisted by Dr Susann Wiedlitzka.

The current volume represents one of two initiatives stemming from the September conference. The aim of this book is to present a selection of the reform ideas discussed at the conference to a wider audience. The task for authors in this volume has been to present the best case for a particular criminal law reform, as well as to explore *how* this reform might be best achieved; although each proposal began life as a consultation response to the Law Commission, several chapters recognise and explore alternative potential routes to reform that might be more appropriate to the proposal under discussion. In this manner, the book aims to provide a snap-shot of contemporary reform ideas within the criminal law, practical insights into how these ideas might best be taken forward, as well as expert commentary on each chapter from a second expert. Our ambition is to host similar conferences, and to produce collections of this kind, in line with future Law Commission consultations on reform.

The second initiative stemming from the conference has been the establishment of a new *Criminal Law Reform Now Network* (www.clrnn.co.uk). Launched in 2017, and supported by AHRC funding, the CLRN Network's mission is to facilitate collaboration between academics and other legal experts to gather proposals for criminal law reform, and to disseminate them in an accessible way to the wider community. It aims to include members of the public and mainstream media as well as legal professionals, police, policy makers and politicians. Its proposals will sometimes require legislation, but it is not restricted to such projects. Reforms that public bodies such as the Home Office, Police or CPS can bring about by internal policies may be explored, as well as reforms that require the support of some of the judiciary, bearing in mind the proper constraints on judicial law making. The first two projects undertaken by the CLRN Network are reviews of the Computer Misuse Act 1990 and of the current mechanisms for private prosecution.

We would like to thank all those who have contributed to this collection, and the publishing team at Hart, as well as those involved in the other projects discussed above. Criminal law reform is one of the most direct ways in which experts can engage with and improve the legal landscape in which they work, and in which we all live; it is a project we believe in passionately.

1

Reflections on Proceeds of Crime: A New Code for Confiscation?

MICHAEL LEVI*

The reform of law is a political process, and the elements of underlying political pressures – as well as the difficulties thrown up by cases brought or wanted to be brought – have a strong influence on prioritisation of issues in the scarce space available in Parliamentary timetables. This chapter will review the cultural and political background behind measures to combat proceeds of crime, the history of legislation and implementation, and the contemporary case for change.

The proceeds of crime confiscation are socially and politically attractive for a range of reasons. Confiscation and forfeiture are socially restorative in a visible way that takes away something criminals have acquired and feel that they have ownership of, even if they know it is not legal; they offer a prospective general deterrence or at least crime reduction, through the common sense assumption (not proven empirically) that criminals will not offend at all or will offend less if they become aware that they will not be able to keep the funds that they have 'acquired'; and they offer some compensation to identifiable victims, to society and (via a sometimes controversial incentives scheme) to cover police, prosecutors and the courts for enforcement costs in the use of financial investigation, asset freezing and other mechanisms to pursue assets.[1] Confiscation and asset recovery also offer something for diverse political and even ideological constituencies. For NGOs and development aid agencies in the Global North and South, there are prospects of deprivation of the proceeds of Grand Corruption (which usually involves offences committed in other jurisdictions, in which the UK or

* I would also like to thank Tristram Hicks and Russell Smith for their comments on an earlier draft.

[1] Whether this amounts to actual profit in the UK or other parts of Europe is doubtful, since it would be a rare individual case in which the sums actually confiscated outweighed the total investigation cost, and even if that were true for an individual case, it would be unlikely to be true for enforcement costs as a whole. I exclude here those crimes for which compensation is paid out of a confiscation order. Note that this demand for profitability in asset recovery is not applied to other areas of policing and ignores other social benefits of confiscation.

other major financial centres are trusted locations for assets and may also be where the bribe-paying companies – if not their actual bribe-paying intermediaries – are located).[2] Sanctions and asset freezing supplement banking and corporate due diligence by placing some funds 'beyond use', thereby reducing terrorism capacity for legally designated individuals, networks and Rogue States[3] – an impact also claimed for freezing and confiscation on transnational organised criminals. For the public, stripping undeserving criminals – from local dealers to transnational traffickers and from full time criminals to otherwise respectable fraudsters – of the fruits of their crimes offers the hope that this will reduce the extent to which they serve as negative role models for young people in their communities and offers some symbolic satisfaction. In societies which crave public signals to offenders to deter them from vice and to show the virtuous that crime does not pay, proceeds of crime freezing and recovery is important.

Consequently, the *public* failure to achieve those objectives counts as humiliation for the State and civil society. Levels of proceeds confiscation have failed to meet official hopes for major financial impact. The public, like the media and indeed governments, may not 'connect up' the large (if empirically contested by scholars) 'estimates' of money laundering and the 'costs of organised crime' with the relatively puny criminal assets confiscated or even frozen: however it is not intellectually tenable to argue that confiscation is successful at the same time as asserting that criminals are making sums in the trillions while confiscation globally barely struggles into the billions of dollars, euros or pounds.[4] It appears that criminals are cocking a snook at the State's efforts to inhibit their lifestyle. Added to the dramatic demonology of crime itself, this somehow makes the grievance of lack of redress and 'just deserts' worse. If it turns out that offenders' vehicles and other apparent 'assets' are hired or borrowed and are beyond the reach of confiscation or forfeiture, and that suspects and convicted persons cannot be stopped from making use of these 'undeserved' facilities, it may evoke the same resentments (or sometimes envy) at lack of entitlement as the stereotype of social security fraud, and even worse if the public can see (or imagine) them continuing to do visible harm in their neighbourhoods. It may contribute to de-legitimate the State's claims about its capacity and motivation to control 'serious crime'. Hence the long-term efforts of the police to monitor and act against the Adams 'gangster' family in London, which have occupied the courts in relation to Serious Crime Prevention Orders and confiscation.[5]

[2] See, eg, *A&A v DPP* [2016] EWCA 1393, a case very competently heard by a single judge, confirmed on appeal, involving funds allegedly stolen or skimmed from the Kuwaiti government.

[3] Though except for Iranian and Libyan funds, the sums frozen for designated individuals and networks are very modest.

[4] One can bulk up confiscation data with civil racketeering penalties and those for financial services 'misconduct': but these stretch the concept and fines may not reflect levels of laundering.

[5] It took a decade from the confiscation order following a money laundering conviction in 2007 for the courts to get Terry Adams to repay the confiscation order which, with substantial interest, amounted to £1.1 million. See *Adams v CPS* [2017] All ER 169. Even this sum would buy only a modest house in their part of London.

Despite the narrow framework of recent National Audit Office and Parliamentary reports (reasonably in the case of the NAO progress updates)[6] – excluding HMRC civil fraud recovery and police cash forfeitures – it is important to appreciate that the problems of pursuing offender assets are neither new nor are they restricted to the British and formerly British Isles (including the Irish Republic). A reader of the above reports would be unaware of the EU network of MS Asset Recovery Offices, the Europol-based Camden Asset Recovery Inter-Agency Network,[7] and the wealth of British, Dutch and Italian – indeed pan-EU and Council of Europe – empirical as well as legal research on this subject.[8] Whether pre- or post-Brexit, the UK must deal with its crime problems on a national basis as well as by cooperation or pressure in international cases, which has improved in recent years. In reviewing existing approaches, the UK should consider practices in non-Anglophone countries and also what might be possible in international applications. Though modest regular recoveries from lower level criminals may have more crime reduction effect, more critical detailed attention is needed to the sorts of cases that generate larger and unsuccessful recoveries internationally, to examine whether success and failure are associated with case mix rather than particularities of confiscation regimes, and also whether more can be done to recover criminal assets held overseas that were neglected when POCA was drafted.[9] The Public Accounts Committee noted with resignation:

> While the amount confiscated has increased from £133 million in 2012–13 to £175 million in 2015–16, the number of confiscation orders imposed has fallen and debt has soared to £1.9 billion. Furthermore, weaknesses previously identified, such as unclear objectives and ineffective incentives for the many bodies involved in the system and poor performance information, still remain.[10]

The figures above are simply gross and net confiscation order values. However, the choice between metrics of asset recovery performance – per capita population, per recorded crime (or sub-set of crimes), per amount *reasonably* estimated to be proceeds of crime domestically and imported, per amount frozen or only actually confiscated or recovered – have not received serious analysis in formal papers by the Financial Action Task Force (hereafter, FATF), International

[6] National Audit Office, *Confiscation Orders: Cost Estimate Methodology* (2013); National Audit Office, *Confiscation Orders: Progress Review* (2016); Home Affairs Committee, *Proceeds of Crime: Fifth Report of* Session 2016–17 (HC 25, 2016).

[7] This rotates but, in 2015, the CARIN Steering Group Member jurisdictions were Bulgaria, Czech Republic, Guernsey, Hungary, Ireland, Netherlands, Spain, Sweden and the USA.

[8] K Ligeti and M Simonato (eds) *Chasing Criminal Money: Challenges and Perspectives On Asset Recovery in the EU* (Hart, 2017); C Atkinson, S Mackenzie, and N Hamilton-Smith, 'A Systematic Review of the Effectiveness of Asset-Focussed Interventions against Organised Crime' (2017) *ESRC, What Works: Crime Reduction Systematic Review Series* 9.

[9] Personal reflections, as a member of the Performance and Innovation Unit steering group and later discussions with officials. For a collection of information on major corruption cases, see *Digest of Asset Recovery Cases* (UNODC, 2015).

[10] *Confiscation Orders: Progress Review* (HC124, 2016) 3.

Financial Institutions (IMF, World Bank), governments or the National Audit Office internationally. Although we should be much warier than the evangelists of change usually are about whether there is a universal 'what works' package to be found in this realm, these experiences may and should teach us that there are broader issues we need to consider even if we are focused solely on restraint and confiscation cases in the UK or England and Wales. Indeed the 'in' here should be carefully considered: the assets of offenders convicted (or investigated) in the UK may be overseas, while assets may be held in the UK by offenders (including but not restricted to kleptocrats) who reside overseas. The Law Commission cannot itself determine extra-territorial restraint and confiscation (though Worldwide Freezing Orders – formerly known as Mareva injunctions – were developed by the English civil courts to deal with financial claims, including misconduct such as Grand Corruption[11]).

Implicit in many reports is the assumption that criminals are Protestant ethic capitalists bent principally on accumulation and on integration of their illicitly acquired proceeds into the respectable economy. It is true that empirical studies of offender lifestyles are thin on the ground, but *Freakonomics* insights such as its chapter 'WHY DO DRUG DEALERS STILL LIVE WITH THEIR MOMS?', as well as more formal academic studies, yield some grounds for scepticism about the centrality of accumulation in criminal motivation.[12] One quantitative study of serious fraud cases in Australia and New Zealand found that more than half of fraudsters simply spent the proceeds of their crimes on luxurious goods and services, with gambling and living expenses accounting for most of the other proceeds. Only 5 per cent of losses were recovered from offenders.[13] And offender expenditure of significant sums on restaurants, clubs, gambling, holidays as well as on personal drugs consumption is unavailable for recovery. (Doubtless, betting firms and casinos would put more effort into customer due diligence if the money lost by criminals from criminality was repayable by them!) Unless confiscation can be made to occur much earlier in the criminal life cycle, this high lifestyle expenditure (by an unknown percentage of serious offenders as well as by most

[11] M Levi, 'Pecunia non olet: Cleansing the Money Launderers from the Temple' (1991) *Crime, Law, and Social Change* 217–302. Brexit may have a negative effect on the cooperation the UK gives and receives from EU MS.

[12] S Levitt and S Dubner, *Freakonomics* (William Morrow & Sons, 2006). PC Van Duyne and M Levi, *Drugs and Money: Managing the Drug Trade and Crime Money in Europe* (Routledge, 2005); PC Van Duyne, 'Mobsters are Human too: Behavioural Science and Organized Crime Investigation' (2000) 34.4 *Crime, Law and Social Change* 369–90; PC van Duyne and M Soudijn, 'Crime-Money in the Financial System: What We Fear and What We Know' in M Herzog-Evans (ed) *Transnational Criminology Manual* (Wolf Legal Publishers, 2010); PC van Duyne, 'Crime-Money and Financial Conduct' in B Unger and D van der Linde (eds) *Research Handbook on Money Laundering* (Elgar, 2013) 232; R Naylor, 'Towards a General Theory of Profit-Driven Crimes' (2003) *British Journal of Criminology* 81–101; D Hobbs, *Lush Life: Constructing Organized Crime in the UK* (OUP, 2014).

[13] RG Smith, *Serious Fraud in Australia and New Zealand* (Australian Institute of Criminology and PricewaterhouseCoopers, 2003).

petty offenders) undermines some of the deterrence argument for proceeds confiscation, which relies on a significant proportion of the proceeds being saved rather than spent as offenders go along.

Thus, the elapsed time between the offence or obtaining proceeds and access to funds being stopped by post-conviction orders or pre-conviction asset restraint becomes the critical period both for deterrence and for asset recovery prospects. Some criminals are apprehended by the police or HMRC in possession of cash, which can be seized immediately with, one might expect, stronger cognitive effects. However, to understand deterrence and deterrability better, we need to avoid the tendency to lump different 'types of criminal' together so that it becomes hard to distinguish motivation and to identify how to discourage. We might therefore look at the difference between criminals who fit the definition of criminal lifestyle and those who do not. As defined by POCA 2002, 'criminal lifestyle' is not about how the money is spent but about how (and how repeatedly) it is obtained. However, we might consider also how money is spent or saved.[14] To the extent that offenders have saved their proceeds, those funds or assets purchased with them will still be available in theory: but whatever moral position POCA 2002 and politicians may adopt in relation to their recuperability, it is unrealistic to think that would ever happen, and the high proportion of outstanding debts accumulating interest among the uncollected totals[15] suggests that writing off those hypothetical obligations would be a sensible policy. Then free of this unnecessary hostage to the public discrediting of system efficiency, we can start again.

I. A Short History

There is a centuries-old tradition of legal rulings and academic disputes about the nature of post-felony confiscation which has influenced common law internationally, but which is not germane here and can be found elsewhere.[16] However, it might be instructive 23 years on to revisit the executive summary of the first British empirical research study,[17] and to see how 'the system' has fared: despite the substantial *percentage* rise in confiscation, massive expansion of the anti-money laundering regime in the private sector and legislation globally, and the attention given to the proceeds of crime issues at regular cross-government committees, many weaknesses identified then remain. This suggests that more substantive

[14] Not that this assumption is true either of the lifestyles of wealthy businesspeople: culturally, we are a world away from Max Weber's Germany.

[15] National Audit Office, *Confiscation Orders: Progress Review* (2016); Home Affairs Committee, *Proceeds of Crime: Fifth Report of* Session 2016–17 (HC 25, House of Commons, 2016).

[16] K Kesselring, 'Felony Forfeiture in England, c.1170–1870' (2009) *The Journal of Legal History* 201–26.

[17] M Levi and L Osofsky, *Investigating, Seizing, and Confiscating the Proceeds of Crime* (Home Office, 1995) 6–8.

changes, rather than mere consolidation changes, may be needed in any Code for Confiscation to generate change.

> No one who reviewed the current state of confiscation of the proceeds of crime in England and Wales in any detail would be likely to judge it a success. To summarise, the main difficulties are as follows:
>
> (1) Relatively few 'Mr Bigs' have been convicted in the courts and consequently, few are available to have their assets confiscated. Indeed, few have been charged, and therefore have not even had their assets frozen.
>
> (2) The confiscation order cannot 'reclaim' the past 'entertainment' expenditures of proceeds of crime by people … who have no apparent assets. Our interviews and what criminological evidence there is on persistent offenders' lifestyles suggests that – except for cash 'floats' and other assets found directly on them, plus sometimes ostentatiously decorated homes – most medium and low-level offenders 'spend as they go' and have low savings ratios …. In fraud and other property crimes where the offender is not caught very soon after the offence, there are unlikely to be sufficient funds remaining even to compensate victims, let alone to yield any surplus to the Treasury.
>
> (3) It is only the recent provisions of the Criminal Justice Act 1993 (CJA 1993) which make it easier to come back to the court if assets are discovered subsequent to the making of a confiscation order, and thus may generate greater sums confiscated in the future …
>
> (4) There is generally no organisational incentive for anyone to deal vigorously with confiscation matters … There are no obvious performance indicators which translate measures of high-level political concern into the working practices of police, prosecutors, and courts. The only possible impact on performance measures within the present framework would be if the financial … incapacitation of individuals subjected to confiscation orders led to a large, visible and attributable diminution in levels of recorded crime in the same geographical areas covered by the unit of investigative/prosecutorial cost. Most of those interviewed in this study agreed that this is unlikely.
>
> (5) Perhaps because confiscation cases are dispersed among so many counsel and judges, and because the issues are essentially civil in nature and consequently are alien grafts upon the criminal justice system, few people are able to gain any real expertise and many still appear to find the process of deciding on benefit and realisable assets confusing and unattractive …
>
> (6) Once an order is imposed, there is little reason for prosecutors or court staff to spend money on enforcing it unless the sums likely to be recovered are estimated obviously (at the time) to exceed the costs of enforcement …. While the pursuit of those offenders' assets which are less than the costs of receivership may deprive offenders of their unlawfully obtained assets – the key principled objective of the legislation – it provides no net benefit, or even generates a net cost, to the prosecutors ….
>
> (7) ….
>
> (8) … the only sanction for defendants' non-co-operation in liquidating assets held overseas to repay confiscation orders was imprisonment …. The extent to which offenders would be prepared to suffer an additional prison sentence in lieu of payment may have been underestimated by those drafting the early legislation.

(9) There are costs and difficulties involved in assessing realisable assets of defendants. The … reluctance of police financial investigators to indicate an amount of realisable property that might be lower than the offender's benefit from crime (which allows the offender to profit from his crimes) mean that some confiscation orders are therefore made in over-optimistically large sums ….

(10) Combined, these factors may explain why confiscation orders constitute such a small proportion of the estimated proceeds of drugs trafficking and other major crimes, and why, in many instances, the amount recovered from cases where orders are imposed is so modest.

In summary, inefficiency and ineffectiveness combine with a lack of timeliness and lack of focus to dilute the deterrent effect to the point of irrelevance. As far as can be deduced from their judgments, some trial and appellate judges at that time were unenthusiastic about or actively resistant to the changes in post-conviction reversal of the burden of proof, and the very limited submissions by legal insiders to the Home Affairs Committee (2016) allege that the judiciary – taken as a whole – still are largely unmotivated and not always well-informed on this complex area of law.[18] The attempt to concentrate expertise was one reason why initially all restraint orders nationally were channelled through a small number of judges at the High Court in London. However, the political enthusiasm for increasing the number of restraint and confiscation cases led to the abandonment of that model, and there has been insufficient empirical analysis of the reasons behind what is generally agreed to be the under-utilisation of restraint orders, which have declined in the latest dataset. Interviews by this author for the then Prime Minister's Strategy Unit a decade ago suggested that the main reasons were the reluctance to employ receivers due to the high gross and net of recoveries prices of the specialist accounting firms; the cost to a constrained CPS budget of applying for orders; and the pressurising impact of restraint orders on the time available to complete the investigation: there is no reason to think that this has changed substantially, despite the lowering of thresholds in the Serious Crime Act 2015.

Most of the attention given to proceeds of crime efforts focusses on the police and anti-organised crime agencies, but as the scope of 'organised crime' has broadened, it is important for the Law Commission and other reformers to take account of its use (or non-use) by non-police agencies. The evidence shows how little financial investigation is used as a tool in dealing with environmental crimes. This may be partly because these violators are not unknown members of organised crime networks who need to be traced or proven to be connected with the violation but are rather otherwise licit corporations. However, the shading between licit and illicit commerce may be difficult to discern in the case of Small and Medium-sized Enterprises (SMEs) and individuals targeted by the Scottish Environmental Protection Agency (SEPA) and, to a lesser extent, the UK Environment Agency, which find difficulty in financing proceeds of crime provisions against local offenders.

[18] Home Affairs Committee, *Proceeds of Crime* (HC 25, 2016).

Thus, SEPA obtained in 2015–16 confiscation orders for £2,356; £41,131; £28,538; and – its largest ever – £345,558.43 under the Proceeds of Crime (Scotland) Act 2002.[19] In one other case, there was a fine of £200,000. The most powerful Scottish gangs were undercutting legitimate operators by ignoring environmental standards or avoiding tax by mixing high-harm waste – that attracts higher rates of taxation for dumping – with low-risk rubbish. In England and Wales, proceeds of crime orders were made in 106 Environment Agency cases in 2011–14 for a total of £9,725,956, averaging £91,754.[20] Subsequently, there have been other cases, some of which show the disparity between modest identified saved assets that have been confiscated and huge profits from crime already spent or hidden away.[21] The footnoted case above had a press notice which does not indicate this disparity but bravely stresses the lifetime burden on waste-dumpers of millions of pounds that are due if those convicted come into assets subsequently. However, to make this a reality would require the surveillance of such offenders, which has a lower institutional priority than for drugs traffickers.

The remainder of this chapter deals with the question of to what extent these 'under-performance' issues are due to problems with legislation, and to what extent they are to do with attitudes, culture, resources and finance. This may require reform of both law and institutions of legal administration: but are these necessary but not sufficient components for enhancing proceeds confiscation, or indeed are they neither necessary nor sufficient conditions? If, for example, the legal mechanisms have little to do with the 'under-performance', then what is likely to have impact on the output or outcome?[22]

II. Proceeds of Crime Recovery: Some International Experiences

It is common for UK studies to look westwards to the United States for thoughts about how to improve the effectiveness of crime control. Superficially, this looks

[19] SEPA, 'Waste Recycling Firm given highest Confiscation Order for Environmental Offences in Scotland' (Press Release, 2016).

[20] Data supplied by the Agency. This does represent a rise from previous levels of orders.

[21] Environment Agency, 'Payback for Illegal Waste Crimes' (Press Release, 2017).

[22] The author has been involved intermittently in proceeds of crime issues since 1993 (and before, if one includes the repealed Criminal Bankruptcy Orders that were once a sanction imposed). He was a member of the Steering Committee of the Performance and Innovation Unit study which led to POCA; worked for the former Prime Minister's Strategy Unit on improving asset confiscation; a Scientific Expert for the Council of Europe conducting studies of how the reversal of the burden of proof was treated in some jurisdictions; the co-author of Matrix Insight and RAND Europe studies of the subject for the European Commission, for the Regulatory Impact Assessment underpinning their political initiative – DIRECTIVE 2014/42/EU OF THE EUROPEAN PARLIAMENT AND OF THE COUNCIL of 3 April 2014 on the freezing and confiscation of instrumentalities and proceeds of crime in the European Union – and a member of the EC Asset Recovery Office expert group from its inception to the present.

promising, for, although the US makes it extraordinarily difficult to work out what the amount confiscated is (and from whom, whether from financial intermediaries or from the primary offenders themselves), there is no doubt that they confiscate a great deal more than the UK does (or indeed than the rest of the world together). The ten-year average of Assets Forfeiture Fund (AFF) is roughly $2 billion per year in deposits and associated expenses. However, the average for the past two years is $1.78 billion per year, essentially the same as it was a decade ago if the dollar amounts are adjusted for inflation.[23] There has been a 40 per cent drop in the number of all cash assets forfeited during the past five years, but their value in 2016 was still $377 million, only $50 million of which was the result of criminal judicial proceeds, the rest mostly arising from administrative proceedings:[24] even this reduced cash seizure total dwarfs the total value of confiscations seized by any mechanisms in the UK. However, that is only part of the story because – as is common in US claims of effectiveness – there is scant empirical evidence, and many components are particular to their system and may not be readily transferrable.[25]

Offenders hide some of their assets and law enforcement agencies fail to trace some or all of them. The police might believe and even have good reason to believe that an offender has assets, but there may be no actual signs of them.[26] Some or all of those assets may in fact have been spent, and unless vendors have been paid over value or recipients have been paid under value in some *provable* exchange, they are, in practice, irrecoverable. Recovery is hindered by the fact that parts of some offenders' assets are located abroad. The analysis of the assets of organised crime offenders in the Netherlands by Kruisbergen et al[27] showed that

[23] US Department of Justice, *10-yr Summary of Financial Report Data* (2017).

[24] US Department of Justice, *5-yr Summary of Seizure and Forfeiture Trends* (2017). Note that in the US Federal jurisdiction, **Criminal forfeiture** is an action brought as a part of the criminal prosecution of a defendant. It is an *in personam* (against the person) action and requires that the government indict (charge) the property used or derived from the crime along with the defendant. If the jury finds the property forfeitable, the court issues an order of forfeiture. For forfeitures pursuant to the Controlled Substances Act (CSA), Racketeer Influenced and Corrupt Organizations (RICO), as well as money laundering and obscenity statutes, there is an ancillary hearing to give any third parties the chance to assert their interest in the property. Once the interests of third parties are addressed, the court issues a final forfeiture order. **Civil judicial forfeiture** is an *in rem* (against the property) action brought in court against the property. The property is the defendant and no criminal charge against the owner is necessary. **Administrative forfeiture** is an *in rem* action that permits the federal seizing agency to forfeit the property without judicial involvement. The authority to start an administrative forfeiture action is found in the Tariff Act 1930, § 1607. Property that can be administratively forfeited is merchandise the importation of which is prohibited; a conveyance used to import, transport, or store a controlled substance; a monetary instrument; or other property that does not exceed $500,000 in value.

[25] M Levi and A Smith, *A Comparative Analysis of Organised Crime Conspiracy Legislation and Practice and their Relevance to England and Wales* (Home Office Online Report, 2002).

[26] K Bullock, D Mann, R Street and C Coxon, *Examining Attrition in Confiscating the Proceeds of Crime* (Home Office, 2009) 14–19; M Fleming, *An examination of the means of establishing the efficacy of asset recovery and anti-money laundering policies* (PhD thesis, University of London, 2008), 86–89.

[27] E Kruisbergen, E Kleemans, and R Kouwenberg, 'Explaining attrition: Investigating and confiscating the profits of organized crime (2016) 13(6) *European Journal of Criminology* 677. See also PC Van Duyne, W de Zanger and F Kristen, 'Greedy of crime money: The reality and ethics of asset recovery'

more than one-third of the real estate and companies owned by them was located in a foreign country, for example in their country of origin (eg, Turkey), making it difficult and comparatively expensive to pursue.[28] As Van Duyne et al argue,[29] a financial investigation is partially a mental attitude, a way of looking at things that can be integrated into the daily routines of police work, and research in several European countries shows that this seldom happens.[30] Although the Dutch Court of Audit concluded that capacity and expertise have improved since 2008,[31] studies show that policy-makers' invocations of the importance of financial investigations are not always implemented.[32] The problem of inconsistent downward policy transmission may be especially acute where (as in England and Wales) constabulary forces are answerable to their Police and Crime Commissioners as well as to government, but it applies even in more centralised systems like the Netherlands.

Kruisbergen et al found that attrition takes place in all phases.[33] For the 102 cases they analysed in detail, the initial public prosecutor's claims totalled €61,928,210. At the end of the court procedure, this was reduced to €27,463, 899 (44 per cent), of which €11,325,036 (41 per cent, or 18 per cent of the original claims) was actually paid. As they conclude:

> Spending behaviour and losses during criminal transactions are partially ignored when estimating the amount of money an offender should pay. Ignoring expenditures and losses may be well justified given the ideological position that 'crime should not pay'. However, it also increases the chance that offenders are simply not able to pay the confiscation amount in full.[34]

in PC van Duyne (ed) *Corruption, Greed and Crime Money: Sleaze and Shady Economy in Europe and beyond* (Wolf Legal Publishers, 2014) 235–66.

[28] R Brown and S Gillespie, 'Overseas financial investigation of organised crime: Examining the barriers to effective implementation' (2015) 18(3) *Journal of Money Laundering Control* 371–81; P Cabana, 'Improving the recovery of assets resulting from organised crime' (2014) 22 *European Journal of Crime, Criminal Law and Criminal Justice* 19–21; M Levi, *Drug Law Enforcement and Financial Investigation Strategies* (International Drug Policy Consortium, 2013) 1.

[29] PC van Duyne, M Pheijffer, HG Kuijl, ATM Van Dijk and GJCM Bakker, *Financial Investigation of Crime* (Koninklijke Vermande, 2001), 89–94.

[30] K Bullock, 'The confiscation investigation: Investigating the financial benefit made from crime' (2010) 4(1) *Policing: A Journal of Policy and Practice* 8, 12, 13; B Vettori, *Tough on Criminal Wealth: Exploring the Practice of Proceeds from Crime Confiscation in the EU* (Springer, 2006); Brå (Brottsförebyggande rådet) [The Swedish National Council for Crime Prevention], *Criminal Assets Recovery in Sweden* (2008) (English summary of Brå report No.2008:10 Stockholm: Brå, 23); JD Meloen, R Landman, H de Miranda, J van Eekelen, S van Soest, PC van Duyne and W van Tilburg, *Buit en besteding: Een empirisch onderzoek naar de omvang, de kenmerken en de besteding van misdaadgeld* (Nationale Recherche Informatie, 2003) 23–24; Inspectie Openbare Orde en Veiligheid [Inspectorate of Public Order and Security] *Follow the Money! Een onderzoek naar financieel opsporen door de politie in het licht van het landelijk programma FinEC Politie* (Inspectie Openbare Orde en Veiligheid, Ministerie van Veiligheid en Justitie, 2012) 10.

[31] Court of Audit, *Combating Money Laundering: State in 2013* (Court of Audit, 2014) 6–8.

[32] B Slot, L de Swart, I Deleanu, E Merkus, M Levi, and E Kleemans, *Needs Assessment on Tools and Methods of Financial Investigation in the European Union: Final Report* (Ecorys, 2015).

[33] E Kruisbergen, E Kleemans and R Kouwenberg, 'Explaining attrition: Investigating and confiscating the profits of organized crime' (2016) 13(6) *European Journal of Criminology* 677.

[34] ibid, 691.

In short, as the Home Affairs Committee also note,[35] our attitudes can get in the way of a rational approach to handling the pursuit of proceeds. One issue that the Law Commission should tackle is this unrealistic accumulation of hypothetical proceeds within the confiscation statistics (and the interest charged upon it).

One approach to incentivisation has classically been that of the US, where asset sharing and Federal/State Joint Task forces have been used to improve inter-agency cooperation as well as single agency work. This has led to critiques from the libertarian right as well as from more traditional civil liberties groups, most dramatically two decades ago in *License to Steal*,[36] but continuing to the present, despite reforms.[37] There is no space here to discuss details of legal tensions in the US system, but some of the earlier abuses have been removed, even if issues of proportionality have not been resolved. What researchers have hitherto hardly done, however, is to examine the composition of US cases. To the extent that white-collar crime, bribery and money laundering prosecutions have gone after primarily legitimate financial intermediaries, for example, asset recovery is not difficult, because the firms have relatively high sunk capital and both want to and are able to carry on trading after payment of financial penalties. Some transnational bribery cases involving foreign kleptocrats have given larger problems, and some are currently going through the courts: but the Malaysian 1MDB and FIFA cases, etc offer examples where the creative use of extra-territorial reach generates substantial asset recovery.[38] There used to be no procedures by which victims could be compensated out of confiscated funds – a source of embarrassment that may have reflected the origins of these procedures in anti-organised crime and drugs trafficking measures. However, the prospects of parallel proceedings and triple penalties under RICO and 'no win, no fee' litigation partly filled that gap. Curiously, the US has not conducted the sort of attrition research studies carried out in England and Wales, or the Netherlands. However, some modest studies in the 1980s indicated the distorting effects that an asset-recovery reinvestment model can have on policing priorities, so the Law Commission should reconsider the appropriate balance between incentivisation and other objectives

[35] Home Affairs Committee, *Proceeds of Crime* (HC 25, 2016).

[36] L Levy, *License to Steal* (University of North Carolina Press, 1996).

[37] For an excellent review, see S Cassella, *Asset Forfeiture Law in the United States*, 2nd edn (Juris, 2012). For the UK equivalent, see M Williams, M Hopmeier and R Jones, *Millington and Sutherland Williams on The Proceeds of Crime*, 4th edn (OUP, 2013). See B Kelly and M Kole, 'The effects of asset forfeiture on policing: A panel approach' (2016) 54(1) *Economic Inquiry* 558–75; D Carpenter II, L Knepper, A Erickson, J McDonald, *Policing for Profit: The Abuse of Civil Asset Forfeiture*, 2nd edn (Institute for Justice, 2015).

[38] See updates on the US Department of Justice website: www.justice.gov/opa/pr/us-seeks-recover-approximately-540-million-obtained-corruption-involving-malaysian-sovereign; www.justice.gov/opa/pr/sixteen-additional-fifa-officials-indicted-racketeering-conspiracy-and-corruption. The French Courts found the son of the President of Equatorial Guinea guilty of money laundering and ordered him to hand over €150 million in assets, mostly in France (*The Times*, 28 October 2017) where they had already been identified. The change in the Malaysian government in 2018 is expected to generate more mutual legal assistance to increase recoveries.

of financial investigation; any Code it develops should contain clear boundaries on incentive schemes.

As Fazekas and Nanopoulos note,[39] despite the adoption of new legislation in this field and the stronger institutional framework introduced by the Treaty of Lisbon, the legal rules still present a number of deficiencies, and the emphasis on formal legal solutions has come at the expense of broader questions of transposition and utilisation within the EU, which are crucial to ensuring what they term effective recovery (though it might be preferable to conceptualise this as efficient, since 'effective' implies impacting on broader goals than merely more money).

III. Incentivising Civil Society to Attack Offending

Asset recovery is expensive, and the UK government (like many others) has been reluctant to spend large sums of money to recover it, whether or not on balance, there may be a net profit. A Confiscation Code will not solve this investment in enforcement problem unless it makes it radically easier to freeze and actually recover funds. One issue the Law Commission might consider is the role of the private sector in supplementing law enforcement. There are essentially two models: (i) hourly or daily paid firms engaged on a 'normal' basis (like POCA receivers who were largely stopped because of concerns that they were costing more than they recovered – a view that ignored any (usually unmeasured) impact on disruption and offending levels but reflects the fear of marginal net costs); (ii) venture capital firms operating on a conditional fee basis. Potential business and criminal targets include:

(1) Planned wholly criminal enterprises where the business is just a tool for crime and is expected to self-liquidate when the crimes are judged to be sufficiently completed (eg, telemarketing frauds; VAT carousel frauds);

(2) Part-time criminal enterprises where the ongoing business activity is substantially legitimate but where offending – perhaps quite serious offending – is instrumental and is not perceived (at the time) as being high risk or is conducted as an unauthorised operation by deviant or over-zealous executives (price-fixing cartels and misleading customers; major firms that dump toxic waste without 'cut-out' intermediaries; domestic and transnational bribery on behalf of or against UK businesses);

(3) Enterprises where the business is on a slippery slope to failure and crime is seen as a way of propping up the business which would otherwise fail. This group may be morally opprobrious but not very good candidates for substantial forfeiture gains.

[39] M Fazekas and E Nanopoulos, 'The Effectiveness of EU Law: Insights from the EU Legal Framework on Asset Confiscation' (2016) 24(1) *European Journal of Crime, Criminal Law and Criminal Justice* 39–64.

Usually, in civil litigation, initial recoveries fund further work, so the 'client' can maintain some level of control over costs. Even in the civil courts, because of its moral imputations, the burden of proof test for claims of fraud is higher than, say, for breaches of contract or statutory duty. Consequently, in the case against corporates for breaching their statutory duty not to rig the market for the sale of pharmaceuticals to the NHS, the claim was not fraud but breach of duty. Asset freezing is unnecessary where the deep pockets are large enough and the companies are ongoing; but it may well be needed where the 'offender' is in a marginal situation and has little or no 'sunk capital' in the jurisdiction. In the latter cases, my interviews suggest that the attrition between arrest and confiscation enforcement was mostly due to assets abroad that could not be secured, plus permitted expenditure on living expenses in long-running cases.[40] Increasing the final asset recovery take rests arguably on freezing more in the first place, which hinges on better investigation, international cooperation and automatic or at least quicker freezing: the latter will require the Law Commission to weigh up difficult issues of fairness to defendants.

In all cases, the evidence has to meet judicial tests of there being a sufficient cause of action. There may be other examples of price-fixing which are suitable for the kind of treatment given in the NHS cases (then funded by the NHS Counter-Fraud and Security Management Services, now NHS Protect), which yielded some £34 million in settlements.[41] However, although environmental damage might appear to be an area of promise on social grounds, in order to get to the 'deep pockets', one might have to prove collusion between the toxic sources and the intermediaries who dump the waste. There is no systematic UK research on patterns of waste dumping that tells us whether the identified 'dumpers' are financially healthy firms, but knowledge about this is dependent on the quality of intelligence collections. An Environment Agency report noted:

> In 2011–2012 we stopped 759 illegal waste sites, either by closing them down or helping them to move into legal compliance and get the right permit or exemption to operate. The number of successful prosecutions against illegal waste activity also rose to 335 last year. This included closing one of the highest risk illegal waste sites in south-east England, where a multiple offender received four years in prison for money laundering and waste offences. We believe that the custodial sentence imposed, and the fact he must now hand over nearly £1 million of profits he made from his illegal waste business, will send a strong message to illegal operators about the consequences of their crimes.[42]

We have no idea whether that message was absorbed by and deterred other criminal operators. The use of money laundering provisions is difficult for the

[40] Confidential interviews, 2007.

[41] The SFO's criminal investigations and prosecutions of the companies were very expensive and despite their failure, the prosecutions in Operation Holbein may nevertheless have had a deterrent impact on individuals and firms: whether any more effect than publicised settlements remains open to question.

[42] Environment Agency, *Cracking Down on Waste Crime* (2012).

Environment Agency. Anecdotal research on fines suggests that courts find difficulty in fining 'proportionately' at the high end, so whether confiscation would yield more than regulatory sanctions is unknown. However, one might think about 'lifestyle polluters' or 'reckless traders' in the same way as 'lifestyle criminals' under POCA, especially if the Environment Agency/Trading Standards were given powers of arrest.

Venture capitalists typically purchase for a nominal sum (sometimes £1) the assignment of the cause of action in exchange for 20 per cent of the revenues from the action, though both the initial investment and the reward may vary. This particularly helps where there are a large number of relatively poor victims who otherwise would not be able to fund legal actions singly.[43] Whether such firms would act on a conditional fee basis against carousel or MTIC fraudsters or other targets is unknown. In general, the prosecution of a multi-jurisdictional concealed asset recovery investigation involves both extra-judicial and judicially assisted investigative procedures. Hitherto, accounting firms have in practice not displayed much enthusiasm for taking on the costs of difficult cases when presented with the opportunities to pursue them: but especially in light of judicial criticisms of the contracting out of parts of criminal investigations to the private sector,[44] the Law Commission would need to extend itself beyond normal crime investigation and prosecution agencies without infringing on the rights to civil action by injured parties.

A. The Corrupt Enrichment Order – An Irish Import

At a policy level, some overseas cases have been stymied by concern about return of assets to still-corrupt regimes. At the domestic level, there remains a view that the UK has comparatively little corruption (unless one wishes to include in the latter category the kind of 'pretexting' under which private investigators obtain information in violation of the data protection legislation, which could be liable to proceeds of crime confiscation).[45] Outside of some notorious local authorities, there has been comparatively little evidence of corrupt planning or contracting (some of which might fall within civil RICO provisions). Nevertheless, not least as part of a mutual legal assistance model for proceeds of crime cases that it would be in the UK's interest to develop, consideration might be given to enacting parallel provisions which could also be used if such cases developed.

When the Irish legislation was developed in 1996, it was a response to conventional crimes such as drugs trafficking and its associated threats of corruption

[43] In other cases, they act for wealthy victims, and no government intervention is needed for such persons as market provision is adequate.

[44] See *Zinga* [2014] EWCA Crim 52; *Tchenguiz v SFO* [2012] EWHC 2254.

[45] This is not an uncontested claim: for a view that Britain is very corrupt, though using a very broad construct of corruption, see D Whyte (ed), *How Corrupt is Britain?* (Pluto Press, 2015).

and violence in a small jurisdiction. A series of judicial tribunals, prompted by whistle-blowing among aggrieved participants (without prospective financial benefit), led to a series of revelations about extensive corruption in property development, planning permission and other matters involving businesspeople, ministers, Lord Mayors, planning officials, etc. This coincided with a reduction in drugs and terrorism cases with a large asset recovery component, as the low hanging fruit had been picked and assets overseas looked irretrievable: despite the powers granted to the Criminal Assets Bureau (CAB), some of these cases go back to the 1990s.[46] In the light of this, and of the risk that the political class had been de-legitimated, the Proceeds of Crime (Amendment) Act 2005 Act modernised and clarified the scope of the Criminal Assets Bureau (CAB) in relation to corruption. To ensure that it was ECHR-compliant, CAB was not allowed to make direct forensic use of information supplied under compulsion. Rather, since there was no use-immunity ('fruit of the poisoned tree doctrine') on that sort of information, they used the evidence obtained under compulsion to lead to other results, which they could use. CAB officers were able to freeze goods based on reasonable grounds for believing that they were Proceeds of Crime.

Before this, there were a very limited number of corruption cases under which proceeds were recovered.[47] In July 2006, using the new legislation, CAB secured a High Court order freezing lands at Carrickmines, Co Dublin, owned by Jackson Way Properties, after claiming that a €53 million increase in the value of some of the property stemmed from corrupt conduct. That conduct had allegedly led to the 'corrupt enrichment' of Jackson Way Properties (via an English-registered company) under the Proceeds of Crime (Amendment) Act 2005. CAB contended

[46] In an interview with Cormac O'Keefe, the head of CAB outlined recent work including: A massive investigation into money laundering by drug-trafficking organisations, centred on the bogus motor trade, but expanding into the horse-racing industry and other sectors, including gyms; actively and successfully pursuing vacant possession of John Gilligan's (who spent 17 years in prison for trafficking and is believed to have ordered the murder of *Sunday Independent* journalist Veronica Guerin in 1996) final three properties, which he and family members were required by a Supreme Court order to leave by 6 June 2017; issuing tax demands against up to 10 leading members of the Rathkeale Rovers international criminal network – with a total bill believed to be in excess of €10m; targeting 34 middle-ranking members of organised crime groups through Gardaí seconded to CAB and working specifically for the Special Crime Task Force; investigating a global mail fraud scam involving the seizure here of an estimated €4m in bank accounts; and conducting investigations into 20 suspected members of the Cork Wall burglary gang network. See C King and C Walker, (eds) *Dirty Assets: Emerging Issues in the Regulation of Criminal and Terrorist Assets* (Routledge, 2016); K Ligeti and M Simonato, (eds) *Chasing Criminal Money: Challenges and Perspectives on Asset Recovery in the EU* (Bloomsbury, 2017).

[47] Those pursued by CAB under the old legislation included former Minister for Justice Ray Burke and former Lord Mayor of Dublin, Michael Keating. Burke was jailed for tax evasion in January 2005. CAB investigators found documentation in his house, which showed he had undeclared income, and served him with a €2 million tax bill. Burke pleaded guilty to furnishing incorrect information during the government's 1993 tax amnesty by failing to declare an income. Keating was a more conventional target. He and his former business partner, Peter Bolger, were the subject of a CAB investigation in 1997/1998 after Gardaí discovered they were carrying money for a leading drug-trafficker. They were also involved in a VAT fraud in England during the early 1990s. Keating subsequently made a settlement of €250,000 with CAB.

that these lands had been re-zoned on 16 December 1997 by Dún Laoghaire-Rathdown County Council from agricultural to industrial after Frank Dunlop bribed and made corrupt payments to councillors to secure their support in the re-zoning vote. That vote increased the value of 17 acres of the property from €8 million to €61 million. CAB later withdrew its case against the company following a failed prosecution for corruption against Mr Kennedy and a number of councillors. The Bureau said its case could not proceed due to unavailability of witnesses. In addition to suing Dún Laoghaire-Rathdown County Council, JWPL then sued CAB for damages for misfeasance in public office. CAB denies the claims. So as with other areas of confiscation law over time, this has not been a smooth path in practice. The import of this experience has been to demonstrate that legislation introduced with a positive aim still may founder upon evidential processes which are unlikely to be resolved in a Code for Confiscation alone.

B. Unexplained Wealth Orders

The latest popular area for development is the Unexplained Wealth Order (UWO), enshrined in the Criminal Finances Act 2017. Part 1, sections 1–9 of the Act require a person who is suspected of involvement in or association with serious criminality to explain the origin of assets that appear to be disproportionate to their known income. To assist asset recovery, a failure to provide a response gives rise to a presumption that the property is recoverable. Those who make false or misleading statements in response to a UWO commit criminal offences.

The intention was to restrict this provision to cases over £100,000, but a Lords' amendment was accepted reducing this amount to £50,000. There is provision for a compensation scheme in relation to the interim freezing orders that can accompany an UWO, which may inhibit their use but is more respectful of the right to property under the ECHR.

In common with many other measures, the UWO has attractions for many constituencies, including those seeking more recoveries from Grand Corruption, human rights violations, and the full range of crimes. There has been some resistance against this in the Australian courts, and there is a long history of over-optimism in the practicability of such measures, which like others, depend on levels of financial investigation and the speed with which assets are frozen.

One international review notes:[48]

> Several countries have debated the possibility of introducing UWOs into their legal systems, but most have decided to maintain traditional confiscation regime, *in personam* following conviction, and *in rem* proceedings targeting property. Few have ventured into the area of UWOs, and some of those that have done so have faced constitutional

[48] BA Hamilton, *Comparative Evaluation of Unexplained Wealth Orders* (National Institute of Justice, 2012) 1.

> and legal challenges. For example, in Italy the Constitutional Court declared law *12 quinquies* to be unconstitutional after two years of use determining that shifting the burden of proof violates the Italian constitution. Other countries have adopted only some aspects of UWO laws, eg, United Kingdom, South Africa, some states in Canada, and New Zealand, have a presumption in favor of forfeiture for unlawful activities or specific offenses, but not full UWOs. Other countries have, under the umbrella of the United Nations Convention against Corruption (UNCAC), enacted illicit enrichment offenses targeting the proceeds of corruption where the reversed burden of proof is part of the offense but yet apply only to political officials and not to all crimes and individuals as do UWO laws. A similar approach was followed by France with an amendment to its criminal code which introduced reversed burden of proof forfeiture measures targeting certain specific criminal offenders but it is still a post-conviction method. Only three countries thus far have adopted full UWOs – no proof of the property being connected to a crime and a reversed burden of proof. These are Australia, Colombia, and Ireland.

The report goes on to note that neither Australia nor Ireland have made major inroads by using UWOs, and my discussions in 2017 with informed insiders assert that there has been significant judicial resistance in Australia.

Research conducted in Australia also casts doubt on the workability of the enforcement process there, some of which is attributable to variations arising from the devolved State and Federal systems, but other components are more general, relating to communications, data sharing, speed of action, etc. The authors conclude:

> In Western Australia, $6.9m has been paid into the Confiscation Proceeds Account from unexplained wealth investigations over a 10-year period. Unexplained wealth orders in New South Wales have recovered a total of $2.6m in three years and, when orders that could only have been commenced as unexplained wealth orders but were settled as other orders are also counted, this rises to $14.4m. The Tasmanian Government has stated that unexplained wealth orders 'for the forfeiture of over $820,000 in cash, assets and firearms were issued in 2015–16 ….[49]

A number of interviewees highlighted the New South Wales Crime Commission's ability to achieve settlement in short periods of time, while sacrificing little unexplained wealth in the negotiation process, as an important element of its success. A key advantage of the New South Wales Crime Commission model is the ability to issue a notice to give evidence in a coercive hearing or 'star chamber'. Court hearings are impartial and lack the power and effectiveness of a star chamber. In jurisdictions where more than one agency is involved in investigating unexplained wealth cases and obtaining orders, and particularly where the Director of Public Prosecutions is involved, there are issues associated with communication, coordination and agency functions. As far as possible, unexplained wealth cases should be managed by a single agency.

[49] M Smith and RG Smith, *Procedural Impediments to Effective Unexplained Wealth Legislation in Australia* (Trends & Issues in Crime and Criminal Justice No.523, 2016) 7–8.

The likely sums are quite modest: over the last decade, Australia has confiscated $44 million per annum on average, and that includes proceeds of crime from both 'organised criminals' and corrupt public officials, whether or not connected to the former. For the year 2013–14, it was estimated that the total proceeds of serious and organised crime in Australia amounted to $21 billion,[50] while national confiscations for that year alone were only $45 million. The value of unexplained wealth orders was even smaller, although this is now beginning to grow.[51]

Nevertheless, Transparency International enthusiastically proposed UWOs as a way of dealing with the problem of transnational corruption, citing the fact that in 2014, UK law enforcement agencies were only able to take action on seven individual reports of suspicious financial transactions that were identified as the possible proceeds of international corruption.[52] The report is light on the general issues of proceeds of crime legislation and institutions, but notes that non-conviction based asset forfeiture (NCBAF) civil powers are 'under-used' in cases of grand corruption (though it is not obvious what level of utilisation would defeat that criticism). Placing the burden on the defendant might in principle get around the non-cooperation in the alleged kleptocrat's host country. But irrespective of the merits in principle of this proposal, there will remain the issue of resourcing and judicial reaction to the proposals, which can be expected to receive challenge. The procedural justice and fairness in the selection of targets for such interventions will also be an interesting political issue, not addressed by any of the above studies or by TI itself. One could imagine what would be the reaction in 2018 if Russian/Middle Eastern-origin super-rich or Chinese-origin holders of UK 'golden visas' were targeted.

IV. Shifting Targets for Asset Recovery

A. Prosecuting/Civil Recoveries from Professionals in Primary/Ancillary Roles

The main law enforcement targets historically have been full-time 'core nominals' (ie, people identified through law enforcement intelligence as high-level offenders). The confiscation yield from those offenders has been modest, especially from assets held overseas, whose 'true proportion' does not seem feasible to estimate plausibly but is unlikely to be anywhere near as low as the 2 per cent of

[50] Australian Crime Commission, *The Costs of Serious and Organised Crime in Australia 2013–14* (2015).

[51] M Smith and RG Smith, *Exploring the Procedural Barriers to Securing Unexplained Wealth Orders in Australia: Report to the Criminology Research Advisory Council* (2016) 51.

[52] Transparency International, *Empowering the UK to Recover Corrupt Assets: Unexplained Wealth Orders and Other New Approaches to Illicit Enrichment and Asset Recovery* (2016). This figure may be an underestimate. See also F Keene, *Unexplained Wealth Orders: Global Lessons for the UK Ahead of Implementation* (RUSI Occasional Paper, 2017).

guesstimated proceeds of crime currently recovered globally.[53] One of the major legal transformations since the serious development of anti-laundering legislation in the 1990s has been to create liabilities for ancillary parties by giving them particular legal duties beyond the mere refusal to enter into a positive criminal conspiracy, a view developed in the Serious Crime Act 2015. To the extent that these ancillary roles are pursued by regulatory or DPA sanctions rather than as criminal prosecutions, may reduce formal confiscation in those cases, though it is arguable we should include relevant regulatory fines within the confiscation fold. Prosecutions of professionals have not been a major focus to date, and in areas of insider trading, solicitor fraud and assistance to money laundering, and accountants assisting frauds and corruption, many difficulties have been experienced, only some of which have been mitigated by the Fraud Act 2006. Despite NCA rhetoric, solicitors suspected of involvement in money laundering and high-yield investment frauds – and sometimes acquitted in the criminal courts, though more often 'convicted' in Solicitors Disciplinary Tribunals – have not hitherto been the focus of many criminal enquiries.[54] Sums involved in these high-yield investment frauds can be as high as £100 million – the mean and median have not been calculated by agencies involved but would always be in the millions.

It should be clear that this does not apply to all lawyers involved in financial misconduct. Many lawyers who have been successfully prosecuted for fraud (especially mortgage fraud) have been presiding over unprofitable firms and therefore do not have many assets to confiscate once their victims have been compensated (to the extent that they have been). Though the data are not split out in statistics, there have been very few prosecutions of wealthy individual bankers or banks for money laundering or for failure to report suspicions or for failing to have adequate measures in place: it is they and professionals whose criminality may be too difficult to prove 'beyond reasonable doubt' who may be suitable targets for civil forfeiture mechanisms on a lower standard of proof and different evidential rules. Arguably, these should be counted in totals of proceeds of crime confiscation totals.

B. Action Against Persistent Insolvents/Repeat Trading Standards Complainees

In 2016–17, the Insolvency Service disqualified 1,214 directors and made 430 referrals to prosecuting authorities for possible criminal conduct. Acting as

[53] The denominator against which confiscated sums should be judged for efficiency purposes remains obscure. Those who use high guesstimates of money laundering to attract attention to the harmfulness of particular forms of criminality end up being hoist with their own petard when the recovery percentage is used against them to demonstrate their inefficiency or ineffectiveness.

[54] D Middleton and M Levi, 'Let Sleeping Lawyers Lie: Organised Crime, Lawyers and the Regulation of Legal Services' (2015) 55(4) *British Journal of Criminology* 647–68. See also R Choo, RG Smith, J Walters and S Bricknell, 'Perceptions of Money Laundering and Financing of Terrorism in a Sample of the Australian Legal Profession' (2013) 122(1) *Research and Public Policy Series* (Australian Institute of Criminology).

trustee and liquidator, it distributed over £46m to creditors in that year in dividend payments, but otherwise, there is no indication of asset recoveries from the egregious cases that it wound up.[55] There is a more general reservoir of 'delinquent directors' who exploit victim inertia at a level unlikely to attract private law firms, but (though they may not be carrying much cash) are probably more profitable than the local drug dealers targeted by the police for cash seizures. There has been no update subsequently and there is no reason to think that the data would not be the same, but data from global credit risk group Experian show that in mid-1999, 212,028 directors (6.66 per cent of the total UK director population) on its databases were 'serial failures' (undefined, but meaning two or more previous failures): indeed, 2,385 male and 331 female directors – 0.085 per cent of all directors in 1999 – had more than ten failures each. One in four directors nationally has been involved in a failed company (though there is no detailed analysis of one potential implication: it is not clear what the expected probability is that a past failure will predict a future failure, especially a suspected fraudulent one).[56] The riskiness in different areas of the UK roughly corresponds to the proportions of directors there, though directors in London and the South East are most likely to have more than 10 failures.

There is scope for better information sharing to identify and take more aggressive action against recidivist delinquent directors and their assets than has occurred in the past. However, whether there would be a significant asset recovery dividend net of investigative costs or even gross is an open question, since quite apart from any high lifestyle expenses that are irrecoverable, such serial 'failures' are likely to have hidden their assets competently in anticipation of liquidator efforts, whether or not this is treated as 'asset recovery'. Here, the metrics of success might be assets recovered from rogue insolvencies, but they may also be fraud losses prevented by early intervention, which would not show up in asset recovery data.

V. A Code for Confiscation

The argument of this chapter has been that reform of the law of confiscation is neither a necessary nor a sufficient condition for enhancement of the levels of proceeds of crime actually confiscated by the authorities. Inviting comments on the need for reform, the Law Commission has observed:

> The law on the confiscation of proceeds of criminal conduct has changed significantly and frequently over the last three decades. The principal source is now the Proceeds of Crime Act 2002 (PoCA), but that Act has been repeatedly amended, most recently by Chapter 1 of the Serious Crime Act 2015.

[55] *The Insolvency Service Annual Report and Accounts 2016–17* (HC 209, 2017).
[56] It is a failure from the perspective of the creditors, but not from that of a fraudster.

The law in this area is notorious for being difficult to apply and enforce. These difficulties have at least 2 principal causes:

- The complexity and unwieldy nature of the PoCA regime which must be considered by courts faced with an application for an order which can lead to protracted litigation around the making of orders. Figures published by the National Audit Office in December 2013 estimated the total annual cost of court hearings and appeals on confiscation orders to be £31.8 million.
- The inefficiency of enforcement processes and the lack of discretion available to enforcement agencies and the courts when it comes to the enforcement of orders once made. Figures published by the National Audit Office in December 2013 estimated the total annual cost of confiscation enforcement was estimated at £3.2 million.
- The complexity of the law is legendary. Even after detailed consideration by the Supreme Court in *R v Waya (Terry)* [2012] UKSC 51, the law remains unclear. The effect of this decision was to cast doubt on much of the case-law which had grown up around PoCA over the preceding decade, and the Supreme Court has heard five further appeals on the issue of confiscation since *Waya*.
- A disappointingly small fraction of the total monies ordered to be paid under confiscation orders has been collected. In March 2016 the National Audit Office published figures that showed an outstanding debt on unpaid confiscation orders, as at September 2015, of £1.61 billion (an 11% increase on the year before). Only 17.5% is estimated to be realistically collectable.
- Often defendants facing confiscation orders do not have the means to pay them. It can, however, be extremely difficult for the courts to rule that a defendant's assets are inadequate to pay an order under the current provisions. Usually the courts have no option but to impose the obligatory default sentence, and thereafter the chances of successful collection decline drastically. Only 2% of orders were paid off in full in cases where the default sentence was imposed in 2012.
- A confiscation regime should have a simple purpose, namely to strip wrongfully acquired assets from those convicted of crime, and should be capable of being applied and understood in the busy criminal courts by practitioners, judges and indeed self-represented defendants. The current law clearly fails in that respect, and also fails in practice in its purpose of stripping those convicted of acquisitive crime of their assets.[57]

It is not clear to the present author whether the imposition of a default sentence is the cause of fewer confiscation debts being paid, or merely a coincidence. There is no research on this matter. Certainly, some defendants (like Terry Adams, as deduced from his eventual payment in 2017) are capable of repaying but are unwilling to do so, and it is not easy for a judge or other administrator to determine in advance whether they are dealing with a recalcitrant offender or an impecunious one. However, in other cases, the logic of the existing legal rules would repay revisiting, and the rules about interest payments on notional sums create a false 'debt'

[57] Law Commission Website: www.lawcom.gov.uk/confiscation/.

that stands in the way of a sensible assessment of 'effectiveness' (which should more accurately be termed 'efficiency', since mere recovery of proceeds is not the only objective of asset recovery and certainly not the only objective of financial investigation). Although the Criminal Finances Act 2017 deals with a small number of major policy areas, there remain many aspects of civil and criminal asset recovery that would repay systematic revisiting and a Confiscation Code would be one way of addressing that.

However, unless it mandated particular actions, a Code cannot magically resolve the under-resourcing of financial investigations, the relative (in)attention by police and non-police agencies given to some offences such as fraud and environmental crimes, and the reluctance of some prosecutors to apply for Restraint Orders, nor the neglect of much-trumpeted civil recovery mechanisms (whose appropriateness in the light of experience a Code could revisit). These require attention to the underpinnings of financial investigation that, beyond the formal process of FIU-training and accreditation, do not show intensive change since Levi and Osofsky's study in 1993–4. Besides, early financial investigation can be important to conviction of primary and 'enabler' offenders, and to crime reduction via a better understanding of the *system* of crime, as well as to proceeds recovery.

Freezing and confiscation law is very technical, and though a succession of appellate cases have clarified a series of issues, there are grounds for increasing decision-making speed and competence through the use of specialised courts, as was the case when asset freezing needed to go to High Court judges in London pre-POCA. However, unless there were several such courts, they would be distant from many courts of prosecution, and it would mean that 'confiscation judges' would not have heard the evidence as trial judges.

Ian Dennis makes the following observations in support of creating a Code of Criminal Procedure:

> (1) Looking back at the codification project, one can see three kinds of arguments used in support of a criminal code … First, there are the constitutional arguments. These are partly focused on the legality of the criminal law. They claim that the law should be reasonably clear, accessible and known in advance, so that citizens may regulate their conduct accordingly … The argument goes accordingly that a code would enable citizens to find the law more easily and to understand it better than if they had to search through the mass of statutory and common law sources that we presently have. A related claim concerns the legitimacy of the criminal law …
>
> (2) Secondly, there are arguments of principle for a code. These relate to the moral quality of the law. They claim that the process of codification enables us to maximize the fairness of the criminal law and to ensure that it adheres to the ethical standards that we wish to respect.
>
> (3) Third, there are arguments relating to efficiency in the administration of criminal justice. The argument is in essence that a code will make the jobs of those working in criminal justice easier. Judges, lawyers, magistrates, police officers, and other criminal justice players will all be able to find and use the criminal law more quickly and efficiently. Since many of these people will not be trained lawyers,

> or may not have much experience of administering and enforcing the criminal law (for example, part-time judges), a code offers the great advantage of a common authoritative starting point, drafted in a clear and consistent style.[58]

Provided there is a risk that a Code might lead to the ossification of issues that may require change in the light of the ongoing dynamics of what is seen as 'serious and organised crime'[59] – which in addition to all-crime money laundering offences, increasingly includes cyber-dependent crimes and cyber-enabled economic crimes within the mandate of the UK National Crime Agency and its foreign equivalents. However, a Code that takes into account the broader issues of incentivising financial investigation/asset recovery and the human rights of suspects would be a useful development.

VI. Conclusion

Faced with this succession of failures and after a series of contested legal cases that have generated first the initial need for legislation and second, the difficult legal and political history of civil recovery and the Assets Recovery Agency,[60] a systematic re-examination of the freezing and confiscation process by the Law Commission looks attractive. Though the jurisprudential principles will be contested and have to be weighed alongside the costs and benefits, the UK now has enough experience of criminal confiscation and (largely neglected after the initial post-POCA global heralding) of civil forfeiture to draw up a more coherent framework, whether that be merely a codification and consolidation of existing case and statute law or something more reforming in nature. The social deliberation involved in the shaping of the Code and its possible adoption may increase its perceived legitimacy within the legal and judicial profession, which remains bifurcated between a minority of enthusiasts who dominate the literature and appeals before the higher Courts, and the indifferent or actively hostile. So it is also in the rest of Europe, where the patchy Eurostat data – albeit out of date now – indicates that in many Member States, there remains policy indifference and mixed performance that has been difficult to shift into the active harmonised whole evangelised by the European Commission and Union.[61]

[58] I Dennis, 'Codifying the Law of Criminal Evidence' (2014) 35(2) *Statute Law Review* 107. See also JR Spencer, 'The Case for a Code of Criminal Procedure' [2000] *Crim LR* 519.

[59] M Levi 'Foreword: Some Reflections on the Evolution of Financial and Economic Crimes' in B Rider (ed), *Research Handbook on International Financial Crime* (Elgar, 2015).

[60] Lasting from 2003 to 2008, ARA had 180 staff at its peak in 2005, and an annual budget of £15.5m: however, by the time of its demise, it had recovered only £4.6m – though £68.45m was frozen in June 2006.

[61] Directive 2014/42/EU. Subsequently, there has been a controversial proposal for a Regulation on freezing and confiscation orders. See European Commission, *Strengthening the Mutual Recognition of Criminal Assets' Freezing and Confiscation Orders* (Inception Impact Assessment, 2016).

Overall, it remains to be seen what appetite politicians and the public have for further legislative and institutional change. The global history of proceeds of crime forfeiture – whether civil or criminal – is a history in which expectations and rhetoric are not matched by criminal justice inputs (financial investigations and processing of cases to criminal and regulatory action nationally and internationally), outputs (like funds frozen and/or confiscated) or outcomes (like demonstrable impacts of such freezes, forfeitures and confiscations on different forms of criminal behaviour). This chapter has reviewed a range of material that is relevant to understanding those challenges, without repeating case law that can readily be found elsewhere. A Code of Confiscation may perform some useful functions in enhancing legitimacy and pulling together issues arising from the now quite extensive case law that have not been dealt with in the Criminal Finances Act 2017 or its prospective Codes of Practice. The extent to which a Code is able to enhance the other elements analysed here may highlight the limitations of seeing 'law reform' as a sufficient rather than as a necessary but not sufficient part of social welfare.

Comment on Chapter 1

Reforming Confiscation Law?

COLIN KING

It is trite to say that *crime should not pay*. Most people would accept the logic of such a statement. When it comes to 'proceeds of crime' the UK has enacted a vast – at times unwieldy – legislative framework to ensure that criminals should not benefit from their illegal activity. Modern confiscation law can be traced to the decision of the House of Lords in *R v Cuthbertson*.[1] In that case, three people – Cuthbertson, Todd and McCoy – had pleaded guilty to conspiracy in relation to manufacturing and supplying Class A drugs.[2] They were sentenced to 11, 13 and 3 years' imprisonment, respectively. Following their conviction, forfeiture orders were granted pursuant to section 27 of the Misuse of Drugs Act 1971. On appeal to the House of Lords, the appellants did not dispute that the assets ordered to be forfeited were acquired through the manufacture and supply of Class A drugs. They contended, however, that those assets could not lawfully be subject to a forfeiture order under the Misuse of Drugs Act (on the basis that they were convicted of conspiracy, which was not an offence under that Act). Their appeal was allowed – albeit 'with considerable regret' on the part of the House of Lords.[3] While it might be argued that Parliament surely must have intended that the Act of 1971 would extend to those convicted of conspiracy (as was contended by counsel for the Crown), the question for the court was a matter of law, 'a pure question of construction of section 27 read in the context of the Act of which it forms a part'.[4] As Lord Diplock stated: 'Parliament's intention must be ascertained from the actual words which Parliament itself approved as expressing its intention when it passed the Act in the terms in which it reached the statute book.'[5] Ultimately, it was held 'that there was no jurisdiction to make any order for forfeiture in the instant case, even of tangible things, since the conviction in respect of which the order was made was one of conspiracy and not of any substantive offence.'[6]

[1] [1981] AC 470.

[2] They had been detected as part of a police operation – 'Operation Julie'.

[3] [1981] AC 470, 479, per Lord Diplock. Or, in the words of Lord Edmund-Davies, 'the most reluctant conclusion' (485).

[4] ibid, 480, per Lord Diplock.

[5] ibid, 480, per Lord Diplock.

[6] ibid, 485, per Lord Diplock. The appellants had been convicted of conspiracy contrary to common law, as the offences had taken place prior to the enactment of the Criminal Law Act 1977. It would have made no difference, however, had they been convicted under the 1977 Act: ibid, 480, per Lord Diplock.

The Drug Trafficking Offences Act 1986 was subsequently enacted,[7] providing for confiscation orders where a person has benefited from drug trafficking.[8] The Criminal Justice Act 1988 extended this confiscation regime beyond drug trafficking offences.[9] The Criminal Justice (International Co-operation) Act 1991 contained further provisions, for example relating to interest on sums unpaid under confiscation orders,[10] applications for an increase in the amount to be recovered under the confiscation order,[11] and seizure, detention and forfeiture of money being imported or exported that represents proceeds of drug trafficking.[12] The Criminal Justice Act 1993 was introduced to amend, and enhance, the confiscation provisions.[13] The Drug Trafficking Act 1994 further consolidated the confiscation regime, implementing many of the recommendations of the Working Group on Confiscation.[14] The Proceeds of Crime Act 1995 set out the procedure that the court must follow when considering confiscation orders,[15] as well as a number of other incidental provisions. In 2000, however, a report published by the Cabinet Office emphasised:

> The UK has extensive powers to deprive offenders of the proceeds of their crimes, but these powers have developed in a piecemeal fashion, are not well understood, and are spread across a range of statutes with differences in the treatment of the proceeds of drugs and non-drugs crime. There are also deficiencies in the application of these powers by law enforcement and prosecution authorities. And the court system is complex with the High Court, Crown Court and Magistrates' Court all having a role to play.[16]

Ultimately, in 2002, the Proceeds of Crime Act 2002 (POCA 2002) was enacted to provide an all-encompassing legislative framework for confiscation law and this legislation continues to govern confiscation law today. As Bullock and Lister note, this legislation was 'intended to bring confiscation law in from the margins, placing it centrally within criminal justice policy responses to crime and insecurity'.[17]

In *Soneji*, however, Lord Steyn ominously stated:

> The aim of the new statute is to create an effective unified regime of confiscation law. Given the almost year by year amendment over the last 20 years of sometimes overhasty

[7] This Act was influenced by the Hodgson Report: see Howard League for Penal Reform, *Profits of Crime and their Recovery: Report of a Committee Chaired by Sir Derek Hodgson* (Heinemann 1984).

[8] Drug Trafficking Offences Act 1986, s 1.

[9] Criminal Justice Act 1988, s 71 and Sch 4.

[10] Criminal Justice (International Co-operation) Act 1991, s 15.

[11] ibid, s 16.

[12] ibid, ss 25–26.

[13] Criminal Justice Act 1993, Parts II and III.

[14] Working Group on Confiscation, *Second Report. Drug Trafficking: Home Office working group on the confiscation of criminal assets: report on part VI of the Criminal Justice Act 1988* (Home Office, 1992).

[15] Proceeds of Crime Act 1995, s 1.

[16] Performance and Innovation Unit, *Recovering the Proceeds of Crime* (Cabinet Office, 2000) 7.

[17] K Bullock and S Lister, 'Post-Conviction Confiscation of Assets in England and Wales: Rhetoric and Reality' in C King and C Walker (eds) *Dirty Assets: Emerging Issues in the Regulation of Criminal and Terrorist Assets* (Ashgate, 2014) 53.

> criminal legislation, and the great difficulties created for the courts by much of this flood of legislation, it would be innocent to predict that the 2002 Act has solved the problems involved in the criminal process of confiscation.[18]

Lord Steyn's prediction proved correct; POCA 2002 did not solve the 'confiscation problem', nor was it the end of legislative development. Subsequent piecemeal developments include, *inter alia*, the Serious Organised Crime and Police Act 2005, the Serious Crime Act 2007, the Crime and Courts Act 2013, the Serious Crime Act 2015, and the Criminal Finances Act 2017. Unsurprisingly, such piecemeal developments have been accompanied by a wave of caselaw on various aspects of the confiscation regime.[19]

Given criticism of the confiscation regime – both of the law and of its application in practice[20] – it is no surprise then that POCA is touted as being ripe for widescale reform. As Laird states, 'past experience suggests that piecemeal reform is not the most effective method of ensuring legislation is effective at separating criminals from the proceeds of their crimes. Perhaps the time has come for a holistic review of POCA?'[21] The prospect of review has also been welcomed by the courts.[22] And while confiscation was not included in the Law Commission Thirteenth Programme of Reform,[23] the Commission will commence a review of the law in this area in September 2018 by way of Ministerial Reference.[24]

For this commentary, my (somewhat daunting) task is to set out relevant legal developments (see above), to outline any areas (whether of law or in practice) that are of particular concern, and to consider whether codification is necessary and/or desirable – and to do all this within a limited word count. Against this backdrop, this commentary focuses on two specific aspects of the confiscation regime that have attracted particular attention, namely: (1) suggestions to have specialist confiscation courts or judges, and (2) the role of incentivisation. It then moves on to consider the thorny, and topical, issue of codification.

Before proceeding further, however, it is important to stress that – when considering reform of POCA – we must look beyond the *law*, to also consider wider issues that impact upon the operation of that law. Indeed, a recurring

[18] [2005] UKHL 49, [3].

[19] Notable recent examples include *Waya* [2012] UKSC 51; *Ahmad* [2014] UKSC 36; *Harvey* [2015] UKSC 73. See M Hopmeier and A Mills, 'Post-Conviction Confiscation in England and Wales' in C King, C Walker and J Gurulé (eds), *The Palgrave Handbook of Criminal and Terrorism Financing Law* (Palgrave, 2018).

[20] See, eg, National Audit Office, *Confiscation Orders* (Stationery Office, 2013); House of Commons Committee of Public Accounts, *Confiscation Orders* (Forty-ninth Report of Session 2013–14, HC 942); National Audit Office, *Confiscation Orders: Progress Review* (Stationery Office, 2016); Home Affairs Committee, *Proceeds of Crime* (Fifth Report of Session 2016–17, HC 25); House of Commons Committee of Public Accounts, *Confiscation Orders: Progress Review* (Seventh Report of Session 2016–17, HC 124).

[21] K Laird, 'The Criminal Finances Act 2017 – an Introduction' [2017] *Crim LR* 915, 939.

[22] See, eg, *Guraj* [2016] UKSC 65, [36], per Lord Hughes.

[23] See Law Commission, '13th Programme of Law Reform', available at: www.lawcom.gov.uk/project/13th-programme-of-law-reform.

[24] Law Commission, *Thirteenth Programme of Law Reform* (Law Com No 377, 2017) 23.

thread throughout Professor Levi's chapter in this volume is that there is a lack of empirical research on the confiscation regime.[25] Any review of this area must adopt an evidence-based approach supported by appropriate empirical research. We now turn to consider whether there ought to be specialist courts or judges.

I. Specialist Courts/Judges

An area that has attracted substantial discussion as a possible area of reform is the suggestion that a dedicated system of confiscation courts or judges be established. In his chapter, Professor Levi states:

> … there are grounds for increasing decision-making speed and competence through the use of specialised courts, as was the case when asset freezing needed to go to High Court judges in London pre-POCA. However, unless there were several such courts, they would be distant from many courts of prosecution, and it would mean that 'confiscation judges' would not have heard the evidence as trial judges.[26]

This point was also raised at the 2016 Home Affairs Committee Proceeds of Crime Inquiry, both in its oral hearings and written evidence. Based on earlier empirical research in Ireland,[27] my own suggestion to the Committee was to consider whether expert judges would be appropriate:

> … because you could have a judge being faced with a very complex proceeds of crime case and that judge would never have dealt with a POCA case before, whereas if you had a judge who was specifically dealing with POCA cases the whole week, that judge would be much more adept at dealing with the issues.[28]

This suggestion was also influenced by discussions with UK judges, many of whom have indicated a strong preference for not getting involved in POCA cases. One judge went so far as to say that he delayed a decision in one (non-POCA) case until after lunch to ensure that he avoided being allocated a POCA case that was waiting to be allocated.

A specialist confiscation court was also advocated by other witnesses at the Committee, for example Tim Owen QC stated: 'Most judges do not enjoy or look forward to doing confiscation. I am very strongly in favour of the idea of specialist judges assigned to deal with these cases from the beginning to the end.'[29] The Committee agreed with such views, stating: 'Specialist courts would enable complex confiscation hearings to be dealt with more efficiently and with much

[25] Albeit there are some exceptions, see eg H Wood, *Enforcing Confiscation Orders: From Policy to Practice* (RUSI, 2016).

[26] M Levi, 'Reflections on Proceeds of Crime: A New Code for Confiscation?', ch 1 of this volume, 22.

[27] Though it is recognised that the sheer volume of POCA cases in the UK makes comparisons at a practical level more difficult.

[28] Home Affairs Committee Oral evidence, *Proceeds of crime* (HC 771, Tuesday 8 March 2016) Q.34.

[29] ibid, Q.70. See also Kennedy Talbot QC (ibid, Q.64) and written evidence from the NPCC Financial Investigation and Proceeds of Crime Portfolio, [7.3].

greater expertise, with the added bonus of leaving Crown Courts more time to focus on criminal trials.'[30]

The government roundly rejected this stance, however, contending that specialist courts would not necessarily enable confiscation cases to be dealt with more efficiently; there are likely to be unintended adverse consequences; the likelihood of increased waiting times; and cost factors.[31] Perhaps the strongest argument advanced by the government was that:

> Requiring cases to be listed before specialist judges in a specialist court will result in a lack of listing flexibility which will result in unnecessary delay. It will also involve duplication of work: where there has been a trial, the trial judge is better equipped than anyone else to deal expeditiously with the issues arising in relation to confiscation, because he or she has heard all the evidence at trial. If the confiscation proceedings are transferred to a specialist court, the judge there will have no prior knowledge of the evidence at trial, and will have to start from scratch. This duplication of work also introduces the undesirable risk that the confiscation judge's assessment of the limited evidence they hear may differ from that taken by the judge who had the advantage of hearing all the evidence at trial.[32]

If there are any issues relating to training of the judiciary, that – the government responded – is a matter that should be taken up by the Judicial College and the Lord Chief Justice.[33]

Notwithstanding this resistance to specialist courts/ judges, in their review of confiscation the Law Commission should go beyond the law governing confiscation orders and consider wider issues – including whether specialist courts or judges would be desirable – that impact upon the effectiveness of the law. At the very least, it would be worthwhile undertaking a review (whether in-house or commissioned) of the pros and cons of specialist courts/judges and how that might work in practice.

II. Incentivisation

A crucial question that must be considered is 'what happens to confiscated money?' At present, a 'top slice' is taken to fund key national asset recovery capabilities[34]

[30] See Home Affairs Committee, *Proceeds of Crime* (Fifth Report of Session 2016–17, HC 25), [34–35].

[31] Home Affairs Select Committee, *Government Response to the Committee's Fifth Report of Session 2016 - 17* (HC 25, 2016).

[32] ibid.

[33] ibid. The government undertook to 'work with the Lord Chief Justice to assess whether additional capabilities are required, and whether any additional measures can be put into place to encourage increased knowledge of POCA.' While the National Audit Office (in 2013 and 2016) was in favour of specialist judges and courts, the judiciary have resisted such suggestions on the basis that it is 'unnecessary and too restrictive'. See National Audit Office, *Confiscation Orders: Progress Review* (Stationery Office, 2016) 30.

[34] In 2014–15, this 'top slice' was approximately £5 million.

and then, under the Asset Recovery Incentivisation Scheme (ARIS),[35] monies realised from confiscation orders are allocated to the Home Office (50%), investigation agencies (18.75%), prosecution agencies (18.75%) and HM Courts and Tribunals Service (12.5%).[36] In his chapter, Professor Levi refers to the US approach, and notes how 'some modest studies in the 1980s indicated the distorting effects that an asset-recovery reinvestment model can have on policing priorities'.[37] He suggests that the Law Commission 'should reconsider the appropriate balance between incentivisation and other objectives of financial investigation; any Code it develops should contain clear boundaries on incentive schemes'.[38] I agree. To maintain trust in confiscation law and practice, as well as to avoid potential for (or even insinuations of) 'policing for profit',[39] the ARIS scheme as it currently operates should be reformed. Before looking at possible alternatives, it is worth saying a bit more about incentivisation.

In the US, for example, incentivisation schemes[40] have been heavily criticised – in the media,[41] by NGOs,[42] and by researchers.[43] Advocates of such incentivisation schemes, however, suggest that since law enforcement agencies are responsible for seizing assets, they should at least share in the spoils. Similar arguments are evident in England and Wales. Yet, incentivisation schemes are not the only options for the disposal phase. Other options include transfer of the property (or the proceeds of sale) to the State budget or social reuse of the property in question.[44] In many jurisdictions, the property in question will be transferred to the Central Fund, and will be distributed in accordance with standard budgetary rules (eg, Ireland). In other jurisdictions, the property will be used (directly or indirectly) for social purposes: this can include anti-drug initiatives (eg, work by the Interministerial

[35] ARIS was introduced in 2006, following concern that proceeds of crime powers were not being sufficiently used. Note, ARIS does not apply in Scotland.

[36] Different percentage allocations apply to other POCA powers, including cash forfeiture and civil recovery.

[37] See Levi (n 26) 11.

[38] ibid 11–12.

[39] E Blumenson and E Nilsen, 'Policing for Profit: The Drug War's Hidden Economic Agenda' (1998) 65 *University of Chicago Law Review* 35; J Holcomb, T Kovandzic, and M Williams, 'Civil Asset Forfeiture, Equitable Sharing, and Policing for Profit in the United States' (2011) 39 *Journal of Criminal Justice* 273.

[40] For an overview of equitable sharing, see US Department of Justice, Criminal Division: Asset Forfeiture and Money Laundering Section, *Guide to Equitable Sharing for State and Local Enforcement Agencies* (April 2009).

[41] See, for example, the episode dedicated to civil forfeiture on 'Last Week Tonight, with John Oliver' available at: www.youtube.com/watch?v=3kEpZWGgJks; S Stillman, 'Taken', *The New Yorker* (12 August 2013).

[42] D Carpenter *et al*, *Policing for Profit: The Abuse of Civil Asset Forfeiture*, 2nd edn (National Institute for Justice, 2015).

[43] K Baicker and M Jacobson, 'Finders Keepers: Forfeiture Laws, Policing Incentives, and Local Budgets' (2007) 91 *Journal of Public Economics* 2113; Holcomb, Kovandzic and Williams (n 39).

[44] See Center for the Study of Democracy, *Disposal of Confiscated Assets in the EU Member States* (CSD, 2014). That report notes that the primary distinction between these two options is the level of visibility of the use of the confiscated assets.

Mission in the Fight Against Drugs and Drug Addiction in France), offering the property for charitable purposes (eg, the Charity Council in Hungary), or giving property to community organisations (eg, Cashback for Communities in Scotland).[45] So there are other options available instead of ARIS. Below, I set out three options that would be preferable to ARIS.

One option is to not have an incentivisation scheme, such as ARIS; instead, all realised monies might be sent back to the Central Fund. This approach is adopted in Ireland; for example, monies realised by the Criminal Assets Bureau are transferred to the Minister for Public Expenditure and Reform to be spent as he sees fit. Based on qualitative interviews with Irish practitioners, this is the option that I suggested to the Home Affairs Committee as an alternative to ARIS. In my interviews with these practitioners, there were many areas of disagreement in relation to the operation of the Irish proceeds of crime legislation; one area where there was unanimous agreement, however, was resistance to incentivisation schemes such as ARIS. Even interviewees from the Criminal Assets Bureau advocated in favour of realised monies being transferred to the Minister. Interviewees preferred this option, for example, on the grounds that if the decision as to how such money is spent is in the hands of the government, there can be no criticisms in relation to policing for profit, and it does not interfere with Bureau priorities.

A second option is for law enforcement agencies to not participate in ARIS, but instead receive a fixed amount in lieu. For example, the Serious Fraud Office participated in the ARIS scheme until 2014, but no longer does so. Since April 2014, the SFO instead receives a fixed sum in lieu of entitlements under ARIS; this fixed sum amounts to the cost of running the SFO Proceeds of Crime Unit.[46] Not participating in ARIS represents a better approach to the allocation of realised monies: it provides certainty for the SFO (in terms of budgetary resources and planning) and avoids potential criticism, whether on the basis of 'policing for profit' (as mentioned above) or conflicts of interest.[47]

A third option involves ring-fencing realised monies and allocating them to community projects. One example of this is the Scottish Cashback for Communities programme,[48] whereby funds realised under POCA are invested in communities.[49]

Any of the above three options would provide significant improvements over the current incentivisation approach. Indeed, the Home Affairs Select Committee

[45] For detailed discussion of social reuse, see B Vettori, 'The disposal of confiscated assets in the EU Member States: what works, what does not work, and what is promising' in C King, C Walker, and J Gurulé (eds), *The Palgrave Handbook of Criminal and Terrorism Financing Law* (Palgrave, 2018).

[46] Home Office, *Asset Recovery Statistical Bulletin 2011/12–2016/17* (Statistical Bulletin 15/17, 2017) 9.

[47] See, eg, *Innospec Limited*, Sentencing Remarks, Crown Court at Southwark, 26 March 2010, [36].

[48] For examples of such projects, see CashBack for Communities, *Annual Report 2015–2016* (Scottish Government, 2016). See also Research Scotland, *Impact Evaluation of the Cashback for Communities Programme 2014/15* (2016).

[49] See also suggestions that ARIS monies should be ring-fenced for community spending: Police and Crime Commissioner West Yorkshire, *Proceeds of Crime Act Petition* (25 June 2013).

(HASC) concluded that 'there are significant weaknesses in the Asset Recovery Incentivisation Scheme (ARIS), specifically in that it rewards those who have not been affected or taken a role in the recovery of assets'.[50] Yet its (inadequate) solution was to recommend:

> … that at least 10% of the criminal assets recovered are returned or donated to the communities which have suffered at the hands of criminals, for example through charities. This must not disadvantage the agencies that have worked hard to recover the assets, but instead should be deducted from the 50% portion which the Home Office currently takes.[51]

It is unsurprising to see reform recommended, not least given previous criticism by, *inter alia*, the joint thematic review of asset recovery[52] and the National Audit Office.[53] However, the rather timid approach of the HASC fails to grasp the difficulties that go to the heart of incentivisation. Instead of tweaking around the edges, a fundamental overhaul of the ARIS scheme would be more desirable.

Even more disappointing than the HASC approach, however, was the government response. Underlying this response is an implication that the government is generally happy with the current scheme, though it will 'introduce further reform to ARIS to implement a Manifesto commitment to return a greater percentage of recovered assets to policing. This reform will result in additional incentivisation funds being invested in the multi-agency Regional Asset Recovery teams, which will allow for due consideration to be given to supporting prosecutorial functions'.[54] A fundamental review of the ARIS scheme by the Law Commission would be welcome.

III. A Confiscation Code?

Readers of this book – aptly entitled 'Criminal Law Reform Now' – will likely be all too aware of debates about codification of the criminal law.[55] As recently as 2016

[50] Home Affairs Committee (n 30), [42].

[51] ibid, [43].

[52] HM Crown Prosecution Service Inspectorate, HM Inspectorate of Court Administration, and HM Inspectorate of Constabulary, *Joint Thematic Review of Asset Recovery: Restraint and Confiscation Casework* (Criminal Justice Joint Inspection, 2010) [6.1] et seq.

[53] National Audit Office, *Confiscation Orders* (Stationery Office, 2013) Part 2. See also National Audit Office, *Confiscation Orders: Progress Review* (Stationery Office, 2016).

[54] Home Affairs Select Committee, *Government Response to the Committee's Fifth Report of Session 2016–17* (HC 25, 2016). See also the Government response to the Committee of Public Accounts in November 2016: HM Treasury, *Government Responses to the Committee of Public Accounts on the Thirty Seventh and the Thirty Ninth Reports from Session 2015–16; and the First to the Thirteenth Reports from Session 2016–17* (Cm 9351, 2016) 45.

[55] See, eg, G De Búrca and S Gardner, 'The Codification of the Criminal Law' (1990) 10(4) *Oxford Journal of Legal Studies* 559; ATH Smith, 'Legislating the Criminal Code: The Law Commission's Proposals' [1992] *Crim LR* 396; F Bennion, 'The Law Commission's Criminal Law Bill: No Way to Draft a Code' (1994) 15(2) *Statute Law Review* 108; H Brooke, 'The Law Commission and Criminal Law

the Lord Chief Justice reiterated calls for a Code of Criminal Law, stating that the criminal law:

> … is contained in a maze of innumerable, to some … impenetrable, statutes and common law developments over the centuries, which it is difficult to defend as entirely rational. It is in my view long overdue clarification and simplification. We ought to be able to look to a single document that sets out the nature of criminal conduct, in other words, a modern code.[56]

For many, the same criticisms levied against the current criminal law can be levied against the confiscation regime, and there have been many calls for codification.[57] As mentioned above, reform of confiscation law has been piecemeal – both before and subsequent to the current regime under POCA 2002 being enacted. It was not unexpected then to see the Law Commission identify confiscation as a possible option for reform under its Thirteenth Programme (the reasons for this being set out more fully in Professor Levi's chapter). While confiscation was not formally adopted as part of that Programme, as noted earlier the Commission will nonetheless commence a review of confiscation in September 2018 by way of Ministerial Reference.[58]

In his chapter, Professor Levi states that 'reform of the law of confiscation is neither a necessary nor a sufficient condition for enhancement of the levels of proceeds of crime actually confiscated by the authorities'.[59] He emphasises that there is limited research available to make informed judgment on the need for reform, a point that I heartily endorse. He suggests that 'the logic of the existing legal rules would repay revisiting' and, while there have been some changes (such as under the Criminal Finances Act), he states that 'there remain many aspects of civil and criminal asset recovery that would repay systematic revisiting and a Confiscation Code would be one way of addressing that'.[60] With that in mind, it is worth setting out some of the arguments in favour of a Code for confiscation law.

Arguments in favour of a Code are relatively straightforward: the law is currently disjointed, spread over numerous pieces of legislation (as well as in non-statutory forms). Codification would ensure that the law is clear and accessible; is rationally

Reform' [1995] *Crim LR* 911; Lord Bingham, 'A Criminal Code: Must we Wait for Ever?' [1998] *Crim LR* 694; A Samuels, 'Why do we not have a Criminal Code?' (2003) 67(3) *Journal of Criminal Law* 214.

[56] Lord Thomas, Speech at Dinner for Her Majesty's Judges (6 July, 2016). Available at: www.judiciary.gov.uk/wp-content/uploads/2016/07/lcj-mansion-house-july-2016.pdf.

[57] Some suggestions allude to codification, others to consolidation. For the purposes of the discussion here, it is not necessary to go into this distinction further, though it is worth setting out the difference. According to Ian Dennis, codification involves setting out the law in a single, coherent, consistent, unified and comprehensive piece of legislation, and this 'may necessitate a certain amount of reform'. In contrast, consolidation involves bringing together in one statute provisions relating to the same subject that are contained in a variety of other statutes. With the latter, 'provisions will be restated rather than reformed'. See I Dennis, 'Codifying the Law of Criminal Evidence' (2014) 35(2) *Statute Law Review* 107, 109.

[58] Law Commission (n 24) 23.

[59] See Levi (n 26) 20.

[60] ibid, 22.

thought-out (for example, allowing time to reflect upon judicial pronouncements over the past 16 years, as opposed to ad hoc reactions to particular judicial decisions); is fair and just (including taking into account relevant human rights jurisprudence); and enable the efficient administration of justice.[61] Such reform should be relatively straightforward given that much of the law is currently set out in statutory form, albeit across different pieces of legislation, and so would not require (much) re-drafting. Aspects of confiscation that have provoked discontent, for example in the wake of particular judgments, have often already been resolved by amending legislation[62] (though not always without criticism),[63] which lends further weight to suggestions that codification would not require a great deal of effort.

Clearly, there is a strong argument in favour of codification. Yet, I remain somewhat sceptical whether this will have the desired impact. Two points are worth making here. The first point, which can be dealt with swiftly, is a recurring counter-argument[64] amongst some stakeholders with whom I have spoken about reform of POCA: advocates of the current regime are concerned that a new Code would result in a 'new start', ie that many POCA 2002 issues already resolved by the courts would be opened to further – perhaps even identical – challenge under a new regime. Such concerns could be easily addressed by including a statutory provision to avoid this undoubtedly real concern.[65] The more pressing reason for my scepticism in relation to codification relates not to codification itself, but concern that the extant difficulties that have been identified under POCA are not ones that can be fixed merely by recourse to legislative change alone.

In this regard, the (many) criticisms that have been levied against confiscation are not ones stemming solely from deficiencies in the legislative regime. Other issues (including, inter alia, lack of adequate resourcing; the need for specialist staff; turnover of staff; the need for better training; difficulties in enforcement;

[61] See Dennis (n 57) 109–10 for elaboration of such arguments in favour of codification, in the context of criminal evidence.

[62] See, eg, s 48 of the Crime and Courts Act 2013, enacted in response to the Supreme Court decision in *SOCA v Perry* [2012] UKSC 35 (extra-territoriality of civil recovery). Another example is Sch 4, para 19 of the Serious Crime Act 2015 which purported to put the Supreme Court decision in *Waya* [2012] UKSC 51 (proportionality) on to a statutory footing.

[63] For example, the efforts to put *Waya* on a statutory footing have been criticised: 'It is simply not possible to compress the practical significance of *Waya* into a single sentence. Even judged in isolation, the amendment is arguably deficient. … This is unlikely to cause much genuine confusion, but it is an untidy omission that suggest the amendment may have been a hastily drafted afterthought.' M Sutherland Williams, M Hopmeier and R Jones, *Millington and Sutherland Williams on The Proceeds of Crime*, 5th edn (OUP, 2018) [9.23].

[64] There are many criticisms that can be levied against codification (whether in the context of confiscation law or otherwise), with varying levels of strength. For further discussion, see Dennis (n 57), 112 et seq.

[65] I thank Professor David Ormerod QC for this point.

the level of outstanding orders, as well as the likelihood of enforcement alongside the high interest rate) must also be taken into consideration in any discussion of reforming the current confiscation regime. It is important to explore the 'extent [to which] these "under-performance" issues are due to problems with legislation, and to what extent they are to do with attitudes, culture, resources and finance'.[66] It is hoped, then, that the Law Commission will adopt an all-encompassing approach in its review of the current regime.[67]

[66] See Levi (n 26) 8.

[67] See, eg, the approach of the Royal Commission on Criminal Justice where research was commissioned to inform its review. A full list of the 22 research studies is available at: The Royal Commission on Criminal Justice, *Report* (Cm 2263, HMSO, 1993) 254–55.

2

Rationalising Civil Preventive Orders: Opportunities for Reform

STEPHEN SHUTE*

In this chapter I examine those civil preventive orders (CPOs) which have been introduced solely to control the risk of an offender causing substantial criminal harm to the public or particular members of the public. I am leaving on one side, therefore, CPOs such as Anti-social Behaviour Orders (ASBOs) and their successors Criminal Behaviour Orders (CBOs) which can be imposed where lower levels of harm are envisaged.[1] I am also leaving on one side those CPOs such as Risk of Sexual Harm Orders/Sexual Risk Orders, Slavery and Trafficking Risk Orders, and Restraining Orders under the Protection from Harassment Act 1997 which do not require the persons upon whom they have been imposed to have previously committed a criminal offence.[2]

CPOs which meet these two conditions – (a) the only people who can be made subject to them are those who already have a criminal record, generally involving

* The author would like to express his deep thanks to his wife, Julia, and his three children, Miranda, Catherine, and Helena: without their understanding and forbearance, this chapter could not have been written.

[1] ASBOs were available in England and Wales to anyone aged 10 or older from 1998 to 2014; they sought to protect the public from conduct 'which caused or was likely to cause further harm, harassment, alarm, or distress'; they could only be imposed if deemed 'necessary' to achieve that goal. CBOs, which replaced ASBOs, were introduced by the Anti-social Behaviour, Crime and Policing Act 2014; they are available only on conviction and came into force on 20 October 2014; there is no 'necessity' test: they can be imposed if they would 'help' to prevent an offender 'from engaging in behaviour that causes or is likely to cause harassment, alarm or distress' to any person; they can include requirements as well as prohibitions; if imposed on persons under the age of 18 they must last between one and three years; if imposed on adults they may be no shorter than two years and can last indefinitely.

[2] Sexual Risk Orders, which have replaced Risk of Sexual Harm Orders in England and Wales, were introduced by the Anti-social Behaviour, Crime and Policing Act 2014. Slavery and Trafficking Risk Orders were introduced in England and Wales by the Modern Slavery Act 2015 s 23. Restraining Orders under the Protection from Harassment Act 1997 s 5 are now – as a result of s 5A introduced by the Domestic Violence, Crime and Victims Act 2004 which came into force on 30 September 2009 – available on acquittal as well as conviction. The maximum sentence for breach of a Restraining Order is five years' imprisonment and orders can last indefinitely. I am also setting on one side those orders for which breach is not a criminal offence but is punishable via contempt proceedings. Examples include Forced Marriage Protection Orders under the Forced Marriage (Civil Protection) Act 2007

a serious offence; and (b) the only legal warrant for their imposition is the prevention of further serious crime – are easier to justify than other CPOs, although this has not always been recognised.[3] In another article I explore some of the counter-arguments that might be deployed to attack their legitimacy: (i) that they permit an inappropriate transfer of rule-making authority from Parliament to the judiciary; (ii) that they transgress a principle that criminal prohibitions ought to be general in character; (iii) that they unacceptably preclude some offenders from activities which for others are lawful and harmless; and (iv) that they ride roughshod over a separation which ought properly to be kept between criminal and civil law. My conclusion is that none of these four arguments is of sufficient strength to render such CPOs an illegitimate device for the State to deploy.[4] That article builds on a piece I published almost 15 years ago in which I claimed that the three-stage process lying at the heart of all CPOs – risky behaviour followed by a formal legal warning followed by the possibility of punishment if that warning is ignored – is not in itself wrong.[5] My claim was qualified by concerns about the efficacy of CPOs (given the difficulty of predicting future behaviour and the possibility that those minded to reoffend and those minded to stay out of trouble would do so anyway, irrespective of the order). Nonetheless, despite that qualification, I was of the view that the orders themselves are legitimate. I remain of that view. It is important to recognise, however, that this does not mean that the legislature is duty bound to bring CPOs into being. Nor does it mean that all aspects of these orders are beyond reproach. It simply means there is no argument of general principle which renders their broad structure impermissible. In other words, the orders are a legitimate device for the legislature to have created and, once the legislature has empowered them, for the courts to impose.

However, as we shall see, the fact that each of these orders was brought into being at a different point in time, stimulated by different policy makers' views of the relevant criminal justice needs at that juncture, has meant that inconsistencies

(amending the Family Law Act 1996) and Gang-Related Violence Injunctions under s 34 of the Policing and Crime Act 2009 as amended by s 51 of the Serious Crime Act 2015 (brought into force in January 2011 for those aged 18 or over and in January 2012 for those aged 14 to 17, these orders can last for a maximum of two years: see *Chief Constable of Greater Manchester v Calder* [2015] All ER (D) 185, per Blake J (Queen's Bench Division)). Note that, in one respect, Serious Crime Prevention Orders (SCPOs) fall outside this restriction. In the Crown Court, SCPOs can only be imposed on someone who already has a criminal conviction for a serious offence; but in the High Court they may be imposed where the court is satisfied that the person has been involved in serious crime even though no convictions of any kind have been obtained against him/her. In this author's view, that power (which is in any event very rarely used) is anomalous.

[3] See, eg, House of Lords Select Committee on the Constitution, *2nd Report of Session 2006–07, Serious Crime Bill: Report* (HL Paper 41, 2007) [17]: 'A broad question for the House is whether the use of civil orders in an attempt to prevent serious criminal activity is a step too far in the development of preventative orders.'

[4] The article is entitled 'Individualised Criminalisation: The Rise and Rise of Sexual Offences Prevention Orders and Sexual Harm Prevention Orders in the United Kingdom'. It focuses exclusively on SOPOs/SHPOs.

[5] 'New Civil Preventative Orders: Sexual Offences Prevention Orders; Foreign Travel Orders; Risk of Sexual Harm Orders' [2004] *Crim LR* 417, 439.

now exist between them. Once the totality is considered, it is apparent that there is a strong case for rationalisation and streamlining. This chapter argues that such rationalisation would best be achieved by the introduction of a consolidating statute which brings together all the relevant orders into a single common framework. The goal should be to improve the structures of individual orders and make the overall arrangements more coherent.

I. The Orders

The following CPOs, all designed to prevent serious crime, will be considered: Sexual Offences Prevention Orders/Sexual Harm Prevention Orders; Serious Crime Prevention Orders; Violent Offender Orders/Violent Offences Prevention Orders; Financial Reporting Orders; Drug Travel Restriction Orders; and Slavery and Trafficking Prevention Orders/Trafficking and Exploitation Prevention Orders.

A. Sexual Offences Prevention Orders/Sexual Harm Prevention Orders

Sexual Offences Prevention Orders (SOPOs) were introduced into the courts' armoury by the Sexual Offences Act 2003 and brought into force on 1 May 2004.[6] They are aimed solely at persons with a proven record of sexual criminality. Their purpose is to inhibit these offenders from committing further sexual crimes. They seek to protect the public by adding new layers of protection for potential victims in the form of tailor-made, legally backed, prohibitions. The effect of these prohibitions is to establish a set of new personalised criminal offences for the offender.[7] The orders are available for adults and children aged 10 or over. They cannot be imposed for less than five years and can be made to last indefinitely. Breaches can be punished by a sentence of up to five years' imprisonment.

SOPOs in England and Wales were reformed following the enactment of the Anti-social Behaviour, Crime and Policing Act 2014 with the intention of making the legislation 'more flexible and effective'.[8] These reforms, which took effect on 8 March 2015,[9] did not extend to Northern Ireland or Scotland, where SOPOs

[6] The Sexual Offences Act 2003 (Commencement) Order 2004, SI 2004/874.

[7] Shute (n 4).

[8] Home Office, *Anti-social Behaviour, Crime and Policing Bill Fact Sheet: Overview of the Bill* (2013). The original Bill was introduced to Parliament in May 2013; the late amendments were introduced in October 2013. Simultaneously with the new orders, the Home Office, as required by the legislation, published guidance: *Guidance on Part 2 of the Sexual Offences Act 2003*. One of the first SHPOs was imposed on Bob Thompson: 'Former Lib Dem councillor avoids jail for sex offences involving teenager' *Brighouse Echo* (19 March 2015).

[9] The Anti-social Behaviour, Crime and Policing Act 2014 (Commencement No. 8, Saving and Transitional Provisions) Order 2015, SI 2015/373.

continue to operate. But, in England and Wales, SOPOs were replaced by a new order, the Sexual Harm Prevention Order (SHPO). The threshold for a SHPO's imposition was lowered from a risk of serious sexual harm to a risk of sexual harm. If one accepts the general legitimacy of the scheme, and if one accepts the premise that any sexual harm is – by definition – substantial, this change has advantages. It widens the scope of the orders and avoids the difficulty that has occasionally been experienced of distinguishing between serious and non-serious sexual harm. Two other important differences between SOPOs and SHPOs are that the prohibitions within SHPOs can run for different periods of time and can include travel restrictions (rather than these having to be imposed as part of a separate order as with SOPOs). However, despite a recommendation to the contrary in the Davies report which preceded the change,[10] and despite this now being possible for SOPOs in Scotland and in Northern Ireland following reforms made in November 2011 and June 2014,[11] SHPOs in England and Wales do not, in terms, extend to positive obligations. This restriction has in practice, though, largely been evaded by the courts.

B. Serious Crime Prevention Orders[12]

The genesis of the Serious Crime Prevention Order (SCPO) is to be found in a Green Paper, *New Powers Against Organised and Financial Crime*, which was published by the Labour Government in July 2006.[13] Among other suggestions to tackle organised and 'lifestyle' criminals, the Green Paper proposed the introduction of a new CPO to allow limitations to be imposed on, for example, their travel and communications. Such restrictions, it was argued, would force those subject to the orders to change their ways of working, thus leaving them open to greater law enforcement scrutiny, or risk becoming subject to breach proceedings. A further 'unique feature' of the proposed order was that it was to be extended not just to individuals but also to organisations.

[10] Hugh Davies QC, *Civil Preventive Orders: Sexual Offences Act 2003* (2013) [6.5.13]. Davies proposed adding the words 'or requirements' to the legislation.

[11] The change in Scotland followed two reports: Professor George Irving's review of sex offender notification, *Registering the Risk* (2005); and Lady Cosgrove's report on sex offending, *Reducing the Risk: Improving the Response to Sex Offending – Report of the Expert Panel on Sex Offending* (2001). Both mentioned the lack of a requirement to comply with risk assessment processes; the Scottish police envisaged using the change to extend the information some sex offenders had to provide: see *Sexual Offences Prevention Orders* (Police Circular 2/2012).

[12] The discussion of SCPOs, VOOs, and FROs draws in part on my chapter, 'Managing the Risk Posed by Offenders after the Expiry of Sentence: The British Experience' in PH van Kempen and W Young (eds) *Prevention of Reoffending: The Value of Rehabilitation and the Management of High Risk Offenders* (InterSentia, 2014) 235–61.

[13] (Cm 6875, 2006). See *New Powers against Organised and Financial Crime – A Summary of Responses* (November 2006); and *Powers against Organised and Financial Crime – responses received to the consultation document* (May 2007) (issued following an FOI request).

The power for the courts to create SCPOs was included in the Serious Crime Act 2007 and the orders became available in England and Wales and Northern Ireland on 6 April 2008.[14] However, they were not able to be imposed in Scotland until 1 March 2016, following amendments made to the Serious Crime Act 2007 by the Serious Crime Act 2015.[15] Although breaching a SCPO was always a United Kingdom-wide offence,[16] Scotland initially adopted a wait-and-see approach to the imposition of SCPOs. It wanted to understand their effectiveness in other parts of the United Kingdom before deciding whether the courts in Scotland should be allowed to create them. Nonetheless, by 2013, the Scottish Government had become sufficiently receptive to the idea to open a consultation on their extension to Scotland.[17] It published its response to that consultation on 4 April 2014[18] and subsequently indicated it would ask the United Kingdom Government to amend the 2007 Act to allow SCPOs to be made in Scotland, thus creating a single United Kingdom-wide SCPO scheme.

Like all other CPOs, SCPOs are designed to be preventative not punitive. As indicated above, their aim is to render it more difficult for serious criminals to operate by imposing conditions upon them which prevent, restrict, or disrupt their involvement in serious crime. SCPOs are limited to adults, bodies corporate, partnerships, and unincorporated associations.[19] Unlike SOPOs/SHPOs, they cannot be imposed on persons who are aged less than 18 years. The maximum period across which they can be in force is five years rather than the indefinite period possible for SOPOs/SHPOs and Slavery and Trafficking Orders (STPOs). However, section 16 of the 2007 Act expressly empowered the courts to specify when an order is to come into force and when it is to cease. Consequently, where an offender is in prison it has become common practice for the courts to delay commencement of the order until the offender is released.[20] Furthermore, unlike SOPOs but like SHPOs, STPOs, and Trafficking and Exploitation Orders (TEPOs), the courts can specify different start and finish dates for different

[14] The Serious Crime Act 2007 (Commencement No. 2 and Transitional and Transitory Provisions and Savings) Order 2008, SI 2008/755.

[15] See Serious Crime Act 2015, ss 46–50 (together with Schedule 1) which extended the scope of Part 1 of the Serious Crime Act 2007 to Scotland. The changes were brought in force by the Serious Crime Act 2015 (Commencement No. 5 and Transitional Provisions and Savings) Regulations 2016, SI 2016/148.

[16] On 8 March 2007, the Scottish Parliament adopted a legislative consent motion for that part of the Bill.

[17] Scottish Government, *Serious Crime Prevention Orders in Scotland: A Consultation Paper* (2013). The *Consultation Paper* stated that: 'Experience in England & Wales has shown that these orders make it harder for criminals to carry out their illegal activities and easier for law enforcement agencies to intervene at an early stage when a breach of an order has been found' [11]. The Paper also said that the orders would be 'highly targeted and used for a relatively small number of individuals/organisations' [13].

[18] Scottish Government, *Serious Crime Prevention Orders in Scotland: Summary of Consultation Responses* (2014). Nine responses were received, the majority of which were in favour of introducing SCPOs to Scotland.

[19] See s 6.

[20] CPS, *Serious Crime Prevention Orders Guidance* (CPS Website, updated 2018).

provisions in a SCPO, as long as the total period across which the order runs does not exceed the five-year limit. As with many other CPOs, the maximum penalty for breach of a SCPO is five years' imprisonment. There is no bar to imposing SCPOs alongside other CPOs such as Drug Travel Restriction Orders (TROs) or SOPOs/SHPOs.[21]

The power to impose a SCPO differs from the power to impose a SOPO/SHPO in some other important respects. Unlike SOPOs/SHPOs – and departing from the suggestion in the Green Paper that SCPOs would need to be *both* necessary and proportionate[22] – there is no 'necessity' requirement for a SCPO to be created. Section 19 of the 2007 Act simply empowers the court to impose a SCPO on an individual, following his or her conviction for a specified serious offence, if there are reasonable grounds to believe that the imposition of the order would protect the public by preventing, restricting, or disrupting his/her involvement in serious crime.[23]

SCPOs in England and Wales can be made only by the Crown Court or the High Court.[24] They cannot be made by magistrates' courts. Where they are available – unlike, for example, SHPOs – they can impose positive as well as negative obligations on an offender. Section 5 offers an extensive list of examples of the types of prohibitions, restrictions, or requirements that may be imposed which includes placing controls on an individual's ability to travel outside the United Kingdom. But the section does not limit orders to any of the listed examples. This means that almost any prohibition, restriction, or requirement the court deems appropriate may be included in a SCPO as long as it will help to protect the public from serious crime.

SCPOs have been relatively sparingly used. By 31 March 2014, the National Crime Agency (NCA) – the successor body to the Serious Organised Crime Agency (SOCA) – was able to give the Home Office details of 317 SCPOs that had been imposed by the Crown Court (and one by the High Court) since their introduction

[21] See, eg, *Brooks (John Alan)* (n 36).

[22] (Cm 6875, 2006) [3.1].

[23] SCPOs in England and Wales can only be made on an application by the Director of Public Prosecutions, the Director of Revenue and Customs Prosecutions, or the Director of the Serious Fraud Office (s 8). However, that power can be delegated to a Crown Prosecutor: see Schedule 2 [1–21]. The definition of 'involvement in serious crime in England and Wales' is provided by s 2 of the 2007 Act. It refers to a person who has committed an offence which is specified (or falls within a description specified) in Part 1 of Schedule 1 to the Act *or* is one which, in the particular circumstances of the case, the court considers to be sufficiently serious to be treated for the purposes of the application or matter 'as if it were so specified'. The latter alternative appears to give the court the power to extend the reach of the list of offences where it deems that appropriate. The list of 'specified' offences is long. It includes, inter alia, offences relating to 'drug trafficking', 'people trafficking', 'arms trafficking', 'prostitution and child sex', 'armed robbery', 'money laundering' (contrary to the Proceeds of Crime Act 2002, ss 327 and 328), 'fraud', 'corruption and bribery', 'counterfeiting', and 'blackmail'. The list has a certain degree of overlap with the specified offences which could trigger a Financial Reporting Order (see n 59).

[24] The High Court is given this power by s 1 of the 2007 Act. Applications to the High Court can be made without the need for a prior conviction; these applications thus fall outside the restriction set on the scope of this article in the introduction.

in April 2008: an average of around 45 per annum.[25] In June 2010, the NCA began the practice of publishing a *Register* of ancillary orders on its website.[26] This gave information regarding the offender's name, date of birth, the offences committed, the start date of the order, its duration, its terms, and whether the offender was in prison or had been released from custody. The names of 199 offenders subject to SCPOs could be found on the NCA's website as at 1 September 2017.[27] An analysis of these orders by the author reveals that more than 90 per cent (184: 92.5 per cent) had been imposed for the maximum period of five years. The remainder had been made for three years (11: 5.5 per cent) or four years (4: 2 per cent). More than eight out of ten of these orders were imposed for drugs offences (137: 69 per cent) or money laundering (25: 12.5 per cent). The rest had been imposed for offences of fraud, including cyber fraud (18: 9 per cent); people trafficking or other immigration offences (11: 5.5 per cent); firearms offences (4: 2 per cent); unidentified conspiracy offences (2: 1 per cent); and perverting the course of justice (1: 0.5 per cent).[28]

SCPOs have also been rare in Scotland. The first Scottish order was not imposed until June 2017, some 16 months after the power became available. The offender, Isabella Jackson, had been given a sentence of 45 months' imprisonment after pleading guilty to sending death threats to the then Home Secretary and now Prime Minister, Theresa May. Her five-year SCPO, which will only become active once she is released from prison, restricts her use of mobile communication devices and requires her to notify the police of all her online and social media accounts.[29]

Despite being little used, SCPOs are regarded by the Home Office as an 'important tool' for disrupting organised and financial crime, including the relatively new and rapidly increasing area of cyber crime (although it appears from the analysis above that very few orders have been imposed thus far specifically to guard against this risk).[30] Applications for SCPOs to the courts are rarely refused. Home Office data reveal that, of the 180 applications made to the courts for a SCPO up to 31 March 2012, 164 were granted and just 16 were refused: a success rate of 91 per cent. Most of these orders were constructed to become active only following the offender's release from prison.[31]

[25] See *Explanatory Notes to the Serious Crime Act 2015* [150]. But, as footnote 12 of the *Explanatory Notes* points out, these figures represent those SCPOs known to the NCA and the SOCA. Other SCPOs may have been granted which were not reported to either of these bodies.

[26] See *A Memorandum to the Home Affairs Committee and the Justice Committee* which was submitted by the Home Office as part of the post-legislative scrutiny of the Serious Crime Act 2007 (Cm 8502, November 2012) [48].

[27] Details are also given of persons subject to FROs and TROs. The list, though, is not a complete list of those subject to any of these orders (see n 25).

[28] One offence was recorded as 'Not Known'; the two conspiracy offences were not further identified.

[29] 'Fife woman sentenced for bomb threats' (Crown Office and Procurator Fiscal Service media release, 15 June 2017).

[30] *A Memorandum to the Home Affairs Committee and the Justice Committee* (n 26) [90].

[31] ibid, gives details of the year-by-year build-up of the 164 SCPOs that had been imposed up to 31 March 2012 (all in the Crown Court): 19 orders were secured in 2008–09; 43 in 2009–10; 39 in 2010–11; and 63 in 2011–12.

As with other CPOs, the Court of Appeal has considered a number of appeals involving SCPOs. These give a flavour of the issues that can arise, the sorts of circumstances in which the orders may be made, and the types of conditions – positive and negative – which the Crown Court may include. Five cases – three involving frauds and two involving the supply or importation of drugs – are offered as examples:[32]

Batchelor (Andrew John):[33] Batchelor was a 'professional' criminal who appealed against a five-year SCPO and sentences of imprisonment totalling five years which had been imposed for 29 offences of fraudulent trading, obtaining property by deception, and fraud by false representation. The offences related to jewellery scams. They involved an abuse of trust placed in the offender by his victims. The Court of Appeal described Batchelor's offences as 'serious, substantial and heartless'. His SCPO contained six detailed clauses which, inter alia, prohibited him from working within a business engaged in the jewellery trade; being in possession of any article for use in the jewellery trade; and entering a pawnbroker's establishment in England and Wales without leave of the court. The Court of Appeal upheld both Batchelor's sentences and his SCPO. Giving the judgment of the Court, Lord Judge, the Lord Chief Justice, said it was clear that SCPOs were not confined to violent or sexual offences but could also apply to crimes of dishonesty. (Indeed, as we have seen, very few SCPOs are issued following convictions for violent or sexual offences and the vast majority are imposed on drug importers, drug dealers, people traffickers, money launderers, and fraudsters.) In the circumstances, the Court concluded, it was 'entirely reasonable and utterly proportionate' for the sentencing judge to have imposed a SCPO on Batchelor to disrupt the possibility of him committing similar offences again.

Heayns (Christopher Francis):[34] Christopher Heayns had originally been known as Christopher Poulton but changed his name by deed poll to Heayns in January 2013. Aged 35 at the time of his appeal, he was a 'determined and experienced confidence trickster' with a long history of offending. During his adult life he had used 13 different surnames and three different birth dates, served five different prison sentences, and appeared before the courts on 15 previous occasions for 131 offences. In total, he had accumulated 77 previous convictions for fraud and similar offences. He also had a history of failing to comply with SCPOs

[32] See also *Barnes (Michael Jackson) and Another* [2012] EWCA Crim 2549, per Rafferty LJ, where the SCPO placed restrictions on the offender's involvement in motor cycle clubs, including the 'Outlaws Motorcycle Club'; and *Corkovic (Paul Robert Joseph) and Others* [2013] EWCA Crim 1117, per Rafferty LJ, where the order placed restrictions on the offender wearing a motor cycle helmet. See also *Hancox and Duffy* [2010] EWCA Crim 102, per Hughes LJ (as he then was) (appeals against SCPOs imposed on both offenders were dismissed). To assist prosecutors in drafting orders, the CPS has published an extensive *SCPO Precedent Library* (December 2015) containing examples of successful applications.

[33] [2010] EWCA Crim 1025, per Lord Judge CJ.

[34] [2017] EWCA Crim 465, per Gilbart J. As might be expected, the case attracted considerable interest from both broadcasting and print media. Examples include '"Slick" fraudster posed as multimillionaire to con woman he met on dating site out of £250k' *The Sun* (21 July 2016), and 'Doctor left penniless after being tricked by Plenty of Fish conman lover' *Mail Online* (29 July 2016).

and twice had received sentences of imprisonment for breaching these orders: in January 2012 and February 2013. In October 2007, he had been made subject to a Bankruptcy Restriction Order which remained effective until September 2020. His original SCPO, taken out in June 2010 and extended in November 2012 until June 2017, included a term that he was not to use a name other than Christopher Poulton 'in all aspects of his life'. Nor was he to use a birth date other than 26 June 1981. He was also prohibited from holding more than one authorised bank account; from borrowing money from any person other than a family member; and from obtaining credit or entering any relationship which resulted in him owing a financial debt of any kind.

Despite these restrictions, in July 2013, within days of his release from prison, Heayns created a dishonest profile on an online dating site, Plenty of Fish, and began a relationship in Newcastle with a 28-year-old hospital doctor, Liz Todd, telling her his name was Christopher Smith. He convinced the doctor that he worked as a barrister with a criminal law practice and owned a number of properties around the country which were worth millions of pounds. Two months later, in September 2013, he persuaded the doctor to take out the tenancy on a large Grade II listed manor house, Sandhoe Hall in Hexham, at a rent of £2,400 per month. The couple moved into the house together and, over the next three months, began to furnish and renovate the property. Heayns persuaded the doctor to take out a £25,000 bank loan to help pay for this work on the understanding he would pay her back when his finances were sorted out. She also used her credit cards to the maximum to pay more bills. Heayns assured her that he had an investment bond worth £250,000 which would mature in February 2014. Similar assurances were given to the doctor's father to convince him to cover other expenses. Yet more debt was incurred when Heayns established a printing and graphic business at the Hall, converting a garage into a studio to do so and persuading the doctor to purchase mobile phones and iPads. The doctor's mother, a former biochemist who had retired and now ran a soft furnishing business, was employed to provide soft furnishings for the Hall. She, too, was duped by him. She was persuaded to take out a £25,000 bank loan which she gave to Heayns. Heayns continued to ask both the doctor and her mother for money and the mother used her credit cards to pay bills and took out a further loan of £17,800 which was paid directly into Heayns' bank account.

Things came to a head in December 2013 when a self-employed builder, who had been hired to carry out work on the Hall and brought in up to 10 employees to help, had not been paid. He became suspicious of Heayns and, having seen a Christmas card in the Hall in the name of Christopher Poulton, carried out an internet search. He discovered that Heayns was a convicted fraudster and sent a text to the doctor with a link to the website of a Bournemouth newspaper which had run an article about Poulton and included a photograph. After that, the doctor's relationship with Heayns deteriorated rapidly and she moved out of Sandhoe Hall in February 2014.

The effect of the fraud on the doctor was 'devastating'. She was 'financially ruined'. When she left the Hall she had just £5 to her name. The fraud also had a significant effect on the doctor's family and on the employees and others with whom Heayns did business. The doctor did not report the fraud to the police until May 2015.[35] Soon after that, Heayns was charged and remanded in custody. Following a not guilty plea, he was convicted by a jury in February 2016 of 14 offences involving fraud and engaging in business and obtaining credit contrary to the Insolvency Act 1986. Five months later, he was sentenced to a total of nine-and-a-half years' imprisonment. He also received a new five-year SCPO to commence on the date of his release from prison. He was described by the sentencing judge as 'the most dishonest person whom the court had ever encountered' and 'totally without morals'. He had spun 'lie after lie about his circumstances'. The judge concluded that there was no prospect of him desisting from his behaviour, which was why the ancillary orders had been made. Heayns appealed against his sentence and his SCPO but, subject to some minor amendments to the wording of the SCPO, both were upheld. The Court of Appeal made it clear that it considered Heayns an offender who would carry on offending: he was someone, the Court said, from whom the public urgently needed protection.

***Brooks (John Alan)*:**[36] Brooks was a 61-year-old drug importer who operated on a major scale. In 2012 he was convicted, after a two-week trial, of a single count of conspiracy to import cocaine. Subsequently, he was sentenced to 28 years' imprisonment for this offence. His prosecution arose after Irish police boarded a yacht called *Dances with Waves* in November 2008. On the yacht, the police discovered 75 bales of cocaine with a street value of around £140 to £150 million. Alongside his prison sentence for what was rightly described by the Court of Appeal as a 'massive drugs conspiracy', Brooks received a Travel Restriction Order (TRO) and a five-year SCPO. Both were timed to take effect on his release from prison. The SCPO, inter alia, placed restrictions on his possession of cash; his use of yachts; his possession of certain documents; his use of Money Service Bureaux; and his use of communication devices. It also placed notification obligations on him relating to any acquisition of a new passport or identification card; any foreign travel; and any use of premises.[37] Brooks appealed against his conviction, his sentence, and his two CPOs. Although the TRO was quashed by the Court of Appeal, his conviction, his 28-year custodial sentence, and his SCPO were upheld.

***McIntyre (Andrew James)*:**[38] McIntyre was a 'very significant criminal' and 'head of a serious criminal gang'. Despite being only in his 20s, he was sentenced to a total of 21 years' imprisonment for firearms offences and two counts of conspiracy to supply Class A drugs. He had 'orchestrated and arranged' drug supply conspiracies in Liverpool while he was in prison serving a previous five-year sentence for conspiracy to rob. He did that by means of mobile phones he

[35] See Northumbria Police, 'High value fraudster jailed' (21 July 2016).

[36] [2014] EWCA Crim 562, per Davis LJ. See also *Brooks v R* [2016] EWCA Crim 44, [2016] 4 WLR 79, per Treacy LJ (confiscation order reduced from £3.6 million to £0.5 million).

[37] See the National Crime Agency website http://www.nationalcrimeagency.gov.uk/.

[38] [2012] EWCA Crim 3085, per Moses LJ.

had obtained illegally. His five-year SCPO required him to notify the authorities of his prison visitors; placed restrictions on his use of the prison telephone system and on his use of prison accounts; prohibited his use of other communication devices; and restricted his communication and association with certain specified persons. McIntyre sought leave to appeal against his convictions, his sentence, and his SCPO. However, the Court of Appeal rejected his challenge to his conviction and his sentence and – subject to a minor modification which allowed contact with his partner, Emma Clay, who was a co-accused – upheld his SCPO.

Haq (Mohammad Izhar-Ul):[39] Haq was convicted in 2012 of an offence of cheating the public revenue. He was sentenced to five years' imprisonment. The fraud was said to be 'a particularly cunning and sophisticated operation' involving the production of bogus bank guarantees. Haq's SCPO placed restrictions, inter alia, on the number of bank accounts and credit cards he could have; his possession of mobile phones; and his entering gambling casinos (the money raised from the fraud had been used to pay gambling debts). It also required him to notify the authorities of his residence. Haq, then aged 60, challenged the terms of his order on the grounds that they were disproportionate and did not sufficiently address the question of risk or the question of the protection of the public. The Court of Appeal disagreed. The terms of the order may have been 'stringent', the Court said, but that was 'precisely because the public needed protection'. It concluded that there was no arguable basis for holding the restrictions to be unnecessary or disproportionate.

C. Violent Offender Orders/Violent Offences Prevention Orders

Violent Offender Orders (VOOs), which took effect in England and Wales from 3 August 2009,[40] were created following the enactment of Part 7 of the Criminal Justice and Immigration Act 2008. Their origins lay in the reaction to the killing by Damien Hanson and Elliot White of an Oxford-educated financier John Monckton in his home in London in 2004. After Hanson and White's conviction (for murder and manslaughter respectively) an inquiry into the affair was ordered by the then Home Secretary, Charles Clarke. Conducted by Andrew Bridges, HM Chief Inspector of Probation, the report was published in February 2006.[41] Two months later, Clarke told the House of Commons that there was 'a strong case' for introducing violent offender orders along the same lines as had proved effective in the case of sex offenders. He promised to publish proposals in the area before the

[39] [2014] EWCA Crim 2212, per Davis LJ.

[40] The Criminal Justice and Immigration Act 2008 (Commencement No. 10) Order 2009, SI 209/1842.

[41] HM Inspectorate of Probation, *An Independent Review of a Serious Further Offence Case: Damien Hanson & Elliot White* (2006).

summer.[42] After the foreign prisoners' scandal in April 2006, and Labour's poor performance in the May 2006 local government elections, Clarke was dismissed as Home Secretary by Prime Minister Tony Blair. However, his successor, John Reid, was no less committed to the idea of VOOs. In July 2006, Reid repeated Clarke's promise to introduce them in a government review of how the criminal justice system might be reshaped to protect society better. Entitled *Rebalancing the criminal justice system in favour of the law-abiding majority: Cutting crime, reducing reoffending and protecting the public*, this review was strongly endorsed by the Prime Minister. A stakeholder consultation paper followed in April 2007 and, although opposition was voiced in some quarters – notably by Liberty,[43] legislation to create the new orders was finally passed in 2008. It covered England and Wales only and did not extend to Scotland or Northern Ireland.

The declared purpose of a VOO is to protect the public from the risk of serious violent harm. Orders seek to achieve this by targeting those offenders who continue to pose a risk of committing serious violent offences after they have been released from prison. VOOs have the same basic structure as SOPOs, SHPOs, and SCPOs, but there are also some important differences. A qualifying offender is defined as a person aged 18 or over who has committed a specified offence and received a sentence of at least 12 months' imprisonment. So, like SCPOs but unlike SOPOs/SHPOs, VOOs cannot be imposed on persons under the age of 18. Also, unlike SOPOs, SHPOs and SCPOs, VOOs are not available on conviction. Nor, in a further marked contrast to SOPOs/SHPOs and SCPOs, can they come into force while an offender is in prison or subject to a supervision order (or a hospital order) or while the offender is subject to statutory licence conditions made in relation to any offence.[44]

Under the enabling legislation, a magistrates' court – because the orders are not available on conviction, they are not available to the Crown Court – is able to impose a VOO if, following an application by a Chief Officer of Police, it concludes that the offender has acted in such a way as to make the order necessary for the purpose of protecting the public from the risk of serious violent harm.[45] 'Serious violent harm' is defined as serious physical or psychological harm caused by the offender committing one or more of a limited list of serious offences: manslaughter; soliciting murder; an offence under section 18 of the Offences Against the Person Act 1861 (for example, wounding with intent to cause grievous bodily harm); an offence under section 20 of the Offences Against the Persons Act (for example, malicious wounding); and attempted murder or conspiracy to commit

[42] HC Debates, vol. 445, col. 245 (20 April 2006).

[43] *Liberty's Response to the Home Office Consultation on Violent Offender Orders* (2007).

[44] An example of a SCPO imposed on prisoners before their release from custody is that imposed on two large-scale drug smugglers, Cavan Hanna and James Hanna, who had five-year restrictions placed upon them which required notification of prison visitors and imposed restrictions on the use by them of the prison telephone system.

[45] Criminal Justice and Immigration Act 2008, s 101(3)(b).

murder. The restrictions that can be included in a VOO are set out in an exhaustive list contained in section 102 of the 2008 Act. This allows VOOs to contain prohibitions from specified areas or places; prohibitions from attending specific events; and prohibitions from having any or particular kinds of contact with specified individuals. As a result, the limitations that can be included in a VOO are considerably more constrained than those that can be included in a SOPO/SHPO or SCPO.[46] Furthermore, unlike SOPOs/SHPOs which can last indefinitely, VOOs cannot run for less than two years and cannot last longer than five years. Breach of a VOO, like breach of a SOPO/SHPO or SCPO, leaves the offender liable to a maximum penalty of five years' imprisonment.

From what has been said above, it can be seen that a VOO is a much more bounded order than a SOPO/SHPO or even a SCPO. Its focus is on the top end of seriousness: 'the critical few' as they are sometimes called. For this reason, the Home Office initially estimated that only about 125 VOOs would be made annually.[47] By 2010, the Home Office had downgraded even this prediction to between 60 and 120 orders annually.[48]

As mentioned above, the jurisdiction for VOOs does not extend beyond England and Wales. However, a variant of the VOO – the Violent Offences Prevention Order (VOPO) – was eventually introduced into Northern Ireland by sections 55 to 76 of the Justice Act (Northern Ireland) 2015. While sharing some characteristics with VOOs, VOPOs in Northern Ireland differ in that they *are* available on conviction and *can* be imposed on offenders under the age of 18. The 2015 Act also made it clear that, unlike VOOs, VOPOs may include positive requirements as well as negative prohibitions. Additionally, the permissible restrictions in a VOPO were left open-ended rather than constrained by an exhaustive list as with VOOs. This means VOPOs, but not VOOs, can be constructed entirely flexibly by the court to suit the needs of the individual case. Furthermore, also unlike VOOs, VOPOs can operate during a period of custody and can run alongside licence conditions once an offender has been released from prison. However, VOPOs share with VOOs the fact that they cannot run for less than two years and, like SCPOs, cannot last longer than five years. No order akin to a VOO or a VOPO has been introduced in Scotland.

Although they have been criticised by the Chief Executive of the Howard League for Penal Reform, Frances Crook, who described them as an 'imprecation not a solution',[49] the introduction of VOOs had strong support from the police and was also welcomed by the probation service.[50] Examples of VOOs that have

[46] Criminal Justice and Immigration Act 2008, ss 107–112, also imposed a set of notification requirements on offenders who are subject to a VOO.

[47] *The Telegraph* (5 August 2009).

[48] Home Office, *The Criminal Justice and Immigration Act 2008 (Violent Offender Orders) (Information about Release or Transfer) Regulations – A Targeted Consultation* (2010) [8].

[49] See the entry on her blog for 5 August 2009.

[50] The Vice Chair of the Probation Chiefs Association, Steve Collett, said they would provide a useful additional tool to protect the public from 'a very small group of highly dangerous offenders': see his appearance on *BBC 1 Breakfast TV*, 5 August 2009.

been imposed thus far in England and Wales include the order imposed in 2010 by Leicester magistrates' court on 43-year-old Ricky Michael Simon who had a 20-year history of violence. His VOO prohibited him from entering a large area of the City of Leicester from 6.00 pm to 6.00 am on Mondays to Fridays and at any time on Saturdays and Sundays.[51] A second example is the VOO imposed in 2012 on Bradley Stantiford who was the head of an organised crime group which supplied controlled drugs across the south east of England,[52] Stantiford had been sentenced to five years' imprisonment for causing grievous bodily harm and was prohibited by his VOO from entering any pub, hotel bar, or nightclub in Bedfordshire, Cambridgeshire, Essex, and Hertfordshire.[53] A third example is the VOO imposed in 2013 on Sean Aslam, a 38-year-old man from Stoke-on-Trent whose previous convictions included a sentence of eight years' imprisonment in 2005 for an offence under section 18 of the Offences Against the Person Act 1861 (wounding with intent to cause grievous bodily harm) after he picked up a prostitute in his car and slashed her throat. In the light of this offence, Aslam's VOO banned him from specified parts of the red-light district of the city. Within weeks, however, he was reported as having breached the order by entering the prohibited area: he was spotted in a pub by an off-duty police officer. For this breach, he was sentenced by the Crown Court at Stoke-on-Trent to five months' imprisonment.[54]

The first VOPO to be ordered in Northern Ireland was apparently imposed in January 2017 on Gary Woods. Woods had a significant history of domestic violence which included a sentence of two-and-a-half years' imprisonment imposed in 2015 for an attack on his heavily pregnant girlfriend. According to his Probation Officer, Woods had a 'longstanding hostility' towards women: indeed she told Coleraine magistrates' court that although she had worked with serious violent and sexual offenders for 18 years, she had not come across an individual who was so hostile. Woods' VOPO prohibited him from 'entering into any relationship with a woman without his offending being made known to her'. He was also prohibited from staying away from home without prior approval from the authorities and from possessing a mobile phone or any internet device without registering it with his Designated Risk Manager (DRM). He was, in addition, required to make any such device available for inspection by his DRM and required to engage appropriately

[51] *Leicester Mercury* (27 February 2010). The newspaper report stated that Simon was the 'first person in Leicestershire' to have been made subject to a VOO. As there are no Court of Appeal cases on VOOs (VOOs cannot be imposed by the Crown Court, so appeals against them do not reach that level), these examples are taken from press reports.

[52] Dubbed 'The Beast', Bradley Stantiford was said to be a 'drug kingpin who ran a gang of drug dealers throughout Hertfordshire and Essex': 'Herts and Essex drug kingpin "The Beast" Bradley Stantiford has assets seized' *Hertfordshire Mercury* (2 April 2017). In August 2016, Stantiford was sentenced to eight years' imprisonment for conspiracy to supply cocaine: 'Gang which sold drugs in Cheshunt, Ware, Hoddesdon, Harlow and Essex jailed for combined 46 years' *Hertfordshire Mercury* (19 August 2016).

[53] 'Man given interim violent offender order banning him from pubs and clubs in four counties' *The Hunts Post* (10 January 2012).

[54] *The Sentinel* (16 April 2013). The police in Stoke-on-Trent indicated to the newspaper that Aslam's VOO would be 'proactively policed' when he was released from that sentence.

with his DRM.[55] When granting the order, the judge in the magistrates' court said that the statements from Woods' victims about his crimes were 'chilling', even for someone who had been involved in law for more than 20 years. It is worth noting that neither of the last two groups of restrictions in Woods' VOPO could have been included in a VOO in England and Wales as they are not in the exhaustive list of permissible prohibitions provided by the enabling legislation.

D. Financial Reporting Orders

The power to make a Financial Reporting Order (FRO) was introduced by the Serious Organised Crime and Police Act 2005. It followed publication of a White Paper, *One Step Ahead: A 21st Century Strategy to Defeat Organised Crime*, which had been issued by the Labour Government in 2004.[56] The central idea behind the White Paper was to move beyond merely increasing the chances of the major players in organised crime being apprehended and convicted to a broader strategy which sought to disrupt their activities at an earlier stage and hence reduce the likelihood that further crimes would occur at all. To achieve this, the White Paper floated the idea of a new type of civil preventive order which could be used against those serious acquisitive criminals who the authorities believed posed the most significant long-term threat. Accordingly, under section 76 of the 2005 Act, which came into effect across the United Kingdom on 1 April 2006,[57] courts were empowered to make a FRO when sentencing or otherwise dealing with a person convicted of a specified offence if, but only if, they were satisfied that the risk of the offender committing another specified offence was 'sufficiently high' to justify the order being made.[58]

Section 76 provided an exhaustive, and lengthy, list of the specified trigger offences.[59] If made in a magistrates' court, a FRO could not exceed five years.

[55] 'Thug deemed a risk to women has first ever NI anti-violence order imposed' *Belfast Telegraph* (24 January 2017). See also the VOPO imposed on Jonathan Gregory Wilkinson: 'Violent offences order imposed on man who assaulted court staff' *The Ballymena and Antrim Times* (10 March 2017).

[56] Cm 6167 [6.6].

[57] The Serious Organised Crime and Police Act 2005 (Commencement No. 5 and Transitional and Transitory Provisions and Savings) Order 2006, SI 2006/378.

[58] Section 76 applies to England and Wales; ss 77 and 78 make similar provision in respect of Scotland and Northern Ireland.

[59] Under s 76(4), the Secretary of State may, by order, add or remove offences from the list. Many new offences were added to the list of trigger offences by an order which took effect as of 4 May 2007: see the Serious Organised Crime and Police Act 2005 (Amendment of s 76(3)) Order 2007, SI 2007/1392. Specified offences now include fraud and obtaining services by deception under the Fraud Act 2006; conspiracy to defraud; false accounting; any of the so-called 'lifestyle offences' specified in Schedule 2 to the Proceeds of Crime Act 2002 (which include 'drug trafficking', 'money laundering' offences contrary to the Proceeds of Crime Act 2002, ss 327 and 328, 'directing terrorism', 'people trafficking', 'arms trafficking', 'counterfeiting', certain 'intellectual property offences', offences relating to pimping and brothels, and blackmail); certain offences under the Bribery Act 2010; 'money laundering offences' contrary to the Criminal Justice Act 1988, ss 93A, 93B, and 93C; offences under the Drug Trafficking

But if made by one of the higher courts, the order could last for 15 years or, where the person was sentenced to imprisonment for life, 20 years. The extent of the obligations created by a FRO were explained in section 79. In essence, they required persons subject to an order to make a report on their financial affairs. Reports had to include 'any specified documents' required by the court and had to be made to a specified person, at specified periods, and in a specified format. Under section 79(10), failure to comply with any of those requirements 'without reasonable excuse', or including false or misleading information in a report, was made an offence liable on summary conviction in England and Wales to imprisonment for a period not exceeding 51 weeks.[60] But there was no ability for a breach of a FRO to be tried on indictment. This not only limited the sentencing powers of the court when breaches occurred but also severely restricted the investigative powers of enforcement agencies under the Police and Criminal Evidence Act 1984. In addition, it exposed breaches to the six-month time limit for prosecutions imposed by section 127 of the Magistrates' Courts Act 1980.

Use of FROs was even more limited than use of SCPOs. The original prediction was that around 1,500 FROs would be made annually but, as of 31 March 2014, just 119 FROs had been obtained by the NCA and its predecessor the SOCA since the orders became available on 1 April 2006.[61] In eight years, this amounted to an average of just 15 a year.

As at 1 September 2017, the names of 79 offenders subject to FROs could be found on the NCA's website. This author's analysis revealed that more than half of these orders (42: 53.2 per cent) were imposed for 15 years. The remainder were for 14 years (2: 2.5 per cent), 12 years (7: 8.9 per cent); ten years (19: 24.1 per cent), nine years (3: 3.8 per cent), eight years (3: 3.8 per cent), seven years (1: 1.3 per cent), and six years (2: 2.5 per cent).[62] As with SCPOs, more than eight out of ten of these orders had been imposed for drugs offences (54: 68.4 per cent) or money laundering (12: 15.2 per cent). The rest had been imposed for offences of fraud (10: 12.7 per cent) or illegal immigration (3: 3.8 per cent).

Low usage of FROs, combined with the fact that breaches had limited consequences and were difficult to investigate and prosecute, produced a momentum

Act 1994; offences under the Terrorism Act 2000; offences under the Proceeds of Crime Act 2002, s 329 ('acquisition, use and possession of criminal property'); cheating in relation to the public revenue; fraudulent evasion of duty under the Customs and Excise Management Act 1979; offences relating to VAT under the Value Added Tax Act 1994; fraudulent evasion of income tax under the Taxes Management Act 1970; and tax credit fraud under the Tax Credits Act 2002.

[60] Or in Scotland a period not exceeding 12 months or in Northern Ireland a period not exceeding six months.

[61] See the *Explanatory Notes to the Serious Crime Act 2015* [153]. Again, as the *Explanatory Notes* point out (footnote 12), these figures represent those FROs known to the NCA and the SOCA and other FROs may have been granted which were not reported to either of these bodies. As at February 2010, the SOCA was managing just 72 FROs: see *Memorandum to the Home Affairs Committee, Post-Legislative Assessment of the Serious Organised Crime and Police Act 2005* (Cm 7974, 2010) [19].

[62] One FRO set at 10 years two months has been rounded down to 10 years for the purposes of this analysis.

for reform. In 2015, the decision was taken to consolidate FROs into the financial reporting requirements that can be imposed under a SCPO.[63] There was already considerable overlap between FROs and SCPOs, as the latter could be used to impose very similar information requirements. Furthermore, SCPOs and FROs were often imposed by a court simultaneously on the same offender (see, for example, *Baybasin and others* which is discussed below). Folding FROs into SCPOs, therefore, helpfully simplified the CPO landscape. At the same time, it ensured that any breach of information requirements was an indictable offence. In this way, the investigatory and prosecutorial disadvantages which had so hampered the effective use of FROs were side-stepped. The provisions abolishing FROs in England and Wales and Northern Ireland came into force on 3 May 2015;[64] the provisions abolishing these orders in Scotland came into force on 1 March 2016.[65] From those dates, it has not been possible to create a free-standing FRO. While this change has, as indicated above, a number of significant advantages, the downside is that an order which could last for up to 15 years when made in the higher courts (or 20 years if the offender had been sentenced to life imprisonment) has been folded into a SCPO which can last only for a maximum of five years.

When they were available to judges, a number of cases on FROs reached the Court of Appeal. Although new orders can no longer be created anywhere in the United Kingdom, existing orders have not been revoked and some will continue for many years to come. So the appellate cases remain important. They also give an insight into how the enhanced SCPOs will be used. Six cases involving fraud, money laundering, concealing the proceeds of crime, and drug importation and supply will be considered here. Despite the challenges made by these offenders, none was successful in his attempt to have his FRO quashed.

Adams (Terence George):[66] This was the first FRO case to come before the Court of Appeal. It was heard in April 2008. Adams' 10-year FRO had been made in May 2007 in the Crown Court after he pleaded guilty at an earlier hearing to one count of conspiracy to conceal the proceeds of criminal conduct contrary to section 93C of the Criminal Justice Act 1988. For that money laundering offence, he received a sentence of seven years' imprisonment.[67] In addition, a confiscation order for £750,000 was imposed. The Court of Appeal described Adams, who was then aged 52, as someone who had been, for a significant period of time, a highly

[63] The change was brought about by the enactment of s 50 of the Serious Crime Act 2015. This section removed the sections in the Serious and Organised Crime and Police Act 2005 which established FROs and amended the provisions relating to SCPOs in the Serious Crime Act 2007 by inserting a new s 5A covering the verification and disclosure of information.

[64] The Serious Crime Act 2015 (Commencement No. 1) Regulations 2015, SI 2015/820.

[65] The Serious Crime Act 2015 (Commencement No. 5 and Transitional Provisions and Savings) Regulations 2016, SI 2016/148.

[66] [2008] EWCA Crim 914.

[67] Originally this particular 'money laundering' offence was not included as a specified offence in s 76(3) of the Serious Organised Crime Police Act 2005 and so was not a trigger offence. It was added by the Serious Organised Crime and Police Act 2005 (Amendment of s 76(3)) Order 2007, SI 2007/1392, 3 May 2007, which took effect on 4 May 2007.

successful career criminal and was well known as such. (Adams is widely recognised as head of the notorious Clerkenwell Adams crime family – 'the A-Team' – and has been described as 'Britain's most ruthless gangster'.[68]) The Court noted that Adams had amassed a considerable fortune from his criminal activities which had been expended on a lavish lifestyle involving, according to the prosecution, 'significant numbers of first class flights to different destinations around the world, expensive jewellery, private education for his child, and the acquisition of antiques, works of art, and other property'. Yet Adams had paid no income tax for a long period. The Court dismissed his appeal against both his sentence of seven years' imprisonment and his FRO which required him to make reports on his financial position every six months while he remained in custody and every four months after his release.[69] Giving the judgment of the Court, Latham LJ, the Vice-President of the Court of Appeal (Criminal Division), held that the requirements of Adams' FRO were 'proportionate to the problem presented by the fact that [he] had for so long manipulated his financial activities to hide the proceeds of crime'. Latham LJ also expressed the opinion that a FRO was not a penalty under the terms of article 7(1) of the European Convention on Human Rights. Rather, it was a preventive measure which was designed to enable the courts to 'keep control over those in respect of whom there is the risk that they may indulge in criminal activity'. In August 2011, Adams was sentenced to eight weeks' imprisonment after pleading guilty to breaches of his FRO.[70]

Wright (Brian Brendon):[71] Six months after the Adams' appeal, in December 2008, another major case involving a FRO came before the Court of Appeal. It again involved a career criminal who operated on 'an enormous scale'. Wright, aged 61, was described by the sentencing judge as 'a master criminal, manipulative, influential and powerful'. He had, at various times, been 'the controlling mind and financial backbone' behind an international drug smuggling ring operating in South America, particularly Columbia, through the Caribbean to the United Kingdom. Dubbed 'The Milkman', because he always delivered,[72] the benefit Wright obtained from his drug trafficking activity was colossal. It was assessed in confiscation proceedings as amounting to no less than £45 million. Wright was said to be a man who, throughout his adult life, had lived outside the system. There was, it was observed, 'no or virtually no recorded trace of his existence'. He gave evidence in his trial, which lasted three months, that he owned no property, paid no tax, had no social security or National Insurance, no bank accounts, and had no car registered in his name. Yet he maintained a

[68] See 'Busted: The fall of Britain's most ruthless gangster' *The Independent* (8 February 2007).

[69] The focus in the 2004 White Paper was on the value a FRO might provide after an offender was released from custody. Indeed, it was considered that these obligations might usefully run for between five and 10 years after that happened. Under the terms of the Serious Organised Crime and Police Act 2005, however, (and as *Adams* illustrates) a FRO can run while a prison sentence is being served.

[70] See *Adams v Crown Prosecution Service* [2015] EWCA Civ 1495, per Gloster LJ.

[71] [2008] EWCA Crim 3207, per Hughes LJ (as he then was).

[72] 'Guilty: The Milkman – international cocaine smuggler who always delivered' *The Guardian* (3 April 2007).

lavish lifestyle which was supported almost entirely by cash. At the conclusion of his trial, he was convicted of offences of importing and supplying cocaine over a period of about three years in the late 1990s and was sentenced to a total of 30 years' imprisonment. In view of the length of that sentence and his apparent wealth, it is perhaps not surprising that the risk which the FRO was designed to confront was money laundering rather than further drug offences. The FRO was made to last 10 years. Wright appealed against this order but his appeal was dismissed. Giving the judgment of the Court, Hughes LJ, as he then was, observed that it was a case in which the temptation on Wright to deal with his enormous assets in a way which constituted an offence of money laundering was so great that 'any, even limited, prospect of restraint' by means of a FRO justified the order being made. Hughes LJ added that, while the paradigm case for a FRO was the offender who had a history of unsatisfactory business or financial dealing, there was no doubt that it also embraced persons such as Brian Wright. He stressed that judges who were asked to make FROs should give careful consideration to whether the order 'would actually achieve anything' and – in a statement that presaged FROs' abolition as a free-standing order – said they should 'look at alternative powers which are available to financial investigators' to see if these powers would have much the same effect.

***Davies (Jonathan Robert)*:**[73] This case involved a 42-year-old offender who was the organising mind behind a major conspiracy to supply heroin. He was convicted in June 2008 of one count of conspiracy to supply a class A drug (diamorphine). He was finally sentenced for this offence in August 2009 at the Crown Court in Liverpool and received 17 years' imprisonment. In addition, he was made subject to a FRO for 14 years. He appealed against his conviction, his sentence, and his FRO. All these appeals were dismissed. The Court of Appeal concluded that Davies' conviction was safe and that he had had a fair trial. It acknowledged that a 17-year prison sentence was 'towards the upper end of the range' but considered it 'well within the permissible bracket' as Davies was the prime organiser of a major conspiracy. Finally, given the offender's history of drugs and financial dealings, the Court held that the sentencing judge had been entitled to conclude that the statutory requirements for a FRO were made out and indicated that it was alive to the benefits FROs could offer.

***Baybasin and others*:**[74] This case also involved a very substantial Liverpool-based conspiracy involving Class A drugs. In a judgment given by Lord Judge, the Lord Chief Justice, the Court of Appeal refused one of the offenders, Anthony Geraghty, leave to appeal against a 15-year FRO which had been imposed on him alongside a SCPO and a 20-year prison sentence for his role in the conspiracy which was described as involving 'highly organised drug trafficking on a vast scale'.

[73] [2010] EWCA Crim 2720, per HHJ Rook.

[74] [2013] EWCA Crim 2357, per Lord Judge CJ. See also *Geraghty (Anthony)* [2016] EWCA Crim 1523, per Turner J; and 'Merseyside gang jailed in £4 billion cocaine bust – run from Liverpool city centre phone box' *Liverpool Echo* (26 October 2011).

One of the charges to which Geraghty pleaded guilty related to a conspiracy to import approximately two tonnes of cocaine. Geraghty, who was aged 43, argued that imposing a FRO – which required him to report on all his financial transactions, bank accounts, and assets[75] – for the maximum period of 15 years was manifestly excessive. The Court of Appeal took a different view. Given the risk he presented of future offending, it concluded that the order was necessary, proportionate, and of the appropriate length. Its duration took account of the fact that Geraghty would be in prison for some time and that important parts of the order would not become operative until he was released.

Bagnall (Darren John) and another:[76] This was an appeal against a confiscation order and a FRO imposed on a wealthy businessman who claimed he made his money from the wholesale distribution of mobile telephones but was suspected by Her Majesty's Revenue and Customs (HMRC) of substantial VAT fraud. After examining the money that had passed through his personal bank accounts, his wife's accounts, and the accounts run by his companies, HMRC originally estimated that, during the six years prior to his conviction, Bagnall's benefit from his general criminal conduct had been in excess of £50 million. In the end, however, HMRC decided not to prosecute him for VAT fraud due to the resource implications and lack of evidence.[77] Instead, proceedings were brought for a money laundering offence contrary to section 328 of the Proceeds of Crime Act 2002 (entering into or becoming concerned in an arrangement involving criminal property). This offence arose when Bagnall was found in 2005 in Manchester in possession of a bag containing £99,200 in Bank of England notes. For that offence, he was sentenced in 2007 at the Crown Court in Manchester to 15 months' imprisonment. Three years later, in 2010, after a process described by the Court of Appeal as 'tortuous and lengthy', the same judge (HH Judge Atherton) made a confiscation order against Bagnall for £1,818,619.97 and a FRO. Bagnall appealed against both these orders. His appeals were dismissed by the Court of Appeal, subject to a £200K reduction in the size of the confiscation order. Later, Bagnall's failure to pay the compensation order led to his extradition from Cyprus in 2015 after a European Arrest Warrant had been issued. Following his return, a six-year default prison sentence for failing to pay the compensation order was activated.[78]

Mullen (Kenneth Ross), Davison (Adrian), and Bingham (Andrew):[79] This case involved a 'boiler room fraud', so-called because of the pressure put on

[75] See the National Crime Agency website http://www.nationalcrimeagency.gov.uk/.

[76] [2012] EWCA Crim 677, per Moses LJ. Leave to appeal to the Supreme Court was refused by the Court of Appeal on 18 April 2012.

[77] *Bagnall v The United Kingdom – Statement of Facts and Questions* [2014] ECHR 514 and [2014] ECHR 1411. Bagnall's application to the European Court on Human Rights (Application no. 54241/12) was lodged on 8 August 2012 and communicated on 6 May 2014.

[78] HMRC Press Release, 14 October 2015. See also 'Jailed South Yorkshire businessman will lose £1.8 m' *The Star* (23 April 2012); and 'South Yorkshire money launderer who fled to Dubai extradited back to UK' *South Yorkshire Times* (17 October 2015).

[79] [2012] EWCA Crim 606, per Lloyd Jones J (as he then was). See also 'Conman who signed his emails 'R Hood' is jailed for seven years after persuading OAPs to invest in fake property near Olympic Park' *Mail Online* (3 February 2011).

victims, often retired, to buy either shares in companies that do not exist or worthless shares in companies that do exist. Davison was the architect of a 'sophisticated, well-organised and well-planned' version of this type of fraud. Six offenders were involved in all. They used 'glossy brochures, elaborate fake websites and convincing share certificates' to mislead their vulnerable victims who lost a total of around £434,500. The offenders all received prison sentences for a range of offences, the most serious of which (involving five of the six offenders) was conspiracy to defraud. The Court of Appeal described their offences as 'mean and despicable'. They involved 'the cynical targeting of vulnerable individuals and the application of repeated pressure on them'. The predatory nature of these offences called for substantial custodial sentences. Davison's sentence of seven years' imprisonment was upheld by the Court of Appeal, as was Bingham's sentence of five years' imprisonment. Four of those convicted also received FROs, two of which (those imposed on Davison and Bingham) were ordered to run for 15 years. Leave to appeal against these FROs was refused. The Court of Appeal concluded that the persistent and repeated criminality involved in Davison's offences, and Bingham's previous history of dishonesty alongside the pivotal role he played in acting as Davison's 'right-hand man', amply justified the trial judge's conclusion that the risk of their committing similar offences in the future was sufficiently high to warrant making the orders.

E. Drug Travel Restriction Orders

Drug Travel Restriction Orders (TROs) were created by the Criminal Justice and Police Act 2001. They were brought into effect on 1 April 2002.[80] Their purpose is to reduce the risk of drug traffickers committing a further drug trafficking offence. Their introduction was linked to the Labour Government's *Ten-Year Strategy for Tackling Drugs Misuse*, particularly its commitment to reducing the flow of illicit drugs into the United Kingdom.[81] TROs were defined by the legislation as orders which prohibit an offender from leaving the United Kingdom at any time within a specified period. As a consequence – and unlike travel controls in SCPOs which, as we saw in *Brooks (John Alan)*, can be imposed simultaneously with a TRO – TROs have to be all or nothing: they cannot prohibit travel only to a named country or set of countries. Nor do they allow for exclusion of a named country or countries. This has sometimes led to difficulties when courts recognise that curtailing an offender's travel to certain high-risk places would be desirable but conclude that a total travel ban would be disproportionate.[82] The maximum duration of a TRO

[80] The Criminal Justice and Police Act 2001 (Commencement No. 4 and Transitional Provisions) Order 2002, SI 2002/344.

[81] *Tackling Drugs to Build a Better Britain: The Government's Ten-Year Strategy for Tackling Drugs Misuse* (Cm 3945, 1998).

[82] See, for instance, *Sacco* [2006] EWCA Crim 1391, per HHJ Gordon (five-year TRO would cause 'undue hardship' and was therefore quashed and replaced with a two-year TRO; Court said the hardship

is 15 years. It cannot be made to last indefinitely. The minimum duration is two years.[83] Orders take effect once an offender is released from prison because it is only then that he/she can travel overseas.

Under section 33 of the 2001 Act, a court must, when imposing a sentence of four years or more for a drug trafficking offence,[84] ask itself whether it would be appropriate for the sentence to include a TRO. This duty is not, as some sentencing judges have erroneously concluded, a duty to *impose* a TRO. It is only a duty to *consider* doing so, and a TRO should not be 'axiomatic' on conviction for a drug offence, even an offence of importation.[85] The sentencing threshold of four years' imprisonment is designed to confine the court's power to impose TROs to serious cases. To ensure orders are obeyed, section 33(4) gives the court the power to require the offender to surrender his or her passport to the court. If a TRO is considered appropriate, the court must fix the relevant period. If it concludes that an order is not appropriate, it must state its reasons.[86] In assessing the risk of reoffending, the court must have regard to factors relevant to that risk, such as the offender's circumstances, previous convictions, travel patterns, employment, and any family and other connections both in the United Kingdom and overseas.[87] The Court of Appeal has made it clear that light will be thrown on this by the nature, quantity, and quality of the drugs involved in the previous offence along with its sophistication.[88] Contravening a TRO by leaving the United Kingdom at a time when an offender is prohibited from so doing by the TRO is an offence punishable by a maximum sentence of five years' imprisonment. Failure by an offender to comply with a direction in a TRO to deliver up his/her passport is a summary-only offence and is punishable by a maximum term of imprisonment of six months.

As of 1 September 2017, the names of just 16 offenders subject to TROs were included on the NCA's website. Analysis by the author reveals that one of these orders was imposed for 15 years, one for 12 years, one for ten years, two for eight years, one for six years, five for five years, one for four years, two for three years, and two for two years.

could be overcome if Italy – Sacco's home country – could have been excluded from the order but noted that that was not possible under the legislation: 'no power is provided to exclude a country or otherwise limit geographically the operation of such an order').

[83] In the case of an order of between four years and 10 years, the offender may apply for revocation or suspension of the order after four years; in the case of an order of four years or less, the offender may apply to revoke or suspend the order after a period of two years.

[84] Defined by s 34(1)(a) and including offences under the Misuse of Drugs Act 1971.

[85] *Gee (Stewart Carl)* [2009] EWCA Crim 1843, per Cranston J (TRO quashed). See also *Omishakin (Oluwatosin)* [2011] EWCA Crim 3003, per Burnett J (as he then was) (five-year TRO replaced with two-year TRO); *Powell (Karlton)* [2014] EWCA Crim 1606, per Keith J (TRO quashed); and *Graham (Lesley Elizabeth)* [2011] EWCA Crim 1905, per Swift J (TRO quashed).

[86] *Mee* [2004] EWCA Crim 629, per Newman J (15-year TRO quashed and replaced with five-year TRO), and *Williams (Kelly)* [2009] EWCA Crim 2165, per Openshaw J (TRO quashed).

[87] See n 85.

[88] ibid.

F. Slavery and Trafficking Prevention Orders

Originating in the Modern Slavery Act 2015, trailed in the government's *Modern Slavery Strategy*,[89] and supported in general terms by Frank Field's Modern Slavery Bill Evidence Review panel,[90] Slavery and Trafficking Prevention Orders (STPOs) came into force in England and Wales on 31 July 2015.[91] Their purpose is to protect the public by imposing legally backed conditions on offenders who have previously been involved in slavery or human trafficking with the aim of preventing, restricting, or disrupting their becoming involved in such offences again. Only persons with a conviction (or other finding or caution) for an offence of slavery or human trafficking listed in Schedule 1 to the Act (or an equivalent offence in another jurisdiction) can be made subject to a STPO. The order can be imposed immediately on conviction or later following an application to a magistrates' court from a chief officer of police, an immigration officer, the Gangmasters and Labour Abuse Authority, or the Director General of the NCA. To be created in the latter circumstances, the offender must, subsequent to his/her conviction, have behaved in such a way that there is a risk he/she will commit a further slavery or human trafficking offence. Orders are available for adults and children aged 10 or over. They cannot last for less than five years and can be made to last indefinitely. They may include any prohibition (but not a positive requirement) that is necessary to protect persons generally, or particular persons, from the physical or psychological harm that is likely to arise should the offender commit another similar offence. Orders may, for example, prohibit an offender from participating in a particular type of business; operating as a gangmaster; visiting a particular place; working with children or other vulnerable persons; organising transport or accommodation for others; contacting previous victims; retaining other people's passports or bank cards; carrying more than a stipulated amount of cash; or travelling to a specified country. Unlike TROs, foreign travel restrictions in a STPO can include not only prohibitions on the offender travelling *anywhere* outside the United Kingdom but also prohibitions on the offender travelling anywhere with an *exemption* for any country or countries named or described in the order or prohibitions *confined* to a country or countries named or described in the order thus leaving the offender free to travel anywhere else. Following the pattern set for SHPOs, the legislation allows each prohibition in a STPO to have a different duration although, with the exception of restrictions on foreign travel, they must, like the order itself, last for a minimum of five years. Prohibitions on foreign travel within a STPO, however,

[89] *Modern Slavery Strategy* (HM Government, 2014) [5.25].

[90] *Establishing Britain as a world leader in the fight against modern slavery, Report of the Modern Slavery Bill Evidence Review*, Frank Field MP (chair), December 2013 [4.5]. The panel, working with Field's Centre for Social Justice, was established in October 2013 by Theresa May when she was Home Secretary.

[91] The Modern Slavery Act 2015 (Commencement No. 1, Saving and Transitional Provisions) Regulations 2015, SI 2015/1476. See also *Guidance on Slavery and Trafficking Prevention Orders and Slavery and Trafficking Risk Orders under Part 2 of the Modern Slavery Act 2015* (Home Office, 2017).

cannot exceed five years although they can be renewed at the end of that period. The maximum punishment for breach of a STPO is five years' imprisonment. According to the Crown Prosecution Service, the first STPO in England and Wales was made by the Crown Court at Warrington on 11 December 2015.[92] By the end of March 2016, 16 STPOs had been made on sentencing in the Crown Court and three in the Magistrates' Courts.[93]

STPOs are also available in Northern Ireland under section 11 of, and Schedule 3 to, the Human Trafficking and Exploitation (Criminal Justice and Support for Victims) Act (Northern Ireland) 2015. But, unlike orders in England and Wales, STPOs in Northern Ireland are not available for offenders aged under 18. A further difference is that STPOs in Northern Ireland can include requirements as well as prohibitions. Northern Ireland STPOs came into force on 1 April 2016.[94]

In Scotland, Part 4 of the Human Trafficking and Exploitation (Scotland) Act 2015 created Trafficking and Exploitation Orders (TEPOs). These bear many similarities to STPOs in Northern Ireland. They can include prohibitions and requirements and cannot be imposed on offenders aged less than 18. But, in a significant departure from the STPO structure elsewhere in the United Kingdom, TEPOs in Scotland, which came into force on 30 June 2017,[95] cannot be ordered to last indefinitely.

It is early days for these orders but it is worrying that HM Inspectorate of Constabulary and Fire and Rescue Services (HMICFRS) recently reported that, in the 10 forces it visited in England and Wales, only 'limited use' was being made of the orders and some investigators were unaware of their existence or appeared confused about their use.[96] That confusion is, perhaps, further confounded by the fact that SCPOs can be (and, as we have seen, are) also used for offenders convicted

[92] See *The Crown Prosecution Service in London*, 15 January 2016. See also the STPOs imposed in *Mohammed Rafiq* [2016] EWCA Crim 1368, per Treacy LJ ('Boss guilty of trafficking Hungarian slaves at Dewsbury factory that made beds for John Lewis' *Yorkshire Post* (20 January 2016); 'Batley bed firm boss jailed over 'slave workforce' *BBC Online* (12 February 2016)); *Joyce (Timothy)* [2017] EWCA Crim 337, per HHJ Munro (indefinite STPO) ('Redbridge Hollow traveller Timothy Joyce jailed at Oxford Crown Court after using 'wrath and anger' to force men to work' *The Oxford Times* (17 December 2015)); and *Zielinski* [2017] EWCA Crim 758, per Davis LJ (ten-year STPO) ('Man jailed for locking slaves in attic and forcing them to urinate in bottles' *Metro* (30 October 2017)).

[93] Caroline Haughey, *The Modern Slavery Act Review* (2016) [13]. The *Review* concluded [30] that there was 'still too little awareness of the far reaching impact of [STPOs] and the particular benefits and protections they offer victims who wish to return to the area from where they were trafficked'. It argued that there was room 'to extend their applicability further still' by expanding Schedule 1 'to incorporate any other exploitative offences, such as prostitution, child grooming and other sexual offences', as well as 'Immigration Act 1971 section 25 assisting unlawful immigration'.

[94] The Human Trafficking and Exploitation (2015 Act) (Commencement No. 2) Order (Northern Ireland) 2016, 2016 No. 61 (C.3).

[95] The Human Trafficking and Exploitation (Scotland) Act 2015 (Commencement No. 3 and Transitional Provisions) Regulations 2017, SSI 2017/140.

[96] *Stolen freedom: the policing response to modern slavery and human trafficking* (HIICFRS, 2017) [78].

of people trafficking offences.[97] HMICFRS's findings were reinforced by an inspection report from HM Crown Prosecution Service Inspectorate (HMCPSI) published two months later which revealed, in the six Crown Prosecution Service (CPS) areas the Inspectorate visited, there was 'limited knowledge' among CPS staff about STPOs and an 'inconsistent approach' in forces 'as to whether they should be used at all'.[98]

II. Opportunities for Reform

It is clear from the above discussion that there are many differences in the way those CPOs which are designed to control the risk of offenders causing substantial harm to the public have been constructed. Some of these differences are an understandable reflection of the nature and purpose of the order. Others are much harder to justify. The following discrepancies fall into the latter category:

A. Length of Orders: Maximum and Minimum Periods

Why is it that SCPOs, VOOs, and VOPOs can only be made to run for a maximum period of five years and TROs for a maximum of 15 years when TEPOs can be ordered for any fixed period of five years or longer and SOPOs/SHPOs and STPOs can be ordered to run indefinitely? Are there going to be problems now that FROs, which were able to last for up to 15 years (or 20 years in the case of an offender sentenced to life imprisonment), have to be included within SCPOs which can run only for a third of that time? And why is there no minimum period for SCPOs when VOOs, VOPOs, and TROs (and indeed adult CBOs) cannot run for less than two years? (Note: Football Banning Orders can only run for a minimum of three years and a maximum of five years and CBOs imposed on persons under the age of 18 cannot last less than a year or more than three years. SOPOs/SHPOs, TEPOs, and STPOs cannot run for less than five years.) Should there not be a rationalisation of these periods across the different orders? It is surely telling that the position is now so complicated and haphazard that judges are making mistakes. For example, in 2016 a judge at Maidstone Crown Court erroneously imposed a SCPO for a period of 10 years when, under the Serious Crime Act 2007, the maximum period across which such an order can be in force is five years. This fault was corrected by the Court of Appeal eight months later but, unless simplifying reforms are introduced, more mistakes are almost inevitable.[99]

[97] See text at n 28. FROs have also been used for persons convicted of offences involving illegal immigration (see text at n 62).

[98] *The CPS response to the Modern Slavery Act 2015* (HMCPSI, 2017) [1.14], [5.28].

[99] *Cooper (David)* [2017] EWCA Crim 1153, per HHJ Mark Brown. Cooper's appeal against a total of eight years' imprisonment for five offences of domestic burglary and one offence of attempted burglary involving the homes of elderly residents was unsuccessful.

B. Length of Individual Prohibitions

Allowing prohibitions to run for different periods (within the maximum period for the order) is a positive arrangement. To require each component in a long and complicated order to last for exactly the same length of time was never desirable. But, if that is right, why has this change been introduced in SHPOs, SCPOs, STPOs, and TEPOs but not across all CPOs which are designed to prevent substantial harm to the public? Would it not be sensible, for example, for Scotland and Northern Ireland to allow the same flexibility in the SOPOs they have retained that courts in England and Wales now have for SHPOs? And should this flexibility not also be available for VOOs and VOPOs? Moreover, where flexibility is allowed, why does this not extend to empowering the court to allow a term in an order to last for a period that is shorter than the minimum length of the order as a whole? Is it not strange that (other than restrictions on foreign travel) prohibitions in SHPOs and STPOs cannot last for less than the minimum five-year period set for the full order?

C. Positive Obligations

Why do some of the CPOs which are designed to protect the public from substantial harm expressly allow the order to contain positive obligations and requirements as well as negative prohibitions when others do not? Isn't it time for the legislation governing VOOs, SHPOs, and STPOs in England and Wales to be amended expressly to permit positive obligations to be included – as is the case with SCPOs, VOPOs, SOPOs, STPOs in Northern Ireland, TEPOs, and CBOs – rather than leaving the issue to judicial interpretation?

D. Eligibility

Why is it appropriate that SOPOs, SHPOs, VOPOs, STPOs in England and Wales, and CBOs can be imposed on persons as young as 10 when SCPOs, VOOs, STPOs in Northern Ireland, and TEPOs can only be imposed on persons aged 18 or older? Perhaps the danger from organised criminals targeted by SCPOs is only likely to be of sufficient intensity when a person is 18 years of age. But it seems anomalous that the risk of sexual harm posed by a 10-year-old can be controlled by a SOPO/SHPO (and the risk of harm from slavery or human trafficking posed by a 10-year-old in England and Wales can be controlled by a STPO) when the risk of violent harm posed by someone of the same age cannot be controlled by a VOO (and the risk of harm from slavery or human trafficking posed by someone of that age in Northern Ireland or Scotland cannot be controlled by a STPO or a TEPO). Also, why is it that TROs can only be imposed on offenders who have received custodial sentences of four years or more, and VOOs are limited to offenders who have received custodial sentences of 12 months or more, when other CPOs discussed in this chapter are not so limited? And why is it that SCPOs can be imposed not just on individuals but also on bodies corporate, partnerships, and unincorporated associations when that power is not available for other cognate orders such as STPOs and TEPOs?

E. Availability

Why are other CPOs, including VOPOs in Northern Ireland, available on conviction when VOOs in England and Wales are not? And is it appropriate that a VOPO can operate while an offender is in prison, or subject to a supervision order (or a hospital order) or subject to statutory licence conditions, when this is not possible for a VOO? Also, would it not now be sensible to include a power in the legislation governing all CPOs to allow the court, in appropriate circumstances, to postpone or suspend the prohibitions or requirements they contain during periods when the person subject to them is detained in custody? Such a power exists for SCPOs but there is no similar power in relation to SOPOs or SHPOs or STPOs or TEPOs or VOPOs. It is also interesting to reflect on the fact that SCPOs cannot be created by the Magistrates' Courts when other high-end CPOs – such as SOPOs, SHPOs, STPOs, TEPOs, VOPOs, and VOOs – can be made at that level. Indeed, VOOs can *only* be made at that level. This issue has been put into sharper focus now that free-standing FROs have been abolished and rolled up into SCPOs. As a result, the restrictions FROs used to permit are no longer available to the lower tier courts.

F. Grounds for Imposition

Is it not time to ensure that a 'necessity' requirement is a condition precedent for the imposition of all CPOs? This is the test for SOPOs, SHPOs, VOOs, VOPOs, STPOs, and TEPOs. But the test for SCPOs is simply that there must be reasonable grounds for the court to believe that the imposition of the order would protect the public by preventing, restricting, or disrupting involvement by the person in serious crime. And the test for TROs is whether the order is 'appropriate'. (When it was available, the test for a FRO was that the court must be satisfied that the risk of the offender committing another specified offence was 'sufficiently high' to justify the order being made.) Despite judicial suggestions that this difference in wording will make no 'significant difference in practice',[100] there is surely a compelling argument to rationalise these tests and upgrade them all to the level of necessity.

[100] *Hancox and Duffy* (n 32).

G. Content

Why does the legislation authorising the creation of some CPOs include exhaustive lists of the terms they can contain (VOOs) whereas others list examples (SCPOs) and some say nothing at all (SOPOs/SHPOs/VOPOs/STPOs/TEPOs)? Should this piecemeal approach not be reformed? And has the time not come to allow TROs to be made more flexible rather than taking the form of a single blanket ban on all foreign travel, especially as SHPOs, STPOs, and TEPOs explicitly allow for that flexibility (and SCPOs do so implicitly)?

The case for a new consolidating, streamlining, statute in this area thus seems overwhelming. Not only would it bring all the orders into a single place, making them more comprehensible and accessible, it would also offer the opportunity to provide a more rational structure to the orders by allowing changes to be made which would introduce greater commonality of approach.

III. Desiderata for the Consolidating Legislation

If a new consolidating statute were to be introduced, what form should it take? The statute should begin with a clear statement of the purposes these orders serve. The wording should explain in unambiguous language that the orders have no punitive function. They should not be imposed because they are somehow thought to be deserved. Nor should they be seen as a form of sentence.[101] They are not designed to punish. Rather, their purpose is to serve the public by disrupting, restricting, preventing, or inhibiting the opportunities some convicted offenders – those who present sufficient risk to the public to warrant legally backed restrictions being placed on their freedom of action – have to cause serious criminal harm. Placing these principles on the face of the statute would make explicit something that thus far has only been implicit in the existing legislation and has had to be teased out by the courts. Such provisions would also give legislative force to the many judicial rulings that CPOs do not amount to 'penalties' within the terms of the protections provided by the European Convention on Human Rights.

Once that has been done, the new legislation should set out the core statutory safeguards that ought to apply to every CPO. In particular, the legislation should state that no order can be imposed unless the court concludes, on the basis of the evidence presented to it, that it is *both* necessary *and* proportionate. This would bring home to all involved that CPOs are strongly freedom-inhibiting and the constraints they impose on the rights of those subject to them can only be justified if they are truly necessary to protect the rights of others and if the controls they create are genuinely proportionate to the risk the offenders pose.

[101] ibid.

In addition, the legislation should drive greater consistency by providing a set of features that would be made common to all CPOs. It would be desirable, for example, if it were stated that every order may include positive requirements as well as negative prohibitions. This change would ensure that courts are expressly empowered to mould and shape the contours of an order as they deem necessary in the particular circumstances of the case rather than feeling constrained to include in SHPOs, VOOs, and STPOs in England and Wales only terms which are phrased in negative prohibitory language. It would also be constitutionally more honest as it would remove the temptation from the courts to use judicial fiat (or, less politely, barefaced distortion) *ex post* to read clauses in these orders as if they created merely negative prohibitions when at first blush they would straightforwardly seem to fall foul of the bar on using positive conditions.

A second unifying provision that could usefully be introduced would be to allow terms in these orders to run – within the maximum period available for the order – for whatever period the court considers necessary. This could be a useful reform even where the legislation establishes a mandatory minimum period across which the order as a whole can operate. It, too, would allow the courts full flexibility to tailor the terms of an order to the risk the offender poses and not require some terms to run for longer periods than is necessary because the legislation requires them to be shoe-horned into a period which equals or exceeds the minimum period set for the entire order. In this way, the structure of these CPOs would support more fully and effectively, and remain truer to, the overarching principle of proportionality.

A third unifying provision would be to allow any term in a CPO to be postponed or suspended in appropriate circumstances while the offender is in custody or subject to any other legally-imposed constraint (such as a licence condition or another CPO) which renders the term unnecessary during that period. By avoiding such duplication, this reform would ensure that the way orders are structured is able to support more fully and effectively, and remain truer to, the overarching principle of necessity.

A fourth unifying provision would be to allow all CPOs to be imposed in the Magistrates' Courts as well as the Crown Court. This would ensure greater consistency of approach across the range of orders and enable them to be created in a forum which enshrines relevant due process but without unnecessary delay, cost, or complexity.

A fifth unifying provision would be to include in the legislation for all CPOs a set of illustrative examples of the types of terms they may contain while shying away from the temptation to provide exhaustive lists which (as with VOOs) tie the hands of the judiciary and prove unhelpful when the risks in a particular case come to be considered. At the same time, the opportunity should be taken to rationalise and consolidate the rules on restrictions on foreign travel, specifying how these may be framed, avoiding wording which compels all or nothing approaches, and extending the power to impose these prohibitions in appropriate circumstances to all the CPOs.

Finally, it would be helpful if the introduction of new consolidating legislation were preceded by a full review of the CPOs discussed here to allow a coordinated and consistent position to be reached on other areas which are harder to resolve as a matter of *ex ante* principle and are more closely connected to political judgment. These include issues such as the period of time across which orders ought to be able to run. For example, whether there ought to be legislatively-imposed minimum durations for any orders; whether any orders ought to be able to run indefinitely; and whether and what variation between orders in these respects is warranted. The review should also embrace issues such as whether orders should be capable of being imposed on persons aged less than 18 (a question which intersects with the age at which criminal responsibility is set in the three United Kingdom jurisdictions) and whether STPOs and TEPOs, like SCPOs, should be capable of being imposed on bodies corporate, partnerships, and unincorporated associations as well as individuals. The suggested review could either be in the form of a Government White or Green Paper or a Law Commission Consultation Paper and then Report. Ideally, the review should take the form of a joint project run across all three legal jurisdictions in the United Kingdom, with the different governments and/or Law Commissions working together to reach a common agreed position. That will not necessarily be easy, of course. And it will need to be done in a way which is sensitive to, and does not undermine, the rights of the devolved governments to determine the shape of their own criminal justice systems, while at the same time recognising the desirability of United Kingdom-wide solutions. But, on important matters such as these, the broader the expertise involved the more likely it will be that the ensuing legislation will be sound, will endure, and will command respect and support across a wide range of criminal justice stakeholders and the broader population.

IV. Conclusion

The CPOs that have been the subject matter of this chapter represent one of the ways in which the State can deliver on its positive duty to protect its citizens from substantial harm. Nonetheless, the piecemeal way in which CPOs have developed across the last 20 years has meant that there is now a strong case for rationalisation and streamlining of these orders. The argument in this chapter is that can best be done through the enactment of a new consolidating statute.

Comment on Chapter 2

Offenders' Rights and Public Safety

ZACHARY HOSKINS

Stephen Shute offers a thorough and persuasive case for reform of the host of civil preventive orders (CPOs) currently implemented in the United Kingdom, measures whose aim is to reduce the risk that people with criminal records will cause substantial criminal harm to members of the public.[1] Shute focuses on Sexual Harm Prevention Orders (in England and Wales), Sexual Offences Prevention Orders (in Northern Ireland and Scotland), Serious Crime Prevention Orders, Violent Offender Orders (in England and Wales), Violent Offences Prevention Orders (in Northern Ireland), Financial Reporting Orders, Drug Travel Restriction Orders, Slavery and Trafficking Prevention Orders (in England and Wales, and Northern Ireland), and Trafficking and Exploitation Prevention Orders (in Scotland). He contends that these various CPOs, which were created and have developed in a piecemeal fashion, should now be consolidated and streamlined into a new statute that would bring a more rational structure to the orders and bring more coherence to the overall practice of prevention orders. In particular, he calls for rationalisation and coherence with respect to seven main issues: (a) the maximum and minimum durations of the orders, (b) the durations of individual elements within orders, (c) whether the orders may impose positive as well as negative obligations, (d) who is eligible to be subject to an order, (e) the conditions for creation and implementation of the orders, (f) whether the orders must be determined to be necessary as well as proportionate to be permissible, and (g) how specifically and exhaustively the orders spell out the potential restrictions.

Overall, I found Shute's argument in favour of a more rational, coherent structure among these various orders largely persuasive. Why, for example, should there be no minimum period for Serious Crime Prevention Orders but a two-year minimum for Violent Offender Orders? Why is it that some CPOs, such as Sexual Harm Prevention Orders and Sexual Offences Prevention Orders, can be imposed on children as young as 10, whereas other orders, such as Violent Offender Orders and Serious Crime Prevention Orders, cannot be imposed on people younger than 18? This is not to say that there may not be rationales for

[1] S Shute, 'Rationalising Civil Preventive Orders: Opportunities for Reform', ch 2 of this volume.

these or other differences among the orders, although Shute often indicates scepticism about whether the differences are justifiable. But his more central point, I take it, is that because these various orders have developed piecemeal, they have not as a group been subject to scrutiny to determine where consistency is rationally warranted and where differentiation is appropriate. This is why a consolidating statute is much needed, as it would provide occasion for just this sort of rational scrutiny.

In this commentary, I first briefly flesh out a couple of the prescriptions Shute offers for particular reforms to make CPOs more consistent. Then, I examine two normative claims that frame Shute's discussion of particular reforms, but on which he does not elaborate in this chapter: first, that CPOs for those with criminal records are easier to justify than CPOs for others, and secondly, that there is no in-principle argument against CPOs targeting people with criminal records. I contend that there is an in-principle argument grounding at least a strong presumption against CPOs generally. I also highlight two possible answers to the question of why CPOs are easier to justify for those with criminal records than for others, one of which is plausible and one of which is not.

One of the dimensions Shute considers along which various CPOs differ is with respect to whether they claim to impose only negative prohibitions (as Sexual Harm Prevention Orders do, for instance), or both positive obligations and negative prohibitions (as do Serious Crime Prevention Orders). His proposed consolidating statute would make clear that all of the CPOs considered here may impose positive requirements as well as negative prohibitions. As he recognises, this approach is more honest than attempting to maintain the somewhat contrived distinction between negative prohibitions and positive duties. The key weakness of the positive-negative distinction is that complying with a negative prohibition frequently will require taking any number of positive steps. To give an example from the US context, some years ago in Englewood, Colorado, the town passed a statute barring people convicted of certain sex offences from living within 2,000 feet of schools, playgrounds, or parks, and within 1,000 feet of licensed day-care centres, recreation centres, swimming pools, recreational trails, bus stops, or walking routes to schools. (The law was struck down by a US District Court in 2013 as unconstitutional because it left virtually all of Englewood off limits to those subject to the restrictions.) Although it might initially be tempting to characterise the statute as imposing a host of negative prohibitions, it in fact creates all sorts of positive requirements, too. Don't go near parks, schools, or playgrounds: negative. Do your grocery shopping one town over, since the stores in Englewood are all in forbidden zones: positive. Don't go near bus stops: negative. Buy a car to get to work, since you cannot take the bus: positive. Rather than adhere to the somewhat contrived distinction between positive requirements and negative prohibitions, I agree with Shute that it is preferable to acknowledge explicitly that the fulfilment of negative prohibitions will typically require a variety of positive steps.

Shute also contends that the consolidating statute should make clear that the CPOs considered here must all be both necessary and proportionate (some CPOs, such as Serious Crime Prevention Orders, do not require necessity). Requiring necessity and proportionality, he writes, 'would bring home to all involved that CPOs are strongly freedom-inhibiting and the constraints they impose on the rights of those subject to them can only be justified if they are truly necessary to protect the rights of others and if the controls they create are genuinely proportionate to the risk the offenders pose' (p 64). Both the necessity constraint and the proportionality constraint admit of different interpretations, so it is worth clarifying which interpretation of each is relevant here.

One way of reading the necessity condition is that some measure is necessary if it is the only way to achieve a given aim. Thus, in our context, a given CPO might be deemed necessary if it is the only way to protect the safety and security of members of the public. But this cannot be the sense of necessity relevant in this context. If we had multiple variants of CPOs that would accomplish the given public safety aim, then this construal of necessity would appear to prohibit all of them, as none would be the only way to achieve the aim. We might try to avoid this worry by instead construing necessity in this case to apply to the set of candidate CPOs: If the only way to achieve the public safety aim is to implement *one or the other* of them, then we might conclude that the necessity condition is satisfied when we choose one from the set of candidate CPOs to implement. The problem with this construal of necessity, however, is that it provides no way of adjudicating between the candidate CPOs. It tells us only that we are permitted to choose from among the effective options.

A more promising construal of the necessity condition holds that a given measure is necessary if there is *no less burdensome alternative means* of achieving the same aim. This is the standard construal of necessity in philosophical debates about the rules of war.[2] Unlike the first construal of necessity considered above, this version does not hold that if multiple CPOs could achieve the public safety aim, they are all therefore impermissible. Unlike the second construal considered above, this version does provide some basis for adjudicating between candidate CPOs. Necessity requires that the CPO under consideration be the least burdensome available means of achieving the public safety aim.

Now let us turn to the proportionality constraint. Proportionality is often invoked as a key consideration in the criminal justice context, although the term is often used to refer to different principles. In punishment theory, for example, several different uses can be identified. Proportionality may refer to the principle that the severity of a sentence should be no more severe than an offender deserves given the seriousness of the crime. It may refer instead to the idea that a sentencing scheme should punish equally serious crimes equally severely, and should punish more serious crimes more severely than less serious crimes. Or it may mean that the benefits generated by punishment should outweigh its harms. Shute is careful

[2] See, eg, J McMahan, 'Proportionate Defense' (2013–14) 23 *Journal of Transnational Law and Policy* 1, esp 2–3.

to highlight, however, that the purpose of CPOs is preventive rather than punitive. Thus, the relevant sense of proportionality here is forward-looking rather than backward-looking: the controls created by CPOs should be 'genuinely proportionate to the risk the offenders pose' (p 64). One might interpret this phrase as holding that CPOs should be no more severe than is required to avert the risk. But on this interpretation, proportionality would amount to nothing more than the necessity constraint discussed above, which requires that the CPO be the least burdensome available means of achieving the public safety objective (because if there are less burdensome means of achieving the objective, then the given CPO is more severe than is required). Instead, we should interpret the proportionality constraint as holding that the likely harms to be averted by a given CPO should outweigh the burdens it is likely to create. Taken together, then, the necessity and proportionality constraints require that a CPO be the least burdensome available means of reducing a given risk, and that the burdens the CPO is likely to create are outweighed by the harms it is likely to avert.

Having examined some of Shute's particular prescriptions for a more coherent system of CPOs, I want to devote the remainder of this commentary to consideration of two more general normative claims he makes at the beginning of the chapter: first, that CPOs targeted only at people with criminal records, 'generally involving a serious offence', are 'easier to justify than other CPOs' (p 37), and secondly, that regarding such CPOs, 'there is no argument of general principle which renders their broad structure impermissible' (p 38). In what follows, I first offer an in-principle argument for the conclusion that CPOs targeted at people with criminal records are, at least presumptively, impermissible, in that these orders deny to people with criminal records access to goods and opportunities that others enjoy.[3] I acknowledge that the presumption against such measures can be overridden in a fairly limited range of cases on grounds of risk reduction. But I believe it is important to emphasise that our starting point must be a strong presumption against such measures, and that when we do impose such measures, we should do so reluctantly and with a clear sense of their costs. Secondly, I distinguish two possible answers to the question of why CPOs targeted at people with criminal records are easier to justify than other CPOs. I contend that only one of the two answers is plausible.

The in-principle case against CPOs generally begins with the idea that in a society that values liberty and equality, there should be a presumption against measures that single out certain groups of individuals for the imposition of restrictions of liberty to which other individuals are not subject. This presumption can be strengthened if we take a step back to consider the significance of punishment itself within a liberal democratic polity. As I mentioned, Shute emphasises that CPOs are preventive rather than punitive, but my account of their presumptive

[3] For a fuller articulation of the brief argument I offer in what follows, see Z Hoskins, *Beyond Punishment? A Normative Account of the Collateral Legal Consequences of Conviction* (OUP, forthcoming), ch. 5 and ch. 7.

permissibility requires that we consider the significance of punishment to glean insights about the permissibility of imposing additional restrictive measures outside the context of punishment.

Liberal political philosophers, such as Hobbes, Locke, Rousseau, Kant, and more recently, Rawls, have recognised that for exercises of state coercion to be *justified*, they must be *justifiable* to those subject to them. Thus, the institution of criminal law and punishment, as perhaps the paradigmatic exercise of state coercion, must be justifiable to those subject to it. It must be justifiable to us as subjects bound by the law, as citizens in whose name the law coerces, and whose values the law claims to represent. It must also be justifiable to those of us who violate the laws and are thus subject to punishment. We must ask, then, what would be required to justify the institution of punishment to all of us, including those of us who commit crimes?

On one type of liberal account, state coercion is justifiable to those subject to it if they have expressly or tacitly consented to it. Such accounts are empirically implausible, however: many people do not consent either expressly or tacitly. Other theorists, most notably Rawls, instead suggest that coercive state institutions are justifiable if they would be endorsed by individuals in certain idealised conditions.[4] The problem faced by these *hypothetical* consent views is that consent itself does not appear to be doing any normative work. If people in idealised conditions would endorse certain institutions, they would do so for certain reasons, presumably because these institutions have certain features that make them legitimate. If so, then the coercive institutions will be justifiable in virtue of these legitimate-making features, and we still need some account of what these features are.

Other theorists have sought to justify coercive state institutions by appeal instead to the benefits such institutions provide. One version of a 'benefits' account holds that coercion of a person is justified by the benefits this creates for that same person. But liberals typically reject as unappealingly paternalistic the idea of a State's restricting a person's liberties for her own good.[5] A more promising 'benefits' account, I believe, is grounded in the benefits of State coercion to others in society. Christopher Heath Wellman develops such an account. He contends that 'what ultimately legitimizes a state's imposition upon *your* liberty is not merely the services it provides *you*, but the benefits it provides *others*'.[6] Wellman claims that each of us has a duty of Samaritanism to help others 'when they are in dire need and one can help them at no unreasonable cost to oneself'.[7] The relevant benefit

[4] J Rawls, *Political Liberalism* (Columbia University Press, 1993), esp 137. See also see S Dolovich, 'Legitimate Punishment in Liberal Democracy,' (2004) 7(2) *Buffalo Criminal Law Review* 307–442; and C Brettschneider, 'The Rights of the Guilty: Punishment and Political Legitimacy,' (2007) 35(2) *Political Theory* 175–99.

[5] See, eg, JS Mill, *On Liberty*, ch 1.

[6] CH Wellman, 'Liberalism, Samaritanism, and Political Legitimacy,' (1996) 25(3) *Philosophy and Public Affairs* 211, 213–14.

[7] ibid, 216. Wellman's principle is similar in obvious respects to Peter Singer's argument in his seminal article 'Famine, Affluence, and Morality,' (1972) 1(3) *Philosophy and Public Affairs* 229–43.

provided by coercive state institutions is the protection of people's moral rights.[8] Thus each of us has a duty, insofar as it does not generate unreasonable costs on us, to help others stay out of the dire circumstances in which moral rights are unprotected. And because rights can be assured only in the context of general submission to coercive state institutions, none of us has a right to be free from such coercion. Note that on Wellman's account, punishment must not impose costs on anyone that unreasonably outstrip the benefits to them. My Samaritan duty to help keep others out of peril may require me to submit to institutions that make me somewhat worse off overall, but it is not reasonable to coerce me to bear inordinate burdens for others' sake.

For punishment to be justifiable to those subject to it, on this account, it must be the case that it helps to protect citizens' moral rights (by helping to reduce crime) without imposing unreasonable costs on those punished. My contention, which I have fleshed out more fully elsewhere, is that a system of proportionate punishment (proportionate in the sense mentioned earlier of being no more severe than is deserved) that functions as the payment of an offender's debt to society, and completion of which restores her to full standing as a member of her political community, does not impose unreasonable costs. A system of punishment that does not treat the completion of a term of punishment as the full payment of the offender's debt, and thus allows the imposition of additional burdens on offenders, is unreasonably costly and thus not justifiable to those subject to it.[9]

If this account is correct, then we should take seriously the conception of punishment as the means by which offenders pay their debts and restore themselves to full standing as citizens in their polity. But if an offender's standing as a citizen is thereby restored, then she is entitled to the same legal rights and privileges as everyone else. Thus, just as there is a presumption against subjecting citizens who do not have criminal records to restrictive preventive measures, the same presumption should count, and with equal weight, against subjecting offenders to such measures.

Now, presumptions may be overridden, so it is possible that in some limited range of instances, the risk to be averted by CPOs will be substantial enough to override the presumption against them. One question we should ask, however, is what the basis is for Shute's claim that the presumption against such measures is more easily overridable for those with criminal records than for everyone else.

One answer might be that when a person commits a crime, she thereby makes herself liable to be subject to prevention orders, whereas law abiders do not make themselves liable to such orders. But if we are to take seriously the notion that offenders who complete a term of punishment thereby pay their debts and thus

Singer offers two versions of a duty-to-aid principle, the more modest of which holds that 'if it is in our power to prevent something very bad from happening, without thereby sacrificing anything morally significant, we ought, morally, to do it' (231).

[8] ibid, 217.

[9] Hoskins, (n 3).

restore their standing as members of the political community, it is unclear how we can justify continuing to subject them to onerous treatment to which others are not subject.

A more plausible account of why it is easier to justify subjecting offenders to CPOs than everyone else is epistemic rather than normative: It is not that the offender's moral standing is different (outside the context of her punishment) from anyone else's, but rather that the prior criminal offence provides important information about the person's relative likelihood of offending in the future, whereas there is no such information about those without criminal records. Here, it is worth noting that researchers have suggested factors other than past criminality that correlate with future criminality: factors such as education level and intelligence level, among others. Many people would be uncomfortable with the state's imposing CPOs on the basis of a person's education, intelligence, or similar factors. Why, then, should it be easier to justify imposing CPOs based on a criminal record? The answer should not be simply that a criminal history more strongly correlates with future offending. Even if age, race, and sex were shown to correlate with future offending more strongly than does past offending, many of us would regard it as unjust to subject people to risk assessment based on age, race, or sex. Why is subjecting some offenders to risk assessment not similarly unjust?

The relevant difference between criminal histories and age, race, or sex as grounds for CPOs is that criminal histories are responses to a person's prior culpable actions. Imposing restrictive orders based on a person's age, race, or sex is not consistent with respecting her as an autonomous agent, because such orders are not responsive to her own autonomous choices. By contrast, taking a person's previous autonomous behaviour into account in imposing CPOs is consistent with respecting her as an autonomous agent. Such engagement is responsive to the person's autonomous choices. Indeed, failing to consider someone's prior choices in predicting her future behaviour arguably fails to respect her agency.

This is not to say that past behaviour should be a *decisive* consideration in our predictions of others' future behaviour. Respecting each other as autonomous agents involves acknowledging that we are always free to make choices for different reasons from those that guided us in the past. But acknowledging that past behaviour is not deterministic of future behaviour is consistent with shaping our engagements with others based in part on predictions of their future behaviour that are responsive to the previous autonomous choices they have made. Thus, it is at least sometimes consistent with respect for offenders as autonomous agents for the state to take prior convictions, and the prior public wrongdoing that such convictions certify, into account in imposing CPOs. When I say it is at least sometimes consistent, I mean that it is consistent in those cases where there is a sufficiently compelling interest to be served, when the CPO would effectively serve this interest without generating offsetting harms, and when no less burdensome alternative is available.

In principle, it might also be permissible to subject people without criminal convictions to CPOs – although, again, there is a strong presumptive case against such measures. In practice, CPOs on those without criminal convictions will be infrequently justified. This is because when there is clear, publicly available evidence of previous autonomous behaviour that is sufficiently indicative of a risk of serious future wrongdoing to justify restrictive measures, there will typically also be a conviction. But there might be cases in which, despite clear evidence that a person has previously behaved in ways indicative of risk of serious future wrongdoing, there was no conviction: as one example, perhaps the conduct, although now criminalised, was not criminalised when the person committed it. Generally, if there is clear, publicly available evidence of past autonomous behaviour that is sufficiently indicative of a serious risk of future wrongdoing, the presumption against CPOs may be overridden. But if everyone may in principle be liable to CPOs based in part on prior behaviour, then subjecting those with criminal records to such measures does not violate their right to equal treatment.

Thus, I maintain that there is an in-principle case against all forms of CPOs. But this case doesn't inflict a fatal wound. Rather, it grounds a strong *presumption* against such measures, but a presumption that may be overridden in a narrow range of cases based on considerations of risk reduction. And in the limited range of cases in which CPOs can be justified, Shute is right that they should be more rational and coherent in their administration. His proposed consolidating statute would be a welcome improvement on the current system of disconnected, and frequently inconsistent, CPOs.

3

Reforming the Law of Criminal Attempt: Take Two

SHACHAR ELDAR

There is little disagreement that the law of criminal attempt is in need of reform,[1] but the correct formula for restructuring it is elusive. The present article traces the failed effort to amend the law governing criminal attempt carried by the Law Commission in its report no. 318, from 2009.[2] Learning from the mistakes of the past, I propose guidelines for what may be a more theoretically sound and viable solution, particularly in relation to: (a) delineating the lower boundary of attempt liability, (b) excluding offences from the applicability of attempt liability, and (c) exempting cases of abandonment from liability.[3]

Following a brief review of LC 318 in Part I, I suggest in Parts II and III that a clear distinction between criminal conduct and mere non-criminal preparation is more likely to be achieved by diversifying attempt law to make it content-sensitive and offence-specific, with regard to both its physical and mental elements. The practical technique I propose consists of a methodical, or perhaps, more realistically, piecemeal exclusion of offences from the ambit of attempt liability by specifically and as clearly as possible delineating the lower boundaries of these offences. Parts IV and V elaborate this proposal and compare it with similar solutions suggested previously. Finally, in Part VI I discuss the defence of abandonment,

[1] The backdrop of any reform proposal is the Criminal Attempts Act 1981, s 1, which states as follows: 'If, with intent to commit an offence to which this section applies, a person does an act which is more than merely preparatory to the commission of the offence, he is guilty of attempting to commit the offence.'

[2] The Law Commission, *Conspiracy and Attempts* (Law Com No 318, 2009) (hereinafter LC 318), which followed The Law Commission, *Consultation Paper, Conspiracy and Attempts* (CP No 183, 2007) (hereinafter CP 183). In the title, 'take two' refers to this recent endeavour, although the Commission paid some attention to the Criminal Attempts Act on previous occasions, most notably in LC 143 (1985), and LC 177 (1989). The Act itself was the outcome of The Law Commission, *Attempt and Impossibility in Relation to Attempt, Conspiracy and Incitement* (Law Com No 102, 1980). As I reveal in the concluding section, the title of this chapter is deceptive in yet another way.

[3] Some have suggested that the mens rea of attempt may also be ripe for reform. See JJ Child and A Hunt, 'Pace and Rogers and the Mens Rea of Criminal Attempt: Kahn on the Scrapheap?' (2014) 78 *Journal of Criminal Law* 220. I will touch only one aspect of this subject below, in Part III.

presently unavailable in English law. I argue that a varied, offence-specific attitude toward attempt liability makes the doctrine of abandonment better suited for its purpose and therefore more attractive to lawmakers.

I. Past Endeavour: CP 183 and LC 318

The Law Commission published its consultation paper on conspiracy and attempt in October 2007. Close to 80 pages were devoted to the law of attempt, with a view to a deep and comprehensive reform. The Commission proposed to divide the sphere of attempt into two separate offences: 'criminal attempt', covering the last acts necessary for the commission of the offence, and 'criminal preparation', covering behaviour that 'had proceeded beyond the stage of mere preparation' to commit the offence.[4] It stated that the two categories of 'attempt' and 'criminal preparation' were meant to cover together the scope of attempt liability as it was designed to be interpreted under the Criminal Attempts Act 1981;[5] however, it recognised that the proposal exceeds the scope of attempt liability as it was in fact interpreted by the courts.[6] The Commission further proposed guidelines in the form of statutory examples aimed at clarifying the distinction between criminal preparation and mere preparation,[7] and asked consultees to consider the prospect of repealing the exemption of conspiracy as a predicate offence to attempt.[8]

These aspects of the proposal attracted much criticism.[9] First, it was noted that the dividing line between the proposed offences of attempt and criminal preparation was left vague by resorting to the test of 'one of the last acts' necessary for the completion of the offence. The Commission illustrated that under this test, the category of attempt was meant to include the act of a person who aims a gun at a would-be victim and removes the safety catch but does not shoot, as well as the act of someone who tries to break into a house by striking a hammer at the bolt on the front door but is caught before delivering the effective blow.[10] Commentators

[4] CP 183, [1.77–1.78], [12.5–12.7], [16.16].

[5] CP 183, [1.76], [12.30], [16.19]; LC 318, [8.2].

[6] Particularly in *Geddes* (1996) 160 JP 697 (a defendant equipped with a knife, rope, and a roll of masking tape trespassed in a lavatory with the purpose of capturing and restraining a boy, but was held to be in the preparatory stage, not warranting liability).

[7] CP 183, [16.25], [16.47–16.57].

[8] CP 183, [1.94], [7.36–7.58]. The Commission's treatment of the mental element in criminal attempt was not aimed at reform. Staying close to existing law, the Commission proposed that attempt be based on the actor's intent, where such intent is to be directed at the conduct and consequence elements of the predicate offence and to include oblique as well as conditional intention (LC 318, [8.91–8.95], [8.106]). As for the circumstances of the offence, a mental element of recklessness would suffice unless the predicate offence requires an elevated form of mens rea, such as knowledge (LC 318, [8.116–8.137]).

[9] Most notably in Note, 'The Law Commission and Inchoate Offences' (2008) *Crim LR* 1; CMV Clarkson, 'Attempt: The Conduct Requirement' (2009) 29 *OJLS* 25; and to some extent, J Rogers, 'The Codification of Attempts and the Case for "Preparation"' (2008) *Crim LR* 937.

[10] CP 183, [16.17].

noted that it is highly doubtful that such a complex division, cut as it is by the scissors of terms of art, would be readily understandable and serve the cause of fair labelling.[11] Secondly, commentators questioned the significance of this division, considering that the distinction between criminal attempt and criminal preparation was not meant to entail any consequent difference in doctrine, ie, in the requirement of mens rea or in the level of punishment.[12] Thirdly, commentators noted that the creation of a distinction between attempt and criminal preparation subverts the more important distinction (in its consequences for the accused) between criminal behaviour and mere preparation, because it diverts toward it much of the energy that should be expended on interpreting the latter distinction.[13] Finally, the prospect of criminalising attempted conspiracy did not gain the support of commentators.[14]

The final report of the Commission was published in December 2009. Although the Commission continued to laud its proposed measures, most of them had to be reluctantly abandoned for lack of support from the consultees.[15] Consequently, the Commission offered no change in the conduct element of attempt, other than strongly stressing its preference that attempt be interpreted as being wider in scope than was decided in some Court of Appeal rulings, and recommending that attempted murder including commission by way of omission.[16] The aim of reform was not realised.

II. Reflections on the Lower Boundary of Attempt Liability

Consider the approach advanced by the Law Commission in CP 183, according to which 'substantive criminal law should comprise a body of offences that are

[11] I find that Clarkson (n 9, 33) overstated the argument when writing that 'there appears to be no moral distinction or different wrongs involved in the proposed two separate offences'. The subdivision may marginally serve fair labelling, as there may be a significant enough moral difference between a defendant who has spotted the victim and removed the safety catch in order to shoot there and then, and a defendant who is caught while still lying in wait.

[12] Along these lines, Jonathan Rogers proposed to maintain the distinction but give it practical implications: the offence of criminal preparation would reflect a condemnation of the actor's commitment to offend (defined based on the subjectivist tradition of attempts), whereas the offence of attempt would reflect a condemnation of the danger he has created (defined according to the objectivist tradition of attempts). See Rogers (n 9).

[13] See Clarkson, above n 9, at 33. The Commission rejected this line of criticism, stating in its final report that 'there would only rarely be any dispute as to whether D's conduct constituted an attempt or the offence of criminal preparation' (LC 318, [8.19], [8.35–8.36]). However, in its consultation paper the Commission expressly acknowledged the possibility of subversion when asking consultees 'to focus on the desirability of separating the present offence of attempt into two new offences,' expressing the 'fear that an additional proposal to include statutory examples to supplement the definition of our proposed offence of "criminal preparation" may become the focus of too much attention and thereby distract consultees from this key issue' (CP 183, [16.45]).

[14] LC 318, [3.20].

[15] LC 318, [8.67–8.68].

[16] LC 318, [8.151].

readily understandable to the lay person'.[17] Should not this commendable aspiration for clarity in the rules advising individuals on the limits of sanctioned behaviour also apply to attempt liability? This question becomes particularly salient when taking into account that it is attempt liability, and not the body of discrete offences, which truly delineates the permissible and the impermissible.

However, one striking practical implication of the distinction between acts that are directly criminalised under the definition of an offence and those that are indirectly criminalised as attempts is that attempt liability is exempt from the need to precisely define its contours. While the principle of legality requires that offences be defined as precisely as possible to promote the values of clarity and certainty in formulating criminal prohibitions,[18] all forms of criminal attempt are defined in one statutory provision, which requires only that the act be 'more than merely preparatory' to the commission of the offence.[19] The dividing line between the consummated offence and the attempt, which generally holds no formal punitive consequence, is well defined, whereas the demarcation between a punishable attempt and an acquittal is left vague. It follows that the principle of legality does not demarcate the prohibited from the permitted; it really only marks out one wrong (the complete offence) from another (attempt liability for that offence), and therefore loses much of its practical significance.

The deficiency in clarity and certainty that characterises the law of attempt is the inevitable outcome of maintaining a single, uniform definition of criminal attempt. Undoubtedly, if one definition of attempt is to govern all offences, as is presently the case, its contours must be amorphous and thus at odds with the rule of legality. The Law Commission, in acquiescence, wrote that:

> The definition of attempt … must be flexible and therefore imprecise. If it is not, it will fail to cater for the vast range of substantive offences and factual circumstances to which it must be applied.[20]

[17] CP 183, [16.10].

[18] Recall LL Fuller, *The Morality of Law* (Yale University Press, 1964) 43, 63–65; J Raz, *The Authority of Law – Essays on Law and Morality* (Clarendon Press, 1979) 210–29. It is assumed that the reader is familiar with the disadvantages of imprecision of the legal norm, which include, *inter alia*, the detraction from fair labelling and the impairment of crime prevention caused by the effect of either over- or under-deterrence.

[19] It is sometimes argued with regard to examples of penal indeterminacy that 'those who for no better reason than self-advancement skate at the margins of legality have no compelling ground for complaint if they are not given precise warning as to when they are about to fall in'; discussed in W Wilson, *Central Issues in Criminal Theory* (Hart, 2002) 242. This view may have some validity regarding the core offences of the criminal law, such as murder, rape, or armed robbery, but it fails in other regards. If personal freedom is to be valued and self-advancement not frowned upon, anyone wishing to hold a party should be warned as to when such activity becomes a breach of the peace or an attempt thereof, and anyone wishing to conduct an elaborate financial transaction should be given fair notice as to what is deemed entrepreneurial genius and what is attempted financial fraud. Possibly, there should be some sort of trade-off between scope and certainty; as the margins of criminality narrow, the degree of tolerance to indeterminacy increases.

[20] CP 183, [16.3].

Not content, however, with leaving things as such, the Commission made an effort to achieve some level of clarity, primarily by listing statutory examples that fall within the purview of attempt. This measure is discussed below in Part V. For now, note that clarity comes at the expense of precision in the scope of crime because treating attempt so as to be relevant for all offences, and for all acts and situations criminalised by each offence, dictates anchoring the limits of such examples in simplistic abstractions, ignoring the unique characteristics of each offence. Such a formulation creates a dichotomous divide within the diversity, aspiring, unrealistically, to correctly distinguish the forbidden from the permissible in a manner that will be relevant for both a would-be rapist's ambuscade and a bank clerk's attempt at money laundering.[21]

This reflects the peculiar state of current English law (shared by other jurisdictions), where a court decision that delineates the lower boundary of attempt for any offence is considered a valid precedent regarding the lower boundary of attempt for all other offences, ie, the lower boundary of criminality in general. The cost of this practice, in terms of loss of normative nuance, is illustrated by the observation of Oliver Wendell Holmes that crimes that endanger life 'warrant holding the liability for an attempt to begin at a point more remote from the possibility of accomplishing what is expected than might be the case with lighter crimes'.[22] In earlier days it was clearer than today that the boundaries of attempt would change from case to case according to the offence being charged and the interest that it protects. For example, Francis Sayre stated in 1928, that the act of sprinkling a harmless substance onto another person's plate might constitute a basis for the offence of attempted murder but not for the offence of attempted assault.[23]

The Commission recognised that some communal interests are so important that they justify a wider scope of inchoate liability than others. For example, it proposed to specifically allow for attempted murder by way of omission,[24] and was apparently willing to accept that for drug-related offences and terrorist activity liability should form even before the actors have left the dominion of their home.[25] Based on this recognition, the Commission drew the conclusion that some discrete preparatory offences should be enacted. Supplementing the law of attempt with discrete preparatory offences is a welcome step toward clarity and certainty, but it is not sufficient.

[21] The joint classification of all offences of attempt is reminiscent of the joint classification of women and fire under the category of 'dangerous things': see G Lakoff, *Women, Fire and Dangerous Things – What Categories Reveal about the Mind* (The University of Chicago Press, 1987). See also TW Arnold, 'Criminal Attempts – The Rise and Fall of an Abstraction' (1930) 40 *Yale LJ* 53, 72 ('to discuss whether acts done in an attempted robbery are comparable to acts done in an attempted incestuous marriage, as they relate to the general principle of proximateness, is as valuable as discussing whether Milton is more poetical than a pig is fat').

[22] OW Holmes, *The Common Law* (Little, Brown & Co., 1881) 68–69.

[23] FB Sayre, 'Criminal Attempts' (1928) 41 *Harvard LR* 821, 845–46.

[24] LC 318, [8.151].

[25] CP 183, [15.11].

Acknowledging the need to treat different offences differently cuts both ways, and there will be numerous counter-examples in which the boundaries of liability for attempt are to be drawn particularly narrowly or where there should be no attempt liability (some of these are discussed below, in Part V). The Commission, however, allowed no room for such specific treatment, reasoning that in cases of attempt (and the proposed category of criminal preparation) 'the need to intervene, deter and punish almost always outweighs any concerns related to the rights of the individual to non-intervention and the desirability of affording D an opportunity to abort his or her enterprise'.[26] The wide scope of criminalisation favoured by the Commission renders this reasoning unconvincing.[27] The key word is 'almost': in some of the cases presently criminalised by the general outlawing of attempt, the balance between the rights of the individual and the interests of society would favour no liability. While it may be true that criminalisation is appropriate when the conduct examined is sufficiently connected to the commission of the offence, the question still remains as to how we are to determine, for each and every offence, if the actor's conduct is indeed sufficiently connected to the commission of the offence. A uniform standard is, by definition, ill-equipped for the task.

III. Reflections on the Mental Element in Attempt Liability

The classification of a prohibition as a complete offence or an attempt has another implication: whereas complete offences may be defined through a variety of *mentes reae*, the mental element of an attempt is uniformly set at intention, at least with regard to the conduct and consequence elements of the offence.[28] The fruits of the lengthy historical progression that led to the development of a graduated scale of mental elements in crime, including intent, knowledge, awareness, recklessness, and negligence,[29] have not been extended to the domain of criminal attempts.

[26] CP 183, [16.21].

[27] This is surprising when considering the well-articulated support of the Commission of offence-specific inchoate liability for preparatory acts: 'Whether any act of mere preparation should be covered by the criminal law therefore depends on a range of interests. These include: (1) the extent of D's moral culpability; (2) the nature and seriousness of the intended offence; (3) the danger to society; (4) the difficulty of establishing D's intention; (5) the rights and liberties of the individual (at common law and under the European Convention of Human Rights and Fundamental Freedoms); and (6) the extent to which the law should allow persons involved in "mere preparation" to have an opportunity to change their mind (CP 183, [15.12]).'

[28] Regarding circumstances, where the predicate offence does not require more than recklessness, recklessness may also suffice for attempt liability. See above (n 8).

[29] For some accounts of this progression, see A Levitt, 'The Origin of the Doctrine of Mens Rea' (1922) 17 *Illinois LR* 117; FB Sayre, 'Mens Rea' (1932) 45 *Harvard LR* 974; PH Robinson, 'A Brief History of Distinctions in Criminal Law' (1980) 31 *Hastings LJ* 815.

What could justify this state of affairs? It may be argued that it is the intention of the actor to consummate the offence that defines the wrong in the attempt, and it is therefore a necessary constituent element of attempt liability. Despite its conceptual soundness, this answer does not suffice in the context of current law, in which attempt liability is given a distinctive normative role in generally defining the outer limits of the prohibition. If attempt liability is inherently based on intention, then the question becomes whether the contour of criminalisation for each and every prohibition must always be determined by attempt liability. This seems far-fetched when taking into account the plurality of protected interests and the all but infinite types of conduct that warrant criminalisation. There are at the margins of criminal liability some discrete offences that are in substance, if not in form, inchoate, in that their commission does not require the actual occurrence of the mischief at which they are aimed – and some such offences, as offences of reckless endangerment, do not require intention as to the relevant mischief. These offences could carry some of the burden, alongside attempt liability, of outlining the bounds of criminal liability, while enriching the inventory of *mentes reae* from which to draw. Remarkably however, under current English law these offences are subject to the applicability of attempt liability, and thus their contour too is marked by a mental element of intent.[30]

It could be argued that given the inchoate nature of the conduct element of attempt, a lesser mental state than intent simply does not suffice for incurring criminal liability.[31] The doctrine's shift of focus from the factual or objective element of the offence to the criminal's foul subjective intention could be seen as based on the latent assumption that liability is determined by an amalgam of 'harm (or conduct) and culpability', so that the less there is in the harm or conduct dimension, the more that is required in the culpability dimension. This would mean that the augmentation of the required mental element for attempt liability from that of recklessness or knowledge – common in complete offences – to that of intent is needed to compensate for the factual deficit inherent in the definition of attempt. The appeal of this notion is strengthened by the equivalence in the maximum penalties set for the attempt and for the consummated offence. Is the normative conversion of physical and mental elements valid? Notice that its supporting argument must base itself on at least three strong assumptions: (a) mental and factual elements are distinct from one another; (b) they are quantifiable; and (c) they are commensurable. The dualistic approach underlying the first assumption, and the

[30] The difficulty could be alleviated by exempting some of these offences from the ambit of attempt liability, a possibility which I discuss below in Part IV.

[31] The butt of this argument is shared by the aforementioned discrete inchoate offences that are not predicated on a mental element of intent. The argument may alternatively rest on the uncertainty associated with the lower boundary of attempt, a theme which I discuss above in Part II. The requirement of intent thus serves as a rough safeguard against over-inclusiveness of a prohibitory norm which does not properly delineate its act requirement. If this is the case, and the requirement of intent for attempt liability is contingent on the under-determinability of the physical scope of attempt, then the alleviation of the latter (as I propose below in Part IV) will facilitate an independence from the former.

belief in the ability of the law to quantify the unquantifiable (eg, translate physical injury and mental propensities into terms of imprisonment) are such an integral part of criminal law theory that they cannot be questioned without entirely upending the field. The third assumption is more problematic. Like flour and sugar in a cake recipe, the mental and factual components of crime are distinct from one another in nature and are not interchangeable. The problem of commensurability becomes more distinct once we examine more closely what is meant by a conversion between mental and factual elements. There is no apparent reason to believe that the augmented mental state produced by the transformation from knowledge or recklessness, which usually suffice for liability when consummating the offence, to intention, which is required for attempt liability, overlaps the factual deficits of attempt, which may manifest as failure to cause a required outcome, absence of a relevant circumstance, or failure to complete a significant act. Because the augmented mental requirement is at times designed to overcome the lack of a few factual components (in the case of an almost complete attempt), and at others the lack of many such components (as, for example, in the case of first steps having been taken toward the commission of the offence), the conversion between the factual and mental elements can hardly be said to be uniform. Furthermore, for some offences no conversion takes place, because they already include a mental requirement of intention in their complete form.

The Law Commission defended the requirement of intent in attempt liability on yet another ground: it stressed the benefits associated with using ordinary language in criminal legislation, pointing out that in everyday language attempt means 'trying', and trying means 'intending'.[32] The linguistic rationale too fails to persuade, particularly because the Law Commission, in accordance with existing law, defines 'intention' as legal jargon that includes oblique intention, by no means in accordance with everyday usage.[33] The Commission, again in keeping with existing law, also exempts the circumstantial element from the requirement of intention – for this element, a mental state of recklessness usually suffices[34] – and this too is a departure from ordinary language.

In sum, the general applicability of a generic doctrine of attempt liability entails a common mental threshold, which reduces the precision of criminal liability in English law.[35]

[32] CP 183, [16.10].

[33] See above (n 8). The Commission expressly recognised that the availability of oblique intention denotes a departure from the linguistic notion of attempt as 'trying' (CP 183, [14.29]; LC 318, [8.90]).

[34] See above (n 8).

[35] The problems inherent in unifying the mental aspects of attempt are not limited to the rejection of all mental states other than intention, but also have to do with the instability of the term intention itself. Here are some classic examples: when a person shoots at another and misses by a few centimetres, would we describe his mental state as an intention to shoot at another or to shoot in a certain general direction? When a man gets married a second time without knowing that his first wife had already obtained an *ex parte* divorce from him, would we say that he intended to get married or to commit bigamy? When a person tries to smuggle merchandise in order to avoid paying customs duties and it turns out that no customs duties apply to such merchandise, would we describe his mental state as the

IV. Proposal (1): Exempting Offences from Attempt Liability

Because a unified yardstick for attempt may stifle any effort to introduce precision to the limits of the criminal prohibition, I propose a diversified approach, which abandons the quest for a general lower limit of attempt, and focuses instead on specific offences.[36] The method I suggest is an incremental exploration, at a realistic pace, of the preferred lower boundary of discrete offences, geared at exempting offences, one by one, from the ambit of attempt liability. This suggestion moves in the opposite direction of the historical process that gave birth to the doctrine of attempt. The generalised concept of 'attempt' was the creation of eighteenth century English courts. Desiring to expand the definition of offences to include scenarios in which the transgressor was apprehended before completion, courts repeatedly invoked the common law to forge an ever expanding list of crimes for which attempt was prohibited, until finally declaring the general applicability of attempt liability to all Common Law misdemeanours, in *Scofield*.[37] Once the offence was established, the law had to divide it into its physical and mental components, giving birth to the abstractions underlying the general doctrine of attempt. Yet until *Scofield*, attempt liability was offence-specific.[38] In contrast to sporadically bringing specific crimes under the sway of attempt, I propose here the sporadic, and if possible, methodical exemption of offences from the general doctrine of attempt; in other words, that the two and a half centuries-long rule of abstraction slowly give way to the resurrection of the reign of discrete offences.

Undoubtedly, the task of delineating the desirable lower boundary of the prohibition associated with any given offence or protected interest is intimidatingly difficult, as the resilience of the general abstraction of criminal attempt attests. Therefore, I do not suggest that confining attention to discrete offences would achieve maximal precision in the definition of these offences or eliminate the need for judicial discretion. I argue that such a strategy would allow Parliament to enact its prohibitions with greater precision than is currently afforded by the general formula of 'more than merely preparatory', which in turn would enable the courts to reach greater accuracy in their rulings. I also recognise that in drawing

intention to smuggle taxable merchandise or some particular merchandise? These questions require specific, not unified, answers that deal with the context of each offence. Generally, it has been said that isolated from context there can be no decisive legal arguments, only pairs of opposing ones; see D Kennedy, 'A Semiotics of Legal Argument' (1991) 42 *Syracuse LR* 75.

[36] Without entering the argument as to the existence of a unifying wrong to all attempts, I will comment that even if such a unifying wrong is to be acknowledged, it does not follow that this wrong must be criminalised in relation to all prohibitions and to the same extent.

[37] (1784) Cald 397.

[38] See Sayre (n 23) 834–37; PR Glazebrook, 'Should We Have a Law of Attempted Crime?' (1969) 85 *LQR* 28, 29–33.

the limits of criminality, the ideal of clarity must be balanced against society's need for safety, but here again, the balancing is better performed within the context of specific offences.

Suppose we substitute attempted robbery (ie, the implementation of the general doctrine of attempt on the offence of consummated robbery) with a discrete offence prohibiting action that is directed at carrying out a robbery.[39] Even if defined at this crude level, the separate offence may hold several advantages. First, confining attempted robbery to a discrete offence would dissuade courts from their current practice of shaping attempted robbery by relying on precedents created for attempting offences of a dramatically different character, such as attempted bribery, arson, or bigamy – all the while maintaining that analogies between these offences in their completed form are invalid. Concern is not limited to fashioning attempted crime A by reference to a prior treatment of an attempt at a dissimilar crime B. Perhaps more harmful is the habit of shaping attempted crime A with a view to ensuring just treatment in future occurrences of attempted crime B. If crime A is robbery and crime B murder, the court tends to set the limit of attempted robbery early along the timeline of perpetration, but if crime B is some minor offence, the court tends to favour the value of defendants' freedom, and set the limit of attempted robbery at a later stage. In either case, the boundaries of attempted robbery cannot be expected to reach their ideal scope.

Secondly, in time, an interplay between Parliament and the courts is expected to refine the definition of the discrete offence without having to fall back on the abstractions – both physical and mental – of the general doctrine of attempt. Is this prospect over-optimistic? Antony Duff wrote that '[g]iven the diversity of ways in which most offences can be committed, it is not obvious that it would be much easier to specify the conduct element for attempted murder than to specify a conduct element for attempts in general'.[40] Admittedly, the length to which some perpetrators would go in their preparations to kill or rob is not precisely determinable in advance, but it is still possible that narrowing the field of inquiry as much as possible will result in some progress in the delineation of the prohibition, and at the very least will resist complete forfeiture of the rule of law ideals of clarity and certainty.[41] It may also be the case that for some instances of what would now be regarded as attempted robbery a different mental element than intention will prove fitting.

In seeking to draw the proper boundaries of criminalisation, it may turn out that the eradication of attempt liability for some offences, although perhaps not

[39] I mean this offence description to be neutral on the question of the scope of the offence, ie, whether it should include 'first acts' in furtherance of the robbery or be limited to 'last acts' close to its completion. It is inherent in my proposal that the question of scope is to be separately determined for each prohibition or protected interest, according to context.

[40] RA Duff, *Criminal Attempts* (Clarendon Press, 1996) 385.

[41] Arnold (n 21) 58.

for robbery, will require no substitution.[42] Under current law, summary offences are entirely exempt from the application of attempt.[43] Other obvious candidates for a complete exemption from attempt liability are preparatory offences, such as 'being in possession of an article for use in connection with any burglary or theft',[44] and conspiracy (which current English, but not US law exempts from attempt liability).[45] The principle of parsimony in criminalisation suggests the existence of other examples.[46]

Thirdly, focusing on the context of a given prohibition will facilitate the grading function of liability, by layering offences according to their proximity to the infringement of the relevant protected interest.[47] Recall that the Law Commission tried to achieve grading by dividing criminal attempt into two categories: attempt and criminal preparation. The subsequent relinquishment of this proposed measure can be explained by the fact that the categories proposed were not confined to specific prohibitions and particular contexts but rather meant to apply across the range of offences.

[42] This possibility runs counter Gideon Yaffe's 'transfer principle', meaning that attempts are implicitly prohibited whenever completions are: 'if a form of conduct is legitimately criminalized, then so are attempts to engage in that form of conduct'. G Yaffe, 'Criminal Attempts' (2014) 124 *Yale LJ* 92, 102; see also G Yaffe, *Attempts: In the Philosophy of Action and in the Criminal Law* (OUP, 2010). This principle is not suitable to current law, where many prohibitions in their completed form are inchoate in nature, and where policy concerns may inhibit the applicability of attempt liability for some offences (examples follow in the text).

[43] Criminal Attempts Act 1981, s 1(4).

[44] Theft Act 1968, s 25(1). This offence is drawn broadly enough to criminalise a preliminary act in the perpetration of a burglary, which in itself consists of attempted theft, theft being commonly regarded as an attempt to deprive owners of their property (Holmes, n 22, 72; J Hall, *General Principles of Criminal Law*, (Bobbs-Merrill, 1960) 586): making attempted possession of instruments for use in connection with any burglary an attempt of the fourth order, ie, four times removed from the realisation of the harm to the property interests of the owner. The prospect of criminalising attempts of the fourth order while sparing attempts of the second order (there is no recognised concept of 'attempted attempts'), deserves separate attention, apart from the automatic application of the general doctrine of attempt to discrete possession offences. More generally, it needs to be noted that the negative effect of each instance of excessive criminalisation in the formulation of discrete offences is automatically multiplied by the application of the doctrine of criminal attempt.

[45] Rather than expand the list of exemptions from attempt liability to include more offences of inchoate nature, the Law Commission considered the repeal of the exemption of conspiracy as a predicate offence to attempt (see also above, Part I). The Commission stressed the view that conspiracy should be regarded not only as a preliminary step towards the commission of some other offence, but also as a 'free-standing offence', and therefore subject to attempt liability (CP 183, [7.54]). This position is consistent with the general approach by which 'if the preliminary act is prominent enough to serve as a basis of substantive liability, it should also provide a sufficient foundation for attempt liability'. See H Wechsler, WK Jones & H Korn, 'The Treatment of Inchoate Crimes in the Model Penal Code of the American Law Institute: Attempt, Solicitation, and Conspiracy' (1961) 61 *Columbia LR* 571, 620–21.

[46] Apart from attempt liability, the exemption mechanism described in the text may prove relevant to other inchoate doctrines such as conspiracy and incitement. Some jurisdictions limit these doctrines and specify the offences that fall within their scope. See, eg, the Israel Penal Code 1977.

[47] Such a layering of offences may also allay Antony Duff's concern that abolishing the law of attempt will result in defining all discrete offences in the inchoate mode, thereby losing the distinction between potential and actual harm to protected interests. See Duff (n 40) 354–58.

V. Advantages over Similar Proposals

The proposal to substitute or complement attempt liability with discrete offences is not altogether novel, and commentators have made similar suggestions in the past. Following in their footsteps, the present proposal is distinct in the balance it strikes between comprehensiveness and pragmatism. It is, on one hand, farther-reaching than some earlier proposals, and on the other, more subtle in its mode and therefore more realistic in its prospects for reform.

According to Peter Glazebrook, if the doctrine of attempt defines the margins of criminalisation, its proper place is in the special part of the criminal code: correctly placed, attempt liability will continue to expand the boundaries of the various criminal prohibitions, but with greater obligation to precision. Glazebrook proposed to abolish the general doctrine of attempt entirely, and in its stead redraw the true boundaries of every single offence in the special part.[48] I think Glazebrook is right in locating attempt liability in the special part, and my proposal noticeably draws on this insight. His solution offers a cure for the imprecision associated with the general doctrine of attempt, and is therefore theoretically promising. However, abolishing the general law of attempt in one stroke may prove impractical and too drastic to gain approval. As early as 1930, Thurman Arnold lamented the impracticality of this ultimately favourable solution: although regarding the general doctrine of criminal attempt as a 'complete obstacle to intelligible judicial speech and an encumbrance on intelligent judicial action', he observed that the complexity of the issue, the degree of confusion surrounding its statutory provisions, the fact that many books have been written on the subject, and the fact that many interests depend on its definitions prevent the abolition of the generalisation.[49] For this reason, it is arguably better to proceed more cautiously, by keeping the general law of attempt in the books but gradually legislating to remove specific offences from its scope, eg, by amending and layering the law of robbery to include actions directed towards robbery, whilst at the same time exempting robbery from the law of attempt.

Stressing the value of fair labelling, Jeremy Horder suggested supplementing the general law of attempt with an array of ulterior intent crimes, to be placed both at the boundary between attempt and completion, to mark the more grievous occurrences falling under the doctrine, and at the boundary demarcating attempt from mere preparation, to form what he terms 'preparatory ulterior intent crimes'.[50] This is a great leap forward, but it suffers from three drawbacks. First, the layering of the lower and upper boundaries of attempt with discrete offences

[48] Glazebrook (n 38) 42. In a later article, Glazebrook proposed to eliminate the distinctions between attempt, incitement, and conspiracy, opting for a single doctrine, based on the will to commit an offence; see PR Glazebrook, 'Structuring the Criminal Code: Functional Approaches to Complicity, Incomplete Offences, and General Defences', in AP Simester & ATH Smith (eds), *Harm and Culpability* (Clarendon Press, 1996) 195, 202–03, 211. He does not explain the change in approach.

[49] Arnold (n 21) 79.

[50] J Horder, 'Crimes of Ulterior Intent', in AP Simester & ATH Smith (eds), *Harm and Culpability* (Clarendon Press, 1996) 153, 159.

may still leave too broad a middle ground to be governed by the generalisations of attempt. Secondly, it excludes the possibility of a complete exemption of some offences from the realm of attempt. And thirdly, in replacing attempt liability with discrete offences, the law need not be bound by the template of ulterior intent.[51]

Antony Duff favoured the solution of 'defining a fairly narrow general law of attempts, and then defining a range of specific inchoate offences … in so far as these are necessary to deal with particularly threatening or dangerous kinds of conduct'.[52] Combined with other aspects of the solution, Duff appears to answer all three drawbacks identified in Horder's proposal: (a) it allows only a limited space for the general law of attempt; (b) it acknowledges the possibility of complete exemptions by leaving open the question of the scope of offences that should be subject to attempt liability;[53] and (c) it proposes to outline the margins of attempt not only with crimes of ulterior intent, but also with other preparatory offences, such as reckless endangerment.[54]

By drawing the sphere of attempt liability narrowly, Duff's proposal maintains a close relation between attempt and the discrete offences to which it applies. But this positive aspect of the proposal may make it impractical. Similarly to Glazebrook's proposal of abolishing the law of attempt in one sweep, the idea of considerably narrowing its contours may also meet with resistance. It was certainly resisted by the Law Commission, which advocated the converse approach of expanding the limits of the general doctrine by setting the limits of criminality far back from the completion of the offence.

The practical inference that the Commission was willing to draw from Duff is the idea of supplementing the definition of attempt with a set of authoritative examples.[55] Could this measure succeed in adding precision to attempt liability? We can begin the appraisal by examining the examples provided by the Commission of the type of acts that are sufficient for criminal liability. Consider first these: 'D, with a view to committing the intended offence there and then or as soon as an opportunity presents itself: (a) approaches the intended victim or the object of the intended offence, or (b) lies in wait for an intended victim, or (c) follows the intended victim'.[56] It is highly doubtful that these examples can

[51] One possibility is ulterior recklessness, such as in s 1(2)(b) of the Criminal Damage Act 1971 (causing damage to property intending to endanger the life of another or being reckless as to such endangerment).

[52] Duff (n 40) 385.

[53] ibid, 378, 398.

[54] ibid, 385. Notice that in order to keep preparatory offences free from a mandatory mental requirement of intent, Duff would logically need to exempt some such offences from the ambit of attempt liability.

[55] CP 183, [16.34]. For Duff (n 40) 65–66, 393–94. Duff notes that he 'will not even try here to suggest what examples should figure in such a set' (394). On the same point, the Commission was also able to cite in its support the authority of Professors Williams, Dennis, and KJM Smith (CP 183, [16.35–16.36]), as well as the example of s 5.01(2) of the American Model Penal Code (American Law Institute, 1962). In his comment on CP 183, Clarkson also added his support for the formulation of examples, noting that the content of such examples is beyond the scope of his article. See Clarkson (n 9) 40–41.

[56] CP 183, [16.47].

outline an adequate general threshold for liability. For instance, lying in wait for a would-be murder victim with a loaded gun in one's hand is a radically different act, and carries a different moral content, than waiting patiently with a gift in one's hand for the purpose of offering it as a bribe. Should both these acts be treated in the same manner and criminalised? Next, consider this example: 'D commits an offence or an act of distraction or deception with a view to committing the intended offence there and then.'[57] An unsuccessful manoeuvre to reach a loaded gun for the purpose of shooting one's rival might constitute attempted murder, but should someone be criminalised for unsuccessfully trying to distract another in order to obtain her pen for the purpose of forging a document? Clearly, the problem does not lie in the inadequacy of the examples formulated by the Law Commission, but rather in the quest for general examples.[58] Any such examples will accord with the concrete predicate offences conjured up in the mind of whoever is in charge of formulation, but will not have persuasive general applicability.[59]

VI. Proposal (2): Taking a Fresh Look at the Wilful Abandonment Defence

Abandonment of a criminal endeavour, however voluntary and honest, is no defence once the actor has passed the threshold of attempt to commit an offence. Although there has been academic support for the introduction of the wilful abandonment defence – one leading textbook going as far as commenting that 'no argument of deterrence, reformation, or prevention seems to require the punishment of one who abandons his attempt before he has done any harm, being truly repentant'[60] – the Law Commission did not propose to recognise a defence of abandonment, and LC 318 is silent on this issue.[61]

[57] CP 183, [12.39].

[58] The mechanism of examples may be more helpful where it is applied by the courts, rather than by the legislature, depending on how much confidence we should have in the common law method of case-by-case reasoning, which precisely involves the comparing and contrasting of specific cases rather than the derivation of conclusions from general rules.

[59] The Law Commission abandoned all its initial proposals to reform the conduct element of attempt, stating that 'although several of our consultees supported a single offence of attempt in tandem with guiding examples of the sort we proposed, there was no wider consensus that it was the right response to the problems we identified with the present offence or on where the examples should be set out. Nor was there sufficiently clear or broad support for our view that the situations described in our proposed list of examples should be covered by a general offence' (LC 318, [8.75]). This result was inevitable, and any innovation or progress in the definition of the conduct element of attempt will have to rely on sensitivity to the variety of enacted offences.

[60] R Card, *Card, Cross & Jones Criminal Law*, (OUP, 2010) 640. See further AP Simester, JR Spencer, F Stark, GR Sullivan and GJ Virgo, *Simester and Sullivan's Criminal Law – Theory and Doctrine*, (Hart, 2016) 355–56. The defence is also recognised in s 5.01(4) of the Model Penal Code, and available in other jurisdictions, such as Germany and Israel. See Strafgesetzbuch, s 24; Israel Penal Code 1977, s 28.

[61] The Law Commission's neglect of the abandonment doctrine is particularly at odds with its inclination to broaden the breadth of the combined sphere of attempt and criminal preparation. A defence

There are two accepted rationales for exempting someone who has reconsidered his actions before completing the commission of an offence. One is a political preference of prevention over punishment, achieved by providing criminals with an incentive to cease their activity before realising the potential harm that it entails.[62] The other is the assumption that honest repentance either negates the culpability incurred by the actor's bad intent and initial steps toward the commission of an offence, or reveals the actor to be innocuous and therefore undeserving of punishment.[63] In this respect, the Law Commission is begging the question when it states that '[i]t is of course illogical to provide a defence of withdrawal in relation to inchoate liability given that D's liability crystallises at the time he or she does his or her relevant preparatory act with the required [fault element]'.[64] The question as to when exactly liability crystallises should be determined according to the underlying rationale of the defence.

The advantages of the wilful abandonment defence notwithstanding, however, resistance to it is understandable. Arguably, it may be explained by the fact that although abandonment is considered and deliberated as a generally applicable defence, its rationales apply differently in different contexts and with regard to different offences. This produces a rupture between the point at which wilful abandonment would no more be considered exculpating and the point at which each offence is consummated. For example, it seems desirable to waive conviction for attempted theft if it provides an incentive to the offender to desist, thereby preventing the additional harm embodied in the offence. But does this rationale lose its validity once the theft is formally consummated and the object is removed, if it can still be returned without being detected? It seems that the difference between lightly touching the object (attempted theft) and slightly moving it (consummated theft) is not significant enough so that once the latter occurs it is no longer worthwhile exchanging conviction for the negation of harm. In certain cases of theft, therefore, the completion of the offence does not obviate the rationales for the defence. Conversely, in other contexts, the defence may not be justified even if the offence has not yet been consummated. This may be the case with an abandoned

of abandonment may not be necessary when the contours of liability are narrowly drawn and do not leave much space for withdrawal in the timeframe between the commencement of the attempt or the criminal preparation and the completion of the offence. It may be that the narrow approach to the actus reus of attempt characterising much of English case law explains the absence of an abandonment defence, indeed the lack of interest in this doctrine: William Wilson has commented that given the narrow ambit of attempt liability in English law, it is not surprising to find only ten lines on the subject in *Smith and Hogan* and only two lines in *Glanville Williams*. Wilson (n 19) 245. The broad definition of attempt put forth in the Commission's reports, may mandate an introduction of this defence, as '[a] cognate defence of voluntary withdrawal is an important antidote to the test of attempts drawn so widely'. Wilson, ibid.

[62] 500 years after *Utopia*, it is worthwhile rehashing 'the principle that it must always be safer to abandon a criminal undertaking than to go ahead with it'. Thomas Moore, *Utopia* (Penguin Books, 2009 [1516]) 23.

[63] Duff (n 40) 70–72; GP Fletcher, *Rethinking Criminal Law* (Little, Brown & Co., 1978) 184–97.

[64] CP 183, [14.70].

attempted attack that has already caused alarm to bystanders. When, in the course of an attempt and before its abandonment, one completes some lesser offence, one may be held accountable for it; but when actions taken before the abandonment cause a harm that is presently confronted only by the prohibition against the attempt, such harm is left unanswered. Attempted attacks that harm the sense of security fall into this category.[65]

The last illustration points at yet another idiosyncrasy of a generally applied defence of abandonment, ie, its inapplicability to preparatory offences already committed before the abandonment. Although, as a matter of positive law, it is true that liability obtains when the preparatory offence is perpetrated, it is also true that preparatory offences criminalise acts that are partial with respect to some other, more severe offences, and are contained in the attempt to perpetrate these offences. It may therefore seem an anomaly to fully excuse someone who comes close to completing an unarmed robbery, and wilfully abandons it, while refusing such concession to someone who has left his home with an iron claw, and then returned immediately, after abandoning his criminal intentions. This would be difficult to justify either from the point of view of retribution or of utilitarian theory.

All these anomalies are removed, or at least reduced, once the questions of attempt and abandonment are decided within the context of specific offences,[66] rendering the defence more attractive to law reformers who may wish that English law benefit from the values associated with the rationales of abandonment.

VII. Conclusion

The general applicability of the doctrine of attempt to almost all offences forces the law to formulate attempt liability through abstractions, which in turn reduce precision in criminalisation and hamper efforts at reform. The antidote can be found in making the law of attempt more content – or context – specific, that is to say, more closely related to the various types of discrete offences. The lesson derived from the disappointing experience of the Law Commission's effort to reform attempt liability should not be one of complete pessimism, but rather, it should teach us that the nature of the doctrine dictates reform at a more concrete level of conceptualisation.

[65] See Duff (n 40) 73. In the case of a complete attempt with a pending result, for example where D sends V a mail bomb, the abandonment defence will still be advantageous in that it saves V, but the availability of the defence should be limited by a requirement that D takes the necessary steps to prevent the harmful consequence from occurring.

[66] Leaving the issue of abandonment to serve as a mitigating factor in sentencing may provide the needed flexibility, but at the cost of harm to clarity. It would also be a less effective message than an explicit rule of liability.

Following this insight, the article formulates two proposals: (a) beginning a process of exempting offences from attempt liability and redrawing their contours more precisely, and (b) re-considering wilful abandonment as a defence in attempt liability. The two proposals are linked because making the law of attempt more offence-related makes the doctrine of abandonment better suited for its purposes, and therefore more attractive.

In reaching the end, it turns out that the proposal is in fact not about reforming attempt at all. If the above analysis is correct, it should have the following practical implication for the Law Commission's work: whenever the Commission sets its efforts at reforming a specific offence or area of criminalisation, it ought to consider loosening the safety net of attempt liability and endeavour to draw the true limits of the prohibition.

Comment on Chapter 3

Should we Retain 'Criminal Attempts' as a General Offence?

JJ CHILD

A decade has passed since the Law Commission last identified criminal attempts as 'ripe for reconsideration',[1] prompted by perceived problems with the narrow application of the offence. As Professor Shachar Eldar sets out in the early part of his chapter,[2] the Commission criticised the narrow application of the actus reus of attempts, but rather than recommending reform of the actus reus directly, it originally sought to address the problem by proposing a new supplementary general pre-attempts offence of 'criminal preparation'. The proposal for a new offence was abandoned following consultation, as were other options for the direct expansion of the actus reus of attempts, and so no reform recommendations were eventually provided.[3] Despite the lack of success from 'take one',[4] however, Eldar's chapter makes the case for the Commission to take a second look. And there is every reason to support this request: the actus reus problems previously identified by the Commission persist, and in addition we now have a fundamental clash of case law on the interpretation of mens rea.[5] The argument for legislative review is stronger now than ever.

The nature of this review however, and the best way forward, remain predictably contested. The approach advocated by Eldar is an extreme one: systematically creating new bespoke attempt offences (eg, attempted murder, attempted theft, and so on) and removing the corresponding substantive offence (in this case, murder, theft, etc) from the general offence of attempts. Over time, this approach

[1] Law Commission, *Conspiracy and Attempts* (Consultation No 183, 2007) [12.4].

[2] S Eldar, 'Reforming the Law of Criminal Attempt: Take Two', ch 3 of this volume.

[3] Law Commission, *Conspiracy and Attempts* (Law Com No 318, 2009) Part 8. The only recommendations for attempts related to mens rea and clarification on omissions.

[4] In terms of legislative reform at least. For discussion of what 'success' means for the Commission, including success beyond legislative impact, see M Dyson, J Lee and SW Stark, *Fifty Years of the Law Commissions The Dynamics of Law Reform* (Hart, 2016).

[5] Between appeal cases *Khan* [1990] 2 All ER 783 and *Pace* [2014] EWCA Crim 186. See Child and Hunt, '*Pace and Rogers* and the Mens Rea of Attempt: *Khan* on the Scrapheap? (2014) 78 *Journal of Criminal Law* 220.

is intended to eliminate the general offence of attempts entirely, filling the gap with many hundreds (perhaps thousands[6]) of bespoke attempt offences. Eldar contends that the flexibility created by such an approach, allowing us to individually construct each bespoke attempt offence, provides the best route to resolving current difficulties – defining the actus reus, and thus enabling official intervention, in a way that is sensitive to differences between substantive offences (potentially including no attempts intervention at all); similar flexibility across the range of potential mens rea requirements; and the individual consideration of defences such as abandonment.[7]

In this comment, I focus on Eldar's central recommendation to replace the existing general attempts offence with a series of bespoke attempt offences, and caution against such a reform. Although it is hard to disagree with much of Eldar's critique of the current law, there is reason to be wary of the greater proliferation of bespoke inchoate offences. Indeed, as I discuss briefly in the final section of this comment, we already face considerable challenges in our treatment of the bespoke preparatory offences that exist within current law.

I. Moving Attempts to the Special Part

Eldar's approach would (over time) eliminate the general offence of criminal attempts, and replace it with multiple special part bespoke attempt offences. It is a move (General Part to Special Part) that has been advocated before, most prominently by Glazebrook.[8] However, Eldar's approach is different in two crucial respects. First, Eldar recognises that the abolition of criminal attempts at a single stroke would be 'impractical and too drastic to gain approval',[9] and so recommends a phased withdrawal: creating bespoke attempt offences and narrowing the general offence in the course of systematic review. Secondly, Eldar's approach would maintain the position of attempts as supplementary to substantive crimes: whereas Glazebrook favoured reforming substantive offences to fill the inchoate void left by the abolition of attempts,[10] Eldar would rather create a series of separate bespoke attempt offences.

Whilst the first of these differences is correctly highlighted by Eldar as demonstrating the greater practicality of his approach, it is perhaps the second difference

[6] Eldar emphasises that attempts need not apply to many offences, though he does not specify where this will be the case.

[7] For discussion of the abandonment defence in relation to attempts, see A Duff, *Criminal Attempts* (OUP, 1996) 66–75, 395–97; Yaffe, *Attempts* (OUP, 2010) 287–309.

[8] Glazebrook, 'Should we have a Law of Attempted Crime?' [1969] 85 *LQR* 28.

[9] Eldar, (n 2) 86.

[10] Glazebrook (n 8) would achieve this by expanding current substantive offences to include inchoate conduct (42), with only a minority of result crimes retained where the result is particularly central to the purpose and understanding of that offence (43).

that is more significant. Maintaining the separation between substantive offences and bespoke attempt offences provides some important advantages, maintaining the conceptual distinction between completed and attempted harms, as well as the ability to give that distinction practical effect through varying mens rea standards, labelling, punishments, and so on.[11] However, Eldar's approach also gives rise to notable problems, both in terms of complexity (through the sheer number of new varying offences), but also in our conception of what these new bespoke attempt offences are trying to do.

If attempts liability is to occupy a separate conceptual space from the substantive offences that are attempted, whether in the form of a single general attempts offence or multiple bespoke offences, we still need to understand what it is to 'attempt'. Only when we agree in identifying the central or unifying mischief of attempts can we then construct and apply a coherent legislative response.[12] This task, of course, is very far from straightforward, and many of the problems correctly identified by Eldar in the current general offence can be traced back to the contested ground within this underlying challenge. However, just because the concept of attempt is contested, there are advantages to maintaining attempts as a single general offence. This is because, with a single general offence, courts and commentators are forced to consider the application of the concept across multiple substantive offences – maintaining points of consistency where possible and debating points of divergence as the offence develops within the common law.[13] This process results in considerable academic and judicial debate and disagreement, but also maintains attempts as a broadly coherent route to liability, consciously applied to like cases in a like manner.

If we were to move from a general attempts offence to a series of bespoke attempt offences, the danger emerges that courts and commentators will lose focus on attempt as a unifying concept, leading to *unprincipled* divergence between attempt offences. It is a danger that is not fully acknowledged or defended within Eldar's proposal. Rather, arguing in the opposite direction, Eldar presents the current law as adopting a position of rigid and unnecessary consistency, stifling the potential separate development of attempt in different areas by comparisons across and between offence categories.[14] The same logic is applied in Eldar's critique of statutory examples as a method of guiding courts on the actus reus of attempts.[15] It is a critique of the current law that has clear merit – few would argue for 'unnecessary' rigid consistency in the application of the concept of attempt,

[11] Noted by Eldar (n 2) in Part IV, and footnote 47.

[12] See, eg, A Duff, *Criminal Attempts* (OUP, 1996), for a conception of attempts based on 'attacks'; and Yaffe, *Attempts* (OUP, 2010), for a conception based on 'trying'.

[13] On divergence within the actus reus of attempts, see C Clarkson, 'Attempt: The Conduct Requirement' (2009) 29 *OJLS* 25. On mens rea, see, Child and Hunt (n 5).

[14] Eldar (n 2) Parts IV and V in particular.

[15] ibid, Part III.

and, indeed, this is why the statutory definition of the actus reus in particular has remained somewhat flexible.[16] However, although Eldar is right to question the rationale behind certain points of consistency (eg, particularly in his concerns about statutory examples), his conceptual basis for embracing divergence remains unclear.

The main advantage of moving attempts to the special part, for Eldar, is that bespoke attempt offences provide the freedom to vary actus reus and mens rea requirements.[17] This is undeniably true. However, without a conceptually clear target for such bespoke offences, it is difficult to see where this added freedom gets us: without understanding the wrong(s) or mischief(s) being targeted, the potential for greater precision in drafting becomes irrelevant. Eldar presents these underlying conceptual debates as secondary and perhaps peripheral to his primary thesis, commenting in a footnote that 'even if such a unifying wrong [for attempts] is to be acknowledged, it does not follow that this wrong must be criminalised in relation to all prohibitions and to the same extent'.[18] This statement rather begs the question as to the content of any such wrong, but it is also potentially misleading. In line with the accompanying discussion, Eldar seems to present the flexible construction of bespoke attempt offences as an advantage of his approach independent of conceptual context. But if we are to abandon (even partially) our focus on a unified conception of attempts, how do we begin to construct and apply such bespoke *attempt* offences?

The danger of embracing the flexible bespoke construction of attempt offences, moving away from a focus on a unifying conception of attempt, is that the resulting offence definitions will be unprincipled and arbitrary. Indeed, this is exactly what we see in the growing number of bespoke preparatory offences already existing within the current law (discussed further in the next section). Unburdened by any apparent desire to maintain conceptual coherence, offences are created as if in perfect isolation from one another, often by different drafting bodies, subject to different (and usually immediately pressing) political priorities, and with wildly varying culpability requirements. Eldar may be correct that the precise balancing of principles can be 'better performed' within a bespoke (as opposed to general) attempt offence,[19] but without prior clarity on what those principles are, and what weighting they should be given in the definition of an *attempted* crime, little progress can be made. The result of the current growth of bespoke preparatory offences has been an apparently perpetual drift towards widening criminal liability and overcriminalisation, a result that few (and certainly not Eldar) would support.

[16] The Law Commission highlight the importance of 'flexibility' within any definition of attempts (n 1, [16.3]), criticised by Eldar in Part II.

[17] Eldar (n 2) Parts IV and V. See also Glazebrook, (n 8), 85.

[18] Eldar (n 2) footnote 36.

[19] Eldar (n 2) 84.

II. Understanding and Evaluating Bespoke Preparatory Offences

Having cautioned against the expansion of bespoke preparatory offences in general terms, it is useful to provide some further discussion here of their role within our existing criminal law.[20] Such offences vary considerably in their construction, but include possession offences (eg, drugs, weapons, etc), endangerment offences (often related to driving or employment), and, increasingly, substantive offences that have been defined or reformed to apply inchoately (eg, fraud, bribery etc). These offences occupy an interesting political space – being popular despite often exhibiting the lack of collective coherence discussed at the end of the previous section – as well as an interesting analytical space – perhaps still too often side-lined as peripheral within academic debate about the limits of criminalisation.[21] Yet, as Eldar highlights, such offence constructions have continued to proliferate across all manner of criminal behaviour. The breadth of bespoke inchoate liability is so great in fact that the Law Commission could not identify a single case falling short of criminal attempt that would not have been caught by some such preparatory crime (aside from hypotheticals).[22]

The first challenge presented by existing preparatory offences is to control how they interact with general inchoate offences such as attempt. The issue here is one of potential overcriminalisation through double or infinite inchoate liability: stretching an already preparatory offence beyond acceptable limits through its combination with another inchoate offence.[23] Eldar uses the example of a possession offence: 'being in possession of an article for use in connection with burglary or theft'.[24] Whilst this offence may be justifiable on its own terms, it is questionable whether liability should *automatically* be stretched further to include attempts at such possession (or conspiracies etc). Given the breadth of and overlap between existing preparatory offences, the potential for such combinations is wide ranging and difficult to control.[25]

[20] For a growing discussion and critique of the prevalence of such offences and their construction within the current law, see A Ashworth and L Zedner, *Preventive Justice* (OUP, 2014); A Ashworth, L Zedner and P Tomlin (eds), *Prevention and the Limits of the Criminal Law* (OUP, 2013); GR Sullivan and I Dennis (eds), *Seeking Security* (Hart, 2012); JJ Child and A Hunt, 'Risk, Pre-Emption, and the Limits of the Criminal Law' in T Beech et al, (eds) *Whose Criminal Justice? Regulatory State or Empowered Communities* (Waterside Press, 2011) 51.

[21] See Child and Hunt (n 20); B McSherry, 'Expanding the Boundaries of Inchoate Crimes: The Growing Reliance on Preparatory Offences' in S Bronitt et al (eds) *Regulating Deviance: The Redirection of Criminalisation and the Futures of Criminal Law* (Hart, 2009) 141.

[22] Law Commission, (n 1), Appendix C.

[23] Assuming, of course, an identified limit to acceptable criminalisation.

[24] Eldar (n 2) 85, and footnote 44. Paraphrasing from the Theft Act 1968, s 25.

[25] For example, the Law Commission proposed in 2007 to expand double inchoate liability to include attempts to conspire (n 1) [7.36–7.58]. This was rejected at consultation as expanding liability too far, and yet the Commission casually concedes that all their examples of potential attempt to conspire could be alternatively charged as assisting or encouraging a conspiracy (n 3), [3.22].

For Eldar, of course, this first challenge is best addressed through the bespoke construction of attempt offences, allowing the specific tailoring of an attempt offence or for no attempt offence to be employed. Although I cautioned against such an approach in the first section of this comment, the need to identify ways to control double inchoate liability remains pressing. There is only space here for limited comment, but I would highlight two alternative options, both of which I believe should be pursued. First, it is important to remember that even general inchoate offences need not apply to *all* substantive crimes. Liability for criminal attempts, for example, is already excluded for all summary only offences as well as for a few other listed offences,[26] and this approach has been taken substantially further within the more recent codification of assisting or encouraging offences, where multiple preparatory offences are listed for exclusion.[27] I have been critical of this approach in previous writing,[28] largely because (as we see with assisting and encouraging) lists of this kind are often incomplete and may be neglected in future reform.[29] However, although not a complete solution, the explicit listing of excluded offences remains a sensible measure to be encouraged; and should be considered when new preparatory offences are created and/or existing ones reviewed.[30] Alongside this, it is also important to maintain a narrow interpretation of double inchoate liability in cases where it does arise. The best way to achieve this, as I have argued elsewhere,[31] is to recognise the separate status of *ulterior* mens rea from mens rea as to action, circumstances and results. Only when this separation is made does it become possible to individually specify a mens rea requirement (eg, for attempts) as to such ulterior mens rea: for example, requiring D to intend any ulterior mens rea elements within an attempted offence.[32]

The second challenge presented by existing preparatory offences is more comprehensive, and not one that I can hope to resolve within this comment – it is simply the question of how such preparatory offences (so prevalent and varied across the current criminal law) can begin to be rationalised and controlled. The challenge to understand attempts liability is daunting enough, but outside of this familiar concept it becomes difficult to identify clear boundaries and/or concepts to help us negotiate preparatory offences that (it should be remembered) will often apply to conduct some way before possible attempts intervention.[33] There are

[26] Criminal Attempts Act 1981, s 1(4).

[27] Serious Crime Act 2007, s 49(4) and (5), with excluded offences listed in Sch 3.

[28] JJ Child, 'The Structure, Coherence and Limits of Inchoate Liability: The New Ulterior Element' (2014) 34(4) *Legal Studies* 537.

[29] ibid, 17–18. This is particularly likely within an uncodified jurisdiction like England and Wales, where criminal prohibitions are scattered across multiple statutes and/or exist only at common law.

[30] This is an area where the systematic review approach recommended by Eldar can be usefully employed.

[31] Child, (n 28).

[32] The control provided through this separate element is even more important in the context of other *less* proximate inchoate offences. See n 28.

[33] This statement is sometimes doubted on the basis that attempts liability will standardly apply to such offences (ie, attempting to commit the preparatory offence), and so attempts logically retains its

two logical paths that we might take here (either independently or in combination), but I remain uncertain as to which offers the best way forward.

The first option is the more pragmatic, but also (perhaps) less likely to achieve its aims: this is an approach that accepts the multiplicity of bespoke preparatory offences across the criminal piste, but seeks to identify and entrench minimum standards and principles of criminalisation in order to encourage coherence within their future evolution. This approach is likely to be supported by academics such as Eldar who place particular value on the potential precision of bespoke offences, but the difficulty will lie in agreeing principles of general application and ensuring that these are acknowledged in reform. It should be observed that this approach mirrors traditional discussions about the reform and rationalisation of so-called substantive offences, highlighting once more that the role of preparatory crimes may not be as exceptional as it is sometimes presented.

The second option is more radical, to embrace and expand the use of general inchoate offences to replace existing bespoke preparatory crimes. Something of this approach can be seen in the (ultimately unsuccessful) consultation proposals put forward by the Law Commission in 2007,[34] recommending a new pre-attempts general offence of criminal preparation and advocating the expansion of conspiracy liability to apply in cases where bespoke offences would otherwise be relied upon. There are a number of specific reasons why these proposals were not successful,[35] and why calls for other potential general preparatory offences (such as a general endangerment offence) have not been taken forward. We should also ask whether general offences of this kind would give rise to *unnecessary* gap-filling and overcriminalisation of the kind cautioned against in Alldridge's chapter later in this volume.[36] However, in each case, the rationalising potential of such offences is clear, allowing for the repeal of multiple bespoke preparatory offences in favour of a single offence that can be applied consistently across different cases.

III. Conclusion

When debating the reform of criminal attempts, as with much legal reform, it is always easier to identify problems than it is to propose solutions. Eldar's approach offers a unique and valuable contribution to this debate, setting out a clear route to a new way of constructing and understanding attempts liability. For my part,

role in defining the limits of criminalisation. However, this will not always be the case. For example, where the preparatory offence applies a mens rea short of intention (which is common), and the particular case involves a non-intending defendant, then liability for attempts will not be relevant.

[34] Law Commission, (n 1).

[35] See, eg, J Rogers, 'The Codification of Attempts and the Case for "Preparation"' (2008) *Crim LR* 937.

[36] See P Alldridge, '"Lawyers' Law" and the Limitations and Flaws of the Role of Reform Bodies in Criminal Law', ch 10A of this volume.

in this comment I have taken the easier route, highlighting some of the problems inherent in the recommendations Eldar puts forward and defending the (admittedly imperfect) place of attempts within the general part. However, whether one is convinced by Eldar's case for bespoke special part attempts or not, this comment has also sought to emphasise the continued central importance of a clear conceptualisation of what it means to attempt and an identification of the mischief targeted: understanding the target of criminalisation must always precede our construction and evaluation of its mechanisms. The simple logic of this statement should be guarded preciously within the development of the law of attempts, and should guide our evaluation of, and efforts to rationalise, the existing bespoke preparatory offences.

4

Done to Death? Reform of Homicide Law

SALLY KYD

In 2000 a collection of papers first presented at a conference in Oxford was published, edited by Andrew Ashworth and Barry Mitchell, the purpose of both being political: to 'relaunch debate on the future of the English law of homicide'.[1] At that time, the Law Commission had recently reviewed the law of manslaughter,[2] but not homicide as a whole. Mitchell was motivated to seek Ashworth's help in organising the conference because, having spent much of his professional life researching homicide, he was clear that the law causes injustice and requires reform. Eighteen years later, much debate has occurred. In its 2004 report, *Partial Defences to Murder* the Law Commission described the law on murder as 'a mess' and recommended a complete review.[3] In 2005 a consultation took place, and the Law Commission published its report, *Murder, Manslaughter and Infanticide* in 2006.[4]

Of the recommendations, only those relating to the partial defences of provocation and diminished responsibility were adopted by the Government, which elected not to proceed with reforms to the structure of homicide as a whole. The Coroners and Justice Act 2009 introduced those reforms of the partial defences to the existing law of murder, bringing some clarification to the definition of diminished responsibility, and both broadening and narrowing the defence of provocation by replacing it with loss of control. Whatever the strengths and weaknesses of the new definitions of those partial defences, they were originally proposed as part of a package of reform, and operate very differently transplanted into the existing law than they would have done had the other recommendations been adopted. They will not be considered further here.[5]

[1] A Ashworth and B Mitchell, *Rethinking English Homicide Law* (OUP, 2000) 1.

[2] Law Commission, *Legislating the Criminal Code: Involuntary Manslaughter* (Law Com No 237, 1996).

[3] Law Commission, *Partial Defences to Murder* (CP No 290, 2004).

[4] Law Commission. *Murder, Manslaughter and Infanticide* (Law Com No 304, 2006).

[5] Other issues beyond the scope of this chapter include the question of whether duress should be a defence to murder; the offences/defences of infanticide, encouraging or assisting suicide and killing in pursuance of a suicide pact; abortion; mercy killing/euthanasia.

In putting forward the law of homicide as a potential project for law reform, I must face the objection that discussion of reform of homicide law has been 'done to death', but that in no way diminishes the strength of the need for law reform in homicide, nor the importance of the issues it covers. My recommendation is for consideration of the whole law of homicide, although I have space in this chapter only to consider involuntary manslaughter in detail. I concede that the obstacle to the Law Commission committing further resources to this issue is that its efforts need to be directed towards reforms that are most likely to be implemented. There seems to be little political will to see legislative change in this area. And yet, there has been the political will to introduce new statutory 'regulatory' homicide offences over the past two decades. The political mileage to be made in creating highly punitive offences penalising death on the roads has driven parliament to create three new constructive homicide offences in the past 12 years,[6] as well as a new offence of corporate manslaughter.[7] Additionally, it is now 14 years since the familial homicide offence of causing or allowing the death of a child or vulnerable adult was created.[8]

Promisingly, there has in fact been some interest in revitalising the discussion of reform of the law of murder, with a debate taking place in the House of Commons in June 2016,[9] leading to an evidence session on the law of homicide held by the Justice Select Committee on 14 September of that year, a day after I presented this paper at a conference. Although the Minister of State for Courts and Justice was clear at the time that the government had no plans to reopen the consultation on reform in this area, he said that he would keep an open mind; and Professor David Ormerod QC is clearly in favour of taking forward a proposal for reform based on the recommendations made in 2006 following a further review process.[10] The suggestion here is that the law can and should most definitely be improved, and an attempt is made to build on the Law Commission's previous recommendations, as well as some of the suggestions of Jeremy Horder, writing from his experience as Law Commissioner at the time of the latest review of homicide offences.[11] The focus is on involuntary manslaughter and, unlike the Law Commission, I have considered the need to examine how (some[12]) existing statutory offences might fit within a codified version of murder and manslaughter. Specific homicide offences regulating certain forms of causing death fell outside the terms of reference for the Law Commission in 2005. Although Horder advises strongly against 'grandiose schemes for the codification of all the law relevant to the commission of homicide',[13] I see a need to rationalise the existing offences to

[6] Road Traffic Act 1988, ss 2B, 3ZB and 3ZC.

[7] Corporate Manslaughter and Corporate Homicide Act 2007.

[8] Domestic Violence, Crime and Victims Act 2004, s 5.

[9] Hansard Reports, *Homicide Law Reform* (30 June 2016, Volume 612).

[10] The Justice Committee, *Evidence session on the law of homicide* (8 September 2016).

[11] J Horder, *Homicide and the Politics of Law Reform* (OUP, 2012).

[12] I do not here consider all the offences that may be ripe for reform, such as the offence under Domestic Violence, Crime and Victims Act 2004, s 5.

[13] Horder (n 11) 113.

establish how a codification of the common law could sit alongside a rethinking of the regulatory or 'bureaucratic-administrative' model of offences.[14]

I. Horder's Models

By way of explanation of the rationale underpinning the proposals made here, a basic summary of the existing models of law explicated by Horder will be provided briefly, before the suggestions for reform are made in that context. These models are the traditional-codifcatory model and the administrative-regulatory model. In explaining the traditional-codificatory account of law-making which has been used by the Law Commission in relation to homicide, Horder draws on the work of Kamenka and Tay[15] in employing two German terms to portray the significance of particular elements of this model of reform: *gesellschaft* and *gemeinschaft*.[16] The former represents the idea that law puts in place rules that are exhaustive, requiring statutory provisions to be drafted using broad language in order to capture every example of wrongdoing that warrants the label of a particular offence such as murder or manslaughter. These labels are then used under the *gemeinschaft* ideal of law to infuse the law with moral judgments.

The bureaucratic-administrative model, on the other hand, employs the law in order to regulate potentially harmful activities, rather than to adjudicate in cases where a harm has been caused as to who is at fault and ought to face retributive punishment. Many such laws will relate to activities carried out for profit, but perhaps the most universal example of this model's use is in relation to driving offences under the Road Traffic Act 1988. This model jettisons the value-laden labels used by the traditional-codificatory model and provides more utilitarian labels for offences, such as causing death by dangerous driving.[17] Similarly, the purposes of punishment have been seen as utilitarian rather than retributive, particularly in the sense of aiming at general deterrence in order to increase road safety. The original rationale behind such offences employing the bureaucratic-administrative model has not endured in relation to some such offences, however:

> The offence of causing death by dangerous driving (together with its punishment) has in effect outgrown its origin merely as a heavy-duty tool for reinforcing a deterrent regulatory message about road safety. The offence has become more like a traditional common law crime, in which the public interest in securing retribution typically predominates over other (more forward-looking) concerns. It has proved difficult, then, for Governments to have their cake and eat it too. It has not been easy to satisfy the perceived need, for deterrence reasons, to increase road safety through increasing

[14] Horder, (n 11) 75.

[15] E Kamenka and A Tay, 'Beyond Bourgeois Individualism: the Contemporary Crisis in Law and Legal Ideology' in E Kamenka and RS Neale (eds), *Feudalism, Capitalism and Beyond* (Edward Arnold, 1975).

[16] Horder (n 11) 71.

[17] Road Traffic Act 1988, s 1.

> numbers of prosecutions and convictions for causing death on the roads (taking the administrative-regulatory approach, rather than leaving homicides to be dealt with as potential manslaughters), whilst also satisfying the demand for sentences of a retributive kind that would certainly have fitted the crime, had it remained manslaughter.[18]

It is these forms of killings that will be the focus of discussion later in this chapter.[19] An attempt will be made at 'imaginative solutions'[20] to the problem of killing with cars, taking on board what Horder suggests about the advantages of what might be seen a hybrid of his two models: corporate manslaughter. He notes that corporate manslaughter has the advantage of adapting a 'general common law crime, with its value-laden and retribution-orientated *gemeinschaft* label (manslaughter), to fit a specific regulatory context'.[21] There are other contexts in which such a traditional-codificatory-regulatory-bureaucratic hybrid model might also be employed,[22] but they are beyond the scope of this chapter.

II. Codifying the Common Law Offences

My primary focus, in terms of proposing anything of novelty, will be on the regulatory homicide offences, but if they are to work alongside codified versions of murder and manslaughter, it is surely necessary to consider what these should be.[23] In making my suggestions, one of my priorities is to give effect to the correspondence principle, meaning that in my view any fault element in a homicide offence should make reference to a risk of causing *death*. This is not to take an exclusively subjective/cognitive approach to blameworthiness and mens rea, but rather to at least require an obvious risk of death to be proved at all levels of homicide.

A. Murder

Despite being singled out as the most serious offence in England and Wales in that it leads to a mandatory life sentence,[24] murder is currently a fairly broad offence, as a result of it requiring either an intention to kill *or* an intention to cause grievous bodily harm as constitutive of malice aforethought.[25] Given the broadness of the

[18] Horder (n 11) 74.
[19] See Part III below.
[20] Horder (n 11) 88.
[21] Horder (n 11) 72.
[22] Examples suggested by Horder include medical manslaughter, armed police officers killing in the execution of their duty and parents failing to prevent the death of their child through physical abuse. See Horder, (n 11) ch 2.
[23] Excluded from consideration, however, are issues of complicity and how the proposed offences might apply to secondary parties.
[24] Murder (Abolition of Death Penalty) Act 1965, s 1.
[25] *Cunningham* [1982] AC 566.

current offence, the Law Commission proposed splitting murder into two degrees, each with different mens rea requirements. Consultees provided a 'good deal of support'[26] for the Law Commission's 2004 proposals which required that for first degree murder D must have an intention to kill.[27] Although the Law Commission went on to loosen the requirement for mens rea for that offence,[28] which it might have hoped would lead to the recommendations finding more political favour, the original proposals are stronger in their rational structure, providing clarity in singling out the most heinous of homicide offences. If the substantive law is to be specific enough to assist in the task of sentencing killers, rather than relying wholly on a provision equivalent to Schedule 21 of the Criminal Justice Act 2003, and/or guidelines from the Sentencing Council,[29] it seems desirable to divide the general homicide cake into three rather than two layers.[30] Slicing off the top layer as *the* most serious offence worthy of a mandatory life sentence would allow the offence to be reserved for the most blameworthy state of mind: an intention to kill. Below that, second degree murder would incorporate those who intend to cause serious injury. But in order to comply with the correspondence principle, I would require more than just that. Taking Tadros' view of how the correspondence principle could be complied with by objectivists,[31] I see it as sufficient to require that D be liable for second degree murder where D killed V with intention to cause serious injury in circumstances where D had created a foreseeable risk of death.

If that were the case, then second degree murder should also include those who are 'recklessly indifferent' to death.[32] This test was replaced in the 2006 recommendations by a mens rea requirement of intention to cause injury or a fear or risk of injury where D was aware of a serious risk of causing death.[33] This, unlike my suggestion above, is a *subjective* test, requiring that death be foreseen rather than merely foreseeable. In most cases, D will be unlikely to foresee death unless an objective risk of death is present, but even if others in D's shoes would not have foreseen death as a result of D's actions, the fact that D did so would suggest that D is sufficiently blameworthy to be convicted of second degree murder. If first degree murder is confined to those who intend to kill, meaning that D must either act with the purpose of causing V's death or foresee it as a virtual certainty,[34] then those who intend to cause serious injury and foresee death as likely, but not

[26] Law Com 304, [2.53].

[27] Law Commission, *A New Homicide Act for England and Wales?* (CP No 177, 2005), [5.26].

[28] Law Com 304, [2.50].

[29] At the time of writing the Sentencing Council had recently published a consultation on sentencing in manslaughter cases (both voluntary and involuntary). The proposed guidance on sentencing in cases of manslaughter by loss of self-control makes reference to culpability factors influencing the minimum term to be served for murder under Criminal Justice Act 2003, Sch 21: Sentencing Council, *Manslaughter Guideline Consultation* (July 2017) 30.

[30] Horder, (n 11), 95.

[31] V Tadros, *Criminal Responsibility* (OUP, 2005) 95.

[32] CP No 177.

[33] Law Com No 304, [2.116].

[34] The test for intention as laid down in *Woollin* [1999] AC 82.

virtually certain, ought to be liable for second degree murder. It may be desirable to include what Taylor refers to as 'advertent lethal risks'[35] within the mens rea of a lower level murder offence.

B. Manslaughter

Setting aside the issue of voluntary manslaughter and the question, which is beyond the scope of this chapter, of whether the existing partial defences to murder should apply to reduce first degree murder to second degree murder or manslaughter, the next issue to deal with in rationalising homicide law is that of involuntary manslaughter. The current law encompasses two or, perhaps, three forms of involuntary manslaughter[36] in a way that lacks coherence and breaches the correspondence principle. Unlawful act manslaughter is seen as particularly controversial and would require extensive reform if codified in statute. This form of manslaughter encompasses deaths caused as the result of any unlawful and dangerous act,[37] such as a single punch. The Law Commission recommended that a form of unlawful act manslaughter be retained but with the requirement that by the unlawful act D either intended to cause injury or was aware there was a serious risk of causing injury.[38]

i. Unlawful Act Manslaughter

Horder labels 'one punch' manslaughter as 'the pure form of manslaughter'[39] and has no doubt that it should continue to amount to manslaughter. This is one issue upon which he and Mitchell do not agree, being on different sides of the objectivist/subjectivist divide.[40] Distilling the issue down to one of objectivism versus subjectivism might be seen as an oversimplification of their views on the relevance of the correspondence principle, but it is difficult to see how this debate can be resolved without resort to 'intuition' regarding the relevance of the moral luck argument. Horder argues that '[w]hen someone intentionally attacks

[35] R Taylor, 'The Nature of "Partial Defences" and the Coherence of (Second Degree) Murder' [2007] *Crim LR* 345, 356.

[36] Unlawful act manslaughter and gross negligent manslaughter clearly exist as separate species of manslaughter. Some doubt exists over the third species of reckless manslaughter, previously recognised by the Law Commission: Law Com No 237, [5.15]; CP No 177, [1.10]. Stark's analysis suggests good reason to harbour such doubts, and provides an explanation for why reckless manslaughter is not mentioned in the Sentencing Council's *Manslaughter Guideline Consultation* (see above, n 29): F Stark, 'Reckless Manslaughter' [2017] *Crim LR* 763.

[37] *DPP v Newbury* [1977] AC 500.

[38] Law Com 304, [1.67].

[39] Horder (n 11) 140.

[40] See B Mitchell, 'More Thoughts about Unlawful and Dangerous Act Manslaughter and the One-punch Killer' [2009] *Crim LR* 502.

another's physical integrity, they attack an interest in preserving that integrity – an interest wherein being alive is a constituent element',[41] and relies on Duff's distinction between intentional attacks and endangerments[42] to support a law that categorises as manslaughter those criminal acts which amount to attacks on V's physical integrity, but otherwise does away with manslaughter based on unlawful acts falling outside the family of offences against the person. An attack on physical integrity amounts to something more than a mere trespass to the person,[43] but is otherwise not clearly defined; what is clear, however, is that Horder's suggestion is *not* based on the dangerousness of the attack:

> [U]nderstanding it in this way is not to make an implicit claim that attacks on physical integrity are more dangerous to life than attacks on property. That may be a false claim, for example, in cases of arson. Manslaughter committed through an intentional attack on V's physical integrity does not rely *at all* for its rationale on an assessment of the danger to life or limb posed by such conduct. It is enough that D caused death, in the meaning given by law to the notion of 'caused', by such an attack.[44]

Others agree that unlawful act manslaughter ought to be confined to offences against the person. At the 2000 conference, Clarkson similarly suggested that constructive manslaughter should be retained but only for unlawful acts of personal violence involving at least a common assault with intention or foresight of some injury.[45] I remain unconvinced about the retention of liability for manslaughter for those whose act may not create an obvious risk of death, but who lose their temper and lash out, whilst excluding liability for manslaughter for those who create an obvious risk of death in other ways. The example provided by Clarkson[46] of a case not falling within his proposal, of setting a car alight, seems to be as blameworthy as punching someone. In both cases a prudent individual who stopped to think about the consequences of their actions would realise the risks involved, and the risk of death to anybody caught in a fire is perhaps higher than the recipient of a punch. I suggest that if we are to retain any form of constructive manslaughter,[47] it should be based on creation of an obvious risk of death, whether an attack or an endangerment, which was, if not foreseen, then foreseeable to D. Again, this is to emphasise the importance of the correspondence principle. It would not require

[41] ibid.

[42] A Duff, *Answering for Crime* (Hart, 2007) 148–58.

[43] Horder (n 11) 149.

[44] Horder (n 11) 143.

[45] CMV Clarkson, 'Context and Culpability in Involuntary Manslaughter' in Ashworth and Mitchell (n 1) 160.

[46] *England* (1995) 16 Cr App R 777.

[47] It might be questioned whether there is a need to retain a form of constructive manslaughter at all, and rather simply define manslaughter as killing when D acts having created an obvious risk of death, where D had the capacity to foresee such a risk, and D acted unreasonably in taking that risk. However, I wonder whether there are political reasons to propose offences that *generally* follow the contours of the common law; there may be more chance of such proposals being adopted and reform going ahead.

D to have foreseen a risk of death, but it could involve a reformulation of the *Church*[48] test to include a requirement that sober and reasonable people would recognise the risk of *death,* rather than of *some harm.*

Although my proposal would adhere to the correspondence principle, it would do so in a way that might offend a strict subjectivist. The strict subjectivist could criticise the suggested offence construction on the basis that it could make manslaughterers of those who did not advert to a risk of death. The proposal put forward for manslaughter in the appendix does at least adopt a modified version of 'objective' recklessness, however, in order to avoid a situation where those who were mature enough to realise that starting a fire might cause damage to property[49] but who failed, perhaps due to incapacity, to realise the inherent risk of death, could be labelled manslaughterers. The addition of a clause to ensure that only those with the *capacity* to have realised an obvious risk of death be held liable for manslaughter is thus required, although further amendment might be needed here in order to avoid the provision being too clumsy.[50] It can also be seen that the suggested provision incorporates a requirement that the risk of death exists *by virtue* of the act being unlawful. This is to ensure that there is a connection between the unreasonableness of the risk D is taking in committing the unlawful act and the causation of death, in order to avoid D being liable for the causing of death through a combination of unfortunate events leading on from the commission of an offence which would not normally give rise to a risk of death in and of itself.[51]

Such a change would not necessarily cover every example of Horder's 'pure' manslaughter, in that a punch struck in anger might not create an obvious risk of death, but only of some lesser physical harm, depending on the circumstances. But it could cover unlawful acts from other families of offences, such as arson. Thus, unlike Horder, I do think that the dangerousness of the underlying act, rather than an attack on physical integrity, is what is important. This suggestion could have the result of extending the way in which manslaughter is prosecuted to incorporate appropriate cases of killing with a motor vehicle.[52]

[48] [1966] 1 QB 59.

[49] Satisfying the mens rea requirement according to *G* [2003] UKHL 50.

[50] A more detailed provision could be drafted with Hart's comments regarding negligence and capacity in mind: HLA Hart, 'Negligence, Mens Rea and the Elimination of Responsibility' in *Punishment and Responsibility: Essays in the Philosophy of Law* (OUP, 1968) 152–57.

[51] There is a need to avoid an offence formulation that risks labelling as manslaughterers those who commit a regulatory offence such as driving without insurance and are involved in a fatal collision, such as the defendants in *Williams* [2010] EWCA Crim 2552 and *Hughes* [2011] EWCA Crim 1508 (prior to the reversal of the Court of Appeal decision in *Hughes* [2013] UKSC 1356). It might be argued that there is always an obvious risk of death involved in driving a motor vehicle, but principle requires that there must be a serious risk of death relating to the underlying offence in order for D to be called to answer for the death.

[52] However, as will be discussed below, as I am also proposing a separate offence of vehicular manslaughter there would not be a need for this generic form of manslaughter to be prosecuted in driving cases.

ii. The Relationship between Manslaughter and Regulatory Offences

Since *Andrews v DPP*[53] it has been assumed that a driving offence can never form the basis of a prosecution for constructive manslaughter. This is based on Lord Atkin's determination that the unlawful act must be unlawful for some reason other than it was negligently performed.[54] Driving is seen as a lawful activity, which only becomes unlawful if D fails to adhere to the rules of the road and other regulations put in place to promote road safety. Such a determination was made in a period of history when driving was less prevalent than it is today, a preserve of the upper classes, and there was less regulation.[55] I suggest that in modern times, and in order to underline the road safety purposes of regulation, it would be preferable to present driving as an unlawful activity only made lawful if certain conditions are met.[56] Wells similarly questions the way in which driving is perceived as lawful and the point in time when it becomes unlawful, comparing it to the lawful social activity of going on a pub crawl which later turns into a brawl.[57]

Although there was less regulation of driving at the time of *Andrews*, there was of course some, and it is worth pausing to examine in more detail Lord Atkin's statement in relation to this regulation and how it has been interpreted since. Lord Atkin specifically referred to regulation on the roads as follows:

> [T]he Road Traffic Acts ... have provisions which regulate the degree of care to be taken in driving motor vehicles. They have no direct reference to causing death by negligence. Their prohibitions, while directed no doubt to cases of negligent driving, which if death be caused would justify convictions for manslaughter, extend to degrees of negligence of less gravity. Sect 12 of the Road Traffic Act, 1930, imposes a penalty for driving without due care and attention. This would apparently cover all degrees of negligence. Sect 11 imposes a penalty for driving recklessly or at a speed or in a manner which is dangerous to the public. There can be no doubt that this section covers driving with such a high degree of negligence as that if death were caused the offender would have committed manslaughter. But the converse is not true, and it is perfectly possible that a man may drive at a speed or in a manner dangerous to the public and cause death and yet not be guilty of manslaughter: and the Legislature appears to recognize this by the provision in s 34 of the Road Traffic Act, 1934, that on an indictment for manslaughter a man may be convicted of dangerous driving. But, apart altogether from any inference to be drawn from s 34, I entertain no doubt that the statutory offence of dangerous driving may be committed, though the negligence is not of such a degree as would amount to manslaughter if death ensued. As an instance, in the course of argument it was suggested that a man might execute the dangerous manoeuvre of drawing out to

[53] [1937] AC 576.

[54] At 585.

[55] For a discussion of the history of the regulation of driving and construction of 'car crime' see C Corbett, *Car Crime* (Willan, 2003).

[56] See S Cunningham, 'Vehicular Homicide: Need for a Special Offence?' in CMV Clarkson and S Cunningham, *Criminal Liability for Non-Aggressive Death* (Ashgate, 2008), 101.

[57] C Wells, *Corporations and Criminal Responsibility* (OUP, 2001) 118–19.

> pass a vehicle in front with another vehicle meeting him, and be able to show that he would have succeeded in his calculated intention but for some increase of speed in the vehicles in front: a case very doubtfully of manslaughter but very probably of dangerous driving. I cannot think of anything worse for users of the road than the conception that no one could be convicted of dangerous driving unless his negligence was so great that if he had caused death he must have been convicted of manslaughter. It therefore would appear that in directing the jury in a case of manslaughter the judge should in the first instance charge them substantially in accordance with the general law, that is, requiring the high degree of negligence indicated in *Bateman's* case[58] and then explain that such degree of negligence is not necessarily the same as that which is required for the offence of dangerous driving, and then indicate to them the conditions under which they might acquit of manslaughter and convict of dangerous driving. A direction that all they had to consider was whether death was caused by dangerous driving within s. 11 of the Road Traffic Act, 1930, and no more, would in my opinion be a misdirection.[59]

Much has changed since 1937, and it is no longer the case that the Road Traffic Acts make no direct reference to causing death by negligence. Causing death by reckless or dangerous driving was first introduced by the Road Traffic Act 1956, and has gone through a number of iterations, with the current law being established through the Road Traffic Act 1991 amending the relevant provisions of the Road Traffic Act 1988.[60] It is still the case, however, that where a driver's negligence in causing death meets the degree of grossness required under *Bateman* and, now, *Adomako*,[61] he can be liable for gross negligence manslaughter. However, the effect of *DPP v Andrews* on charging practice has been that no offence under the Road Traffic Acts is ever treated as the underlying unlawful act on the basis of which unlawful act manslaughter is constructed. The online CPS legal guidance states that: 'Driving carelessly or driving dangerously do not, on their own, amount to unlawful acts for the purpose of unlawful act manslaughter.'[62] Death by motor car does sometimes get charged as manslaughter based on an unlawful act, but only where the car was used as a weapon of offence, or where the driving injects danger into an offence such as burglary.[63]

Although drivers are not prosecuted for unlawful act manslaughter on the basis of an offence under the Road Traffic Acts, it is not unheard of for offences under such Acts to form the basis of such a charge. In the case of *Meeking*[64] the

[58] (1927) 19 Cr App R 8.

[59] *Andrews v DPP* [1937] AC 576, 584–85.

[60] Section 1.

[61] [1995] 1 AC 171.

[62] CPS, *Road Traffic Offences – Guidance on Charging Offences arising from Driving Incidents* (CPS Website, updated February 2018).

[63] As seen in *Bristow* [2013] EWCA Crim 1540. A recent example of this approach may have been that of Michael Johnson, who was sentenced to 5 years and 3 months' imprisonment after pleading guilty to manslaughter for running over and killing the victim whilst he was in the process of stealing a trailer from the farm on which the victim lived. It is not clear whether manslaughter was charged on the basis of an unlawful act and, if so, whether the unlawful act was an assault or some theft-related offence.

[64] [2012] EWCA Crim 641.

defendant was charged with manslaughter, having pulled on the handbrake of a car in which she was the passenger, causing a collision which killed her husband, the driver. The prosecution argued their case on the basis that D had committed the unlawful act of interfering with a motor vehicle so as to endanger road users, contrary to section 22A(1)(b) of the Road Traffic Act 1988. This provides that:

> (1) A person is guilty of an offence if he intentionally and without lawful authority or reasonable cause –
>
> (a) causes anything to be on or over a road, or
> (b) interferes with a motor vehicle, trailer or cycle, or
> (c) interferes (directly or indirectly) with traffic equipment,
>
> in such circumstances that it would be obvious to a reasonable person that to do so would be dangerous.

As noted by Ashworth, this offence appears to be both a crime of negligence and a crime of intention.[65] But Ashworth's interpretation of the provision is that it is essentially a crime of negligence,[66] and that intention only forms a small part of the wrong involved in qualifying the means adopted in such negligence. Intention here is used in the sense used by Lord Atkin in the quotation above, when he provides an example of a case which he thinks would amount to dangerous driving but not to manslaughter, where D has a 'calculated intention' to overtake other vehicles.

Another example of a case of unlawful act manslaughter which could have been based on an offence of similar construction (a crime of negligence where intention was relevant to the way in which such negligence was carried out) is in fact the leading House of Lords case of *Newbury*.[67] Here the House of Lords was determining whether a defendant could be convicted under unlawful act manslaughter where he did not foresee that his act might cause harm to another. The answer was clear: yes; meaning that the convictions for manslaughter of the two 15-year-old boys, who had dropped a paving slab from the parapet of a bridge onto a train below, killing the train guard, were upheld. What the House of Lords did not address was what the unlawful act was on which the charge of manslaughter could be based, given that the appellants accepted that they had committed an unlawful act and this was not an issue before the court.

The Law Commission has suggested a number of unlawful acts the defendants in *Newbury* may have committed. The first of these is the offence of doing or omitting anything to endanger passengers by railway, under section 34 of the Offences Against the Person Act 1861:[68]

> Whosoever, by any unlawful act, or by any wilful omission or neglect, shall endanger or cause to be endangered the safety of any person conveyed or being in or upon a railway,

[65] A Ashworth, 'Commentary to R v Meeking' [2013] *Crim LR* 333, 334.
[66] ibid.
[67] [1977] AC 500.
[68] Law Commission, *Involuntary Manslaughter* (CP No 135, 1994), [2.10].

> or shall aid or assist therein, shall be guilty of a misdemeanor, and being convicted thereof shall be liable, at the discretion of the court, to be imprisoned for any term not exceeding two years.

The Law Commission note that the elements of this offence are unclear:

> The section stipulates that the 'omission or neglect' which forms the basis of the offence must have been 'wilful'. 'Wilful' in this context means that the omission or neglect was deliberate and intentional, not accidental or caused by inadvertence. Although the word 'wilful' does not qualify 'unlawful act', it can perhaps be assumed by implication that the required mental element is that the act was done voluntarily and intentionally.[69]

Thus, it would appear that 'wilful' here has the same meaning as 'intentionally' under section 22A of the Road Traffic Act 1988, according to Ashworth's analysis. Although the Law Commission goes on to identify alternative offences which could have formed the unlawful act upon which the defendants' convictions for manslaughter in *Newbury* were based, it does appear that Lord Atkin's rule of excluding offences of negligence for this purpose is sometimes overlooked.[70]

Whether or not it is right that dangerous driving should be capable of amounting to the unlawful act upon which an allegation of constructive manslaughter is made, the fact that statutory offences have been introduced under the bureaucratic-administrative model makes it highly unlikely that the limits of Lord Atkin's judgment will be further tested. He was clear that manslaughter should not be based on driving without due care and attention, and yet there now exits a separate offence penalising the causing of death in this manner.[71] The use of bureaucratic-administrative homicide offences has additionally been extended to offences requiring not even the merest degree of negligence, with the offences of causing death by driving whilst uninsured and unlicensed,[72] and causing death by driving whilst disqualified,[73] constructing liability for the causing of death based on underlying crimes of strict liability. There does not, at present, exist an offence of homicide penalising the causing of death by drunk driving *simpliciter*; under section 3A of the Road Traffic Act 1988 a drink driver may be convicted of causing death if he drove carelessly as well as being over the drink/drug drive limit. The question arises as to whether such causing of death should amount to manslaughter under the proposals put forward here.

Horder suggests that the existing offences under sections 3A, 3ZB (and now) 3ZC 'could – and should' amount to unlawful act manslaughter: 'Each involves the commission of an unlawful act – respectively, driving under the influence of drink or drugs, and unlicensed, disqualified, or uninsured driving – that may pose a danger of causing some harm, but is not unlawful solely in virtue of involving

[69] ibid.

[70] See also M Dyson, 'The Smallest Fault in Manslaughter' (2017) 6 *Archbold Review* 4.

[71] Causing death by careless driving is an offence under s2B of the Road Traffic Act 1988.

[72] Road Traffic Act 1988, s3ZB.

[73] Road Traffic Act 1988, s3ZC.

negligent or careless conduct'.[74] Presumably, then, Horder would be content to see convictions for the proposed manslaughter offence in any of these situations, as well as in cases of causing death by dangerous driving. His argument in relation to dangerous driving is that 'the public interest in strong measures being taken against those whose driving poses a danger of death seems to me to justify in law *treating* a death so caused as gross negligence manslaughter'.[75] Under the proposal here, some of the present causing death by driving offences could amount to the revised 'unlawful act' version of manslaughter, provided that there existed an obvious risk of death, whilst others might fall under the alternative version based on gross negligence.[76]

That is not to say that any death resulting from a collision involving a driver who has committed a regulatory offence ought to be liable for manslaughter. In many cases, even dangerous driving would not be sufficient, given that the definition of 'dangerous' under section 2 of the Road Traffic Act 1988 requires only a risk of injury or serious damage to property. The proposed requirement that the unlawful act involve an obvious risk of death would mean that dangerous driving *could* form the basis of a manslaughter charge, but only if the driving was so bad as to satisfy that requirement. Likewise, the offence of drink/drug driving *could* lead to a conviction for manslaughter, but only where D was so intoxicated as to create a foreseeable risk of death to another road user from driving in such a condition. This might exclude those whose blood alcohol concentration is only just above the legal limit, depending on how the alcohol affected them and their ability to drive.[77]

iii. Gross Negligence Manslaughter

The proposal is that any codified version of manslaughter should cover both a redefined version of unlawful act manslaughter to comply with the correspondence principle, and a version of gross negligence manslaughter. The latter would give the opportunity to clarify the test in *Adomako*, and should be fairly uncontroversial. Its inclusion in this proposal is to take a 'belt and braces' approach; depending on whether the suggestion below is also agreed to, it may only be necessary to fill the gaps. Despite the House of Lords seemingly laying down a clear test for gross negligence two decades ago, recent cases have shown that there are elements of the offence with which the courts continue to struggle. The recent cases of *Rudling*[78] and *Rose*[79] illustrate this, resulting in the Court of Appeal inserting

[74] Horder (n 11) 82–83.
[75] Horder (n 11) 82.
[76] As discussed at Part II.B.iii below.
[77] The effect of alcohol depends on numerable factors. See P Callow, 'The Drink- and Drug-Driving Offences and the Criminal Law Paradigm' (PhD thesis, University of Sheffield, 2014). The risk of driving after consuming alcohol was famously analysed in the *Grand Rapids* study: Borkenstein et al, *The Role of the Drinking Driver in Traffic Accidents* (Bloomington, 1964).
[78] [2016] EWCA Crim 741.
[79] [2017] EWCA Crim 1168.

an additional test into that laid down by Lord Mackay in *Adomako*. Lord Mackay's test is fourfold, requiring that:

(a) the defendant owed a duty of care to the victim;
(b) the defendant breached that duty of care;
(c) the breach of that duty caused the death of the victim; and
(d) the breach of duty should be characterised as gross negligence and therefore as a crime.[80]

However, in citing cases such as *Misra*,[81] in which Judge LJ had referred to the case of *Singh*,[82] the Court of Appeal in *Rudling* identified an additional requirement which was subsequently inserted between requirements (b) and (c) above in *Rose*, namely that:

> … it was reasonably foreseeable that the breach of that duty gave rise to a serious and obvious risk of death.[83]

It is not tolerably clear that Lord Mackay would have approved of the addition of this requirement, given that he did not include it in his own test and was at pains to avoid the language of recklessness used in *Lawrence*[84] in setting out the law in relation to manslaughter. In his speech he talks instead of the seriousness of the *breach* being relevant, and acknowledges that it is a risk of death which is relevant in determining the extent to which D's conduct departed from the proper standard of care. Thus, he was leaving it to the jury to determine whether the risk of death was sufficiently 'serious and obvious' to class D's breach of duty as a crime, without seeing the need to direct them in those terms. That the last element of Lord Mackay's test is problematic is without controversy: it has been criticised as being circular and unhelpful to the jury, although it has been held not to breach articles 6 or 7 of the European Convention of Human Rights.[85]

In *Rose* an optometrist had failed to carry out an examination of the deceased's eye which, had she done so, would have revealed an obvious and serious risk of death and necessitated referring him for medical investigation. At trial the judge had directed the jury that the Crown must have proved that it was reasonably foreseeable that D's breach of her duty of care gave rise to a serious and obvious risk of death and yet despite this direction, the jury convicted D of manslaughter in circumstances in which it was not foreseeable at the time of D's breach that there was an obvious and serious risk of death. The Court of Appeal quashed the

[80] Summarised from Lord Mackay's judgment at 187.
[81] [2005] 1 Cr App R 21.
[82] [1999] Crim LR 582.
[83] At [77].
[84] [1982] AC 510.
[85] *Misra* (n 81).

conviction on the basis that in assessing the reasonable foreseeability of a serious and obvious risk of death, it is not appropriate to take into account what the defendant *would have* known but for her breach of duty.

If the law is to be codified it is likely desirable that the requirement of the existence of an obvious and serious risk of death be incorporated into statute, as suggested in the appendix, in order to avoid criminalising defendants such as Ms Rose. It is desirable that the scope of gross negligence manslaughter be narrowed to exclude defendants who have breached their duty when such a breach did not give rise to an obvious and serious risk of death. To require this risk to be taken into account again ensures compliance with the correspondence principle, and does so in a way which is not open to interpretation in the same way as Lord Mackay's broader test is.

I have additionally taken the lead from the Law Commission[86] in using the language of dangerous driving in specifying the degree of negligence required for manslaughter, in requiring that V's conduct falls far below that which can reasonably be expected of D in the circumstances. However, given the difficulty for juries in determining how bad negligence has to be in certain contexts before it amounts to *gross* negligence deserving of criminal punishment, even if they are assisted by this change in terminology, my proposals do not end there. Below I suggest that manslaughters committed in certain contexts ought to attract their own test and offence label, drawing on the drafting of the Corporate Manslaughter and Corporate Homicide Act (CMCHA) 2007 for inspiration. The proposal put forward is for an offence of vehicular manslaughter, but the same offence model could be used in other contexts of lethal gross negligence, such as medical manslaughter. However, it is unlikely that the legislature would be able to employ the bureaucratic-regulatory model to create separate offences of manslaughter in every conceivable context giving rise to a risk of death, and it would be undesirable to do so in the sense that it would risk creating too many over-specialised offences,[87] and therefore a generic offence of gross negligence manslaughter remains necessary.[88]

[86] Law Commission (n 4), [3.60].

[87] I would not, for example, agree with a suggestion that the regulation of cycling is something that ought to give rise to separate special homicide offences. The recent case of Charlie Alliston gave rise to a review of the law in relation to cycling after he was acquitted of manslaughter but convicted of wanton and furious driving. The manslaughter charge was based on the unlawful act of riding a bike with no brakes, despite the difficulties of arguing constructive manslaughter on the basis of an act which is, like driving, generally lawful. See L Thomas, *Cycle safety review independent legal report* (DfT, March 2018). This report has proposed the creation of a new causing death by dangerous cycling offence, which I do not support. However, there is no reason why the offence I propose in the appendix should not also include cyclists as well as the drivers of motor car vehicles within its remit. For that reason, the draft provision makes reference to 'vehicle' rather than 'motor vehicle' and it is envisaged that it could, therefore, apply to pedal cycles in the same way as the Offences Against the Person Act, s 35.

[88] Gross negligence manslaughter might continue to be employed to cover cases which involve those liable under the current law through an omission where D was under a duty to act. In cases where it is doubtful that any underlying unlawful act has been committed, but where D has owed a duty of care and has been grossly negligent and caused death, liability for manslaughter should ensue.

III. Regulatory Domain Offences

There is a strong argument to be made that killing on the roads should, where it satisfies the test under *Adomako*, amount to gross negligence manslaughter.[89] However, even if the proposals for manslaughter ever did find favour with legislators, the likelihood of drivers being convicted of that offence would still depend on a change in prosecutorial guidance and practice[90] and, perhaps, an increase in jurors being prepared to convict drivers of an offence otherwise aimed at violent offenders.[91] It therefore appears necessary to propose something slightly different.[92] The proposals here would replace existing bureaucratic-administrative offences of causing death by driving. As noted above, Horder recognises that although the statutory causing death by driving offences are constructed upon regulatory offences designed to improve road safety, their punishment is mainly retributive rather than deterrence based,[93] meaning that they depart from one of the characteristics he attributes to the regulatory model.[94]

It seems impossible to turn back time to reinstate causing death by dangerous driving as manslaughter *simpliciter*,[95] but I want to develop Horder's next point:

> [S]upport should be given to the way in which, for example, the corporate manslaughter offence seeks to combine forms of law reflecting different casts of legal thought. Seen in a positive light, such a strategy can be regarded as a way of helping traditional ways

[89] See, for example, Cunningham, (n 56); and S Cunningham, 'The Reality of Vehicular Homicides: Convictions for Murder, Manslaughter and Causing Death by Dangerous Driving' [2001] *Crim LR* 679. Gross negligence manslaughter is rarely charged in the context of driving, and where this happens it is often because an element of dangerous driving cannot be proven for the purposes of causing death by dangerous driving, such as that the driving did not occur on a road or other public place.

[90] As noted (n 62) the CPS Guidance advises against the use of unlawful act manslaughter based on a driving offence. It does, however, allow for charges of gross negligence manslaughter in the worst cases, but these remain rare. An example is the case of *Dobby* [2017] EWCA Crim 775, where D pleaded guilty to a charge of gross negligence manslaughter, having 'driven in a deliberately appalling manner' and was sentenced to 15 years' imprisonment. Leave to appeal against the sentence as unduly lenient was granted 'because of the considerable importance of the case, its unusual circumstances and the fact that manslaughter had been charged'. The Court of Appeal dismissed the appeal.

[91] It may be that the increase in media calls for drivers to be treated as manslaughterers has influenced public opinion and Mitchell found that the public expressed a view that drunk drivers in particular ought to be liable for manslaughter: B Mitchell 'Further Evidence of the Relationship between Legal and Public Opinion on the Law of Homicide' [2000] *Crim LR* 814. However, there may persist a mentality of 'there but for the grace of God go I' amongst jurors making a conviction for generic manslaughter difficult to secure in driving cases (the reason for the introduction of the statutory causing death by driving offence in 1956: see B MacKenna, 'Causing Death by Reckless or Dangerous Driving: a Suggestion' [1970] *Crim LR* 67 and Cunningham, n 89).

[92] I have previously been reluctant to accept additional context-specific vehicular homicide offences: see Cunningham (n 56). However, I am now persuaded that the advantages outweigh the negatives in using corporate manslaughter as the basis for a vehicular manslaughter offence.

[93] See also, S Cunningham, 'Punishing Drivers who Kill: Putting Road Safety First?' (2007) 27 *Legal Studies* 288.

[94] See quotation in text to n 18 above.

[95] Although, as argued above, it might be possible and appropriate to charge the codified version of manslaughter in some cases of driving causing death.

> of thinking and categorizing to find continued meaning and relevance in a modern regulatory context: here, in the shape of a 'bureaucratic–administrative' form of law with a *gemeinschaft* label, 'manslaughter'. The argument may turn out to be, then, that reformers should have adopted such an approach, an approach more supportive of the common law's mixture of *gesellschaft* and *gemeinschaft* forms of law, in the road traffic and perhaps also in other contexts.[96]

What might such a combined offence look like? An examination, even at a very basic level, of the most important provisions of the Corporate Manslaughter and Corporate Homicide Act (CMCHA) 2007 is necessary in order to understand what Horder might envisage.

The CMCHA is a long statute, and any new homicide offence based on the same structure would want to avoid the complexity of the different provisions it contains. However, most of these relate to the complications involved in convicting a legal personality, rather than a human being, of homicide, and are not necessary in other contexts. The essence of the offence can be distilled into a few provisions. Corporate manslaughter requires death to have been caused by a gross breach of a duty of care owed by the defendant organisation to V. In defining a 'gross breach', section 1(4) borrows from the definition of dangerous driving under section 2A of the Road Traffic Act 1988, which states that a person is regarded to have driven dangerously if the way he drives falls far below what would be expected of a competent and careful driver. Under corporate manslaughter, the way in which an organisation's activities are managed or organised amounts to a gross breach of its duty of care if it falls far below what can reasonably be expected of the organisation in the circumstances.[97] A jury, in making the decision as to whether there has been a gross breach of a duty of care can, in turn, take into account any failure to comply with health and safety legislation.[98] In doing so, the jury can consider how serious the failure was and the risk of death it posed. Thus, although a jury might struggle with judging whether the organisation fell far below what could have been expected of it, they are assisted in making that judgment with reference to something tangible. Existing regulatory offences under health and safety legislation provide a good measure for what can be expected of any company engaged in potentially dangerous activities and adherence to those rules exemplifies conduct expected of such an organisation.

I have taken the essential elements of the CMCHA (particularly section 8) and drafted basic provisions for an offence of vehicular manslaughter. One clear benefit of this proposal as compared to the current regulatory offence is that unlike causing death by dangerous driving, reference is made to the specific regulatory document that should be known to any driver: the Highway Code. This ought to make the determination of whether D is liable easier, insofar as it avoids the current problem of juries having to think about what can be expected of a 'competent and careful

[96] Horder, (n 11), 74.
[97] CMCHA 2007, s 1.
[98] CMCHA 2007, s 8.

driver' with little guidance other than their own experience.[99] An objection might be made that for vehicular manslaughter to truly follow the contours of corporate manslaughter, a gross breach ought to be determined by reference to offences under the Road Traffic Act or other statutes, rather than a document which does not carry the full effect of the law. However, there is a potential road safety benefit to be had by making reference to the Highway Code, a document which every licensed driver ought to know. Few drivers will be aware of the full content of the Road Traffic Act 1988, but all can be expected to know and remind themselves of the content of the Highway Code and referring to it might actually promote the regulatory aspect of the offence, by encouraging drivers to be so knowledgeable. If such a provision were passed, efforts ought to be made to publicise the content of the new law, in order that this benefit may accrue.[100]

The label of vehicular *manslaughter* is important in ensuring that the offence is imbued with a sense of gravity, and may well go a long way to satisfying bereaved families that justice is seen to be done in such cases,[101] but the sentence may also remain important. Despite the continued ratcheting up of sentences for death by driving offences, there remain loud calls for sentences to be increased yet further, with campaign groups such as Brake seeking to push the issue up the political agenda and the Government having recently conducted a consultation exercise.[102] I am not in favour of the present causing death by driving offences attracting higher sentences than the existing maximum of 14 years' imprisonment, not least because if proportionality in sentencing is to be maintained then an offence which is prosecuted where it is thought that gross negligence cannot be proved should attract a lower maximum penalty than that of life for gross negligence manslaughter.[103]

[99] For problems with the current test see S Cunningham, *Driving Offences: Law, Policy and Practice* (Ashgate, 2008).

[100] See A Ashworth, 'Ignorance of the Criminal Law, and Duties to Avoid It' (2011) 74 *MLR* 1.

[101] The need to take into account the needs of victims is discussed in Cunningham (n 56) 117–22.

[102] Ministry of Justice, *Driving offences and penalties relating to causing death or serious injury* (Cm 9381, 2016). Following this consultation the MoJ has announced that it intends to bring forward proposals, when parliamentary time allows, to increase the maximum penalty for the offences under the RTA 1988, ss 1 and 3A to life imprisonment: Ministry of Justice, *Response to the consultation on driving offences and penalties relating to causing death or serious injury* (Cm 9518, 2017) [57].

[103] Despite the calls to increase the maximum penalty for causing death by dangerous driving to life, in line with manslaughter, it is questionable whether raising the maximum penalty would, or should, result in an increase in sentences passed for such offences, in comparison to sentences for manslaughter. An example of a recent case of manslaughter by motor vehicle is that of Matthew Gordon and Peter Wood, convicted at Bristol Crown Court of manslaughter resulting from faulty brakes on a the tipper truck they owned/serviced (S Morris, 'Bath tipper truck crash: haulage company owner and mechanic jailed' *Guardian Online* (27 January 2017)). The sentence given to Gordon of seven-and-a-half years is well within the 14-year maximum for causing death by dangerous driving. The case of *Dobby* (n 90) is unusual in resulting in a sentence of more than 14 years' imprisonment, and this sentence in and of itself provides an explanation for the Crown's decision to charge manslaughter rather than an offence under ss 1 or 3A of the RTA 1988. Under the Sentencing Council's proposals for sentencing guidelines for gross negligence manslaughter, a starting point for the least culpable form of the offence is given of two years' imprisonment, compared to a starting point of three years' imprisonment laid down in relation to a case falling within level 3 (the least serious) of the current causing death by dangerous driving guidelines. See Sentencing Council (n 29) 27, and Sentencing Guidelines Council, *Causing Death by Driving: Definitive Guideline* (2008) 11.

However, since my proposed vehicular manslaughter offence would require a level of blameworthiness equivalent to that required for gross negligence manslaughter, albeit expressed in a way which provides more guidance to the jury in making that decision, there is reason to suggest that it should attract the same maximum penalty as other codified versions of manslaughter.[104]

The proposed offence would likely cover most of the offenders currently caught by the offence of causing death by dangerous driving, and might be broader in covering other drivers who kill, such as drunk drivers. Allowing a drunk driver to be convicted of an offence carrying the label of manslaughter would accord with the results of the public opinion research conducted by Mitchell, whose interviewees argued that the drunken motorist who killed a pedestrian in a scenario should be convicted of manslaughter 'at least':

> … interviewees frequently pointed to the mass of publicity warning of the potential horrors that are likely to ensue from bad driving. People are well aware that cars and lorries are potentially 'lethal weapons' and that other road-users are very much at the mercy of drivers. It is therefore reasonable to place road traffic homicides on a par with traditional murders and manslaughters. Failure adequately to reflect the gravity of such incidents – the harm and personal culpability – would merely bring the legal system into disrepute.[105]

However, it would not necessarily include those who can presently be convicted under the other causing death by driving offences. That is to its benefit, in that those whose blameworthiness does not amount to a gross breach of a duty of care arguably ought not to be punished for the unfortunate result of causing death. However, the advantage of the proposal is that it *could* cover those who might presently be liable for causing death by driving whilst disqualified under section 3ZC of the Road Traffic Act 1988, but only where D's decision to drive, despite being disqualified,[106] amounts to a gross breach of the duty D owes to all road users. It is not the case that every person who is disqualified from driving poses a significant risk of death by deciding to drive and this will depend on the specific facts leading to D's disqualification, as well as the degree to which D otherwise departed from the Highway Code.[107]

[104] This is where my proposal departs from the suggestions put forward by Horder, who is of the view that a truly condemnatory offence label would do some of the punitive work required of any homicide offence, implying that a lesser maximum penalty than even the current statutory causing death offences might be warranted: Horder, (n 11), 87.

[105] Mitchell, (n 91), 824.

[106] This is where the question of whether D's breach was an intentional violation or not becomes particularly useful. The current offences under ss 3ZB and 3ZC of the RTA 1988 are based on strict liability, in that D need not even know that he is driving without insurance or a licence or whilst disqualified to be convicted of the offence. Under this proposal, D's state of mind in relation to the underlying breach becomes important in deciding whether the breach was gross, with juries being more likely to find such a gross breach where D knew he was breaking the rules. This would mean that those who drove without insurance because, for example, their policy had expired without their knowledge, would not be liable for a homicide offence as they might be under current law.

[107] In relation to uninsured driving it would be difficult for any case of vehicular manslaughter to be made out on the basis that D intentionally violated the law by driving without insurance, since presumably the risk of death involved in driving would not be increased solely by the fact that D was uninsured.

The proposal includes a clause which allows the jury to take into account whether the breach of the Highway Code was intentional, and therefore can be categorised as a 'violation'. An intentional violation of the Highway Code would indicate a far higher level of blameworthiness than an unintentional 'lapse' or 'error'.[108] The terms 'violation' and 'error' are used in very specific ways by psychologists in the field of driver behaviour, who have demonstrated that the cognitive processes involved in committing violations and errors are very different, requiring different corrective responses.[109] Under the current law, those guilty of causing death by careless driving will often have committed an error in their driving; a momentary loss of attention which leads to catastrophic consequences.[110] The reference to whether a breach of the Highway Code has been intentional or not will likely lead to a narrowing of the types of cases prosecuted, in that it is unlikely that many of those who are guilty of causing death by careless driving will pass the evidential test in the Code for Crown Prosecutors for the purposes of a vehicular manslaughter charge. However, those who for example use a mobile phone whilst driving might more readily be charged with vehicular manslaughter than they are with causing death by careless or dangerous driving, since this will be seen as a *violation* of the Highway Code and, depending on the circumstances, might also be defined as a gross breach of a driver's duty of care to other road users creating a high risk of a fatal collision.[111]

IV. Conclusion

Horder's suggestion for developing new homicide offences based on the corporate manslaughter model was first made in an edited collection resulting from a conference examining the question of whether specific homicide offences are needed for negligent killings in particular contexts.[112] There is a need to inject some coherence into the law, which has developed in a piecemeal fashion under the

[108] For a suggestion of how this distinction might be used in relation to driving offences more generally, see Cunningham, (n 93).

[109] See, for example, J Reason, *Human Error* (CUP, 1990); J Reason, A Manstead, S Stradling, J Baxter, and K Campbell, 'Errors and Violations on the Roads: A Real Distinction?' (1990) 33 *Ergonomics* 1315–32.

[110] S Kyd Cunningham, 'Has Law Reform Policy been Driven in the Right Direction? How the New Causing Death by Driving Offences are Operating in Practice' [2013] *Crim LR* 711.

[111] Current guidance suggests that using a mobile phone whilst driving is an example of both careless and dangerous driving, which is far from helpful. Dangerous driving will be charged where a driver's use of the mobile phone caused them to be not only avoidably distracted but *dangerously* distracted by such use: see CPS (n 62). It can be argued that *any* use of a mobile phone whilst driving is dangerous. See: P Burns, A Parkes, S Burton, R Smith and D Burch, *How dangerous is driving with a mobile phone? Benchmarking the impairment to alcohol* (TRL Report, TRL 547, 2002).

[112] J Horder, 'Homicide Reform and the Changing Character of Legal Thought' in CMV Clarkson and S Cunningham, *Criminal Liability for Non-Aggressive Death* (Ashgate, 2008).

two distinct models identified by Horder. This can be achieved partly by adopting reforms similar to those recommended by the Law Commission under the traditional-codificatory model, but with the addition of further manslaughter offences. It might be argued that to develop a third, hybrid model, based on corporate manslaughter, will do no more than to muddy the waters even further. However, so long as certain principles are followed to ensure coherence within the law, Horder's reasons for suggesting the development of such a model are persuasive. In concluding a discussion of whether the law should rely on generic offences of manslaughter, or develop further nominate offences to deal with killings in specific contexts, Ashworth puts forward the principle that the law should aim to ensure the equal treatment of offences of equal seriousness.[113] In applying that principle, he suggests that even where nominate offences are thought advisable for some types of homicide, the thresholds of liability for such offences should be the same. Thus, the proposals put forward here are aimed at adhering to this principle in a way which takes into account practical issues too.

Killing with cars is a problem that has plagued the law and its subjects since the motor vehicle became a popular mode of transport. While there has been a general decline in the number of people killed on the roads there are still too many deaths caused by unnecessary risk-taking.[114] I have argued elsewhere that the criminal law ought to be used in order further to reduce such death toll, but that this can only be achieved through enforcement of the regulatory offences contained in the Road Traffic Act 1988, which are generally conduct crimes not requiring the occurrence of any particular harm.[115] On the other hand, those who are blameworthy in taking irresponsible risks involving a high risk of death ought to be treated the same, whether they take such risks by driving at high speeds or by engaging in street violence. The advantage of the model of vehicular manslaughter put forward here is that it underscores the link between the regulation of driving, in making reference to the Highway Code, and the ultimate harm (death) which regulatory offences are designed to avoid. If a homicide statute were to make reference to the Highway Code it may be that drivers would become more aware of the moral reason for the existence of some driving offences, providing drivers with a moral incentive to abide by the rules of the road, leading to normative compliance.[116] That does not mean that anyone involved in a fatal collision who has breached the Highway Code would face vehicular manslaughter charges though; only where there is a *gross* breach will such charges be appropriate.

A question remains for those cases of road death that might fall under the generic version of manslaughter, either through commission of an unlawful act

[113] A Ashworth, '"Manslaughter": Generic or Nominate Offences' in Clarkson and Cunningham (ibid).

[114] There were 1,730 deaths on Great Britain's roads in 2015: Department for Transport, *Reported Road Casualties Great Britain: Annual Report 2015* (2016).

[115] Cunningham (n 93).

[116] A Bottoms, 'Morality, Crime, Compliance and Public Policy' in A Bottoms and M Tonry (eds), *Ideology, Crime and Criminal Justice* (Willan, 2002) 25.

such as drink driving, or through their gross negligence. Should a restriction be put in place to necessitate such cases being prosecuted as vehicular manslaughter? In the past I have always been clear that such cases should be prosecuted as generic manslaughter but, if a nominate offence of vehicular manslaughter were created, it might be accepted that this should be the only offence to apply in a case of road death. On the other hand, where a car has been used as a weapon of offence there might be scope for charging second degree murder, so long as intention to cause serious injury could be proved. Vehicular manslaughter should be available as a lesser included offence to such a charge, even though it might be possible to prove generic manslaughter in such a case.[117] This is not intended to undermine the seriousness of the wrongdoing by labelling killing by motor vehicle as a distinct offence; on the contrary, use of the label manslaughter is to highlight the gravity with which the offending ought to be treated. The reason why it is being proposed is mainly a pragmatic one: to employ the censuring function of the law and use a separate offence in a communicative endeavour.

Appendix: Proposed Homicide Offences

1st degree murder D kills with intention to kill

2nd degree murder D kills with

i. intention to cause serious injury, and there is an obvious risk of death;

or

ii. intention to cause serious injury *and* foresight of death.

Manslaughter D intentionally commits an unlawful act which amounts to a criminal offence; D's act creates an obvious risk of death which D had the capacity to foresee; the risk of death is created by virtue of D's act being a crime; and D's act in fact causes the death of V;

or

D breaches a duty of care owed to V; it is reasonably foreseeable that the breach of that duty gives rise to a serious and obvious risk of death; that breach causes V's death; and D's conduct falls far below that can reasonably be expected of D in the circumstances.

[117] At present it is likely that a charge of murder in a case of road death, if not made out, will result in conviction for causing death by dangerous driving. That was, at least, the position at the end of the last century. See Cunningham, (n 89).

Corporate manslaughter as under the CMCHA 2007

Vehicular manslaughter

1. D commits vehicular manslaughter where D is a driver of a vehicle and the way in which D drives:
   (a) creates a foreseeable risk of death; and
   (b) causes another person's death; and
   (c) amounts to a gross breach of the duty of care owed by D to other road users.
2. Gross breach: factors for jury

   This section applies where it is established that D caused the death of another road user and it falls to the jury to decide whether there was a gross breach of the duty of care owed to other road users.

   The jury must consider whether the evidence shows that D failed to comply with any provisions of the Highway Code, and, if so:
   (a) How serious that failure was;
   (b) Whether D's failure to comply can be categorised as a violation (an intentional breach of the Highway Code).

   This section does not prevent the jury from having regard to any other matters they consider relevant.

Comment on Chapter 4

Reform of the Law of Murder?

SIMON McKAY

This is a response to Sally Kyd's excellent chapter, 'Done to Death? A Reform of the Law of Murder'.[1] The response is by necessity shorter than the substantive argument for reform and seeks to approach the case against reform by looking at the underlying rationale advanced for reform, the offence of causing death by dangerous driving, and some conclusions. At the outset, nothing in this response should take away from Kyd's analysis or arguments; its express purpose is to offer counter-argument and widen debate on the issue. At the conference in 2016, which conceived the idea of pulling together these papers, the oral response was on a theme of Monty Python's dead parrot sketch – the idea of further reform had 'passed on, is no more, kicked the bucket … etc'; this was to lighten the topic for attendees, rather than passing a verdict on further or future reform. In reality, reform may just be resting, and better law may await its awakening in due course. Again, nothing in the response is designed to undermine the importance of aspiring for reform, and this is the easier to achieve when the subject is given the excellent treatment evidenced in Kyd's chapter.

I. Reform: Problems with the Underlying Rationale

A. The Law Commission and Further Calls for Reform

The law of murder is, as the Law Commission reported in *Partial Defences to Murder*, 'a mess'.[2] It did, as Kyd concedes, recommend a review but this was not, contrary to her interpretation of it, expressed as a 'complete review'. The Commission in fact said there was 'every reason to believe that a comprehensive consideration of the offence and the sentencing regime could yield rational and sensible conclusions about a number of issues', but it limited the scope of the proposed review to four discrete areas, two of which had nothing to do with the

[1] Ch 4 of this volume.
[2] Law Commission, *Partial Defences to Murder* (Law Com No 290, 2004).

substantive offence but rather sentencing and whether children should be subject to the same regime as adults.[3]

The report that followed, *Murder, Manslaughter and Infanticide*,[4] recommended the introduction of a new Homicide Act. The government rejected this recommendation, but it did adopt suggested reforms of provocation and diminished responsibility. Kyd argues that these reforms were intended as part of 'a package of reform' and operate differently than intended when grafted onto the existing framework.[5] In fact, there is no evidence to support this assertion. For example, during the passage of the Coroners and Justice Bill in the House of Lords Baroness Murphy supported the change in the law from 'abnormality of the mind' to 'abnormality of mental functioning' because it offered:

> … a legislative route towards ensuring that conditions put forward in the defence come within accepted diagnostic criteria … That will avoid the idiosyncratic diagnoses that have been offered in the past by many experts … We would like to see the definition narrowed, and I accept that the new definition will ensure consistency.[6]

The recommendation that found its way into the Law Commission report had its origins in submissions by the Royal College of Psychiatry, the overall effect of which 'would be to encourage better standards of expert evidence and improved understanding between the courts and experts'.[7] The provision, as enacted in section 52 of the Coroners and Justice Act 2009 (the 2009 Act), may not have ultimately provided the narrowness envisaged by Baroness Murphy, but the new defence encompasses any recognised medical condition (so includes both physical and psychological conditions). This is positive and a development that has been able to work effectively notwithstanding it was not part of overarching homicide law reform. But if Kyd is right, then Albany's cautionary words in Shakespeare's King Lear may be apposite when he said that in 'striving to better, oft we mar what's well'.

Kyd has been encouraged by recent parliamentary debate. Alex Chalk, a Conservative MP, was behind the motion for Homicide Law Reform that was debated on 30 June 2016. He used two examples to advance his case for reform. The first was that of a retired colonel with an unblemished record who has served his country with great distinction, and is known for his charitable work. A neighbour tests the colonel's patience to breaking point by making a persistent nuisance of himself. The colonel confronts his neighbour (with a cricket bat) at 3am. Disgruntled by the neighbour's dismissive and rude attitude, the colonel strikes his neighbour's toe with the intention of breaking it. The neighbour falls back, hits his head on a crate of beer standing in the hallway and is knocked unconscious.

[3] ibid, [274].
[4] Law Commission, *Murder, Manslaughter and Infanticide* (No 304, 2006).
[5] Kyd, (n 1) 101.
[6] Hansard HL Vol.712, col 177 (30 June 2009).
[7] Law Commission (n 4), [5.114].

The police and ambulance service arrive. Unwisely, perhaps, the colonel tells them exactly what happened. The neighbour is rushed to the local hospital, diagnosed with a bleed on the brain and dies. According to Mr Chalk, the only offence the colonel could be charged with is murder. He goes further and states the colonel must plead guilty. Due to the operation of the mandatory life sentence, the colonel gets life with a minimum term of 25 years.

In his second example, the defendant assaults a female in a nightclub queue. He has a string of criminal convictions for assault and criminal damage. He strikes the victim repeatedly and hard to the side of the face with his open hand. She falls back, hits her head on the kerb and is knocked unconscious. The victim later dies, and the post-mortem shows that she suffered bruising – albeit no fracture – to her cheekbone and the fatal injury was caused by the impact on the kerb. The police arrest the defendant, who denies everything, but CCTV proves his guilt.

Again, according to Mr Chalk the law requires the defendant to be charged only with unlawful act manslaughter, because the harm that he caused (or, presumably, that he intended to cause) falls short of grievous bodily harm. The net effect is that he will be convicted of an offence that carries a far lesser stigma than murder and for which there is no mandatory requirement for a life sentence; if he gets a determinate sentence, he will serve only half of it. The zenith of Mr Chalk's argument follows:

> Is that thug, I ask rhetorically, less culpable than the retired colonel or his wife? The only distinction is that the colonel intended to break a toe and the thug intended to commit a marginally less serious assault. In my view, that is a distinction without a difference – it is a distinction that is completely lost on the general public and, frankly, on me.

The examples advanced by Mr Chalk, laced it has to be said with latent prejudices, are defective, self-defeating and do not withstand any forensic scrutiny. Ironically, the retired colonel, even if charged with murder – that decision remains a matter for the prosecutor taking all of the facts into account – is now afforded a partial defence of provocation following the reforms provided for in the 2009 Act. Under the reforms to the offence of murder proposed by Kyd, the colonel would still be guilty of murder, albeit 'second degree'; the 'thug' is still probably only guilty of manslaughter. It is not clear that the examples provided by Mr Chalk move reform forward that much and unlikely to be in the direction Kyd would prefer. Such optimism Kyd may have had in renewed interest from parliamentarians may have been, on reflection, misplaced.

What the two examples really underscore is, first, the difficulty of proving intent; and secondly, the question of sentencing. In the colonel's case, if convicted of murder he receives a mandatory sentence of life in prison. In reality the punitive aspect of his sentence, the so-called 'tariff' would be significantly lower than 25 years and could even be in single figures.[8] Equally, the drunk could expect a

[8] See by way of example *Blackman* (or Marine A) [2015] 1 WLR 1900 (8 year tariff for the murder of an insurgent in Afghanistan); Blackman was later cleared of murder.

significantly higher tariff. The question of sentencing is addressed later in this reply. There are a number of conclusions that can be reached from the recent debate on the need for reform. First, it was predicated on an understanding of the law and how it is applied in practice that was at best questionable and probably self-serving. Secondly, there is no evidence that the debate resulted in a change in the government's stance that systemic review or reform is not part of its political agenda. Thirdly, regardless of how strong the case for reform might be, there is little, if any, prospect of it happening in the near future.

B. The Case for Codification

Kyd's primary argument is for codification. She seeks to demonstrate the need for this using Horder's thesis on the existing models: the traditional codificatory model (exhaustive, rules-based statutory code) and the (bureaucratic) administrative model (law infused with moral judgments).[9] Her focus is what she says is the particular problem in causing death by dangerous driving. There is nothing problematic in principle with these models (the Law Commission itself has adopted them) other than that they are conveyed as mutually exclusive concepts, when in fact the law is unlikely to be that clear or proscriptive in reality. It is in fact this that makes Kyd's premise difficult for the logician. She conceives of 'a need to rationalise the existing offences to establish how a codification of the common law could sit alongside a rethinking of the regulatory or "bureaucratic-administrative" model of offences'.[10] Underpinning her argument is a dual and apparently conflicting purpose – codification of the common law *and* re-thinking the existing scheme of regulatory offences – when in fact reform, if there is to be any, ought to be some form of unification of both schemes. Indeed, in the present context, this is Horder's entire raison d'être.

Horder's respected opinion that the offence of causing death by dangerous driving (the offence which Kyd has used as the focus of her discussion) has outgrown its utility as 'a heavy-duty tool for reinforcing a deterrent regulatory message about road safety'[11] is a tremulous basis upon which to resurrect the debate about the exhaustively scrutinised law of murder. It is, after all, only respected opinion. The treatise from which his opinion emerges is *Homicide and the Politics of Reform*.[12] It is true that politicians, when faced with particularly egregious examples of where the law seems inadequate (or, for that matter, a blunt instrument), have a propensity to seek out a change in the law, but this politically driven 'reform' does not fit easily with either of the models explicated by Horder.

[9] J Horder, *Homicide and the Politics of Reform* (OUP, 2012).
[10] Kyd, (n 1) 102–103.
[11] Horder (n 9), 74.
[12] ibid.

Moreover, (and possibly, because it does not), amendments to the law of this nature rarely end well. An obvious and contemporary example is the amendment to the Criminal Justice and Immigration Act 2008 by section 43 of the Crime and Courts Act 2013, the 'use of force in self-defence at place of residence'. The then and uninspired Lord Chancellor Chris Grayling said of the amendment:

> … we really should be putting the law firmly on the side of the homeowner, the householder, the family, and saying 'when that burglar crosses your threshold, invades your home, threatens your family, they give up their rights'.[13]

After hearing lengthy arguments on the correct interpretation of the provisions, the High Court disagreed. *In R (on the application of Collins) v The Secretary of State for Justice*,[14] Sir Brian Leveson held that the court's interpretation of the new defence represented:

> … no more than a refinement to the common law on self-defence. Thus, I do not accept that the construction placed on s. 76(5A) by the editors of Archbold, 2016 at para. 19-48a (to the effect that force in a householder case is only to be regarded as unreasonable if it was grossly disproportionate) represents an accurate statement of law. The position is better expressed by the editors of Blackstone, 2016 at para A3.63 which makes it clear: 'The new provision merely affects the interpretation of "(un)reasonable in the circumstances" so that force is not by law automatically unreasonable in householder cases simply because it is disproportionate provided it is not grossly disproportionate'.[15]

The court was unsurprisingly of the view that the burglar does not give up his rights by trespassing onto a person's property, although it also held that the provision was not incompatible with Article 2 of the European Convention on Human Rights.

The amendment was neither an exhaustively considered rule, nor law infused with moral judgment. It was politically driven and divisive, as the recent case of Richard Osborn-Brooks has exemplified.[16] In that case, Mr Osborn-Brooks' arrest following the fatal stabbing by him of a burglar gave rise to media campaigns for his release that raised questions of contempt of court and the usurpation of due process. In the event, he was released without charge. Insofar as the state of the law of causing death by dangerous driving is concerned, Horder was doing no more than placing the politics of the issue under a forensic lens and hypothesising, no doubt in the hope that if law reform was proposed, government might actually take note of his analysis. A political imperative to change the law relating to death by dangerous driving should be viewed cautiously therefore. It may not in reality be reform at all but mere refinement, or, worse, undermine the efficacy of something that works, albeit not perfectly.

[13] A Lusher, 'Does the law allow you to kill a burglar who has broken into your home?' *Independent* (5 April 2018).

[14] [2016] 2 WLR 1303.

[15] Para 34.

[16] A Lusher, 'Pensioner held for murder over fatal stabbing of home intruder "was just protecting himself", neighbours say' *The Independent* (5 April, 2018).

C. Degrees of Murder

Kyd's proposals for codification of the existing law of homicide and the creation of two degrees of murder have a good deal of support, including from the Law Commission, albeit she parts company with the Commission on the question of a subjective test as to the risk of causing death.[17] She identifies the division between recognised experts, Horder and Barry Mitchell, along subjective–objective lines in the context of manslaughter, aligning herself generally with the objectivist school of thought. Before dealing with the issue of codification, it is worth emphasising that the division is really attributable to the problem of intention. This is rarely straightforward and because of this lends itself better to the existing binary approach to homicide law, rather than a hierarchical scheme of murder by degrees. Intention is a question of evidence (how a defendant's thoughts and actions are interpreted by a jury) and rarely, if ever, a question of legal construction (about which it receives judicial directions).

The difficulty in proposing different categories for murder is that there is little evidence of it working in those jurisdictions that have it, or at least of it working any better than the existing United Kingdom model. Canada, to use one example, has the offences of first and second-degree murder. The former consists, in summary, in planned and deliberate murder including of specified victims or by different categories of offenders (eg, terrorists and organised criminals); the latter covers murders that are not first-degree murder. Its felony murder provisions, not entirely dissimilar to Kyd's manslaughter proposal, were struck down as unconstitutional, principally because of the risk of injustice to defendants. A lack of foresight of death, falling short of effective forensic definition, may also offend Canadian law on the same ground. In at least one paper, 'Homicide in Canada'[18] it is argued that if 'lawmakers got rid of the categories of homicide and simply charged every accused with homicide it would eliminate the difficulties of overcharging'.[19]

Recent developments in the law of joint enterprise reveal the practical difficulties reform could present. In *Jogee*,[20] the Supreme Court, acknowledging that the courts had taken a 'wrong turn' for more than three decades, quashed the appellant's murder conviction and ordered a retrial. In Canada and in other jurisdictions joint enterprise would classically fall within the category of second-degree murder. In the United Kingdom it may be murder or, as Lord Neuberger said in *Jogee*, 'a person who joins in a crime which any reasonable person would realise involves a risk of harm, and death results, is guilty at least of manslaughter'. Jogee was later convicted of manslaughter. He was sentenced to 12 years imprisonment, although he was eligible for release within less than a year due to time served. Under Kyd's proposals, it is not clear where murder as a result of joint enterprise would fit.

[17] Law Commission (n 4), [2.53].
[18] B Walford, 'Homicide in Canada' (1988/89) 1(2) *Journal of Prisoners on Prisons* 1.
[19] ibid, 43.
[20] [2016] UKSC 8.

This is unlikely to satisfy either side of the very polarised division on the issue, which could result in bringing the law into (some may argue further) disrepute. In doing so it would fail to solve the existing difficulties and may create potentially damaging new ones. Rhetorically, would justice have been better served if he had been convicted of second-degree murder?

II. Road Kill

Kyd's central premise is that since *Andrews v DPP*[21] 'it has been assumed that a driving offence can never form the basis of a prosecution for constructive manslaughter'.[22] This is a narrow view. Driving carelessly or driving dangerously does not, without more, constitute an unlawful act for the purpose of unlawful act manslaughter. Ordinarily, the offence of unlawful act manslaughter would be committed where the driver of the vehicle either intended to cause injury to the victim or was reckless as to whether injury would be caused.

Moreover, the Crown Prosecution considers that:

> If the vehicle was intentionally used as a weapon to kill or commit grievous bodily harm, a charge of murder may be considered. If the killing was involuntary, that is to say, where it was not intended, manslaughter may be considered. Manslaughter may arise as unlawful act manslaughter and gross negligence manslaughter. In addition, the charge of corporate manslaughter is also available …
>
> Manslaughter should also be considered where the driving has occurred 'off road' ie other than on a road or other public place, or when the vehicle driven was not mechanically propelled, and death has been caused. In these cases the statutory offences such as causing death by dangerous driving or causing death by careless driving do not apply.

There have been a number of notable examples where murder charges have been levelled in fatal car-related deaths, including in the case of Police Constable Dave Phillips in 2015,[23] (although the defendant was found guilty of manslaughter) and the death of Mohammed Miah in West Bromwich on 17 March 2018.[24]

There is nothing wrong in principle with the concept that if, whilst otherwise driving lawfully, A kills B, whether as a result of speeding, tiredness or other form of negligence – in the search for a relatively neutral term – A is not guilty of homicide. Of course, there will be borderline cases about which some quarters of the media will express outrage, but the function of the State in prosecuting offences is to undertake a sober and objective review of the facts and law and their sterile application without, as the saying goes, passion or prejudice. A violation of the Highway Code resulting in death as a gateway to homicide is repugnant.

[21] [1937] AC 576.
[22] Kyd, (n 1) 109.
[23] 'Clayton Williams convicted of PC Dave Phillips's manslaughter' *BBC Online* (21 March 2016).
[24] 'Murder charge over West Bromwich "'car drag" death' *BBC Online* (20 March 2018).

The law as it stands is flexible enough to accommodate the facts of the individual case. As things stand, the full range of offences is available to the CPS and is being used. The case for reforming road killings is simply not made out.

III. Conclusions

The case for reform of the law of murder has not been done to death. The absence of political will to reform has led to reform withering on the vine. It is easy to relate to Kyd's paper; the current author acted for Private Lee Clegg, a soldier convicted (though later cleared) of murder. The House of Lords in 1995[25] recognised a case in principle for law reform where a soldier or police officer shoots someone dead in excess of reasonable force. The public debate following his conviction was intense: the press and other media campaigned relentlessly for his release on licence, and once this was achieved there were riots, now known unceremoniously as the 'Clegg riots', on the streets of Belfast. Their Lordships were unable to change the law, saying it was a matter for the legislature. It was to no effect. But as Peter Alldridge opined at the conference that preceded this collection, consulting, particularly the public, in matters of law is dangerous. A vote on the re-introduction of capital punishment is the most compelling example: in 2016, for the first time on record since capital punishment was abolished, those in favour of bringing back hanging dropped below 50 per cent; the vote was in fact 48 per cent – the same number that voted that the UK should remain part of the EU. The only time the public should be asked to vote in the context of criminal justice is in the jury room. Politicians legislating to appease public opinion leads to bad law – the Dangerous Dogs Act 1991, and the provisions in the so-called Protection of Freedoms Act 2012 relating to judicial approval of local authority surveillance, are examples that spring to the mind.

The case for codification of the criminal law generally is a persuasive one. The former Lord Chief Justice, Lord Thomas, revived Lord Bingham's calls for codification during a speech before his retirement.[26] Kyd's proposals are limited in scope in the same way as there was implementation of limited reforms following the Law Commission's review in 2006. If there is going to be reform it must be comprehensive. Word count constrained her considering some areas, but there are others, which in current times need to be included in any proposal for reform: the pervasive role of artificial intelligence and where criminal liability lies cries out for consideration and extends from the driverless car (this exposes an immediate lacuna in Kyd's draft offence of vehicular manslaughter) to targeted killing by lethal drone. The criminal law needs to be equipped to deal with the exponential rate of technological change.

[25] *Clegg* [1995] 1 AC 482.
[26] The Right Hon. The Lord Thomas of Cwmgiedd (Dinner for Her Majesties Judges, 6 July, 2016).

But there is something inherently unpalatable about emulating the United States' criminal justice system. It can hardly be held up as a shining light – anyone who watched 'Making a Murderer'[27] can only be convinced that it should be in the dock itself and not emulated any more than it already is. Moreover, the gradation of murder is the subject of criticism by respected commentators. A review of the historical and contemporary literature makes it clear that it is riddled with the same difficulties as those apparent in other jurisdictions. Insofar as there is any commonality between the issues that arise, these relate to the nebulous concepts of intention and recklessness. The basic architecture is the same – it is the inability to clearly define the terms that is the recurring problem here, in the US, Europe and the rest of the world. Even after *Jogee* intention still entangles our greatest legal minds. The Law Commission in 2006 said that any reforms should 'promote certainty … in a way that non-lawyers can understand and accept'. Even Kyd admits that the concept of 'reckless indifference' to death poses some difficulty in where this would fit in to the scheme of new offences.

As to gross negligence manslaughter, there is no real difficulty in the suggestion that this should be embodied in statutory form, but equally juries manage to return verdicts, despite arguments that the definition is circular. Reality cuts through the sterility of academic nuance. Creating a new category of homicidal medical practitioners is more problematic. In light of the *Bawa-Garba*[28] case it is difficult to see where the justice lies in doing so.

Much of the injustice arising in this area could be readily resolved through the abolition of the mandatory life sentence. This is often where the real injustice lies. In cases of, for example, assisted suicide and fatal shootings by the State – unquestionably murder (indeed, first degree murder, based on Kyd's proposal), but falling into a quite unique category of killing – freeing the trial judge up to sentence on the basis of the facts on the case, the aggravating and mitigating facts, and mercy where appropriate, would cure many ills. Where a judge is considered to have been unduly lenient, the Attorney General would remain capable of seeking a review of the sentence.

[27] D Browne, '"Making a Murderer": The Story Behind Netflix's Hit True-Crime Show' *Rolling Stone* (6 January 2016).

[28] [2018] EWHC 76 (Admin).

5

The CPS, Policy-Making and Assisted Dying: Towards a 'Freedom' Approach

ANDREW SANDERS*

In 2016 I evaluated the CPS after its first 30 years of existence.[1] I did this through the lens of the 'freedom model'.[2] This approach acknowledges that most people agree over the principal aims and values of criminal justice, at least at the level of rhetoric. Few people would argue against convicting the guilty, protecting the innocent, protecting everyone from arbitrary and oppressive treatment, treating victims with respect, and pursuing all this efficiently and proportionately.

The problem is that these values and interests often clash. The goals are not controversial, but their prioritisation often is. 'Freedom' can be a kind of common currency that allows us to weigh up, in any situation, how to prioritise. Criminal justice practices reduce the freedom of suspects, but some reduce it more than others. Compare, for example, out-of court disposals by the CPS with prosecutions: the former usually reduce freedom less than the latter. And some crimes – eg sexual offences – erode more freedom for victims and society at large than do others – eg, driving offences. Convicting guilty careless drivers, then, while desirable, should not be as high a priority as convicting sexual offenders. It will be evident from these examples that current law and practice sometimes prioritise 'freedom', but frequently do not.

In an attempt to see what the 'freedom' model would look like concretely, I examined how far the CPS operationalised the three core criminal justice values that are integral to it: 'Justice', 'Democracy' and the 'Three Es' (efficiency, effectiveness and economy). Again, these are not controversial in themselves, but prioritisation between and within them is.[3] I looked at how a range of policies

* I would like to thank Penney Lewis and Trevor Ponman (a physicist!) for their comments on earlier drafts of this paper.

[1] A Sanders, 'The CPS – 30 Years On' (2016) *Crim LR* 82.

[2] Richard Young and I developed this in the 2nd edition of our textbook. See A Sanders et al, *Criminal Justice*, 4th edn (OUP, 2010) ch 1.

[3] For extensive discussion of these values in relation to the CJS in general see my 'Core Values, the Magistracy and the Auld Report' (2002) 29 *Journal of Law and Society* 324; and my 'Reconciling the

and powers were formulated, interpreted and exercised. I concluded that CPS performance was improving, but still seriously deficient across all its work in relation to all three core values. This is due to its organisational culture, implicit and explicit policy choices, and structural position of police-dependence. One of the issues I examined briefly was assisted voluntary dying (AVD). Since space did not permit an extended treatment of this topic, this paper takes that opportunity.[4] For my purposes AVD refers to assisted suicide (AS) and voluntary euthanasia (VE). We shall see that the CPS policy on AVD can be improved, but it will always fail the tests on 'Justice' and the '3 Es'. First we look at the policy on AVD, then at how it operationalises the three core values in turn, and then we will examine what would be needed to operationalise the 'freedom' model.

I. The CPS Assisted Dying Policy

A. Assisted Suicide

In *Purdy*,[5] the applicant was suffering from MS. She wanted the CPS to promise that if her husband helped her to die when she asked him at some point in the future, he would not be prosecuted. The CPS refused, arguing that the Code for Crown Prosecutors gave guidance on this. Mrs Purdy correctly observed that the Code gave no indication of what would be likely to happen, for the 'public interest' factors are unprioritised. Which factor would be most important: the wishes of the 'victim' (Mrs Purdy) or the seriousness of the offence? If the latter, how seriously would assisted suicide be regarded? To counter this, by illustrating how it interpreted the Code in such cases, the CPS website summarised the case of *Daniel James*.[6] This young man had been confined to a wheelchair following a sporting accident. His suicide was assisted by his parents, despite their initial reluctance, after he spent several years trying to adjust to his difficult circumstances. His parents were not prosecuted because they were motivated solely by compassion and Daniel had a voluntary, informed, clear and settled wish to die.

But one case does not make a policy. There was nothing in the Code to lead anyone to believe that the CPS would decide the *Daniel James* case in the way it did. There was no guarantee that the CPS, under a different DPP perhaps, would continue to decide cases like this in the same way in the future. So the House of Lords, as it then was, agreed with Mrs Purdy, ordering the DPP to issue guidelines setting out how this discretion would be used. He was asked to formulate a policy

Apparently Different Goals of Criminal Justice and Regulation: the Freedom Perspective' in H Quirk et al (eds), *Regulation and Criminal Justice* (CUP, 2010).

[4] In the interests of brevity, general CPS matters that are discussed in my '30 Years On' paper (n 1), such as the Code for Crown Prosecutors, will not be referenced in this paper.

[5] *R (on the application of Purdy) v DPP* [2009] UKHL 45.

[6] See CPS website: www.cps.gov.uk.

that would take account of a defendant's 'improper motive'[7] but that would also seek to 'protect the right to make an autonomous choice'.[8] The DPP speedily issued interim guidelines, based on existing practice[9] as illustrated by the *Daniel James* case. There was a brief consultation after which the final version was published.[10]

The main elements of the final version identify prosecution as more likely when:

- the victim was under 18 years of age;
- the victim had not reached, or was not capable of reaching, a voluntary, clear, settled and informed decision to commit suicide and/or was subject to pressure from D or others;
- the victim had not clearly and unequivocally communicated his or her decision to commit suicide to the suspect;
- the victim did not seek the assistance of the suspect personally or on his or her own initiative;
- the suspect was not wholly motivated by compassion;
- the suspect had a history of violence or abuse against the victim;
- the victim was physically able to undertake the act that constituted the assistance him or herself;
- the suspect was unknown to the victim and assisted the victim by providing specific information via, for example, a website or publication;
- the suspect assisted more than one victim who were not known to each other;
- the suspect was acting in his or her capacity as, eg, a medical doctor, nurse, other healthcare professional, a professional carer;
- the actions of the suspect were of substantial assistance;
- the suspect had not sought to dissuade the victim and/or did not act reluctantly.

We know from the fact that AS is rarely prosecuted (see Part IV below) that the guidelines pointing against prosecution are given great weight in practice. People are not prosecuted when they are judged (by police and CPS) to have helped people who express a voluntary, informed, clear and settled wish to die. The guidelines seek to discourage people from helping others to die when they have something

[7] *Purdy* (n 5) (Lord Hope [63]).

[8] Baroness Hale at [65]. The *ratio* of the case is therefore arguable. However, the ECtHR decided in *Pretty* [2002] 35 EHRR 1 that a blanket prohibition on assisted suicide engaged Art 8(1), although under Art 8(2) this was permissible as long as some discretion was exercised in enforcing it. Art 8 considerations (giving effect to autonomy) should therefore have been be paramount.

[9] Which was, in particular, to give 'safe passage' for those assisting the trip to Dignitas (the Swiss life-ending clinic). Of 115 people who were known to have done this until that time, eight were referred to the DPP but none prosecuted: *Purdy* (n 5) [30].

[10] For the final policy, see the CPS, *Policy for Prosecutors in Respect of Cases of Encouraging or Assisting Suicide* (CPS Website, 2010, updated October 2014).

to gain from the death. But whether this policy succeeds in both protecting the vulnerable and preserving the autonomy of those who wish to die is another matter.

The DPP could have formulated a policy that simply said he would not prosecute if the 'victim' had a voluntary, informed, clear and settled wish to die. Instead, the focus on the motivation and role of the perpetrator restricts assisted suicide more than *Purdy* required and in ways that do not relate to the decision's interpretation of Article 8 of the ECHR (the protection of autonomous choices to die).[11] The DPP's policy attempts to compromise between 'autonomy' and 'sanctity of human life' positions.

B. Voluntary Euthanasia

The DPP could have included VE within the AVD policy, but chose not to do so. This may reflect the commonly held view that VE and AS are fundamentally different. Montgomery, for example, views the elements of the policy that stress the virtue of minimal assistance as positive as, in his view, 'this maintains the distinction between suicide and homicide'.[12] But Montgomery makes no distinction between voluntary and involuntary homicide.

We can categorise people who seek VE as follows:

(a) those who are physically incapable of taking the final step;

(b) those who try and fail to take the final step themselves;

(c) those who do not wish to take the final step themselves.

But reality is messy. Each category could include those who would have been able to take the final step with assistance but did not because of the constraints of the AS laws (eg, fear that their assister(s) would be prosecuted or that they would not be successful), or who perhaps tried and were unsuccessful, and who waited until they were desperate to die but were no longer confident they could take the final step themselves.

[11] J Rogers, 'Prosecutorial Policies, Prosecutorial Systems and the *Purdy* Litigation' (2010) *Crim LR* 543. Making compassion a factor has been criticised on various grounds. For example, as motive is not generally part of the substantive law, taking account of compassion (a motive) is said to change 'the law' by the 'back door' (C O'Sullivan, 'Mens Rea, Motive and Assisted Suicide: Does the DPP'S Policy Go Too Far?' (2015) 35 *Legal Studies* 96). The argument is hard to follow, since all guidelines change 'the law' (if we accept this positivistic idea of 'law') by the back door. The fault, if there is one, is therefore that of the court in *Purdy* – which required the DPP to issue guidelines of some kind and which, in some judgments, focused on motive – not that of the DPP. As Lewis observes, different judgments in *Purdy* had different emphases (P Lewis, 'Informal Legal Change on Assisted Suicide: The Policy for Prosecutors' (2011) 31 *Legal Studies* 119). For a philosophical discussion focussing on the 'compassion' element see A Duff, 'Criminal Responsibility and the Emotions: If Fear and Anger Can Exculpate, Why Not Compassion?' (2015) 58(2) *Inquiry* 189.

[12] J Montgomery, 'Guarding the Gates of St Peter' (2011) 31 *Legal Studies* 644, 661.

Nicklinson concerned a middle-aged man with 'locked-in' syndrome following a devastating stroke.[13] After trying to make a satisfying life for a considerable time with this condition he decided he no longer wished to live. He could make his wishes known clearly by using a computer linked to his eye movements, but this was the only movement of which he was capable. He was therefore in category (a). For such people there are currently just three solutions:

(1) travel to Dignitas in Switzerland, which is very difficult with the apparatus most people in category (a) need to live;
(2) self-starvation;[14]
(3) continuing to suffer, which for the appellants in *Nicklinson* was 'undignified, distressing and intolerable'.[15]

Despite this, the appellants (almost inevitably) failed in their claims. One argument concerned Article 8. But since the Article 8 arguments in relation to AS failed (because of the 'margin of appreciation' ie, the leeway given by the ECHR to domestic jurisdictions to order their criminal justice systems as best fits domestic tradition and culture), the Court of Appeal considered that the same would have to be true of the more serious offence of murder even when it takes the form of VE.[16]

A more substantial argument was 'necessity', though as 'necessity' is excluded in cases of murder the appellants were going to struggle with this too. An analogy was drawn with the 'conjoined twins' case, which allowed doctors to separate twins knowing this would kill one of them.[17] But the crucial difference between the two cases is that in the 'conjoined twins' case both would have died without intervention, while in *Nicklinson* all the appellants could live indefinitely. More fundamentally, if there is no defence of necessity for AS, how can there be one for the more serious offence of VE?[18] And how could there be a defence of necessity for AS when section 2 of the Suicide Act criminalises it?[19] Herring attempts to answer this as follows. If the person seeking VE cannot kill

[13] *Nicklinson* [2013] HRLR 36.

[14] The solution adopted by Nicklinson after he lost his case in the Divisional Court. His case was appealed, to the Court of Appeal and then the Supreme Court, on his behalf.

[15] Lord Neuberger [470].

[16] *Nicklinson* [2012] EWHC 2381 (Admin). For critical analyses see C Draghici, 'The Blanket Ban on Assisted Suicide: Between Moral Paternalism and Utilitarian Justice' (2015) 3 *European Human Rights Law Review* 286; J Adenitire, 'A Conscience-based Human Right to be "Doctor Death"' (2016) *Public Law* 613.

[17] *Re A (Children) (Conjoined Twins: Surgical Separation)* [2001] 2 WLR 480.

[18] *Nicklinson* [2013] HRLR 36 [66]. The necessity argument was probably run because this is how VE developed in the Netherlands (S Michalowski: 'Relying on Common Law Defences to Legalise Assisted Dying: Problems and Possibilities' (2013) 21(3) *Medical Law Review*, 337). A 'necessity' argument cannot, of course, co-exist with an autonomy-based argument for voluntary euthanasia: one cannot argue for choice if one is also arguing that there is only one solution. For a more general discussion reaching similar conclusions, see F Stark, 'Necessity and Nicklinson' (2013) *Crim LR* 949.

[19] Unless, as with most offences, the defence were to apply in only some circumstances. But it is difficult to envisage what circumstances would make a difference to whether such a defence would apply to AS or VE.

him/herself, that person's Article 8 rights can only be realised by allowing a person of choice to kill him/her.[20] However, everyone, no matter how disabled, can kill themselves by starving themselves to death. This is precisely what Tony Nicklinson and others[21] did. This gross inhumanity, comparable with torture (violation of Article 3), provides one reason for changing the law. But it is always an option. Herring might respond that it is 'necessary' to allow an option that does not violate Article 3. But exactly the same argument could apply for many people seeking assistance in suicide, as many of them, too, have no humane way to die except with the help of others.

Whatever the precise arguments, it is clear that there will be no judicial development of a VE policy anytime soon, even for people in category (a). So the CPS policy on AS should logically include VE for people in Tony Nicklinson's situation at the very least. But all the policy says is:

> If the course of conduct goes beyond encouraging or assisting suicide, for example, because the suspect goes on to take or attempt to take the life of the victim, the public interest factors tending in favour of or against prosecution may have to be evaluated differently in the light of the overall criminal conduct. [48]

Turning to category (b), Keating and Bridgeman give several examples.[22] Vanessa Cook suffered from MS and depression and unsuccessfully tried three times to kill herself before taking an overdose and asking her husband not to call emergency services before she was dead. Her husband ensured she died by suffocating her. Sarah Lawson attempted suicide three times in the week before a final attempt was reinforced, again, by suffocation, this time by her father. The courts in these cases generally convict of manslaughter on grounds of diminished responsibility (not murder) and award non-custodial sentences, thus demonstrating the absence of doubt about the compassionate and consensual basis of the death. But why convict at all in that case? Moreover, not all defendants in these circumstances are so lucky: when Frank Lund ensured his serially suicidal wife actually died, as she requested, he was convicted of murder and sentenced to 'life'.[23] In similar circumstances, George Webb smothered his extremely ailing wife when her suicide attempt (which he reluctantly assisted) was failing, as she had asked him to do. He pleaded guilty to manslaughter on the grounds of diminished responsibility. This man of 73, with psychiatric problems and suffering the double anguish of his wife's death at his own hands, still served six months' imprisonment

[20] J Herring, 'Escaping the Shackles of Law at the End of Life: *R (Nicklinson) v Ministry of Justice*' (2013) *Medical Law Review* 21, 487–92. This is a version of the 'necessity' defence urged on (but not accepted by) the courts by S Gardner, 'Direct Action and the Defence of Necessity' [2005] *Crim LR* 371.

[21] Such as Jean Davies, an 86-year-old who was suffering from several painful and distressing health problems: A Topping, 'Right-to-die campaigner who starved herself said she had "no alternative"' *Guardian Online* (19 October 2014). Both she and Tony Nicklinson took 2+ weeks to die, though it seems that infections, brought on by their starved conditions, were the technical causes of death.

[22] H Keating and J Bridgeman, 'Compassionate Killings: The Case for a Partial Defence' (2012) 75 *MLR* 697.

[23] R Ford, 'Life may mean just 3 years for "mercy killing" husband' *The Times* (25th May 2007).

before his sentence was reduced on appeal.[24] So he was luckier than Frank Lund, but still suffered abominably at the hands of our justice system for carrying out a last act of love at the request of the 'victim'.[25]

It is clear that the CPS policy remains problematic. But to fully understand this, and before we can begin to plot a way forward, we need to review it using the 'core values' within the freedom approach.

II. First Core Value: Democracy

A consultation process is only an exercise in democracy if consultee responses are taken into account in a principled way. This can only be done if the principles underlying the policy to be consulted on are articulated. No principles were articulated when the CPS consulted on its draft policy. There is insufficient space to analyse the CPS response to all the issues raised in the consultation, but here are the most important examples:

(i) The interim policy included several suspect-oriented factors (eg, whether the suspect had an entirely compassionate, as compared to a financial or malicious, motive). A majority of respondents agreed with these factors, and they found their way into the final policy. But only a minority of respondents agreed with the victim-oriented mitigating factor that found its way into the final policy (that the 'victim' had a voluntary, informed, clear and settled wish to die).

(ii) The interim policy 'weighted' some factors as more important than others. Over 80 per cent of respondents agreed with 'weighting' in relation to seven of the eight pro-prosecution factors (the seven that eventually found their way into the final policy). But the decision was taken not to continue this weighting into the final policy on the bizarre ground that not weighting 'makes the final policy clearer and more accessible' even though 'the particular facts of the case may mean that one factor alone may outweigh a number of other factors which tend in the opposite direction'.[26] This means that although the policy allows for one factor to be weighted more heavily than another, it is claimed that the policy will be clearer and more accessible if no indication is given of which factors will be so weighted, to what extent, and in what circumstances. But this is not self-evident. Nor is there any explanation of how clarity and accessibility were weighed against public approval. Would the

[24] *Webb* (2011) EWCA Crim 152.

[25] Changes to the law on diminished responsibility (Coroners and Justice Act) now make this route to manslaughter less likely to be available in such cases: M Gibson, 'Pragmatism Preserved? The Challenges of Accommodating Mercy Killers in the Reformed Diminished Responsibility Plea' (2017) 81 *Journal of Criminal Law* 177.

[26] CPS, Public Consultation Exercise (February 2010) [4.7 and 4.8].

same decision have been taken if 99 per cent of respondents had approved of the weighting?

(iii) The consultation asked what other public interest factors might have been included in favour of, or against, prosecution. A few suggestions favouring prosecution were adopted in the final policy. But the suggestion that written documentation signifying a wish to die (such as a living will) be a factor against prosecution was rejected. This was on the ground that it was not for the CPS to recognise such a step if Parliament did not. Yet this whole policy takes a step away from a clear Parliamentary decision (ie, retaining the blanket criminalisation of assisted suicide in the Suicide Act, as amended as recently as 2009!)[27]

It is therefore impossible to identify a rationale for the CPS following the lead of respondents at some times but not at others. Even when the principle adopted is clear – such as how great a role the suspect had – this principle might equally have been rejected. Two senior members of the CPS comment that 'Of course, the public's view, whilst persuasive, cannot be determinative of any particular issue … without reference to other considerations.'[28] But they do not tell us what those other considerations were, or how they were balanced against the views of the public. Did the CPS look at how strongly expressed a view was? How widely held? How logical? How consistent with other principles? They argue that the consultation process was nonetheless vindicated because 'The public gave its views and the Director has reflected the vast majority of them.'[29] This quantitative approach is one of several ways in which the consultation failed to comply with the governmental consultation criteria operating at that time.[30] And, while it is true that the final policy does in general reflect the majority of views, we have seen that it is not true in several respects, and that no convincing explanation was given about why some views were accepted and others not.

Thus a two-stage process was adopted, in which the second stage did not follow logically from the first. The DPP seems to have acted on the consultation responses that he liked, and not on others, for no clear reasons and with no guiding principle. The final policy is therefore as muddled as was the interim policy. We shall see that it is also cruel and restrictive of autonomy. This is because the consultation did not identify the fundamental principle that the policy was supposed to safeguard. If that principle was the protection of autonomy we would expect the policy to have two limbs: allowing 'perpetrators' to do whatever victims wish

[27] Section 2 was amended by s 59 and Sch 12 of the Coroners and Justice Act 2009.

[28] R Daw and A Solomon, 'Assisted Suicide and Identifying the Public Interest in the Decision to Prosecute' (2010) *Crim LR* 737, 743.

[29] ibid, 748.

[30] P Lewis, (n 11) whose critique of the way the consultation was conducted is of huge value.

them to do, whether this involves a major part in the suicide or a minor part, whether done reluctantly or as part of a Dignitas-style organisation; and guarding against pressure on victims to commit suicide.[31] Those who have something to gain from suicide are usually family. So the policy's endorsement of family assistance and discouragement of professional assistance is perverse. Where was the evidence base for this choice? In the Netherlands assisted suicide *requires* medical endorsement.[32] Is it plausible that what works best for people contemplating suicide is completely different in two ostensibly similar western democracies?

If the CPS had started from these principles it would logically have had to consider whether VE should be included in its policy. It would then have had to have consulted accordingly. For the essence of VE is allowing 'perpetrators' to do whatever victims wish them to do, whether this involves a major part in a death or a minor part.

Further what kind of public consultation should have been conducted? Unlike theft or drink-driving, laws that regulate AVD do not directly affect 'the public' as a whole. They mainly impact on people who suffer terminal, disabling or serious chronic ailments and those close to them. Yet no consultation was done with these particular groups of people, or indeed with the medical profession. Giving the general public *a* voice is appropriate. But giving the general public the *only* voice is surely irrational. It is also contrary to current government guidelines: 'Consider the full range of people, business and voluntary bodies affected by the policy, and whether representative groups exist. Consider targeting specific groups if appropriate.'[33] And the Northern Ireland government website, for example, states that 'consultation is … about making policies more effective by listening and taking onboard the views of the public *and interested groups*'.[34]

If consultation exercises had been done with different groups of people their responses could have been compared. Even so, comparison cannot be done in a vacuum. Without explicit principles to underpin whatever would become the final policy, comparison would be worthless.

[31] This is a great over-simplification of the nuances and controversies around the concept of autonomy. See, eg, S McLean, *Autonomy, Consent and the Law* (Routledge, 2010); C Foster, 'Autonomy in the Medico-legal Courtroom: A Principle Fit for Purpose?' (2014) 22 *Medical Law Review* 48. There are many critiques of, and warnings against, autonomy as an over-riding legal principle in general, such as M Shehan, 'Deflating Autonomy' in M Häyry and T Takala (eds), *Scratching the Surface of Bioethics* (Rodopi, 2003); C Foster, *Choosing Life, Choosing Death: The Tyranny of Autonomy in Medical Ethics and Law* (Hart, 2009) esp ch 11. See further discussion in Part V.

[32] For examples of the many discussions of the Netherlands see Lewis (n 11); E Delbeke, 'The Way Assisted Suicide Is Legalised: Balancing a Medical Framework against a Demedicalised Model' (2011) 18 *EJ Health Law* 149.

[33] *Consultation Principles: Guidance* (2016) [8]. Available at: www.gov.uk/government/publications/consultation-principles-guidance.

[34] *Public Consultations* (Ni.Direct, 2017). Available at www.gov.uk/government/publications/consultation-principles-guidance.

III. Second Core Value: Justice

'Justice' can have many meanings, and there is no space in this paper to explore them all. I first look at whether, on balance, this policy leaves 'victims' better or worse off than a more permissive policy would leave them. I then examine the way in which 'perpetrators' are differentiated.

A. Justice for Victims

Since 'victims of crime should be at the heart of the [criminal justice] system',[35] the CPS claims that 'Championing justice and defending the rights of victims, fairly, firmly and effectively is at the heart of all we do'.[36] The effect of the final policy is that AS perpetrators are at risk of prosecution when they provide assistance in the following ways.

Provide specialist advice: Anyone who offers organised assistance is likely to be prosecuted, as are health care professionals with a duty of care to the 'victim'.[37] Thus the policy is 'designed to ensure that assistance in suicide remains an amateur activity carried out by inexperienced individuals without the assistance of professionals'.[38] The result is botched suicides: failed attempts and deaths that are more painful and distressing than they need to be, such as the examples given in Part I(B) above. One of the most distressing examples is the first prosecution for AS carried out between the publication of the guidelines and the decision in *Nicklinson*. The perpetrator provided petrol and a lighter to a vulnerable man known to have suicidal intent, and who subsequently suffered severe burns as a result.[39] Defenders of the policy may see this case as vindication of its restrictiveness, enabling prosecution of the irresponsible perpetrator. In reality it serves to condemn that policy, for if the victim had been able to secure better advice and assistance it is unlikely that he would have suffered so horrifically.

Facilitate suicide in an organised way in the UK: Many UK citizens travel to Switzerland to die at Dignitas, generally assisted by friends and/or family who are never prosecuted.[40] But it is likely that anyone organising a Dignitas-type process

[35] *Justice for All* (Cm 5563, 2002), Forward.

[36] CPS website: www.cps.gov.uk.

[37] Para 43, Factors 5, 6, 11, 12.

[38] Quoted by Patricia Hewitt HoC Hansard 10 March 2010, col 403 from P Lewis, 'Out of Focus' (2010) *Solicitors Journal* 10, 11. For a lengthier and highly persuasive discussion see Lewis (n 11). This remains true even though health care professionals giving advice and assistance when not acting in their professional capacities are now (following an amendment to the Policy) treated like anyone else acting for compassionate reasons. See Para 43, Factor 14.

[39] CPS News Brief, 'Kevin Howe convicted of assisted attempted suicide' (12 September 2013).

[40] This is consistent with Para 45, Factors 1 and 2 if, as the CPS sees it, helping the 'victim' to travel to Dignitas is regarded as minor assistance. This seems to be an *a priori* principle. It cannot be reconciled with any kind of reality in relation to people who *need* assistance to travel to Switzerland. Note that neither Dignitas nor Dignitas-style process and institutions are specifically mentioned in the CPS

in the UK would be prosecuted.[41] For example, a tip-off about a 'euthanasia kit' prompted police to raid and (it is reported) break down the door of an 82-year old wanting to end her life, causing her to delay – but not abandon – her suicide in 2016.[42] This is obviously irrational. It is also cruel and unjust to most victims:

- It compounds the suffering of people who wish to die, and that of their friends and family, by requiring travel to a foreign country away from the comfort of one's home and loved ones.
- Travel to Switzerland will often be painful and difficult, particularly for people whose painful conditions are a precipitating factor in leading them to decide to end their life.
- It costs around £8,000 to use Dignitas.[43] Travel costs, for the 'victim' and friends/family are extra. This is unaffordable for many people.

This part of the policy also erodes the second limb of the autonomy principle identified in Part II. It puts pressure on some victims to die earlier than they otherwise would. People suffering degenerative illnesses, in particular, would be able to delay their death longer if they only had to travel to a 'UK-dignitas' than if they have to make the difficult journey to Switzerland. And who knows how many people, knowing that a 'UK-dignitas' would be available as a safety net, would not in fact take, or ask for help in taking, the final step? The implicit push to travel to Switzerland actually encourages AS.

Provide substantial assistance:[44] Three people were arrested in Loder's case. It was decided there was insufficient evidence against one, and that it was not in public interest to prosecute the other two. One had only contributed to the deceased's 'preparations' while the other only had two phone conversations with her.[45] This sends a clear signal to 'perpetrators': do as little as possible to help victims see their final wishes fulfilled. This contributes to the number of botched suicides referred to above, pushes sufferers to Switzerland, and consigns many 'victims' to loneliness in their final and most distressing stages of life. If 'victims' want others to have major roles in their deaths, to make the final steps easier, why deny them their wishes? The logic of this argument then extends, of course, to VE: if the major role that someone wants another to have is to actually take that person's life, there is no reason to deny it. A common objection to AS is precisely this: that it is a 'slippery

Policy, though under Para 43, Factor 16, prosecution is 'more likely to be required if … the suspect was [in] … an organisation or group, a purpose of which is to provide a physical environment … in which to allow another to commit suicide'.

[41] Factor 16.

[42] *Guardian* (22 March 2016).

[43] N Richards, 'Assisted Suicide as a Remedy for Suffering? The End-of-Life Preferences of British "Suicide Tourists"' (2017) 36 *Medical Anthropology* 348.

[44] Para 43, Factor 10 and Para 45, Factor 3.

[45] C Davies, 'No charges against three arrested over academic's suicide' *Guardian Online* (16 August 2010).

slope' to VE and worse. 'Slippery slope' arguments have been comprehensively demolished by Smith and are briefly addressed later.[46]

B. Justice for Perpetrators

Prosecution decisions should differentiate suspects who facilitate the autonomy of victims (by helping them carry out their freely made wishes) from those who subvert it (by persuading them to attempt suicide). Is that what this policy does?

We have seen that it makes the provision of specialist advice hard to secure, leading to botched suicides. But surely detached medical professionals are less likely to persuade people to take their own lives than families and carers who may gain from these deaths. Further, in many suicide attempts made without specialist assistance the assister – unbearably distressed at seeing their loved one suffer the threefold hardship of their original problem, the decision to end their life and the failure to secure this objective – ends up being the actual killer. As we have seen, this 'amateur' VE is technically homicide and is prosecuted more frequently than AS.

We have also seen that the amount of assistance influences prosecution decisions. It is not obvious that taking a greater role indicates more undermining of victim autonomy – more culpability – than where suspects avoid this responsibility.

Take the part of the policy that makes prosecutions more likely when suspects do not seek to dissuade victims and/or do not act reluctantly.[47] This is a random value judgement about culpability. Many suspects who are reluctant to help 'victims' would presumably consider the suicide of those 'victims' to be irrational (for if a proposed suicide were rational why would a 'perpetrator' be reluctant to help a loved one?).[48] But if victims and/or their suicides are considered irrational, surely helping those victims to die would be wrong, as treatment or persuasion might enable the victim to see sense. Yet people who reluctantly assist suicide are less likely to be prosecuted than those who do so with understanding and respect for their loved one's wishes.

Finally, the number of factors in the policy requires extensive police investigation to enable CPS to make a decision in accordance with it. Even though most suspects are not prosecuted, many are arrested, and in all cases investigations are intrusive. This all adds to the distress these loved ones have to endure – losses to their 'freedom',[49] in other words.

[46] S Smith, 'Evidence for the Practical Slippery Slope in the Debate on Physician-assisted Suicide and Euthanasia' (2005) 13(1) *Medical Law Review* 17.

[47] Para 45, Factors 4 and 5.

[48] I am interpreting 'reluctance' as having reservation about helping, as distinct from sadness at the outcome; sadness is normal, and anyone who does not feel sad when contemplating the death of a loved one is indeed worthy of suspicion if s/he helped that person to die.

[49] In the way we use it in *Criminal Justice* (n 2).

IV. Third Core Value: The Three 'Es'

Every assisted suicide that is reported to the police is investigated by them, who then send a file to the CPS. Suspects are interviewed under caution and frequently following arrest. Yet hardly any are prosecuted:

Table 1 Assisted Suicide Referred to the CPS by Police, April 2009–July 2017[50]

Withdrawn by police	28
Not proceeded with by CPS	85
Ongoing	8
Referred for prosecution for other serious offences	7
Prosecuted	2
Not known (*Included as CPS figures do not add up*)	6
Total referred	136

Nine possible prosecutions out of 136 cases is such a low percentage that the expenditure of resources – efficiency and economy – has to be a concern. But this is an inevitable consequence of post-death assessment.

The effectiveness of the policy (the third 'E') is also questionable. First, the fulfilment of victims' wishes is hampered by the co-focus on 'the motivation of the suspect'. Botched and repeated suicide attempts are just the visible examples of this. There are doubtless many others who wish to end their lives but who do not; they continue to suffer because they have no access to expertise or help or because they fear a lonely or botched attempt.

Secondly, the proxies for assessing autonomy are ill-chosen. The policy rightly seeks to protect victims from those who might pressure them into suicide. But as we have seen, those most likely to exert such pressure are those with most to gain from a person's suicide (such as family and close friends), and those least likely to exert such pressure are those with little or nothing to gain (such as professionals). Yet the policy facilitates AS by family and friends, and discourages AS by professionals.

Thirdly, we know that prohibiting activities that are desired by all parties to them does little to reduce them. What happens to such activities – such as drug taking, abortion, prostitution, gambling, American 1920s Prohibition – is that they go underground. The activities are then more difficult to quantify and control. The 'dark figure' of both AS and euthanasia (voluntary and not voluntary), while impossible to estimate, is undoubtedly higher than if it were not (a) criminal; and (b) restricted more than an autonomy-based policy would be.

Medical euthanasia, in particular, is rife. This is often done under the guise of 'palliative care' and 'deep sedation'. It is usually justified, when called to account,

[50] See the CPS, *Latest Assisted Suicide Figures* (CPS Website, updated 2018).

by the doctrine of 'double effect', which was made part of English law in *Adams*.[51] This holds that where a medical intervention is done primarily to alleviate pain and suffering, there is no homicide even if the person administering it knows that death is a virtually certain consequence. Opponents of AS, as well as proponents, should be equally worried. Unlike 'regular' AS or VE, there is no automatic police investigation – in fact, there is usually no investigation at all, even when doctors announce that life-ending was their main motive.[52] But nor is there any system of recording the patients' wishes. We have to trust the medics that this was what the patient wanted and/or that death was imminent anyway.

In a survey of end-of-life decisions, medical practitioners said that over 17 per cent of deaths involved 'double effect' and over 16 per cent involved continuous deep sedation (CDS).[53] Mason and Laurie suggest that '... terminal sedation ... [is] ... likely to represent an instance of euthanasia hiding under emollient terminology'.[54] Huxtable gives numerous examples where 'double effect' is abused – for example, a junior doctor claiming that the lives of elderly terminal patients are sometimes shortened to manage bed shortages. Ironically, it is now thought that Dr Adams was actually a mass murderer akin to Harold Shipman.[55] And what are we to make of Howard Martin GP, who admitted hastening the death of dozens of his patients, some – but not all – at their request? He was tried for murder, acquitted, and then struck off.[56] While mass murderers are hopefully few and far between, mass murder probably is not. Although estimating the 'dark figure' is impossible, is seems that it is far more extensive than most people – including, crucially, respondents to the CPS consultation – imagine. In 1999 it was estimated that up to 100,000 patients a year are quietly helped to die in the UK.[57] In an Australian survey of 683 surgeons, over one-third (247) stated that, when administering drugs to alleviate suffering, they administered more than necessary for this purpose but with the intention of hastening death. Moreover, it may be that the main difference between the 247 and the rest is their self-evaluation of their mental state.[58] Magnusson also estimates that 'a significant proportion of

[51] [1957] Crim LR 773. See discussion in, eg, J Montgomery (n 12); and in D Price, 'Euthanasia, Pain Relief and Double Effect' (1997) 17 *Legal Studies* 323.

[52] R Huxtable, 'Get out of Jail Free? The Doctrine of Double Effect in English Law' (2004) 18 *Palliative Medicine* 62.

[53] C Seale, 'End of Life Decisions in the UK Involving Medical Practitioners' (2009) 23 *Palliative Medicine* 198.

[54] J Mason and T Laurie, *Mason and McCall Smith's Law and Medical Ethics*, 8th edn (OUP, 2000) 580.

[55] R Huxtable, 'Get out of Jail Free? The Doctrine of Double Effect in English Law' (2004) *Palliative Medicine* 18, 62. On Shipman, see D Griffiths and A Sanders (eds), *Medicine, Crime and Society* (CUP, 2013).

[56] D Batty, 'I helped patients die, says doctor cleared of murder' *Guardian Online* (19 June 2010).

[57] R H Tur, 'Just how Unlawful is "Euthanasia"?' (2002) 19(3) *Journal of Applied Philosophy* 219–32.

[58] C Douglas et al, 'The Intention to Hasten Death: A Survey of Attitudes and Practices of Surgeons in Australia' (2001) 175 *Medical Journal of Australia* 511, quoted in *Ost* (2005) Crim LR 355.

the medical profession has participated, illegally, in assisted death' in Australia.[59] Similarly the 1996 BBC Scotland survey on medical AS showed that 12 per cent of health care professionals personally knew another professional who had hastened death, while 4 per cent said they did this themselves.[60] In yet another example, a doctor in Hampshire was found guilty of serious professional misconduct by prescribing opiates and sedatives in 'excessive, inappropriate and potentially hazardous' ways. This is now the subject of a £13m inquiry into hundreds of deaths to which she may have contributed.[61]

Most non-voluntary medical euthanasia is mercy-killing, but there are occasional bounty-hunters and pathological killers. Only rarely is it identified or investigated, and even more rarely prosecuted. The rare example of Howard Martin being prosecuted turned on its extreme facts; and also perhaps on him acting alone.[62] His acquittal will have done nothing to encourage future prosecutions or deter medical killing without consent.

Thus while no doubt many, probably most, of people who die as a consequence of 'double-effect' do wish to die (or would, if they could express an opinion), there will doubtless be some who do not. The policy therefore lacks effectiveness because it fails to protect many of these people, failing to give effect to the second limb of the autonomy principle identified in Part II. As Orentlichter says '… terminal sedation … is also ethically more problematic than either assisted suicide or euthanasia'.[63] Moreover, 'double-effect' is physician-orientated, not patient-orientated: what matters is what the physician wanted/intended, not what the patient wants/intends.[64] This runs directly counter to the victim-centred criminal justice policy espoused by the CPS. Yet not only is a blind eye turned to cases of 'double effect' because medical professionals who assist suicide risk prosecution, it is positively encouraged even by those who oppose assisted suicide and who oppose the exercise of discretion.[65]

[59] R Magnusson, *Angels of Death: Exploring the euthanasia underground* (Melbourne University Press, 2002) 40.

[60] Daruwala, review of J Keown, 'Euthanasia, Ethics and Public Policy' (2003) 11 *Medical Law Review* 256.

[61] *Sunday Times* (20 August 2017).

[62] Team decisions in hospital settings seem to have a cloak of authority: R Rhodes, 'Physicians, Assisted Suicide and the Right to Live or Die' in M Battin, R Rhodes, A Silvers (eds) *Physician Assisted Suicide* (Routledge, 1998).

[63] D Orentlichter, 'The Supreme Court and Terminal Sedation' (1998–99) 24 *Hastings Const Law Q* 947, 960.

[64] E Jackson, 'Whose Death is it Anyway? Euthanasia and the Medical Profession' (2004) 57(1) *CLP* 415, 436. Indeed, it seems that neither opoids nor sedatives need shorten life: N Sykes and A Thorns, 'The Use of Opioids and Sedatives at the End of Life' (2003) 4 *Lancet Oncology* 312, 317. So its foundations in medicine seem fallacious, as well as morally and legally dubious: See, eg, G Williams, *Intention and Causation in Medical Non-killing: The Impact of Criminal Law Concepts on Euthanasia and Assisted Suicide* (Routledge, 2007) ch 2.

[65] For a leading example see J Keown, *Euthanasia, Ethics and Public Policy* (CUP, 2002).

V. Towards a 'Freedom-Based' AVD Policy

A. The Foundations of the Policy

We have seen that the current policy is weak with respect to all three core values. Consequently the freedom of victims is unnecessarily constrained in several ways: many suicides are made unnecessarily distressing; many suicides take place away from family and friends; many assisted deaths are pushed underground, making voluntariness harder to assess. And the freedom of perpetrators is also unnecessarily constrained, putting many of those who genuinely seek to help carry out the wishes of victims at risk of prosecution, and subjecting them to intrusive investigations. It is true that there are very few prosecutions. But that does not mean that few perpetrators are at risk. For example, medical professionals who openly gave substantial assistance would probably be prosecuted, as would organisers of a 'UK-dignitas' and people who sold DIY-suicide death kits. This policy bans initiatives like these that might make the final days of suicidal people easier. If any of the effects that the current policy leads to – starvation, exile to Dignitas, the agony of an overdose, the dismay and pain following a failed suicide attempt, clandestine killing on the pretext of 'double effect' – were forced on one person by another it would be criminal and/or a violation of Article 3 of the ECHR. It is surely 'inhuman and degrading treatment'. This is what is forced onto countless numbers of people who are already suffering beyond endurance.

What would a policy that conformed to the 'freedom' model and its core values look like? First, the consultation would be with the general public, the medical professions, and subsets of people with disabilities, chronic conditions and terminal illness. It would explain why the autonomy principle (with the two limbs identified in Part II) should be the basis of the policy. It would inform consultees of such facts about assisted death as are known or estimated under different kinds of legal regime. The consultation would seek views on the autonomy principle (and compare those of the sets of consultees) and consult on how to articulate that principle. It would consult on the key elements identified in this chapter: how to best give effect to genuinely autonomous wishes to die; the (limited) ways in which the motivation of, and degree of assistance given by, perpetrators are relevant; and how to protect people who may be at risk of being pressured into suicide.

Secondly, we need to be realistic about 'autonomy'. The idea that individuals have completely free choices, made in isolation from outside influences, is – like the free market – a myth. There is a spectrum of choice in all things, from complete freedom of choice to coercion masquerading as choice. In the middle of the spectrum lies the problem of people making choices that they would not make in other circumstances, including making choices that they think others want them to make (whether under pressure or not). 'Autonomy' is not exercised in a vacuum.

Most people therefore make choices of their own free will but rarely in conditions of their own choosing. This is as true of people considering AVD as it is of people considering other choices in life. This is a structured matter, in AVD as elsewhere. George argues that the structural position of women in western society places more pressure on them to choose to die than it does on men: 'For some women, assisted death might not demonstrate their autonomy, but their acquiescence to controlling influences.'[66] We might note the similarly powerful, but different, impact of social class: wealth, for example, widens one's choices greatly. But while we should acknowledge the inadequacy of all conceptions of individual autonomy, it follows that if it is inadequate to the task of driving policy about the types of life/death decisions discussed here, it is similarly inadequate to drive other equally important policies – for example, religious choice, education, and going to war. Like democracy, the concept of individual autonomy should be replaced by a better alternative, but as there is no better alternative we must make the best of it. That includes being vigilant about individual autonomy becoming overwhelmed by the influence of others, and doing what we can about the conditions that distort choice. We therefore need to create the system that best identifies and encourages non-lethal solutions for people who ask to die.

Thirdly, a change of policy will change the climate around AVD. Attitudes, followed by the law and practice, could slide down a slippery slope towards greater acceptance of suicide. This could increase social pressure on the weak, ill and vulnerable to end their lives prematurely. This will make the encouraging of non-lethal solutions all the more important. As Herring observes, 'The central legal message we should be sending out to people wishing to commit suicide is "please don't."' He rightly states that the law and public health system should be aligned to offer 'care, comfort and support'[67] (ie, doing what we can about the conditions that distort choice). Thus the value of human life needs to be placed alongside that of autonomy as the foundation of a new policy. But this is as much a matter of the quality of life as its existence. Adequate palliative care is often unavailable, often ineffective and often inappropriate (eg, where pain is not the problem).[68] The principles of valuing human life and autonomy *necessarily* co-exist. For in a liberal society it is as impermissible to tell someone who wishes to die that s/he cannot, as it is to tell someone who does not want to die that s/he should do so (and it is even more impermissible to have laws that give effect, directly or indirectly, to such commands). The role of law is not to adjudicate between these principles but to ensure they both have space to operate in as unfettered a way as possible. Policy on AVD should therefore be a matter of both criminal justice and public health.[69]

[66] K George, 'A Woman's Choice? The Gendered Risks of Voluntary Euthanasia and Physician-assisted Suicide' (2007) 1 *Medical Law Review* 29.

[67] Herring (n 20).

[68] See, eg, S Carr, P Beresford, T Coldham (eds), *Assisted Dying: Developing the Debate* (Shaping Our Lives, 2017).

[69] Drawing on Coggan, 'Assisted Dying and the Context of Debate: 'Medical Law' *Versus* 'End-of-Life Law' (2010) 18(4) *Medical Law Review* 541, 549.

Keown argues that since autonomy amounts to a right to die and to be killed, this would be incompatible with the 'right to life' in Article 2 of the ECHR.[70] But as Coggan observes, living and dying are not opposites. They are processes that co-exist: the process of dying arguably begins at the start of life, and certainly proceeds by middle age. People who demand control over the process by which they die are asserting control over how they live the final part of their life. Thus the argument of, for example, Greasley, that death is a denial of personal autonomy (since no choices exist to be made following death), and that therefore personal autonomy cannot provide a justification for the legalisation of AVD, is also flawed.[71]

Further, there is no reason why one should not have the right to (apparently) opposite things. For example, 'Having the right to consent to treatment does not render the right to refuse treatment as useless. Consenting to a sterilisation does not stand the Convention on its head, even though it can obviate the exercise of the right to found a family under Article 12.'[72] So, those who are against allowing AVD because they fear the downgrading of certain lives should have no cause for concern, as long as it is regulated in ways that signal the value of everyone's life. The right to life of every person should be seen as underlined, not undermined, by a right to die.[73]

Showing one policy to be less than wholly effective is of limited value unless one can show that another is or would be more effective. The 'dark figure' of illegal killing discussed earlier varies across different regimes. For example, a survey of 3,000 Australian doctors found non-voluntary euthanasia to be five times more common in Australia, where VE is illegal, than it is in the Netherlands, where it is legal. Further, Australian doctors were far less likely than their Dutch counterparts to discuss the decision to hasten a patient's death with the patient herself, or to seek her consent.[74] Evaluations suggest that criminalising VE is less effective in controlling non-voluntary euthanasia than policies like that of the Netherlands.[75]

[70] J Keown, 'European Court of Human Rights: Death in Strasbourg-assisted Suicide, the *Pretty* Case, and the European Convention on Human Rights' (2003) 1 *International Journal of Constitutional Law* 722.

[71] K Greasley, 'R (Purdy) v DPP and the Case for Wilful Blindness' (2010) 30 *OJLS* 301. The same is true of her argument, and others like it, that AD cannot generally be in the interests of the 'victim' because it cannot be better to be dead than alive (she admits of some exceptions here, but they are not central to the argument). Even if this argument were acceptable in principle, it would only work if one has a choice in the matter. But we don't. We all die eventually.

[72] J Coggan, 'Could the Right to Die with Dignity Represent a New Right to Die in English Law?' (2006) 14 *Medical Law Review* 219.

[73] The idea of a 'right to die' is not, readers will not be surprised to discover, straightforward. To keep the discussion manageable, this chapter will not (and does not need to) tackle that problem; see Coggan (ibid) and J Finnis, 'A British 'Convention Right' to Assistance in Suicide?' (2015) 131 *LQR* 1 for different discussions.

[74] H Kuhse, P Singer, P Baume, M Clark, and M Rickard, 'End-of-Life Decisions in Australian Medical Practice' (1997) 166(4) *Medical Journal of Australia* 191–6.

[75] H Biggs, *Euthanasia, Death with Dignity and the Law* (Hart, 2001); M Freeman, 'Denying Death its Dominion: Thoughts on the *Dianne Pretty* Case' (2002) 10 *Medical Law Review* 245; E Jackson (n 64) 431.

If there is a danger of a permissive AVD regime creating a climate of active life-ending, there is an equally high risk of a restrictive AVD regime creating a climate of deception concerning the procuring and administering of drugs, the drugs paper trail, and post-mortem paperwork.[76] In such a climate, not only is AVD tolerated among many health care professionals, but wrong-doing is far less likely to be discovered than in jurisdictions where AVD is allowed in regulated circumstances. So even in the Netherlands, there is deception: AVD by relatives is not permitted, but many doctors are aware of it, occasionally facilitate it, and often report such deaths as 'natural'. The deception is not primarily a product of Netherlands' permissiveness, but of the ban on relative-assisted dying.[77] In the UK this is exacerbated by the cover for euthanasia provided by 'double effect'.

B. The Need for Pre-death Regulation: A Three Stage Approach

A new pre-death system for regulating AVD is needed, whether operated by health care professionals, judicial figures, or another body. The sole criterion should be a voluntary, informed, clear and settled wish to die. But this is not the sole requirement.

A pre-requisite – the first stage – would be better social and palliative care so that all realistic alternatives to death are explored and offered before people decide to take this final step. Take Greasley's objection to an autonomy-based policy. It would allow assisted dying for extreme examples such as teenagers who feel life is not worth living in the absence of their one true love. In Greasley's opinion, the only way of controlling this is to interpose an objective valuation of that stated belief. In deciding that the teenager is unreasonable but others (people objectively suffering hugely such as Tony Nicklinson) are reasonable we are valuing some lives above those of others.[78] This is why some disability-rights groups oppose the legalisation of AVD.[79] However, if the only requirement is a voluntary, informed and settled expressed wish to die, no objective evaluation of the value of other peoples' lives is needed. Nonetheless, the younger the person (and anyone under 18 would be subject to 'best interests' principles anyway) and the less objectively rational the wish, the less likely it is to be 'informed and settled'. This would justify more extensive enquiry and a longer period of reflection than would be needed for, for example, the terminally ill. The issue is not that those lives are of different

[76] Magnusson (n 59).

[77] S Ost and A Mullock, 'Pushing the Boundaries of Lawful Assisted Dying in the Netherlands? Existential Suffering and Lay Assistance' (2011) 18(2) *EJ Health Law* 163, 180 (citing Dutch research by Chabot).

[78] Greasley (n 71) 301.

[79] See L Carr 'Legalising assisted dying is dangerous for disabled people. Not compassionate' *Guardian Online* (9 September 2016).

value but that those people are differentially able to settle on the most important decision of their lives. Ultimately, though, it eventually becomes each individual's sole decision. That is why 'compromise' positions, relying as they do on an element of objective valuation of life,[80] are either incoherent or offensive.

Greasley's underlying concern here is with a 'slippery slope'. Similarly, Ost observes that 'a potential danger of loosening the medical criteria for assisted death is that it becomes harder to identify and maintain boundaries'.[81] But boundaries to *what prompts the wish to die* cannot be constructed. Kay Gilderdale's 31 year-old daughter, Lynn, was neither terminally ill nor as terribly immobilised as Daniel James or Tony Nicklinson. Yet Kay helped Lynn to die because Lynn's suffering for nearly 20 years from ME led her to attempt suicide several times.[82] Edward Downes, aged 85 and suffering from great pain, deafness and blindness, decided to die with his wife, who was terminally ill. He could have continued to live, but did not wish to.[83] In the Netherlands a woman in her twenties, who had suffered sexual abuse from the age of five to 15, suffered so badly from post-traumatic-stress disorder (severe anorexia, chronic depression and hallucinations) that doctors believed she could not be cured; consequently, she requested VE, which was granted.[84]

There is no doubt that the wish to die of all these people was voluntary, informed and settled. Who are we to decide whether they were 'right', and – if we decide they were not – to deny their wishes? Even the most principled objectors to AVD, such as was Bishop Desmond Tutu, sometimes change their views when confronted with a painful and/or distressing decline in their quality of life.[85]

Greasley's argument illustrates another problem for those using 'slippery slope' arguments against legalising assisted dying. They work, if they work at all, both ways. Greasley says that 'the law would not regard the assisted dying of a depressed, lovesick teenager as beyond recrimination … because the teenager, though she might not know it, has everything to live for'.[86] But if the reason for objecting to someone helping such a person to die is the objective fact that she has much to live for, it is not the *assistance* that is the problem. It is her wish to die that is the problem. If we think that people with objective reasons to live should not be helped to die then we should also think they should not be allowed to take their own lives. This argument against legalising AVD is a logical slippery slope leading

[80] For example, R Heywood and A Mullock, 'The Value of Life in English Law: Revered but not Sacred?' (2016) 36 *Legal Studies* 658, side with Greasley in the matter of the lovelorn teenager. For another advocacy of compromise see R Huxtable, *Euthanasia, Ethics and the Law* (Routledge, 2007).

[81] S Ost, 'The De-medicalisation of Assisted Dying: Is a Less-medicalised Model the Way Forward?' (2010) 18(4) *Medical Law Review* 497, 526.

[82] *Guardian* (25 January 2010).

[83] *Observer* (19 July 2009).

[84] *Independent* (11 May 2016).

[85] *Guardian* (7 October 2016).

[86] Greasley (n 71) 321.

to the re-criminalisation of suicide. If we resist the logic of this 'upward' move we should equally resist the logic of the posited 'downward' move.

The second stage would be the establishment of a pre-death regulatory system operated by people involved in social and medical care, and authorised accordingly. A 'conscience clause' would enable people to opt out of authorising AVD, allowing those seeking AVD to find someone who has no such concerns. This kind of transparent system would reduce both the abuse and the well-motivated but 'dark' practices currently carried out by relatives and medical professionals alike. The precise form of this system would be appropriate for public consultation on the lines set out in Part II.

The third stage concerns VE. The irony of the current AS policy is that, because of the way it de facto decriminalises much AS whilst maintaining the probability of prosecution of much other AS, it pushes many people into committing VE. So if the current restrictive policy towards AS is continued, a similar approach (de facto partial decriminalisation) should be adopted for VE. This logic would not necessarily apply if a new system following the two stages outlined above were adopted. If everyone who sought AVD were allowed AS, following the kind of counselling and support described above, VE need only be sought in two circumstances:

(a) individuals who wish to die but not to kill themselves: one way of looking at this is to say that reluctance to carry out the final act indicates that the wish to die is not definitively settled. However, this is surely an empirical matter. Arguably, a requirement that the 'victim' carry out the final act would be a safeguard against abuse. But if such a system is flawed – and what systems are not? – people could still be pressured into AS. And while 'autonomy' undoubtedly requires that people be allowed to seek and find help to die, it does not necessarily require that people be allowed to kill others. These are finely balanced arguments. It is precisely in such circumstances that public consultation has a role, if done as set out in Part II.

(b) Individuals who cannot kill themselves except by starvation: this is what Tony Nicklinson had to do to exercise his one last act of autonomy, a way of death in violation of Article 3 of the ECHR. In *Nicklinson* it was suggested that an eye-movement controlled machine that could administer lethal drugs would be a solution in such cases. It would not, of course, be a solution currently, as the supplier would undoubtedly be prosecuted.[87] But the freedom-based approach advocated here would allow this solution. Until then, and until such machines can be made both effective and freely available, VE should be treated in the same way as for this category of people. Even then, there will remain arguments for VE as set out in (a) above, on which there should be public consultation.

[87] Remember, the police recently raided the home of someone planning to use a 'euthanasia kit' to end her own life (n 47).

VI. Conclusion

Canada's ban on AS was recently challenged in the Supreme Court of Canada. The court decided that this ban was contrary to Canada's Charter of Rights and Freedoms. It gave the government of Canada 12 months to draft a law allowing doctor-assisted suicide. It also recognised the link between AS and VE, deciding that a new AVD policy had to cover both.[88]

In *Nicklinson*, the UK Supreme Court viewed the UK's AS policy as similarly incompatible with human rights. It warned that if Parliament does not deal with the problem, the courts may have to. Parliament did subsequently consider the issue but it rejected the Falconer Bill.[89] This Bill was, in any event, deeply flawed: catering only for the terminally ill, it would not have helped either Mrs Purdy or Mr Nicklinson, and we have seen that any objective criterion for AVD is unacceptable.

At least 12 different jurisdictions (counting six US States separately) now allow some forms of AS and/or VE. Two Australian States are currently legalising AVD, and 20 more US States are actively considering it.[90] The South African judiciary is drifting in this direction.[91] The UK is becoming out of line with other democracies,[92] so if a freedom-based approach to AVD were introduced this would be unexceptional.

The current CPS policy is a sticking plaster that completely fails on all three core values of criminal justice. We have seen that it could be improved, but it will always fail badly. We have an ageing population, many members of which suffer medical problems that would have been terminal not long ago. Keeping people alive in difficult conditions is wonderful for those who wish to continue to live, but harrowing for those who do not. This problem will only increase. It is currently addressed by post-death assessment by non-medical institutions and by clandestine medical killing under the guise of palliative care. This is what happens when society turns a blind eye (such as Greasly commends to us) instead of confronting the problem head-on. Regulating AVD pre-death will not a complete solution to our collective failure to tackle end-of-life problems. But it would be a necessary part of it, and a great advance on the current approach.

[88] *Carter v Canada* [2015] 1 SCR 331. For discussion see, for example, B Chan and M Somerville, 'Converting the 'Right to Life' to the 'Right to Physician-assisted Suicide and Euthanasia': An Analysis of *Carter v Canada*' (2016) 24 *Medical Law Review* 143.

[89] Whether this now settles the matter, as far as judicial development of the law is concerned, is a matter of on-going dispute in *Conway* (n 92).

[90] For a good overview of developments in several jurisdictions, see J Downie, 'Permitting Voluntary Euthanasia and Assisted Suicide: Law Reform Pathways for Common Law Jurisdictions' (2016) 16 *QUT Law Review* 84; also see *Guardian* (20 September 2017) on the Bill in Victoria.

[91] D McQouid-Mason, '*Stransham-Ford v. Minister of Justice and Correctional Services and Others*: Can Active Voluntary Euthanasia and Doctor-assisted Suicide be Legally Justified?' (2015) 8 *South African Journal of Bioethics and Law* 34.

[92] *Conway* [2017] EWHC 2447 (Admin) is the latest refusal to listen to those who seek help to die, in a judgment that put 'sanctity of human life' at its centre; and which, as an aside, denied the existence of non-voluntary medical euthanasia that is evidenced in Part IV [124].

Comment on Chapter 5

Assisted Dying and the CPS

RA DUFF

As Andrew Sanders makes depressingly clear,[1] those who are considering whether to ask another for help in ending their lives, or whether to respond to such requests by providing such help, face a still uncertain, and unsatisfactory, legal position. If they provide assistance to another's suicide, their conduct satisfies the definition of a criminal offence – an offence definition that allows no room for a defence based on, for instance, the earnestness and rationality of the request to which they respond;[2] if what they do amounts to causing the requester's death, their conduct satisfies the definition of criminal homicide.[3] Someone seeking such assistance might think that the law that criminalises it violates the 'right to respect for … private and family life' declared in Article 8(1) of the European Convention on Human Rights (ECHR): the ECtHR has held that 'the right of an individual to decide how and when to end his life … is one aspect of the right to respect for private life',[4] and English courts have accepted that the formal criminalisation of assisting suicide 'represents an interference with' that right.[5] But the courts will not help such a person by declaring that law to be incompatible with the ECHR (or with the English Human Rights Act 1998): for Article 8(2) of the ECHR allows interference with that right if it 'is necessary in a democratic society … for the protection of health or morals, or for the protection of the rights and freedoms of others'; and the courts have held that such purposes as 'protection of the weak

[1] A Sanders, 'The CPS, Policy-Making and Assisted Dying: Towards a "Freedom" Approach', ch 5 of this volume.

[2] Suicide Act 1961, s 2.

[3] The position in Scotland, which has not formally criminalised assisting suicide as such, is different: the assister might be guilty of homicide, if it can be shown that her conduct 'caused' the other person's death, ie (according to the Lord Advocate) whether 'there was a direct causal link between the actings of the accused and the deceased's death', so that her conduct was 'a significant contributory factor to the death' (Letter to Health and Sport Committee considering the Assisted Suicide (Scotland) Bill (Scottish Parliament ASB 178)); but in *Ross v Lord Advocate* [2016] CSIH 12, the Court of Session refused a request to require the Lord Advocate to publish guidelines – partly on the grounds that the law in Scotland was entirely clear, and that the kind of assistance involved in such cases as *Pretty* and *Purdy* was not criminal under Scots law.

[4] See, eg, *Haas v Switzerland* (2011) 53 EHRR 3, [51]; *Conway* [2017] EWHC 2447, [11].

[5] See, eg, *Nicklinson* [2013] HRLR 36.

and vulnerable', and of the moral value of 'the sanctity of life', can thus make such interference legitimate.[6] Someone seeking help, especially if that help would involve killing them rather than helping them to kill themselves (which is not to say that that is a sharp distinction), can thus look for no support from the law; any assistance she can find will need to be, to put it mildly, discreet, from someone willing to commit a crime and to face the prospect of prosecution. If, however, the assistance is relatively minor, and is provided out of compassion by a friend or loved one (rather than by a medical professional), she and her assister might find reassurance in the 'guidelines' issued by the Director of Public Prosecutions, as required by the Law Lords' decision in *Purdy*:[7] for if the situation, and the help provided, fit enough of the 'factors tending against prosecution', and none or few enough of those 'tending in favour of prosecution', they can expect that the DPP will decide that a prosecution is not 'in the public interest'.

For those who believe, as Sanders does, that 'assisted dying' is under certain circumstances morally permissible, and should be legally permissible, this position is very far from satisfactory. Those who need assistance in carrying out what might be an entirely rational choice to end their lives are hindered from securing the (competent, efficient) help that they need; those who would provide such help are likewise hindered by the uncertain prospect of prosecution; those who are 'weak and vulnerable' are still in danger of having their lives shortened by doctors who quietly subvert the law by hastening death. The DPP's guidelines could be improved, but they could not be made fit for *this* purpose; the only satisfactory way forward is a formal reform of the law to make statutory, institutional provision for 'assisted voluntary dying' – though the prospects for that are rather dim, given the repeated parliamentary defeats suffered by proposals to legalise some form of assisted dying.[8]

My aim in this brief comment is not to criticise Sanders' proposals for institutional reform, or to revisit the general debate about the legalisation of 'assisted dying'. I am inclined to agree with the central thrust of his argument; and the experience of other jurisdictions undermines the 'slippery slope' or 'floodgate opening' objections to which critics of legalisation often appeal. But I want to focus on our present position, in which the prospects for legislative reform are dim, and on the role of the DPP in issuing and applying these kinds of 'guidelines' – whether in their present form or in a revised form that took some account of Sanders' objections. How are we to understand the guidelines? What role can such guidelines properly play in what purports to be a parliamentary democracy?

On one reading, the guidelines mark the extent to which the DPP has in effect been rewriting the law, thus creating a significant gap between the formal and

[6] See, eg, *Conway* [2017] EWHC 2447, and further ECtHR and English cases cited there.

[7] Crown Prosecution Service, *Policy for Prosecutors in Respect of Cases of Encouraging or Assisting Suicide*; see *Purdy* [2009] 3 WLR 403.

[8] See recently the fate of the Assisted Dying (No. 2) Bill in the House of Commons in September 2015; also, in Scotland, the fate of the Assisted Suicide (Scotland) Bill in 2015.

the substantive criminalisation of assisting suicide.[9] Formally speaking, every act of aiding another's suicide is criminal, under section 2 of the 1961 Act; every such act renders the agent formally liable to prosecution, conviction and punishment. Substantively speaking, however, only a subset of such acts are to be treated as criminal, and to be in practice liable to prosecution; the guidelines serve to indicate which kinds of formally criminal act will not be treated, substantively, as criminal. That is a reading that both the DPP and the courts have formally denied. The guidelines do not, the document itself insisted, 'decriminalise the offence of encouraging or assisting suicide'.[10] The policy is indeed, officially, a 'policy for prosecutors', and thus belongs, formally, among the 'rules for courts' that tell legal officials how to deal *ex post* with those who have or may have committed offences, rather than among the 'rules for citizens' that give us *ex ante* notice of what we may or may not do.[11] The courts have also been concerned to make clear that changing the law is a matter for parliament, not for them or for the DPP.[12] On the other hand, when the Law Lords explained why the DPP should be required to publish his *Policy*, they were prone to talk as if the point of the *Policy* was precisely to clarify the law in a way that would enable citizens to plan their actions, and to know what they can do 'without breaking the law':[13] the DPP was thus to clarify, it seems, just what the law (as interpreted and applied by him) required of citizens or permitted them to do.

Read as an exercise in substantive legal reform, the *Policy* is of course problematic from a constitutional point of view. Even had the consultation process for the guidelines been less perfunctory; even had it involved some explicit discussion of, and had the *Policy* itself made clear, the principles that underpinned the factors tending for or against prosecution; even had it been a model of deliberative democracy in action:[14] it surely involved a usurpation of the legislature's role – a usurpation aggravated by the legislature's own explicit refusal to legalise any form of assisted suicide.

There are other ways of reading the *Policy* that do not raise this kind of worry (and that also make sense of the way in which the non-professional status of the assister bears on the decision whether to prosecute). Instead of reading it as an exercise in substantive law reform, we could, for instance, read it as laying down guidelines for the exercise of discretionary mercy: what the assister does is indeed a criminal wrong for which there is neither justification nor excuse; but it would

[9] On formal and substantive criminalisation, see, eg N Lacey, 'Historicising Criminalisation: Conceptual and Empirical Issues' (2009) 72 *MLR* 936.

[10] DPP, *Policy for Prosecutors in Respect of Cases of Encouraging or Assisting Suicide* (2010, updated 2014) [6].

[11] See, eg, P Alldridge, 'Rules for Courts and Rules for Citizens' (1990) 10 *OJLS* 487.

[12] See, eg, *Purdy* [2009] 3 WLR 403, [26]; *Nicklinson* [2013] HRLR 36, [126], [134]. Consistently with this insistence, the factors tending for or against prosecution are formally described, in the *Policy*, as factors bearing on whether prosecution would be 'in the public interest' – not on whether the offence had been committed.

[13] *Purdy* [40] (Lord Hope; see also [46]); see also [59], [65] (Lady Hale).

[14] See Sanders' comments on the process in his chapter.

be harsh or inhuman to insist on prosecuting, for instance, someone who reluctantly helped a loved one end his own life, given the difficulty of her situation, the emotional impact it must have had on her, the loss that she has suffered, and so on. Or we could alternatively see the *Policy* as (implicitly) working towards a compassion-based excuse for assisting another's suicide: given the admirable motive of the agent who acts from compassion, as well as the way in which compassion (like other powerful emotions) can destabilise practical reasoning, we should not blame someone who is led by compassion to assist a suicide – although it is still wrong to do so. On this reading, the *Policy* recognises that such assistance can mark a mistaken but reasonable, non-culpable, judgment about what one should do: it is wrong to assist the suicide, but someone moved by compassion for a loved one's plight (as one should be moved) might misjudge, in a not unreasonable way, what she should do.[15] All of these considerations can apply to those who are close to the would-be suicide, and (likely to be) moved by compassion for him: but they do not apply to medical professionals – not because medical professionals will not be motivated by compassion (they surely should be), but because given their training and their experience, along with the lack of close personal or emotional ties to the would-be suicide, they should be better able to think clearly and appropriately about what should be done.

However, I will not pursue these alternative readings of the *Policy* here: I will not ask whether they are plausible readings of what could have been intended. Instead, I want to discuss a third possible reading (though without asking how plausible it is as an interpretation of the *Policy* as produced by the DPP), according to which the *Policy*, and the DPP's use of the discretion as to whether to prosecute, mark not a rewriting or revision of the law; nor a sympathetic or merciful mitigation of its stringency, or a recognition of factors that might exculpate the commission of a genuine criminal wrong: but an ongoing process of working out a context-sensitive determination of the law's substantive meaning,[16] under the (implicit if not explicit) aegis of a (misleadingly titled) '*De Minimis*' principle.[17]

> The Court shall dismiss a prosecution if, having regard to the nature of the conduct charged to constitute an offense and the nature of the attendant circumstances, it finds that the defendant's conduct … did not actually cause or threaten the harm or evil

[15] See further RA Duff, 'Criminal Responsibility and the Emotions: If Fear and Anger Can Exculpate, Why Not Compassion?' (2015) 58 *Inquiry* 189. Note that on this reading the *Policy* does not 'decriminalise the offence of encouraging or assisting suicide' (see n 10): such assistance is still both formally and substantively criminal, but some of those who provide it should be excused for doing so.

[16] On 'determinations' and their importance, see DN MacCormick, 'Reconstruction after Deconstruction: A Response to CLS' (1990) 10 *OJLS* 539, 548–9.

[17] See DN Husak, 'The *De Minimis* "Defense" to Criminal Liability' in Husak, *The Philosophy of Criminal Law: Selected Essays* (OUP, 2010) 362; M B Valentine, 'Defense Categories and the (Category-Defying) De Minimis Defense' (2017) 11 *Criminal Law and Philosophy* 545. The title is misleading because, as we will see, the principle is not concerned only with trivial instances of criminal conduct. A further question, which I do not have space to pursue here, is whether, if a *De Minimis* principle is sound, it should be included in the formal criminal law (as the Model Penal Code includes it).

> sought to be prevented by the law defining the offense or did so only to an extent too trivial to warrant the condemnation of conviction.[18]

The suggestion is that what the Model Penal Code requires of courts, we should also require of our prosecutors.

Sometimes this expectation is made explicit, if not in the statutory legislation itself, at least in the legislature. A nice example is provided by the Bill that became the Sexual Offences Act 2003. During the parliamentary debate, critics pointed out that sections 9 and 13 criminalised consensual sexual activity between young people aged fifteen – which, they thought, was absurd. A minister reassured these critics that that was not the Bill's 'intention', and would not be its 'effect': 'we shall be able to trust the Crown Prosecution Service to ensure that that intention is followed'.[19] The government was asking Parliament to enact a statute whose offence definitions were avowedly over-broad, defining as criminal types of conduct that there was no intention to treat as criminal; and to rely on prosecutors to use their discretion to put that intention into effect. Suppose that two fifteen year olds engage in 'sexual touching', thus satisfying the definition of the offence of 'sexual activity with a child'. The matter comes to the attention of the police, who (perhaps from moralistic enthusiasm) send the case to the CPS; the prosecutor, in line with the government's expressed intention, decides not to prosecute. If this is a matter of CPS policy, as it must be, given the government's (and by implication the legislature's) clear intention, we should say that such sexual activity is criminal in the books, but is not (really) criminal: it was formally criminalised, but is not substantively criminalised, or has been substantively decriminalised, because it does not involve the mischief at which this law is aimed.[20]

In other cases, including that of assisting suicide, the DPP and the CPS have no such explicit steer from the legislature, or from those who proposed the relevant legislation, about when and in what ways they should exercise their discretion over whether to prosecute.[21] Nor will it always be clear (or even as clear as it was in the case of the Sexual Offences Bill, which was not wholly clear) just what 'harm or evil', what 'mischief', is the target of the statute. It will be a matter for rational

[18] Model Penal Code §2.12.

[19] Hansard vol 409, 15 July 2003, col 248; Paul Goggins, a Home Office Minister. But see AP Simester et al, *Simester and Sullivan's Criminal Law: Theory and Doctrine*, 6th edn (Hart, 2016), 496–8, on the extent to which the CPS has shown this trust to be misplaced; see also *G* [2008] UKHL 37.

[20] It is arguable that non-prosecution in such a case should be grounded not in the 'public interest' test, but in the 'evidential' test: the prosecutor should decide not that, although there is sufficient evidence of a (genuine) crime, 'public interest' factors external to the criminal law militate against prosecution, but that there is no evidence that a real crime (conduct involving the mischief at which the law is aimed) has been committed. See J Rogers, 'The Role of the Public Prosecutor in Applying and Developing the Substantive Criminal Law', in RA Duff et al (eds), *The Constitution of the Criminal Law* (OUP, 2013) 53.

[21] But an expectation that such discretion will be especially important in the context of assisted suicide, and that it will at least quite often be used to decide against prosecution, is suggested by the inclusion of subsection 4 in s 2 of the Suicide Act 1961: 'no proceedings shall be instituted for an offence under this section except by or with the consent of the Director of Public Prosecutions'.

reconstruction or interpretation – a task which will become especially hard when there is a diversity of possible accounts of the mischief, as there clearly is in the case of assisted dying. If we appeal to 'the sanctity of life', as some supporters of the existing law clearly do, we will think (or might think, depending on how we interpret 'the sanctity of life') that the mischief at which the law is aimed is implicated whenever a life is intentionally taken, and thus whenever such an intentional taking of life (one's own or another's) is assisted. If instead we focus on autonomy, and the rights discerned by the courts in Article 8 of the ECHR, we will tell a different story, about the protection of autonomy (a story which will include, as Sanders points out, a concern to enable those whose autonomous choice is to end their lives to carry that choice through, but also a concern to protect the autonomy of those who are 'weak and vulnerable'), and we will think that in a range of cases the relevant mischief is not implicated by someone who assists a would-be suicide. If a DPP is to apply a '*De Minimis*' principle, how then should she deliberate, when faced by such conflicting conceptions of the relevant mischief, generating such different conclusions? Should she, perhaps, embark on a consultation process – though one very different from that in which the DPP actually engaged for the *Policy*, since it would require not just (if at all) a listing of potential 'factors' for or against prosecution, but an articulation and discussion of these competing conceptions of the mischief? But that might look again like an attempt to pre-empt Parliament, and to come down on one side of a debate that Parliament itself clearly refused to settle. Or should she play safe, and decline to prosecute only in those cases that clearly did not involve the relevant mischief on any (plausible, 'reasonable') interpretation of the law[22] – which would again lead her to a very cautious *Policy*?

But why should we even think of asking prosecutors to exercise this kind of discretion – to decide not just whether it is in the public interest to prosecute a provable crime, but whether what fits the law's formal definition of a criminal offence is 'really', or in substance, a crime? Surely we should instead expect legislatures to define offences with sufficient precision to avoid having to rely on this kind of official discretion – given all the familiar dangers of official discretion that is often exercised 'discreetly', and that can be hard to make accountable? Here is where a further question about law reform arises from Sanders' discussion of the CPS and assisted dying. Is this kind of discretion something that we should recognise as a valuable (as well as unavoidable) aspect of the criminal law – in which case we need to ask how it can be guided, controlled, exercised, and rendered appropriately accountable? Or is it an inherently dangerous (and undemocratic) power, that we should seek to minimise even if we cannot eliminate it altogether – which might point us towards something more like the 'legality principle' by which prosecutors elsewhere in Europe are said to be bound, requiring them to prosecute whenever there is sufficient evidence of what the law defines as a crime (although it

[22] Or cases that involved that mischief 'only to an extent too trivial to warrant the condemnation of conviction'.

is not clear how far that legality principle in fact prevails in other jurisdictions)?[23] Such a principle at least creates a strong presumption in favour of prosecution, and resists the idea that prosecutors should generally exercise wide discretion in deciding which provable cases to pursue.[24]

How far we should aspire to a legality principle of prosecution depends in part on how far it is realistic to expect lawmakers so to craft criminal statutes that they capture exactly the mischief at which they are aimed – that they are neither over-inclusive nor radically under-inclusive; but it also depends on how far we should see the enterprise of substantive criminalisation, understood as the enterprise of determining which kinds of conduct should be seen, censured and treated as criminal, as one for the legislature, or how far we should see it as an essentially collaborative enterprise in which legislatures and other official bodies (including the police and prosecutors) and lay citizens have a role to play in collectively determining the substantive content of their criminal law. That is not a question I can pursue here:[25] but suppose we think that prosecutors should play the kind of role I sketched above – that part of their role should be to work out, in context-sensitive ways, more precise determinations of the wrongs that criminal statutes define in inevitably imprecise and potentially over-inclusive ways, and to identify more precisely and contextually the kinds of conduct that do involve the mischief at which the law is aimed. What kinds of reform might this require to the institutional structure and practices of prosecution?

It would require, first, that legislatures do more to identify the mischief at which a criminal statute is aimed. This is not to say that they should be expected to define it precisely (for if they could do that, there would be no need for the kind of prosecutorial discretion we are concerned with here), but that they should at least, in the preamble to each statute, give some indication of the relevant mischief. That would, of course, cause some problems in cases in which legislators with very different views on what the relevant mischief is can still agree on the terms of a statute – for instance if those who would appeal to the sanctity of life, and those who would appeal to the need to protect the weak and vulnerable, can still agree that voluntary euthanasia should be criminal: but if people are to be prosecuted, convicted, and so condemned for a supposed wrong, as those convicted in our criminal courts are, they should be able to know what that wrong is.[26]

[23] See, eg, M Damaška, 'The Reality of Prosecutorial Discretion: Comments on a German Monograph' (1981) 29 *American Journal of Comparative Law* 119; A Perrodet, 'The Public Prosecutor', in M Delmas-Marty and JR Spencer (eds), *European Criminal Procedures* (CUP, 2002) 415; S Boyne, 'German Prosecutors and the Rechtsstaat', in M Langer and D Sklansky (eds), *Prosecutors and Democracy: A Cross-National Study* (CUP, 2017) 138.

[24] However, that way of putting the matter risks begging a question noted above (n 20): does a '*De Minimis*' principle bear on the question of whether the (properly understood) evidential test is satisfied; or on whether it is in 'the public interest' to prosecute a case in which that test is satisfied?

[25] But see RA Duff, 'A Criminal Law We Can Call Our Own?' (2017) 111 *Northwestern University Law Review* 1491; also *The Realm of Criminal Law* (OUP, 2018) chs 1.7, 5.

[26] This would also have the further salutary effect of imposing a more explicit burden on legislatures to justify themselves, and thus of providing a clearer focus for critical scrutiny of legislation.

Secondly, it would require clearer guidance for prosecutors in exercising their discretion, and also some way of making that exercise suitably accountable. The former would involve revising the code for prosecutors;[27] the latter would involve working out procedures through which both decisions to prosecute and decisions not to prosecute can be challenged. It might be said that we already have such procedures: decisions to prosecute are in effect challenged in court, when the burden of proof puts the prosecution to the test by requiring it to prove the charge (to prove first, that is, that there is a case to answer, which is also to justify the prosecution); and it is possible for an interested party to challenge a decision not to prosecute through an independent review,[28] or through judicial review (of prosecutorial policies for particular types of crime, or of decisions about particular cases). Two questions arise about such provisions. First, who should have the standing to seek judicial review: should it only be the alleged victim (or someone acting on her or his behalf), at least when the review sought is of an individual decision; or should any concerned citizen have standing, on the grounds that crimes, as public wrongs, are every citizen's business?[29] Secondly, what standard should the court apply in reviewing the decision? English courts are very reluctant to interfere with prosecutorial discretion: an application can succeed only if the court finds the prosecutor's decision to be one that no reasonable prosecutor would have adopted.[30] As for challenging decisions to prosecute, this should be done – to make clear what the challenge is – either before the trial proper starts, on the grounds that a '*De Minimis*' finding constitutes a bar to trial; or, perhaps, as a version of 'no case to answer': for the key claim is that even if the prosecution proves beyond reasonable doubt all the 'factual' claims made in the indictment, even if it proves that the defendant's conduct did satisfy the formal definition of the offence in question, this would not prove that the defendant had committed a mischief of the kind at which the law is aimed. Thus the case is not like that in which the defendant denies, or challenges the prosecution to prove, that he acted in the way that the indictment alleges; nor like one in which he admits the commission of the offence but offers a defence: it is a case in which, he claims, even on the facts alleged by the prosecution, there was no (genuine, substantive) criminal wrong for which he could be called to answer.[31]

I cannot pursue these issues here. My suggestion is, however, that we should embrace, rather than shrink from, this kind of prosecutorial discretion:[32]

[27] Crown Prosecution Service, *Code for Crown Prosecutors* (2013).

[28] See CPS, *Victims' Right to Review Scheme* (Legal Guidance, updated 2016).

[29] See *Metropolitan Police Commissioner ex parte Blackburn (No.1)* [1969] 2 QB 118.

[30] *Associated Provincial Picture Houses v Wednesbury Corporation* [1948] 1 KB 223.

[31] Compare the provision in Scots law for a pre-trial plea challenging the 'relevancy' of the charge – arguing, that is, that the charge 'did not libel a crime known to the law of Scotland' (see eg *Khaliq v HM Advocate* 1984 JC 23; Criminal Procedure (Scotland) Act 1975, s 76(1)(a)).

[32] A discretion that should certainly be, in Dworkinian terms, 'weak' rather than 'strong': RM Dworkin, 'The Model of Rules' (1967/8) 35 *University of Chicago Law Review* 14.

discretion, that is, to determine whether conduct that satisfies the legal definition of a criminal offence really does involve the mischief at which the relevant law is aimed; and to refrain from prosecution if it does not. But if we are to do this, we need to think about ways of reforming the institution and practice of prosecution so that the exercise of that discretion can be suitably guided, and rendered suitably accountable.

6

How Should the Criminal Law Respond to the 'Special Status' of Children?

HEATHER KEATING

In both international and domestic law, recognition is given to the principle that children are not to be treated as if they were adults; and their 'special status' is recognised in a myriad of ways. In international law, for example, the United Nations Convention on the Rights of the Child is the world's most widely ratified human rights convention and it outlines the ways in which governments and individual adults should give effect to the provisory, protective and participatory rights of children identified in the Convention. In our domestic law, for example, local authorities have statutory duties to protect children from abuse and neglect;[1] laws provide for their (compulsory) education;[2] children may be able to consent to medical treatment but not to decline it,[3] and they are precluded from engaging in a very wide range of activities until they are of (different) identified ages.[4]

The substantive criminal law and justice system's recognition of this principle has evolved over hundreds of years. The presumption of *doli incapax*, for example, developed in the fourteenth century and required courts to be satisfied that children who were accused of offences knew that their behaviour was wrong and not merely naughty.[5] A minimum age of criminal responsibility became an established part of the common law during the seventeenth century, when it was set at seven years old.[6] A specialist tribunal – the juvenile court – was created at the

[1] Children Act 1989.

[2] Education Act 1996.

[3] *Gillick* v *West Norfolk and Wisbech Area Health Authority and Department of Health and Social Security* [1986] AC 112; *Re R (A Minor) (Wardship: Consent to Treatment)* [1992] Fam 11; *Re W (A Minor) Consent to Medical Treatment)* 1993 1 FLR 1.

[4] See further, C McDiarmid, 'After the Age of Criminal Responsibility; A Defence for Children who Offend' (2016) 67 *NILQ* 327, 333.

[5] Originally the presumption applied to children under the age of 12. It was extended to the age of 14 in the seventeenth century. *Gorrie* (1919) 83 JP 136.

[6] Although de Bracton's thirteenth-century treatise considered that children below the age of ten would lack mens rea, it did not set a minimum age of criminal responsibility (E Delmage, 'The Minimum Age of Criminal Responsibility: A Medico-Legal Perspective' 13 *Youth Justice* 102, 102,

start of the twentieth century.[7] Judges have frequently acknowledged the significance of the principle: in the House of Lords, Lord Steyn commented that ignoring the special position of children in the criminal justice system is not acceptable in a modern civil society,[8] and Lord Diplock famously stated that 'to require old heads on young shoulders is inconsistent with the law's compassion to human infirmity'.[9] The European Court of Human Rights has emphasised the importance of the criminal justice system's different treatment of children and young people given their 'special situation'.[10]

At first sight, therefore, all of this would suggest that the recognition of the special status of children is deeply entrenched in our law and that reform is not needed. This chapter contends that this is very far from true. A full discussion of this issue would require not only an examination of the substantive criminal law but also for an examination of the entirety of the youth justice system, from initial interactions with the police through to (deteriorating) conditions in youth offender institutions.[11] However, this chapter does not nor could seek to conduct the type of broad assessment undertaken, notably, by Charlie Taylor's review of the youth justice system in 2016.[12] Rather, it argues the case for reform to three areas of the substantive criminal law: the age of criminal responsibility, fitness to plead as applied to children, and the creation of a defence of developmental immaturity. It is argued that these are three key areas where the law does not reflect appropriately the special status of children and their immaturity. In doing so, it takes a multi-disciplinary approach, drawing upon liberal theories of responsibility as well as, for example, findings from neuroscience and child development studies, international conventions and the law in other jurisdictions.

To say that the subject matter is controversial is an understatement: how the criminal law responds to children's harmful behaviour is not some arcane area of law about which only a few cognoscenti might become passionate. In particular, the question of whether the age of criminal responsibility should be increased polarises opinion: between those for whom the case for reform is overwhelming and those for whom any increase would, for example, be a road to anarchy, a failure to recognise that young children are capable of evil or an unpardonable insult to the memory of James Bulger.[13] Somewhere in the midst of this would

citing G Woodbine, *Four Thirteenth Century Law Tracts (De Legibus et Consuetudinibus* Angliae (Yale University Press, 1910)). It is unclear whether there was a minimum age below which children could not be tried before the 17th century.

[7] Children Act 1908.The Criminal Justice Act 1991 replaced Juvenile courts with Youth courts.

[8] *G* [2004] 1 AC 1034, [53].

[9] *DPP v Camplin* [1978] AC 705, 717.

[10] *S and Marper v UK* (2009) 48 EHRR 50, [124].

[11] See, eg, Her Majesty's Inspectorate of Prisons, *Annual Report 2016–17* (HC 208, 2017) 61–69, reporting increasing levels of violence, more children expressing safety fears, increasing time spent locked in cells etc.

[12] Ministry of Justice, *Review of the Youth Justice System* (Cm 9298, 2016), 'Charlie Taylor Review'.

[13] James Bulger (a child of two years old) was abducted and brutally killed by Robert Thompson and Jon Venables (both aged ten years old at the time). The killing and subsequent trial sent shock waves

be those who acknowledge the arguments for reform but take the view that there are ways in which the youth justice system can positively assist vulnerable young defendants – or that reform is politically unachievable. While most attention has focused upon the question of the age at which children should be held accountable for their actions, it is likely that one of the additional reforms argued for here – the introduction of a defence of developmental immaturity – would also divide opinion.[14]

I. The Current Law

In order to make the case for reform this section opens with an explanation of the current law on the age of criminal responsibility and fitness to plead. It also considers briefly the defences which are open to a young defendant and the absence of a defence of developmental immaturity.

A. The Age of Criminal Responsibility

Section 50 of the Children and Young Persons Act 1933 states that 'it shall be conclusively presumed that no child under the age of ten years can be guilty of any offence'. This provision, which exempts such children from criminal liability based upon their age at the time of the offence, was last amended over 50 years ago, when in 1963 the minimum age of criminal responsibility was raised from eight years old.[15] It is remarkable that in the ever-changing context of the youth justice system, this fundamental aspect has remained unchanged although the presumption of *doli incapax* has been removed. This presumption, as noted in the introduction, required the court to establish that a defendant under the age of 14 knew that his or her actions were seriously wrong. It was certainly open to criticism but the reasons given for reform, including the advent of universal education, that children now grow up more quickly, and that conviction no longer led to punishment, do not withstand much scrutiny. The abolition also

through society which continue to reverberate. The boys were convicted of murder at Preston Crown Court in November 1993.

[14] See, eg, the differing views expressed by legal practitioners in relation to the need and desirability of such a reform in K Fitz-Gibbon, 'Protections for Children Before the Law: An Empirical Analysis of the Age of Criminal Responsibility, the Abolition of Doli Incapax and the Merits of a Developmental Immaturity Defence in England and Wales' (2016) 16 *Journal of Criminology and Criminal Justice* 391. See also Law Commission, *Criminal Liability: Insanity and Automatism* (Discussion Paper, 2013) [5.129].

[15] Children and Young Persons Act 1963, ignoring for these purposes the increase to 14 made by s 4 of the Children and Young Persons Act 1969, which was never implemented, the provision being repealed by s 72 of the Criminal Justice Act 1991. At common law the age of criminal responsibility was seven years old.

took place with virtually no evaluation of the impact of doing so.[16] Removing the presumption, however, has left an unfortunate legacy that will be explored shortly: the knowledge of wrong test has not assisted serious reform discussions. Two attempts by Lord Dholakia to raise the age of criminal responsibility to 12 years old by means of private member's Bills have not gone further than relatively short debates in the House of Lords.[17] Although a third attempt is currently underway, given the government's opposition to the Bills, there is little reason to hope that this Bill will fare any better.[18] It is also very disappointing (although not surprising given the political sensitivity of the issue) that the Law Commission, in devising its thirteenth programme of law reform, has decided not to follow its own suggestion to 'look afresh at the age of criminal responsibility'.[19] Nevertheless, for the reasons to which the chapter will turn in Part II, reform is still a pressing issue.

B. Fitness to Plead

The vast majority of cases involving children are tried in the Youth Court, trial in the Crown Court being reserved for serious crimes. There is a long-standing procedure for establishing a defendant's fitness to plead at the time of the trial in the Crown Court.[20] There is no such equivalent procedure for trials in the Youth Court, despite the fact that Article 6 of the European Convention on Human Rights enshrines the right to a fair trial, which includes the right to effective participation, and despite the compelling evidence that participation difficulties are common in the Youth Court.[21] Arthur has argued rightly that this 'represents a fundamental deficiency in the youth justice system'.[22]

[16] During the Committee stage of the Crime and Disorder Bill, James Clappison MP rightly pointed out that, the government not having conducted research on the numbers of children acquitted as a result of the presumption, 'they had no idea how it operated' (Standing Committee B on 12 May 1998). The presumption was abolished by the Crime and Disorder Act 1998, s 34. The presumption may not have prevented the prosecution of many children but it was symbolically important in recognising that childhood is a process of development. See generally, H Keating, 'The "Responsibility" of Children in the Criminal Law' (2007) 19 *Child and Family Law Quarterly* 183 and S Bandalli, 'Abolition of the Presumption of Doli Incapax and the Criminalisation of Young Children' (1998) 37 *Howard Journal* 114.

[17] In 2013 (Hansard HL Deb vol 749, 8 November 2013) and 2016 (Hansard HL Deb vol 768, 29 January 2016).

[18] Age of Criminal Responsibility Bill 2017–2019. The Bill had its second reading in the House of Lords on 8 September 2017; time has yet to be allocated for the Committee stage (Hansard HL Deb, vol 783, col 2187–2211).

[19] Law Commission, *Unfitness to Plead* (Law Com No 364, 2016), [7.54].

[20] Criminal Procedure (Insanity) Act 1964, ss 4 and 4A.

[21] See Law Commission, (n19), [7.33–7.51] and below at Part II where developmental research is considered.

[22] R Arthur, 'Giving Effect to Young People's Right to Participate Effectively in Criminal Proceedings' (2016) 28 *Child and Family Law Quarterly* 223, 224.

There are few options open to a judge in the Youth Court who is concerned about the ability of a child or young person to participate effectively in the trial. The judge may make a hospital order without a conviction if satisfied that the defendant 'did the act or made the omission charged'. However, this provision can only be invoked if the defendant is aged 16 or over, if the individual is suffering from mental disorder, and if the order is the most suitable disposal.[23] As Arthur notes, this will have no application to a young defendant with a learning disability, unless it is associated with 'abnormally aggressive or seriously irresponsible conduct', nor will it apply to the many young defendants 'whose difficulties may arise as a result of communication impairment'.[24]

The alternative option for a judge in the Youth Court is a stay of prosecution as an abuse of process. This rarely happens for a number of reasons. First, according to Smith LJ, consideration should have been given prior to the institution of criminal proceedings as to whether proceedings under the Children Act 1989 would be more appropriate.[25] In addition, the Youth Court sees itself as a specialist tribunal which is equipped to deal with children with participative difficulties,[26] and if the proceedings are stayed the court cannot make any disposal. Yet it is a denial of justice and a potential breach of Article 6 for trials of young defendants to proceed so as to secure a suitable disposal if they have significant participation difficulties. In such a context, a stay of prosecution is the lesser of the evils: separate child protection proceedings could then be initiated if needed.

It has to be borne in mind that the absence of a procedure to ascertain fitness is being exacerbated by the increasing lack of representation for defendants following changes to legal aid. It would, moreover, become even more of a problem if Charlie Taylor's (otherwise welcome) recommendation that there should be a presumption against trial in the Crown court were to be implemented: even more serious offences would be tried in the Youth Court.[27] It is clear that reform is needed so that a statutory scheme for assessing capacity to participate effectively is established.

In the Crown Court the test for determining fitness was established in the nineteenth century in *Pritchard*[28] and was further developed in *M*: the defendant must be capable of understanding the charge(s), deciding whether to plead guilty, challenging jurors, instructing solicitors and counsel and giving evidence.[29]

[23] Mental Health Act 1983, s 37(3). Evidence from two medical practitioners is required.

[24] Arthur, (n 22), 233.

[25] *DPP v P* [2007] EWHC 936 (Admin) [51], [58]. It was regarded as appropriate to stay proceedings in exceptional cases only.

[26] *R (P) v West London Youth Court* [2005] EWHC 2583 (Admin). See further, Arthur, (n 22), 235–36.

[27] Charlie Taylor's Review, (n 12). The earlier Carlile Report into the operation and effectiveness of the youth justice system also recommended that appearances in the Crown court should be the rare exception for those under the age of eighteen. *An Independent Parliamentarians' Inquiry into the Operation and Effectiveness of the Youth Justice System* (2014) iv ('the Carlile Report'). The Law Commission 'strongly agree[s] 'in principle … that there be a clear presumption that all child defendants are dealt with in the youth court' (Law Commission, (n 19), [7.197]).

[28] (1836) 7 C&P 303.

[29] [2003] All ER (D) 199.

Adult and child defendants with significant learning difficulties have been found fit to plead. In *SC v UK* the defendant, an 11-year-old boy had been charged with attempted robbery.[30] He had a limited attention span and the intellectual ability of a child aged six to eight years old. He appeared not to understand the role of the jury nor that a custodial sentence could follow if found guilty. Despite this, the medical expert who examined him concluded he was fit to plead (if proceedings were explained to him in a way he would understand). After his conviction the case was taken to the European Court of Human Rights where the UK was found to have breached Article 6. While the Court accepted the government's argument that Article 6 did not require that a child should understand or be capable of understanding *every* point, it stated:

> However, 'effective participation' in this context presupposes that the accused has a broad understanding of the trial process and of what is at stake for him or her, including the significance of any penalty which may be imposed. It means that he or she, if necessary with assistance … should be able to understand the general thrust of what is said in court. The defendant should be able to follow what is said by the prosecution witnesses and, if represented, to explain to his own lawyers his version of events, point out any statements with which he disagrees and make them aware of any facts which should be put forward in his defence.[31]

Judges are required to take the child defendant's age, maturity and development (intellectual and emotional) into account when considering arrangements for the trial. The Practice Direction states that 'all possible steps should be taken to assist the defendant to understand and participate in the proceedings and that the ordinary trial process should, so far as necessary, be adapted to meet those ends'.[32] However, important although these safeguards are, it is noteworthy that they were first introduced in 2000[33] and, thus, they did not prevent the UK being found in breach in *SC v UK*. They should not be seen as a substitute for a fuller assessment of the ability to participate effectively.

C. No Developmental Immaturity Defence

As the law stands, once a child reaches the age of 10 (and assuming no fitness issues arise at Crown Court trials), there are very few concessions made in the substantive criminal law which reflect the 'special status' of the young defendant. If a child or young person is charged with murder and pleads the partial defence of loss of control, the jury is required to take his or her age (and sex) into account in determining whether another person might have reacted in the same or

[30] [2005] 1 FCR 347.
[31] At [25].
[32] *Practice Direction (Criminal: Consolidated)* [2002] 3 All ER 904.
[33] Following the finding that the UK had been in breach of Article 6 for the manner of the trial of Thompson and Venables (n 13): *V and T v UK* (2000) 30 EHRR (ECHR) 121.

similar way.[34] There is, in addition, the partial defence of diminished responsibility to murder, which is available to defendants young and old.[35] Although there may be cases when this is available to a young defendant who has an abnormality of mental functioning arising from a recognised medical condition, the 'normal' developmental immaturity of a child would not satisfy this requirement.[36] The effect of the defence is that a 40 year-old defendant with a mental age of 10 may well be able to plead diminished responsibility (having a recognised medical condition) but 10 year-old defendant with a mental age of 10 could not, appearing to suggest that the law requires more from children than from adults.[37] But there is no general or even partial defence of developmental immaturity. If the arguments now to be considered are persuasive then reform is needed.

II. Why We 'Shouldn't Require Old Heads on Young Shoulders'

Lord Diplock's reference to law's compassion for human 'infirmity' may well not be the most apposite description of the significance of youth. Youth is not an illness and so we have to look beyond the most obvious meaning of this phrase. It is thought that a distinction being drawn between child and adult defendants was initially to save children, who might not understand fully what they had done, from the very severe punishments (including capital punishment and whipping) which awaited those who were found guilty.[38] Indeed, hundreds of years after Blackstone, the 'fact' that severe punishments no longer existed was given as a reason for the abolition of the presumption of *doli incapax* in the early 1990s.[39]

However, the reference to children, by dint of youth, not fully understanding what they had done, provides a way forward to explore some of the key reasons (it does not claim to be exhaustive) why the criminal law should not hold children responsible or, putting it another way, why we should not require or expect 'old heads on young shoulders'.

[34] Coroners and Justice Act 2009, s 54(1). Another example is the Sexual Offences Act 2003, s 13, which provides for a lower maximum penalty of 5 years' imprisonment, for offenders aged under 18 who are found guilty of anything which would be an offence under ss 9–13.

[35] Homicide Act 1957, s 2.

[36] See further, McDiarmid (n 4) 335. As McDiarmid notes, the general defence of insanity may also be available – but given the narrowness of the *M'Naghten* Rules this would be rare. See further, SR Kyd, T Elliott and M Walters, *Clarkson and Keating, Criminal Law* (Sweet & Maxwell, 2017) 590–603.

[37] Ministry of Justice, CP(R) 19/08, [98].

[38] Sir William Blackstone, *Commentaries on the Laws of England*, vol 4 (1765).

[39] See, eg, the debates on clause 31 (becoming section 34) of the Crime and Disorder Bill in Standing Committee B on 12 May 1998, in which it was stated that rather than punishment, the presumption stood in the way of 'help' or 'protection', citing G Williams' influential article, 'The Criminal Responsibility of Children' [1954] *Crim LR* 493. Whether the criminal law provided 'help' and whether that is the main purpose of a criminal conviction are, of course, deeply contested.

A. Responsibility and Agency

This chapter could have started with a discussion of the concept of responsibility in criminal law and focusing upon it now is certainly not going to do it justice. If we can agree that the criminal law addresses itself to responsible subjects, and that that is why we have defences such as insanity and exempt very young children from criminal liability, then we are left with the deeply contested questions of what responsibility entails and what denying responsibility to children results in. Classic accounts of responsibility, such as that of Hart's, stress both capacity and choice.[40] This two-dimensional account consists of two closely related elements: a cognitive element (the ability to understand actions and their consequences) and a volitional element (the ability to control one's actions).[41] This goes well beyond a simple knowledge of right and wrong. As Lord Dholakia commented in the debate on his Bill in 2016:

> Those who oppose increasing the age of criminal responsibility often argue that children aged 10 and 11 are capable of telling right from wrong, as though it automatically follows that they should therefore be dealt with in the criminal law. That does not logically follow at all. Most six year olds have a sense of right and wrong but no one suggests that they should be subject to criminal conviction.[42]

If we build in what we know about children's development, then there is a strong argument for saying that children aged 10 or so may have difficulty thinking through the consequences of their behaviour – thus lacking cognitive responsibility – and may also be impressionable and suggestible – and thus lack volitional responsibility. This could lead one to support changes in all three areas of law under discussion.

But supporting this is not without difficulty. In relation to the minimum age of criminal responsibility, whilst an increase would protect young children, it could be argued that it would also rob them of status – that they would become objects of concern, rather than subjects. At the very least we would need to be sure that any non-criminal interventions in relation to children's harmful behaviour would be proportionate and subject to due process. More fundamentally, Hollingsworth, for example, has argued that not conferring criminal responsibility on children strikes at the identity of the actor. She states:

> It is justifiable on a conceptual level to distinguish between a child being *presumed* responsible in order to cross the threshold into the criminal law, thus fulfilling the

[40] HLA Hart, 'Varieties of Responsibility' (1967) 83 *LQR* 346.

[41] There is a wealth of literature exploring the meaning of responsibility. See, eg, A Duff, *Answering for Crime: Responsibility and Liability in the Criminal Law* (Hart, 2007) and J Gardner, 'The Mark of Responsibility' (2003) 23 *OJLS* 157.

[42] *Hansard* HL Deb vol 768, col 1664 (29 January 2016). See also, G Smith and N Winkfield, 'The Development of the Moral Compass: A Study Among Children aged 7 to 16 in the UK' (Youth Research Forum, 2011) where the authors report on a survey which suggested that children of 7 years old have a sense of right and wrong.

> ontological function of responsibility and giving effect to the child's autonomy, and then take account of *actual* capacity once within the system.[43]

However, it is argued here that the criminal court is no place for a young child and that there are other, more suitable fora, in which they can exercise developing responsibility.

An alternative way forward could perhaps be the approach taken in France, which does not have a minimum age of criminal responsibility. Instead children are supposedly dealt with on a case-by-case basis. The Centre for Social Justice Report on Youth Justice acknowledged that some 10- or 11-year-old children may have more capacity than some children a good deal older than them, but rejected the French approach, inter alia, on the basis that the theory was belied by routine practice and suggested (without elaboration) that it may result in discrimination.[44] It is, of course, acknowledged that any age limit is arbitrary but the protective net cast by a higher age of criminal responsibility is the approach favoured in this chapter.

B. Developmental Research

Our understanding of childhood development has come a long way in the last 50 years. There is now a wealth of research from neuroscientists, psychologists and psychiatrists which points to the developmental immaturity of young children. The Royal Society, for example, has examined the neuroscientific evidence and concluded that 'it is clear that at the age of ten the brain is developmentally immature and continues to undergo important changes linked to regulating one's own behaviour'.[45] The frontal lobes, which play a significant role in the development of self-control (as well as other abilities) are not thought to mature until the age of 14 or so. The evidence led the Royal College of Psychiatrists to conclude that the age of criminal responsibility is too low.[46] To this evidence from neuroscience can be added the significant body of research from developmental psychology, which supports the view that 'there are fundamental differences between childhood thought, preoccupied as it is with practical issues to do with the here and now, and adolescent thinking which is much more sophisticated'.[47]

[43] K Hollingsworth, 'Responsibility and Rights: Children and their Parents in the Youth Justice System' (2007) 21 *International Journal of Law, Policy and the Family* 190, 197. See further K Hollingsworth, 'Theorising Children's Rights in Youth Justice: The Significance of Autonomy and Foundational Rights' (2013) 76 *Modern Law Review* 1046. This should not be read as Hollingsworth expressing support for the current age of 10.

[44] Centre for Social Justice, *Rules of Engagement: Changing the Heart of Youth Justice* (Centre for Social Justice, 2012) 208. Presumably this would be on the basis of class, ethnic origin etc.

[45] *Neuroscience and the Law* (RS Policy Document, 2011), 14. See also, Delmage, (n 6) 105–07.

[46] *Child Defendants* (Occasional Paper No 56, 2006).

[47] J Fortin, *Children's Rights and the Developing Law* (CUP, 2009) 83. See also, E Farmer, 'The Age of Criminal Responsibility: Developmental Science and Human Rights Perspectives' (2011) 6 *Journal of Children's Services* 86.

The above research focuses upon the development of children generally, but there are also studies which have examined young defendants' understanding of the nature of criminal proceedings. Rap comments that they 'suggest that young people aged 15 and younger are more likely than older adolescents and young adults to be impaired in their ability to understand criminal proceedings'.[48] There is, in addition, very strong evidence about the particular developmental problems of children entering the youth justice system, with, for example, high levels of communication difficulties, higher levels of special educational needs, attention deficit hyperactivity disorder and post-traumatic stress disorder compared with the general and adult population.[49] As Arthur has stated:

> These developmental differences render such children the least ready to … participate effectively in their own criminal proceedings, and the most seriously in need of adult help and guidance. Evidence suggests that young defendants often do not understand legal proceedings or the language used by lawyers, they report feeling intimidated and isolated in court and may not receive a proper explanation of what has happened until after a hearing is over. Children lack the ability to concentrate for long periods and it may be difficult for them to participate effectively in criminal proceedings.[50]

While science should not be determinative of the issues being discussed in this chapter, it can and should play a significant role in determining an appropriate age at which children should bear responsibility for their harmful behaviour,[51] what is needed to ensure effective participation for those who do stand trial, and whether there should be a defence of developmental immaturity.

C. The International Context

The United Kingdom is a signatory to the United Nations Convention on the Rights of the Child (although, unfortunately, this has never been brought into domestic law). Under Article 40(3) States should seek to establish 'a minimum age below which children should be presumed not to have capacity to infringe penal law'. Whilst the current law satisfies the letter of Article 40(3), further comments from the United Nations Committee on the Rights of the Child do not provide any support for it. In 2007 a General Comment stated that a minimum age of

[48] S Rap, 'A Children's Rights Perspective on the Participation of Juvenile Defendants in the Youth Court' (2016) 24 *International Journal of Children's Rights* 93, 100. See T Grisso et al, 'Juveniles' Competence to Stand Trial: A Comparison of Adolescents' and Adults' Capacities as Trial Defendants' (2003) 27 *Law and Human Behaviour* 333.

[49] See Law Com, (n19) [7.34–7.39] and the 'Carlile Report', (n 27) 24.

[50] R Arthur, 'Exploring Childhood, Criminal Responsibility and the Evolving Capacities of the Child: the Age of Criminal Responsibility in England and Wales' 67 *NILQ* 269.

[51] In this context see the role being played by psychology and neuroscience in Supreme Court decisions in the USA on the sentencing of adolescents to life without parole: L Steinberg, 'The Influence of Neuroscience on US Supreme Court Decisions about Adolescents' Criminal Culpability' (2013) 14 *Nature Reviews Neuroscience* 513.

criminal responsibility below the age of 12 is 'not internationally acceptable'[52] and that States ought to see this as the basis from which to increase it further. In its Reports on the United Kingdom, the Committee has been critical of the low age of criminal responsibility.[53] Article 12 of the Convention also upholds the right of the child to have the opportunity to be heard in judicial proceedings – thus supporting the case for procedures to ensure effective participation.

In addition, the Beijing Rules on Juvenile Justice are also relevant. Rule 4 stipulates that the minimum age of criminal responsibility 'should not be set at too low an age level, bearing in mind the facts of emotional mental and developmental immaturity'. The Official Commentary further states 'in general there is a close relationship between the notion of responsibility for delinquent and criminal behaviour and other social rights and responsibilities', a point to be considered shortly. The Rules further stipulate that young defendants should be able to participate and express their views freely in criminal proceedings.

Unsurprisingly, given the above statements of principle, the age of criminal responsibility has come under scrutiny in jurisdictions close to home with a low age of criminal responsibility: Ireland, Northern Ireland and Scotland. In Ireland the age of criminal responsibility was raised from 10 to 12 in 2006 except for the most serious crimes.[54] Whilst this might be a way to render reform more palatable (Lord Dholakia was prepared to consider this option[55]) it sits very uneasily with principles explored above. In Northern Ireland the Minister for Justice, David Ford, commissioned an independent review of the minimum age of criminal responsibility in 2011, which recommended an immediate increase from 10 to 12, with consideration to follow on a further increase to 14. In the consultation which followed, the recommendation was welcomed by the Minister for Justice and the majority of respondents.[56] In 2016, David Ford welcomed the outcome of a new scoping study, which also recommended an immediate increase in the age of criminal responsibility.[57] This proposal was, however, strongly opposed by the DUP: 'whilst in the vast majority of cases children as young as ten would not be criminalised, sadly events such as the horrific murder of Jamie Bulger illustrate perfectly why the safeguard in the law is required'.[58] The long-standing and deep-rooted opposition of the DUP is likely to make reform very difficult to achieve.

[52] UN Committee on the Rights of the Child, *General Comment No.10 (2007): Children's Rights in Juvenile Justice* (CRC/C/GC/10, 2007).

[53] In 1995, 2002 and 2007: UN Committee on the Rights of the Child, *Forty-Ninth Session – Consideration of Reports Submitted by States Parties Under Article 44 of the Convention – Concluding Observations: United Kingdom of Great Britain and Northern Ireland* (CRC/C/GBR/CO/4, 2008).

[54] Criminal Justice Act 2006, s 52, amending the Children Act 2001. The age of criminal responsibility is still 10 years old for murder, manslaughter, rape and aggravated sexual assault.

[55] Although his inclination was to resist exceptions: Hansard HL Deb vol 768, col 1556 (29 January 2016).

[56] 'Age of Criminal Responsibility Could Rise Says David Ford' *BBC News* (23 October 2012).

[57] Ministerial statement by D Ford, 'Children in the Justice System: Scoping Study' (Minister for Justice, 14 March 2016).

[58] 'Ross responds to the Youth Justice Statement' (DUP Press Release, 15 March 2016).

Scotland has the lowest age of criminal responsibility in Europe, at eight,[59] but has already amended the law so that no child under the age of 12 can be prosecuted in a court (although children aged eight and above can be referred to a children's hearing on offence grounds).[60] In March 2016 an Advisory Group Report recommended an immediate increase in the age of criminal responsibility to 12.[61] This was followed by a period of consultation, which closed in June 2016.[62] In December 2016, Mark McDonald, MSP, Minister for Childcare and Early Years announced that a Bill would be introduced to raise the age of criminal responsibility to 12,[63] and in September 2017 was listed as one of the Bills to be introduced this parliamentary session. It has been reported that the only caveat is the need to maintain public confidence in the system when eight to 11 year olds are involved in the most serious violent or sexual crimes.[64]

Beyond these jurisdictions, broader comparisons can be drawn. In the rest of Europe, the age of criminal responsibility is significantly higher than that of England and Wales: it ranges, for example, from 12 in the Netherlands, 14 in Germany, 15 in Sweden to 16 in Belgium.[65] It would be absurd to argue that this is because children in these countries need more protection from the criminal law than in England and Wales as they are unable to distinguish right from wrong. Instead, 'the only sensible way of understanding these higher minimum ages is in relation to the policy view that has been taken in such jurisdictions that it is wrong, as a matter of policy, to subject young people to the rigours of the criminal justice process'.[66] At the very least we ought to be asking the question: if harmful behaviour by younger children in these jurisdictions is being managed without recourse to the criminal law – and without any seeming breakdown of society – then might we have something to learn from them about the way in which the special status of children is recognised?

[59] Criminal Procedure (Scotland) Act 1995, s 40.

[60] Criminal Procedure (Scotland) Act 1995, s 41A (inserted by the Criminal Justice and Licensing (Scotland) Act 2010, s 52). The majority of child offenders in Scotland are dealt with through the children's hearings system rather than the criminal courts: Scottish Parliament Information Centre, *Children and the Scottish Criminal Justice* (2011) 3.

[61] *The Report of the Advisory Group on the Minimum Age of Criminal Responsibility* (2016). The Group was established after the Government agreed to consultation following the tabling of an amendment to the Criminal Justice (Scotland) Bill 2015 which would have increased the age of criminal responsibility to 12.

[62] Organisations such as Howard League Scotland and the Law Society of Scotland have responded to the consultation welcoming the proposals in the Report.

[63] L Brooks, 'Scotland to Raise the Age of Criminal Responsibility to 12 years' *Guardian Online* (1 December 2016).

[64] S Naysmith, 'Change in Age of Criminal Responsibility Looks Inevitable' *The Herald* (13 May 2016). See generally, E Sutherland, 'Raising the Minimum Age of Criminal Responsibility in Scotland: Law Reform at Last?' (2016) 67 *NILQ* 387.

[65] See D Cipriani, *Children's Rights and the Minimum Age of Criminal Responsibility: A Global Perspective* (Ashgate, 2009).

[66] J Fionda, *Legal Concepts of Childhood* (Hart, 2001) 18.

D. Other Age Boundaries

As noted at the beginning of this chapter, the law routinely sets different ages at which children may engage in different activities and, as I have argued elsewhere, these inconsistencies in age boundaries are not per se unjustifiable.[67] But they do need to be justified and it is an uphill struggle to do so. There is a plethora of examples upon which one could draw, but two will be highlighted here. As noted above, the commentary to the Beijing Rules says that there ought to be a correlation between the age of majority and the age of criminal responsibility – in England and Wales there is an eight year difference. Perhaps even more starkly for our purposes, the age of consent to sexual relations is 16 – a six year difference. Any purported consent is regarded as irrelevant in order to protect children from abuse or simply immature sexual experimentation. Unlike the areas of law under consideration in this chapter, immaturity *here* is recognised as worthy of the State's protection.[68]

III. Reform

In all three areas of law under consideration, the Law Commission has either provided a template for reform or has, even though it has declined for now to review it further, made the initial case for change. In the light of its deliberations this section considers the reforms the Government should take forward.

A. Raising the Age of Criminal Responsibility

The Law Commission has already concluded that the age of criminal responsibility is 'not founded on any logical or principled basis',[69] it has acknowledged the 'increasingly loud calls for such a review by clinicians and academics'[70] and in its report, *Unfitness to Plead* it stated that it remained of the view that there 'may be sound policy reasons for looking afresh at the age of criminal responsibility'.[71] Further, the presumption of *doli incapax* was abolished without any real analysis

[67] See Keating, (n 16). See also, B Goldson, '"Unsafe, Unjust and Harmful to Wider Society": Grounds for Raising the Minimum Age of Criminal Responsibility in England and Wales' (2013) 13 *Youth Justice* 111.

[68] See further, H Keating, 'When the Kissing Has to Stop: Children, Sexual Behaviour and the Criminal Law' in M Freeman (ed) *Law and Childhood Studies* (OUP, 2012). See also, J Horder, 'The Age of Criminal Responsibility and the Age of Consent: Should They be any Different? (2016) 67 *NILQ* 345 where it is argued that there are good reasons why these ages could be different.

[69] Law Commission, *Unfitness to Plead*, (CP No 197, 2010) [8.59].

[70] Law Com, (n 19), [7.54]. To which list could be added, inter alia, the Children's Commissioners of England, Wales and Scotland and the Law Society of England and Wales.

[71] ibid, [7.54].

of the effect it would have. It is clear that the question of the age of criminal responsibility is firmly on the agenda in neighbouring jurisdictions, even if in both Northern Ireland and Scotland the reform process is likely to be a difficult one. The reforms being proposed in these jurisdictions and in Lord Dholakia's Bills are, in light of the compelling evidence, relatively modest – an increase in the minimum age to 12. This should be seen as the first in a series of incremental changes – to 13, and then to 14.

One further option for reform should be discussed at this point. As noted earlier, Ireland's reform increased the age of criminal responsibility to 12, except in cases where the child is accused of a very serious offence. The Centre for Social Justice Report recommended that this approach be adopted in this jurisdiction in the short-term (with a blanket increase in the longer term). The Report recognised 'the contradictions implicit in such a recommendation: that is, in continuing to hold children who have committed the most heinous of crimes responsible for their behaviour one likely criminalises those most in need of help'.[72] More than this, it drives a coach and horses through the principle that the criminal law addresses itself to responsible subjects and, thus, even as a short-term measure of political compromise, is not supported here.

B. A Defence of Developmental Immaturity

The Law Commission considered the case for the developmental immaturity of young people under the age of 18 who kill to be brought within the partial defence of diminished responsibility, in its Report on homicide.[73] While the proposals relating to loss of control have (with modification) become law, other proposals, including this proposal, which attracted support from consultees, have not. However, since then the Law Commission has published its report on insanity and automatism. It revisited the issue of a defence of developmental immaturity and concluded that although it was not possible to do justice to it within the context of that project, it did merit 'separate, full, treatment'.[74] In putting the case for such a defence, based upon a lack of autonomy due to lack of capacity and choice, Dr Catherine Elliott has suggested that it ought to be available to defendants aged between 10 and 14.[75] Dr Claire McDiarmid has gone further: first, she argues rightly that the defence ought to be available to children up to the age of 18 (and possibly up to 21).[76] Secondly, McDiarmid has attempted to flesh out what

[72] Centre for Social Justice, (n 44), 211.

[73] Law Commission, *Murder, Manslaughter, Infanticide* (Law Com No 304, 2006) [5.12 et seq].

[74] Law Com, (n 14), [9.24].

[75] C Elliott, 'Criminal Responsibility and Children: A New Defence Required to Acknowledge the Absence of Capacity and Choice' (2011) 75 *Journal of Criminal Law* 289, 308.

[76] McDiarmid, (n 4), 340, citing the evidence given by the Royal College of Psychiatrists to the Law Commission: Law Commission, (n 14), [5.129].

such a defence might look like in Scottish law, based upon the Scottish defence of mental disorder:

> A child [or young person] is not criminally responsible for conduct which would otherwise constitute an offence and should be acquitted if, due to developmental immaturity,
>
> (a) s/he was unable sufficiently to know the full implications of, to understand, and/or to appreciate the nature of, that conduct, its criminality, its wrongfulness and/or its consequences (legal and/or physical); and/or
>
> (b) s/he was severely restricted in his/her ability to judge whether to carry out the conduct, to exercise rational control over the conduct and/or to refrain from carrying it out.[77]

This is a bold attempt which is, as McDiarmid comments, very comprehensive and which could be made more restrictive by the use of more absolute terminology. Given the controversy which would surround the introduction of any such defence, a more narrowly drawn provision is likely to garner more support. However, whilst McDiarmid sees this development as having advantages over an increase in the age of criminal responsibility, because it differentiates 'between individuals in terms of their actual understanding so that child defendants neither "get away with it" nor, more importantly, are criminalised where they lack capacity',[78] it is argued here that both reforms are needed.[79]

C. Fitness to Plead

In relation to fitness to plead, there is a compelling case for procedures to be extended to the Youth Court as a vital first step to ensuring that the participation difficulties young defendants experience can be dealt with in a more appropriate way than under the current law. The Law Commission is entirely persuaded that this reform is necessary.[80] It has recommended that the same new legal test for effective participation, which they have proposed for trials in Crown Courts, should apply to trials in the Youth Courts. Given that this test is heavily reliant upon that set out in *SC v UK*, a case involving a very young defendant, and that the test was formulated by the court with that very much in mind, this is to be

[77] ibid.

[78] ibid, 341.

[79] After considering the evidence from neuroscience, Delmage, (n 6), 107 has suggested that there ought to be a minimum age of criminal responsibility of 14; that there should then be a defence of developmental immaturity, operating as a presumption to be dealt with by the prosecution for defendants aged between 14 and 15 and by the defence for defendants aged between 16 and 17. This seems unnecessarily complicated.

[80] The Law Commission reported that there was overwhelming support for the introduction of a statutory structure to address participation difficulties in the Youth court (and magistrates' court): Law Com, (n 19), [7.52]. It recommended that it should be extended to non-imprisonable offences [7.59].

commended.[81] Further, the Law Commission is right to recommend that hearings to determine capacity to participate should be reserved to district judges with appropriate additional training.[82]

One further, potentially very significant, recommendation is made by the Law Commission concerning the introduction of mandatory screening for participation issues of young defendants coming before the courts for the first time.[83] As an increase in the age of criminal responsibility to 12 is, in reality, unlikely in the short-term and an increase to 14 even more remote, mandatory screening of those under 14 is very much needed. Although there was some criticism that this would undermine the presumption of fitness (or capacity), it can be distinguished from a presumption, as the Law Commission does, on the basis that as well as identifying those who cannot participate, it could also identify those who could participate if supported by adjustments or special measures.[84] Not only would the proposed reform assist in meeting our obligations under Article 6, but it would also support a duty of courts under section 44 of the Children and Young Persons Act 1933 to have regard to the welfare of the child. This provision may have less significance than it once had (given that the principal aim of the youth justice system is now to prevent offending[85]), but it is still in force.

There is, of course, the question of whether mandatory screening should only apply to young defendants under the age of 14 or whether it should extend to all defendants under the age of 18. The Law Commission has come to the view, rightly, that in principle it should extend to defendants until they reach 18.[86] However, this would involve screening almost seven times the number of defendants, and as the Law Commission had no guarantee that appropriate clinicians would be in place to conduct all the screenings it confined its recommendation to defendants under the age of 14.[87] Again (as with the age of criminal responsibility) it has to be hoped that an incremental approach can be pursued to bring about these highly desirable reforms.

D. The Difference Reform Would Make

The overall number of young people in the youth justice system continues to fall. In 2014–15, the latest year for which results are available, compared to 2010,

[81] See above, discussion under section I, Fitness to Plead and Ibid, Law Commission [7.64–7.75].

[82] ibid, [7.85–7.92]. The options were that it be sent to the Crown court to hear (because of complexity), reserved to district judges or available to all, including lay judges. The recommendation to reserve to district judges is a sensible compromise, and should help to ensure consistency in capacity hearings.

[83] Unless previously screened. The Law Commission has acknowledged this author's concern that this should be subject to concerns being raised about a deterioration in the defendant's condition: ibid, [7.129].

[84] ibid, [7.108].

[85] Crime and Disorder Act 1998, s 37.

[86] Law Com, (n 19), [7.129].

[87] ibid, [7.130] (citing figures of just over 1,100 under 14 year-olds and over 7000 under 18 year-olds).

there are 67 per cent fewer children who were first time entrants (FTEs).[88] The average age of FTEs was 15.2 years old in 2014–15. The numbers of 10 and 11 year-olds coming before the courts is small and declining: in 2014–15 the number of children with substantive outcomes[89] aged 10 (at time of outcome not the crime) was 93 (4 F, 89 M) and at aged 11 was 385 (50 F, 335 M).[90] In 2013–14 the corresponding figures were 116 10 year olds and 424 11 year olds.[91] It is worth repeating that whilst the majority of young defendants will be dealt with by the Youth Court, children charged with serious offences will be tried in the Crown Court. Despite the changes made to court processes following the breach of Thompson and Venables' Article 6 rights at their trial,[92] it is highly questionable whether it is appropriate for very young children to face trial in the 'circus'[93] of the Crown Court.[94] The notion of a presumption against Crown Court trial is thus to be welcomed.[95]

One conclusion which might be drawn from the relatively small number of very young children entering the formal justice system is that the age of criminal responsibility is not a significant problem – involving 1 per cent of the numbers of children and young people in the youth justice system. Such a conclusion would be unwarranted. Increasing the age of criminal responsibility to 12 would remove almost 500 young children not yet of secondary school age from the youth justice system. An alternative conclusion might be that, given the numbers involved, society is unlikely to suffer the catastrophic consequences prophesised by some.[96] Before leaving the issue of the difference an increase in the age of criminal responsibility would make, one further point needs to be stressed: 'young children would not be tarred with the stigmatising "offender" label which evidence shows can exacerbate delinquency'.[97]

As far as the other reforms suggested in this chapter are concerned, it is much more difficult to assess the impact that change would have. Clearly, it would depend on the nature of the reforms themselves. For example, a developmental immaturity defence, which only applied to homicide or to children under the age of 14 would have a much more limited impact than one which applied to children until they attained the age of majority. What can be stated with certainty, given

[88] Youth Justice Statistics 2014/15 (2016).

[89] A substantive outcome is an out of court or court disposal.

[90] Youth Justice Statistics 2014/15 Supplementary Tables (2016), Table 3.1. These figures do not include cautions.

[91] Youth Justice Statistics 2013/14 Supplementary Tables (2015), Table 3.1.

[92] *V and T v UK* (n 33), and *Practice Note* (n 32).

[93] A description given by a barrister, which is quoted in the Charlie Taylor Review, (n 12), [105].

[94] See the comments by Hughes LJ in *W and M* [2010] EWCA Crim 1926, [38–40].

[95] This is subject to important caveats: that further training is provided to judges in the Youth court in dealing with more serious cases and that appropriately experienced legal representation is provided: see Charlie Taylor Review, (n 12), [92] and text at n 12.

[96] Whilst the deterrent effect of the age of criminal responsibility upon children aged 10 to 12 is unknowable, given that most offending is impulsive and opportunistic, it would seem unlikely to figure highly if at all.

[97] Centre for Social Justice, (n 44), 209.

the developmental and other issues identified in young defendants by research, is that introducing fitness procedures in the Youth Court, reforming the fitness test and introducing mandatory screening, would increase the range of options open to courts and do much to ensure that effective participation in the trial was facilitated. It would bring much needed 'justice' into the youth justice system.

IV. Conclusion

As was noted at the beginning of this chapter, the special status of children has long been recognised by law. However, there are glaring inadequacies in the approach of the criminal law. This chapter has exposed three such areas, the age of criminal responsibility, fitness to plead and a defence of developmental immaturity, where reform would mark a fundamental shift in attitudes towards children. In one of the areas explored, fitness to plead, the Law Commission has recommended important reforms which would remedy the long-standing injustice in trials in the Youth Court. In the others, although the Law Commission has laid the groundwork or expressed support for reform no firm proposals have been forthcoming. It is thus disappointing that its thirteenth programme will go forward without the inclusion of the issues of the age of criminal responsibility or a defence of developmental immaturity.

It is not, however, surprising. The view taken by successive governments is one of resistance to such reforms. At the conclusion of the House of Lords' debate on Lord Dholakia's Bill in 2016, on behalf of the government Lord Faulks stated: 'children of ten and above are, for the most part, able to differentiate between bad behaviour and serious wrongdoing', and that 'it allows flexibility to deal with young offenders'.[98] In September 2017 Baroness Vere of Norbiton made very similar statements on behalf of the Government: 'the age of criminal responsibility is appropriate and accurately reflects what is required of our justice system'.[99] Such statements would be likely to be repeated in arguing that a defence of developmental immaturity is unnecessary. There is a job to be done in convincing the Government that knowing the difference between right and wrong is far from being the end of the matter. Even very young children have a rudimentary grasp of this, but this does not mean we should regard them as responsible actors for the reasons explored in this chapter: our understanding of child development generally, our knowledge of the particular difficulties pertaining to young defendants, our obligations under international conventions and comparisons with other jurisdictions. Further, restricting the use of the criminal law does not mean that nothing can be done to respond to young children's harmful behaviour – after all, we have to do so when children of six or even nine behave in this way.

[98] Hansard HL Deb vol 768, cols 1573, 1577, 1575 (29 January 2016).
[99] Hansard HL Deb, (n18), col 2211.

Controversial, difficult and drawn-out (given the current demands upon government) reform undoubtedly will be. But what is needed is an increase in the age of criminal responsibility to 12 (with further increases thereafter), which would exempt the very young from liability; the extension of a new legal test of fitness to plead to the Youth Court to ensure that those above that age are only tried if effective participation in the trial is possible, and, finally for those defendants where evidence exists at the time of the offence, a defence of developmental immaturity for defendants under the age of 18.

Comment on Chapter 6

The Child's 'Special Status' and Disenfranchisement

GIDEON YAFFE

Children who commit crimes, or who are suspected of committing them, ought to be treated with greater leniency than they are by the criminal justice systems in the United States and the United Kingdom. While the point is not beyond dispute, Professor Heather Keating and I are in fervent agreement on it. Reform is necessary and it ought to move in the direction of leniency. The harder question, and also the more interesting one, is what form that reform should take. How should legal practices be changed? And, like all questions of this kind, the background question, which is even harder and even (to me) more interesting, is the question of what principles ought to be guiding us in contemplating and instituting reforms. What is the right measuring stick for determining whether one system's treatment of child criminals is better than another's? With what principle ought we be trying to conform our practices? We need to know not just *that* greater leniency is appropriate, we need to know *why*, if we are going to have grounds for our guesses about *how* reform is best instituted.

Keating's excellent chapter is primarily about the question of *how* we should change the law.[1] She has a few plausible proposals to offer. This comment, however, is going to focus primarily on the question of principle: what principles should guide us in assessing proposals like Keating's? As we will see, the answer to this question will help, also, to see what is right, and what is not, in Keating's positive proposals for reform.

I am an advocate for a view that structures all of my remarks here. In my view, children who commit crimes are owed leniency not because of their psychological or behavioural immaturity but because they are denied, for good reasons, as much say over the law as adults; in particular, they are denied the vote and so the law is not *theirs* to the same degree that it is *ours*. This, I believe, is what justifies treating them more leniently than otherwise similar adults, who enjoy a special kind of ownership over the law derived from the fact that they have a say over it.

[1] H Keating, 'How Should the Criminal Law Respond to the 'Special Status' of Children?' ch 6 of this volume.

So, in my view, policies concerned with the treatment of children who commit crimes should be judged by their degree of conformity with the principle that the severity of one's punishment for a violation of the law should be proportional to the magnitude of one's entitlement to exert influence over it. The rough idea is that the more it is *your* law, the more fitting it is to punish you severely for the violation of it. Those who are entitled to exert influence over the law have no grounds for complaint when they are treated harshly for violating it. Children, by contrast, since they are radically diminished in their say over the law, are worthy of more lenient treatment when they break it even when they do not differ at all, either behaviourally or psychologically, from adults who have more say.

Although I may be wrong, I sense in Keating's discussion animation by a different position, a position according to which policies setting treatment for children in the criminal justice system should be aimed at matching treatment to the psychological dispositions and capacities that drove the problematic behaviour. Where I see age as important because of its *political* meaning, she sees it as important because of its *psychological* meaning.

I have argued for my view about this, in contrast to this alternative position, at length elsewhere and will not do so here.[2] But it is worth making one small negative, but, I think, powerful point: Those who claim that children who commit crimes are to be treated differently from adults on the grounds of their psychological immaturity are committed to something that few are in fact willing to embrace. They are committed to the claim that if we had adequate methods for identifying them, precocious children should be treated the same way as adults. This has the implication, for instance, that if girls mature faster than boys, they ought to be treated as adult criminals at an earlier age than boys. It seems to me that there is something deeply wrong with this idea, and I believe my aversion to it is widely shared. For this reason, among others, I think that we need to recognise that our practices of leniency towards children are not grounded in and legitimated by the immaturity of children, but by something else. Children who are developing normally, those who are developing slowly, and also the precocious are equal in the eyes of the law in this very important respect: they are equally diminished in their say over the law. This, I suggest, is the ground on which it makes sense to be lenient to *all* of them, despite the differences in the speed at which they mature.

My position is consistent with the further observation that there is often good reason to treat differently those who differ psychologically, or differ in their capacity to behave well. This is, of course, true. To give just one obvious example, those who intentionally cause harm ought to be treated more harshly than those who cause harms of the same magnitude accidentally, but while aware of the risk that such harm will materialise. This psychological difference matters. It is also already accommodated by the criminal law of excuse and mitigation, independently of considerations of age. So, while it is often the case that a child is in a different

[2] The argument for the view is offered in G Yaffe, *The Age of Culpability: Children and the Nature of Criminal Responsibility* (Oxford, OUP, 2018).

mindset from an adult, even when they cause comparable harms, and it is often the case that the child's mindset is less bad than the adult's, *this* fact is not the one that we should be particularly attentive to when considering juvenile justice policy. It matters to criminal justice policy for *all* defendants of *all* ages. What matters to *juvenile* justice policy, I claim by contrast, is the distinctive *political* role occupied by children in comparison to adults.

It is for these principled reasons that I am opposed to one of Keating's primary proposals: she thinks the criminal law ought to include an affirmative defence of developmental immaturity. *Anyone*, of any age, can be developmentally immature. To be developmentally immature is for one's behaviour or psychology to be like that typical of those younger than oneself and in ways that tend to change over the course of the life-cycle. A 40-year-old who spends his free time playing video games is, by some measures, developmentally immature. A person in his 70s who can solve cognitive puzzles at break-neck speeds is, also, developmentally immature; people in their 70s tend to lose that ability just through normal aging. Developmental immaturity is not, *in itself*, in any way excusing or mitigating. Sometimes, in fact, it is inculpating, rather than exculpating. It is developmentally immature for a 12-year-old to care not at all about others. But callousness does not count in someone's favour. The adult who says 'Grow up!' to a partner with whom he or she is having a fight might have a point. At best, developmental immaturity, in children, is a proxy for the presence of some other factor thought to be excusing, such as a tendency to be easily influenced by peers, or a tendency to overlook the long-term, or even medium-term, consequences of one's actions, or a tendency to have a skewed perception of the risks of harm to others. These factors might not be excusing at all; that's worth discussing. But the point is that it is the factors that developmental immaturity evidences, rather than developmental immaturity itself, that could even potentially matter to criminal culpability. The reason this is important is that we should be very wary of offering affirmative defences the elements of which are not, themselves, sufficient for excuse but, instead, are proxies for excuse.

To see the point, imagine that we discovered a very reliable genetic marker for schizophrenia. It's not that everyone with gene X has schizophrenia, but many do, many more than in the general population. Nor is it the case that everyone with schizophrenia has gene X; there are other ways to contract the illness. But, still, it is a very good marker. Would it be a good idea to have an affirmative defence of possession of gene X? Of course not. It is a good idea to offer an affirmative defence for people whose crimes *are products of schizophrenia*; and the possession of gene X might be evidentially probative of the presence of this excusing condition. But a defence of possession of gene X is both over- and under-inclusive. Further, such a defence also expresses the faulty and problematic idea that people are owed a break thanks to their genes when, rather, they are owed a break when their problematic behaviour is a symptom of a mental illness (perhaps because of their genes). For the exact same reasons, it would be a mistake to have an affirmative defence of developmental immaturity. Of course, we should excuse those who are owed excuses. Children should have the opportunity to offer all the defences that we provide for adults, and the facts are more likely to be in their favour when they do. Perhaps, even, we ought to have more defences available to everyone. For instance, we lack mechanisms through which those who are living in severe deprivation can appeal to that fact in their defence, and perhaps we should have such mechanisms. But to add a defence of developmental immaturity is to fail to recognise what is special about children who commit crimes. It is not their psychological differences that make them special. It is, rather their subordinate political position. If children are owed more leniency than is already available to them under a criminal law that is replete with opportunities for excuse – and they are, and it is – it is because of this special fact about them.

The view I advocate focuses our attention on adolescents; it offers an account of why 16- and 17-year-olds, for instance, are to be treated more leniently than psychologically and behaviourally identical 20- and 22-year-olds. Keating is concerned with this group, but she is also concerned with the minimum age of criminal liability; she is concerned, that is, with the floor below which there should be no criminal liability, and not just with the threshold above which there should be criminal liability of whatever form is appropriate for adults. As I'll try to explain, the question of minimum age is inextricably intertwined, for conceptual and normative reasons, with the issue of the competence of children to plead and to otherwise participate in legal proceedings against them. A central goal of this comment is to articulate a general principle that should guide thinking about where to set the minimum age, and should also guide thinking about which children are fit to participate in legal proceedings against them. It is to that issue that I now turn; but please bear with me because what I want to say about this takes a few steps to explain.

Here's a first thought: a 'crime' by a seven-year-old is no crime at all. Even when a child is old enough that the label 'crime' seems appropriate, a child's crimes are just not as serious as those of an adult. There seems something right about this. But it also seems obviously false. After all, children, like adults, cause a lot of harm. The homicide victims of children are no less dead than those of adults. The property rights of those from whom children steal are no less violated than those from whom adults steal. And so on. Even if, on average, crimes by children are less harmful than crimes by adults – an empirical claim that might turn out to be false when the harms are aggregated properly – particular crimes by children are just as harmful or more harmful than many crimes by adults. Yet, despite this, there is something right about the claim that a child's crimes are not as serious, or, when the child is young enough, not even crimes at all. How can we capture the grain of truth in that idea?

Philosophers of criminal law, like myself, often draw a distinction between wrongdoing and culpability. Acts are wrongful; agents are culpable for wrongful acts. An act is wrongful just in case it is in violation of a norm; it is criminal if the norm it violates has been given legal force by, for instance, being expressed by a valid criminal statute. By contrast, an agent is culpable for a wrongful or criminal act if she is responsible for that act. This distinction makes possible the observation that there is room for criminal conduct that warrants no punishment thanks to the fact that its agent is not culpable for it. Those who have excuses, such as insanity or duress, engage in conduct that falls into this category. They commit crimes, but they are shielded from criminal liability thanks to the fact that they are not culpable for the crimes they commit. By contrast, those who show that they committed no crime – engaged, that is, in no wrongdoing – do not offer an excuse; rather, they undermine the grounds for their criminal liability in a more basic and fundamental way.

It is sometimes noted by moral philosophers, and much less frequently by philosophers of law, that the agent of an act must meet certain conditions of competence if her act is to be *wrongful*. This can seem strange given the distinction between wrongdoing and culpability. Surely, one might think, an act violates a norm just in case it meets the description of prohibited conduct contained in the norm. If that is true, then any act that is of a particular prohibited type is in violation of a norm prohibiting acts of that type. And this idea is appealing. It is very appealing to think that if you took something of someone else's without permission, then you violated the norm against stealing. But this, on reflection, cannot be quite correct. The tiger's killing of the endangered gazelle is not a violation of the norm against the killing of endangered species. The reason is not that the tiger's conduct is not *action*; it is. The reason is not that the tiger's conduct is not *a killing*, or not *a killing of an endangered species*; it is both these things. The reason is not even that the tiger has no idea that the gazelle is *endangered*. It is true that, lacking the very concept, the tiger does not know that. But an agent who kills an endangered species without knowing it's endangered has *an excuse*, and so has negated one of the conditions of *culpability*, rather than wrongdoing. So, the tiger's act cannot fall short of being *wrongdoing* thanks to the fact that the tiger does not know the gazelle is endangered. Nor can we say that the tiger's act is not wrongdoing because it is justified, and so falls under an exception to the norm, in the way that self-defensive killing falls under an exception to the norm against intentionally killing other people. The reason is that the tiger would not have violated the norm against killing endangered species even if she killed the gazelle purely for the fun of it – that is, for no good reason at all, much less for a reason that would justify it, or make it worth doing. Rather, the tiger has not done anything wrong *because it is a tiger*.

So, there are acts that are indeed acts *of killing an endangered species* which do not violate the norm '*Don't kill endangered species!*' What follows is that an act is an instance of wrongdoing only if: (1) the act matches the norm's description of prohibited conduct, *and* (2) it is performed by a certain kind of agent, a kind to which the tiger does not belong. Not just the first condition, but the second also, is necessary for wrongdoing. My hypothesis is that small children are exempt from criminal liability because they fail to satisfy this second condition; they are no more wrongdoers than tigers are.

When criminal liability attaches to an act it does so in part (albeit only in part) thanks to the existence of a certain kind of government that stands in a certain relation to the agent of the act. In the paradigm case, criminal liability attaches to D's act of C-ing thanks in part to the fact that the government imposing liability has given legal force to the norm 'Don't C!', *and* D is a citizen of the State over which the government presides. Add that in democracies the status of citizen is inextricably entwined with the entitlement to exert influence over the law – it is entwined with *having a say* over the law – and we reach the result that, at least in the paradigm case, criminal liability attaches to D's act of C-ing in part because D has a say over the law against C-ing. When we are talking about criminal liability, that is, an agent must not just perform an act that matches the description of prohibited conduct; he or she must also be a certain kind of agent, an agent invested with an entitlement to exert influence over the law that generated the relevant prohibition.

What should we say about the obvious exceptions: adults who are denied the vote but seem unworthy, when they commit crimes, of the special kind of leniency that is appropriate for children? After all, visitors, such as immigrants and tourists, who are not citizens and so are denied a say over the law, commit crimes when they engage in conduct that matches the relevant descriptions when visiting. Why should they be denied leniency? Roughly, the answer is this: The child who is about to be subject to the same punishment that would be given to an adult can say, in his defence, 'This is not my law!' Voluntary visitors, however, cannot offer this complaint, despite the fact that it is true. Part of what it is to voluntarily visit is to agree to 'play by the house rules', as it were, even though they are not one's own. I believe, relatedly, that those on our soil voluntarily, who face the prospect of criminal punishment, could, instead of accepting it, renounce their visiting status, and with it whatever procedural protections our law offers adult citizens. In fact, depending on the nature of the regime, this might be the best course (think of the position of a foreign missionary standing before a North Korean court). Still, what is unavailable to visitors is the shield to full criminal responsibility that the child employs when asserting 'This is not my law!'[3]

Adults in a democracy have a say over the law in two particularly important ways: First, they have the vote. Secondly, they enjoy free speech protections. By voting and by speaking we can exert ourselves to influence the content of the law. Adults are *entitled* to exert such influence – the law protects them from interference in their efforts to exert influence in these two ways. And it is because of this pair of entitlements that they are to be held fully criminally responsible when they violate criminal laws. Children below the voting age lack one of these entitlements, while some of them possess the other, albeit with limits. They lack the vote, but speech by adolescents is protected to some degree, although subject to parental-gating. Parents can control who their adolescent children speak to and

[3] For more detailed discussion, see ch 7 of Yaffe, (n 2). One implication of the position is that we should be lenient towards involuntary visitors, such as, perhaps, asylum seekers, when they commit crimes. Their crimes, however, may undercut their claims to other forms of aid that they may be seeking, having nowhere else to go.

whose speech they hear. But, still, adolescents have some say over the law through speech protections. Roughly, they have *conditional* protection: the right to be heard and to listen, provided their parents' consent. It is my view that it is because they have say over the law to this small degree that adolescent children are rightly held criminally liable *at all*; and it is because they are diminished in their say over the law – both because they lack the vote, and because their speech entitlements are conditional in ways that adults' are not – that they are to be treated more leniently than adults when they commit crimes. From here it is easy to see what the extra agential requirements must be in order to engage in conduct that qualifies as criminal: one must have *some* say over the law, through entitlement to exercise *some* mechanism for exerting influence over the law, either through speech or vote or something else. The minimum age for criminal responsibility, then, is the age below which there is *no* say over the law, not even through minimal, conditional speech protections.

Below what age do children lack any free speech protections? The answer is that it varies from legal system to legal system. In fact, there is good reason to think that the choice of minimum age for criminal responsibility purposes *is* a choice about the age below which one lacks speech protections. The reason is that what comes along with speech protection is the possibility of civil disobedience, of engaging in unprotected speech for political purpose. Below the floor for criminal liability, there is no possibility of civil disobedience. Young children can no more engage in acts of civil disobedience than tigers can. The reason this is important is that if some of your speech is protected, then some of it is not. If you can attend a political rally *provided the rally is permitted*, then you cannot legally attend it, if it is not. If you are not in violation of the law either way, because you are below the minimum age for criminal liability, then you are both immune to penalty for your speech and denied protection when it is taken away. The logic of free speech protection is such that no one who is exempted entirely from criminal liability can also enjoy free speech protection. Therefore, when the legislature sets a minimum age for criminal responsibility, it also, necessarily, denies those below that age free speech protection. As I see it, that is, the argument over the proper floor for purposes of criminal liability is an argument over when we should start protecting the speech of children. That is a question of when we should start giving them entitlements to be listened to, and entitlements to listen to us, as participants in the kind of political deliberative enterprise of which speech is an important part.

Keating sees this idea when she discusses the way in which raising the minimum age for purposes of criminal liability expands the class of people who are mere objects of concern, rather than subjects of legal and moral address. To me, however, this is not, as Keating seems to hold, just a detriment of raising the floor that is to be weighed against the benefits of such a move. It is more fundamental than that. To raise the minimum age of criminal liability is to rob a class of people of the possibility of a kind of ownership of the law that can, of course, be deeply burdensome, but is also essential to the justification of many forms of government treatment of them. We cannot achieve lenience through means that rob us of our grounds for assigning children criminal liability in the first place.

Given this abstract conceptualisation of the issue, where should we set the floor? Consider an analogy: You are working out the seating arrangements for a large dinner party for many adults and their children who vary in age from infancy to late adolescence. You have to decide who to seat at the table with the adults and who, if anyone, to relegate to a separate 'kids' table. A seat at the table comes with certain etiquette- and morality-based speech protections. It is rude and wrong not to let one's tablemates speak and be heard. A natural way to divide things up is to set an age line; send those below a certain age to the kids' table and send those above it to the adults' table. The main reason to use age, rather than something else, is that it is rude and wrong to sort one's guests by merit. If you send one 16-year-old to the adult table and another to the kids' table, that's a way of saying that one of them has a certain kind of merit that the other lacks. Where to set the age line will depend in part on what goods you are trying to maximise. If what you want is mature conversation at the adults' table, you will want to set the age higher – although there may be some over the threshold who are too childish to help in this respect, and some below it who would improve the conversation had they been given access. If what you want is to protect the youngest from bad adolescent influences, then you will set the age threshold lower, and so move the problematic adolescents away from the vulnerable.

The point of this analogy is that while the issue has something to do with the capacities of those who are to be sorted by the age policy – if all those above 15 are scintillating adult conversationalists, then that's good to know – it has everything to do also with the goals that one has in sorting. So, as I see it, until we know what the point is of democratic governance through speech, we cannot say where, as a principled matter, to set the floor for criminal responsibility purposes. Just as we need to know what kind of dinner party we are seeking if we are to know where to set the age line for a seat at the table, we need to know what kind of polity we are seeking to know where to set the age line for exemption from criminal liability. Different polities will have different ideals in this respect. They will care about speech for different reasons. And so we should not expect there to be perfect convergence in this across legal systems. To me, 12 seems like a good choice; I want to hear from kids that age, and I want them to listen to and talk about politics and public policy. I want there to be limits to what people can do to control what they can say and what they can hear. Below that age, not so much. But I have no theory of the point of the polity that supports that judgement. I am afraid that I cannot claim more rigour in the judgement than that it feels about right. What I am confident of is that that feeling is rooted in an unarticulated picture of the purpose of living under a State where people get to say what they like.

It may be clear already how this discussion fits with the question, discussed by Keating, of the criteria that a child must meet in order to be judged fit to plead and fit to participate in proceedings against him or her. Of course, for the purposes of assessing the minimum age for criminal liability what matters is the defendant's age at the time of the putative offense, while what is relevant to the fitness to plead is the age at the later time, the time of the relevant legal proceedings. But the question is, in its fundamentals, the same: Is this someone who is, or should be, entitled to speak and to listen?

So, in short, as I see it, there should be perfect alignment among: (1) the age below which a person is entirely ineligible for criminal liability, (2) the age below which a person is denied free speech protections, and (3) the age below which a person is categorically judged unfit to plead, or to participate in his or her own defence. Just as there should be alignment between the voting age – the age at which a person has a full say over the law – and the age over which there should be no categorical leniency in the face of criminal conduct, there should be alignment in these ages at the floor, as well.

Let me end with a small rumination. On the one hand, the kinds of remarks that I've made here are useless to juvenile justice reformers. They are, necessarily, inconclusive about exactly what should be done, and what should be done differently from the way that it is currently being done. On the other hand, how can reformers do without reflections of this kind? How can we know how our juvenile justice system is to be reformed until we have some sense of what would constitute success? To know that, we need to know what principles ought to be guiding our practices. Only then can we know whether we are practicing principle, or falling short.

7

The Time Limit on Prosecutions for Underage Sexual Intercourse in the Sexual Offences Act 1956: A Continuing Problem

JONATHAN ROGERS*

Before 1 May 2004, offences concerning sexual intercourse with underage girls (under 16 but not under 13) were charged as unlawful sexual intercourse, contrary to section 6 of the Sexual Offences Act 1956 (SOA 1956). When the Sexual Offences Act 2003 (SOA 2003) came into force on 1 May 2004, that offence was repealed[1] and replaced with a new offence of sexual activity with a child.[2] But, the offence in the SOA 1956 still applies in relation to acts committed when that Act was in force, ie, up until 30 April 2004. In relation to men who, before then, had (possibly) consensual sex with girls[3] who were aged 13 or over, but under 16, there arises a serious problem. There was a time limit for commencing prosecutions of one year from the alleged commission of the offence under section 6 of the SOA 1956,[4] which has been assumed to continue to apply. So it has long been impermissible to charge anyone under section 6 of the SOA 1956, even in serious cases of older men who groomed young girls, and threatened or seduced them into silence for long periods of time.

* I should like to express my thanks to those who commented on an earlier draft of this chapter, including participants at the CLRN Conference in September 2016 and members of 6 KBW Chambers who hosted a presentation later that same month. Special thanks are due to my commentator, Hannah Quirk.

[1] SOA 2003, Sch 6, [11].

[2] SOA 2003, s 9 and s 13.

[3] The gender-specific limitations follows from the core definition of the offence, under SOA 1956, s 6(1): 'It is an offence, subject to the exceptions mentioned in this section, for a man to have unlawful sexual intercourse with a girl not under the age of thirteen but under the age of sixteen.'

[4] Section 37(2) gave effect to Sch 2 to the SOA 1956 which concerns modes of prosecution and maximum punishments for various listed offences. Paragraph 10(a) to Sch 2 lists the offence under s 6 and provided: 'a prosecution may not be commenced more than twelve months after the offence charged'. The same limitation applies to attempts to commit the offence.

In the years leading up to the SOA 2003, this unusual time limit proved to be tolerable only because it used to be evaded (!), namely by charging instead indecent assault under section 14 of the SOA 1956, for which the underage girl could also not give effective consent, but for which no time limit was provided in the statute. So 'rough justice' could still be done, and it frequently was.[5] But the House of Lords in *J*[6] belatedly decided by a 4–1 majority that indecent assault under section 14 of the SOA 1956 could not be charged in cases of underage sexual intercourse[7] so as to avoid the time limit attached to section 6 of the SOA 1956. The statute had to be read as a whole, it was said; and Lord Bingham thought it was impossible to interpret it as though it said that prosecutions for underage sex under section 6 had to commence within one year, but if they were not, they could still be prosecuted under section 14.[8] The need for internal consistency went yet further; other acts which were 'indecent assaults' but were, in truth, preparatory measures towards underage sexual intercourse, were to be regarded as time barred by the decision in *J* too.[9] So, if[10] the drafters of the SOA 2003 were content to leave alone the time limit attached to section 6 of the SOA 1956 on the basis that charges under section 14 of the SOA 1956 could still be laid, then the decision in *J*, just a year or so after the SOA 2003 was passed, created a large legal vacuum that no policy maker had anticipated.

We should examine first the reasons for this time limit, which may partly lie in an underestimation of the harms of the offence itself. Then, we shall consider a plausible argument, based on a common law principle of statutory interpretation, that the time limit has *already* been removed for all proceedings for the offence under section 6 of the SOA 1956 since the SOA 2003 came into force. On the assumption that this interpretation might not be favoured by the courts, we shall then consider a plausible human rights argument which may be raised by determined complainants on suitable facts, which, if successful, would *mandate* that interpretation. But, we should rather pass legislation which unambiguously allows allegations of underage sexual intercourse committed up until 30 April 2004 still to be prosecuted under section 6 of the SOA 1956. Finally, we discuss why no such reform has already been considered. Some of these reasons might also defeat attempts at legislative reform today.

[5] As noted by the House of Lords in *J* [2004] UKHL 42, [22], [53], while there had been no objection to prosecutors charging under s 14 in order to evade the time bar, trial judges developed the practice of observing the maximum two-year prison sentence that Parliament had attached to the offence under SOA 1956, s 6.

[6] [2004] UKHL 42.

[7] The convenient label 'underage sexual intercourse', unless otherwise specified, refers to (possibly consensual) sexual intercourse between males (often adult males) and girls who were aged between 13 to 15 years old at the time.

[8] [2004] UKHL 42, [18].

[9] ibid, [25].

[10] It is a big 'if', however; see Part II.

I. The Reasons for the Time Limit

It is hard to state today what good reason there might have been for the time limit attached to section 6 of the SOA 1956. In *J*, two of their Lordships declined to articulate what policy objective it might have served.[11] Those of their Lordships in *J* who considered the point accepted that evidential problems many years after the event could not supply a reason for a time limit to be attached to this offence but to no other sexual offence. The most intuitive reason for having a time limit for the particular offence of unlawful sexual intercourse would seem to be to protect younger men from oppressive prosecutions. Lord Rodger imagined the prospects of a young man's consensual dalliances coming back to haunt him many years later, when he might have a family and career.[12] As far as one can tell, this also influenced the Criminal Law Revision Committee's recommendation as lately as 1984.[13] But this cannot have been the entire explanation. For a start, Parliament in 1956 enacted a 'young man's defence' as a matter of substantive law,[14] presumably to address some such concerns. But moreover, 'young man concerns' do not explain why the time limit was anywhere near as short as one year. The typical young man would hardly have much matured, or his life much changed, just one year after his offence.

More likely, the reasons for the time limit in the 1956 Act are rooted further back in history. Only since 1885[15] has it been an offence for a male to have (possibly consensual) sex with a girl under 16, as opposed to sexual intercourse with a girl under 13. The increase in the age of consent was part of a series of measures aimed primarily against brothels, where many girls between the ages of 13 and 15 were working, rather than flowing from a concern for the wider welfare of young teenage girls in general. Indeed, it was apparently feared that the sort of girl who would agree to sexual intercourse at such a young age was unlikely to be of good character and, if finding herself pregnant, might seek to blame the wealthiest boy of her age known to her. Thus the offence originally carried a time limit of three months, so that any complaint would have to be made before the fact of the girl's pregnancy could be ascertained.[16] This time limit,

[11] Namely, Lord Steyn and Lord Clyde, the latter of whom went so far as to say '*Whatever the precise reasoning behind the imposition of the time limit may have been* … it was still standing in the legislation when the present case arose' [44] (emphasis added).

[12] *J*, (n 6), [58].

[13] See its *Fifteenth Report on Sexual Offences* (Cmnd 9213, 1984) [5.22].

[14] Section 6(3) of the Act provided: 'A man is not guilty of an offence under this section because he has unlawful sexual intercourse with a girl under the age of sixteen, if he is under the age of twenty-four and has not previously been charged with a like offence, and he believes her to be of the age of sixteen or over and has reasonable cause for the belief.'

[15] Criminal Law Amendment Act 1885, s 5.

[16] See the historical summary in the opinion of Lady Hale in *J*, (n 6), [74–76].

unsurprisingly, made the law *too* hard to enforce,[17] and the duration of the limit was steadily raised.[18]

When one considers that (male) lawyers and judges were very slow to understand why females of any age might delay reporting sexual offences, and indeed held that all women were unreliable on matters relating to sexual offences,[19] it is unsurprising that girls between 13 to 15 years old who, by their own account, agreed to sex were considered as especially untrustworthy. Little thought seems to have been given to the point that many girls seduced by older men, especially by those in positions of authority over them,[20] would have expected their truthful accounts to be disbelieved, and dismissed as childish fantasies, had they made them while they were still children. Today, happily, we seem better able to understand that children may be much slower than adults to alert the police to serious offences committed against them.[21]

Thus, much of the explanation of the time limit lies in a toxic mixture of misogyny, prejudice and ignorance. Yet there was probably more to it. If one assumes that underage sexual intercourse is essentially about illicit love affairs between two young people, then the harms from which the girl is being protected are mainly pregnancy or disease. Nowadays, bearing in mind that many offenders are much older than the underage girl, and might have trapped the girl into a longer term abusive relationship,[22] or might have groomed girls from disadvantaged backgrounds (possibly also making them available to friends) we would describe the potential harms in much wider terms. In the words of Lady Hale, we would expect there to be damage to:

> … their self-esteem, their capacity to form ordinary intimate relationships in the future, and their perceptions of how to live in families, all of which are so crucial to their own ability to be effective partners and parents in their turn. Those with professional experience of trying to pick up the pieces, sometimes many years after the event, are in no doubt of the gravity of the risks involved.[23]

[17] Presumably many girls tried to hide the fact of their pregnancy for as long as possible, for many offences were only uncovered when the girl would actually give birth; ibid, [76].

[18] To 6 months by virtue of the Prevention of Cruelty to Children Act 1904, s 27. It was raised twice more by measures of 3 months, so that it already stood at 1 year when the offence was consolidated with that same time limit provided for in Sch 2 to the SOA 1956.

[19] The requirement for the judge to give a corroboration warning in relation to their accounts was only abolished in England and Wales in Criminal Justice and Public Order Act 1994, s 32.

[20] It may also be assumed that there was less understanding that those inclined towards seducing children may actively seek employment which gives them contact with, or some power over, them.

[21] Notably the Criminal Injuries Compensation Authority waives its usual time limit of two years (from the time of the offence) for all claimants who were under 18 years old at the time of an offence of violence. For them, the two-year limit runs from the time when they first contacted the police. See *The Criminal Injuries Compensation Scheme* (MOJ, 2012) [88].

[22] As Lady Hale put it in *J*, (n 6), [80]: '… sexual abusers commonly groom their victims by making them believe that their behaviour is normal. They make their victims fall in love with them.'

[23] *J*, (n 6), [78].

In other words, part of the very wrong of underage sexual intercourse is that the underage girl may be unable to appreciate for a long time that she *is* being exploited; and that she may be afraid or too immature to address the fact of her exploitation until a long time afterwards. The House of Commons Home Affairs Committee independently noted that, according to the Metropolitan Police, 'significant numbers of complainants are aged between 30 to 40 years when they report experiences of childhood abuse'.[24]

Arguably then, the offence of underage sexual intercourse was one of the most inappropriate of all to be time limited. Happily, in 2000, the Home Office, which in due course drafted the Bill which became the SOA 2003, commissioned an independent report which, inter alia, advised against any time bars for sexual offences.[25] There were no time limits for any of the offences in the SOA 2003, and the maximum penalty for the new offence of sexual activity with a child (by an adult) was substantially lengthened to 14 years' imprisonment.[26]

But this still leaves the problems which arise with prosecuting the more serious instances of underage sexual intercourse committed before the SOA 2003 came into force, which can only be prosecuted under the SOA 1956. First, and most fundamentally; are we really out of time to prosecute in all of these cases, where nothing other than underage sexual intercourse or incidental touching towards it can properly be alleged?

II. Legal Challenges to the Time Limit

A. Matter of Statutory Interpretation

Remarkably, it is arguable that the SOA 2003 *did* abolish the time limit which attached to section 6 of the SOA 1956, so that, since the Act came into force, offences properly chargeable under section 6 can now be heard without reference to it; but it takes some legal education to understand why it is arguable. Unfortunately nothing much was said of the matter in *J*, because the time limit had unquestionably been in force when J was tried in 2001. Only Lord Steyn adverted to the future position, saying 'Not surprisingly, Parliament abolished the time limit with effect from 1 May 2004 by the Sexual Offences Act 2003'.[27] Alas, this comment is ambiguous. But probably his Lordship meant only to say that Parliament had provided a new offence (sexual activity with a child), with no time limit, with effect from 1 May 2004; and not that Parliament had, as from 1 May 2004, *also* abolished the time limit which attached to the offence in section 6 of the SOA 1956.

[24] Home Affairs Committee, *The Conduct of Investigations into past cases of Abuse in Children's Homes* (Fourth Report, 2001/2) [88].

[25] *Setting the Boundaries: Reforming the Law on Sexual Offences* (Home Office, July 2000) [3.6.6].

[26] SOA 2003, s 9(2).

[27] *J*, (n 6), [28].

This is how Parliament, in 2003, repealed the offence and the time limit in the SOA 1956. Schedule 6 to the Sexual Offences Act 2003, entitled 'Minor and Consequential Amendments', provides simply:

> 11. In the Sexual Offences Act 1956, omit –
>
> (a) sections 1 to 7, 9 to 17, 19 to 32 and 41 to 47 (offences), and
> (b) in Schedule 2 (prosecution, punishment etc.), paragraphs 1 to 32.

Thus the offence under section 6 SOA 1956 was to be 'omitted' by virtue of paragraph 11(a), and the time limit attached to it in Schedule 2 to the SOA 1956 by virtue of paragraph 11(b). Certainly Schedule 6 to the SOA 2003 means that these sections have no continuing force in respect of acts committed since 1 May 2004, when the SOA 2003 came into force. But Schedule 6 says nothing either way about their validity in respect of acts committed *before* 1 May 2004. For assistance on this, we must look at section 16 of the Interpretation Act 1978, which provides:

> … where an Act repeals an enactment, the repeal does not, unless the contrary intention appears … (b) affect the previous operation of the enactment repealed.

Applying section 16 of the Interpretation Act 1978 by itself, it would seem that the time limit still 'operates' whenever the offence does (ie, because that is what it 'previously' did) in respect of acts committed up until 30 April 2004. In *Silverwood*[28] the Court of Appeal was concerned with the analogous 'omission' of the offence of gross indecency with men,[29] along with the 'omission' of its belatedly attached time limit in section 7 of the Sexual Offences Act 1967, by virtue of the same Schedule 6 to the SOA 2003.[30] The Court referred to section 16 of the Interpretation Act 1978 and instantly concluded that both the offence and time limit still 'operate' together today (ie, as they 'previously' did) in respect of acts committed up until 30 April 2004.

However, this reading overlooks the important common law distinction between the repeal of substantive law and the repeal of adjectival law. Changes made to substantive law are indeed presumed not to have retrospective effect.[31] But the laws of evidence, or any procedural bars to trial, are only addressed to the court *at the time when it tries an offence*, and statutory repeals of these laws are presumed to apply in respect of all future court proceedings, *irrespective* of the time of the alleged events themselves. Coincidentally, or perhaps not, the leading case on the retrospective extension of a time limit to prosecution concerned the first occasion on which the time limit for underage sexual intercourse was raised from three months to six months. The accused committed the offence when the time limit was only three months but was charged after five months, by which

[28] [2015] EWCA Crim 2401, [12].
[29] Contrary to SOA 1956, s 13.
[30] Schedule 6 to the SOA 2003, [15].
[31] Retrospective criminal liability in this sense would in any event normally be incompatible with the ECHR, Art 7.

time it had been increased to six months. He argued, unsuccessfully, that he was protected by the time limit which applied at the time of his offence, but the new time limit was held to have effect, thus enabling the prosecution to proceed. In *Chandra Dharma*, Lord Alverstone CJ said:

> The rule is clearly established that … statutes which make alterations in procedure are retrospective. It has been held that a statute shortening the time within which proceedings can be taken is retrospective and it seems to me that it is impossible to give any good reason why a statute extending the time within which proceedings may be taken should not also be held to be retrospective … [where statute] only alters the time within which proceedings may be taken, it may be held to apply to offences completed before the statute was passed. That is the case here. This statute does not alter the character of the offence, or take away any defence which was formerly open to the prisoner. It is a mere matter of procedure, and according to all the authorities it is therefore retrospective.[32]

Chandra Dharma has not been doubted at common law, and a search of the Westlaw database reveals only cases where it has been considered or mentioned. The issue has apparently received more attention in Australia. The Australian High Court in 1958 recognised in principle the distinction between substance and procedure,[33] and in 1990, the High Court in *Rodway v The Queen* said that:

> … the rule at common law is that a statute ought not be given a retrospective operation where to do so would affect an existing right or obligation unless the language of the statute expressly or by necessary implication requires such construction. It is said that statutes dealing with procedure are an exception to the rule and that they should be given a retrospective operation.[34]

If Schedule 6 to the SOA 2003 is to be read in the light of these authorities, then it arguably preserves the offence in section 6 of the SOA 1956 for acts committed up until 30 April 2004, *but simultaneously* removes the time limit for all proceedings *commenced* since 1 May 2004. There is nothing in the decision in *Silverwood* (where nothing at all was said of *Chandra Dharma*) which suggests that the enactment of section 16 of the Interpretation Act 1978 casts aside the decades-old distinction between substantive law and procedural law when it comes to the effects of repeal. Nor could such a claim be made. Section 16 of the Interpretation Act 1978 only speaks in terms of the law 'operating' as it 'previously' did; and the point is precisely that time limits only 'operate' *as they currently do or do not exist at the time of trial*, in determining whether the court currently has jurisdiction to hear the case. If that was 'previously' the nature of the 'operation' of the time limit in Schedule 2 to the SOA 1956 – that it only operated for as long as it had not been amended – then section 16 of the Interpretation Act 1978 does not support any

[32] [1905] 2 KB 335, 338–39.
[33] *Maxwell v Murphy* (1957) 96 CLR 261.
[34] *Rodway v The Queen* (1990) 169 CLR 515, 518.

proposition that the time limit continues to apply when trials are commenced from 1 May 2004. Speaking of the 'operation' of law may just as easily be a reference to the distinction between adjectival and substantive law as an abrogation of such a distinction.

But, there is still room for argument; for section 16 of the Interpretation Act 1978 also allows for a 'contrary intention' to 'appear' in any statutory repeal or amendment. It is not stated how explicitly any 'contrary intention' should need to 'appear'. However, we might note that Schedule 6 to the SOA 2003 is entitled *Minor and Consequential Amendments*, which may carry the suggestion that all of the amendments are thought to be consequential as though by logic. Having repealed the offence under section 6 of the SOA 1956, it might have been thought to be a logical 'consequence' that the time limit should be removed too (what, after all, would be the point in leaving on the statute books a time limit to a non-existent offence?). For, whilst one might readily expect a contrary intention to the rule in *Chandra Dharma* to be explicitly expressed when a procedural or evidential rule is abolished *by itself*, maybe less explicitness is required when a procedural rule, attached to a particular offence, is abolished *alongside* that offence. It might be added that, the whole of Schedule 6 to the SOA 2003 seems to be an indiscriminate tidying-up exercise in removing both old offences and anything to do with those repealed offences; and that reading the whole package together might draw one to the conclusion that they were all meant to be abolished to the same extent.

Alas, there is no indication in the Explanatory Notes to the SOA 2003 or other sources exactly to what extent Parliament meant to abolish the time limit. Certainly, if the matter were thought to depend more generally to ascertaining Parliament's likely intention, then it is quite possible that Parliament intended the time limit to continue to apply to old cases, mistakenly thinking (as everyone did in 2003) that it could in any event continue to be evaded by charging defendants under section 14 of the SOA 1956. Properly speaking, the issue is whether a contrary intention 'appears' in the text of Schedule 6 to the SOA 2003, so that we should not need to second guess Parliament's intention. But it would be little surprise if some judges were to ask themselves the latter question first, and to be guided by the answer to that, such is the difficulty with deciding the former issue by itself.

So the success of the argument remains quite uncertain; and we proceed here on the basis that a court might reject it.

B. The Human Rights Argument

There is a second line of argument which may succeed in the alternative. It arises if it can be said that a failure to prosecute a case of underage sexual intercourse can amount to a violation of the complainant's rights under Article 8 of the ECHR, and that removal of the time limit would enable the State to avoid the violation. Then it would follow that Schedule 6 to the SOA 2003 must be interpreted if 'possible' to remove the time limit for all proceedings commenced since the SOA 2003 came into force.[35] This would be a new argument for the courts; for it was assumed without argument in *J* that there was no human rights dimension to the application of the time limit.[36] An outline of the argument has already been suggested by this author,[37] but it can usefully be expanded here.

Member States must show some minimal degree of efficiency in investigating and prosecuting certain serious crimes against citizens in its jurisdiction, by virtue of the doctrine of positive obligations. The best known case is *X and Y v Netherlands*,[38] in which it was held that a domestic rule which required victims of sexual offences to make a complaint in person represented an arbitrary barrier to prosecutions, and that its operation meant that the Netherlands violated Article 8 of the ECHR because it thereby failed effectively to prosecute activities which undermined the sexual autonomy of those unable to complain in person. The main strands to the positive obligations argument are that: (1) a duty effectively to prosecute cases of underage sexual intercourse allegedly committed may arise under Article 8 of the ECHR, (2) that the effect of the time limit in Schedule 2 to the SOA 1956, at least when read with the decision in *J*, is, at least in some cases, to prevent the possibility of effective prosecution, and (3) that there are no good countervailing reasons for the time limit.[39] In a domestic court, the final point would be that the legislation providing for the time limit can be read in a way that avoids the incompatibility.[40]

On the first point, it should be noted that the complainant in *X and Y* wished to complain of rape, and so, although successful under Article 8 of the ECHR, she could also have succeeded in establishing a positive obligation arising under Article 3 of the ECHR. But it may be a stretch to say that complainants of (consensual) underage sexual intercourse have also been subjected to inhuman or degrading treatment as the terms are understood under Article 3. The issue then arises whether there can also be a positive obligation effectively to prosecute offences which may Article 8 but *not* also Article 3. However, at least in the present context, strong reliance may still be placed on a passage in *MC v Bulgaria*.[41] Here, the First Section of the ECtHR said that the duty of effective investigations and prosecution under Article 8 extended to ensure effective deterrence against 'grave acts where fundamental values and essential aspects of private life are at stake', and it added that 'children and other vulnerable individuals, in particular, are entitled

[35] Section 3(1) of the Human Rights Act 1998 provides 'So far as it is possible to do so, primary legislation and subordinate legislation must be read and given effect in a way which is compatible with the Convention rights.'

[36] [2004] UKHL 42, [15].

[37] J Rogers, 'Fundamentally Objectionable?' (2007) 157 *New Law Journal* 1252.

[38] (1986) 8 EHRR 235.

[39] For further discussion of how such arguments are broken down, see J Rogers, 'A Human Rights Perspective on the Evidential Test for Bringing Prosecutions' [2017] *Crim LR* 680.

[40] It is important to note that positive obligations can arise independently from the text of individual Convention rights, and so it suffices that the Human Rights Act 1998 has incorporated ECHR, Art 8, and it is immaterial that it has not also incorporated Arts 1 or 13 of the ECHR.

[41] (2005) 40 EHRR 20.

to effective protection'.[42] This would appear to offer plenty of room for argument that the duty effectively to prosecute under Article 8 of the ECHR extends to at least some cases of underage sexual intercourse, whether or not Article 3 is also engaged. It might, for example, apply where the facts include some element of coercion or ongoing grooming by a much older man, such that the complainant's private life was to some extent dictated by ongoing sexual activity or might continue to be affected by it, eg, if the commission of the offence later interfered with her ability to form trusting relationships.[43]

Even so, whether a complainant's rights are engaged under Article 8 of the ECHR would remain fact-dependent. It might also be that a complainant who was 15 years old at the time of the incident is unlikely to succeed. Within European States, the age of consent to sexual activity has typically ranged between 14 to 16 years old.[44] The ECtHR might, then, have some difficulty in declaring an obligation on the UK to effectively prosecute underage sexual intercourse with vulnerable 15 year old girls while some Member States have 15 as their legal age of consent, because the necessary import of such a decision might be thought to be that these Member States need to amend their substantive criminal law too. Conceivably, a domestic court might take into account such an anticipated objection in Strasbourg, if it were unwilling to give a purely domestic interpretation to the Human Rights Act 1998.

However, in cases where the applicant was just 13 at the time of the incident, then, assuming too some of the aggravating features mentioned above, it seems highly plausible that a positive obligation to prosecute underage sexual intercourse effectively can arise under Article 8 of the ECHR. Our confidence can be fortified by reference to the facts in *NXB v CPS*,[45] a case where the complainant argued that the Crown Prosecution Service (CPS) acted unlawfully under section 6 of the Human Rights Act 1998 when it discontinued allegations of other underage sexual offences on evidential grounds. The complainant was allegedly abused during 1991–1993 and began her statement to the police in 2010 by explaining:

> Over the last 18 months I have been seeing a councillor [sic]. One of the reasons I have needed counselling is because of incidents of a sexual nature with a 40 year old man, which occurred when I was 12 years old, through until I was 15 years old. The counselling is due to end and I feel the need to get everything out in the open now that I am 30. I have decided to tell the police everything as I want closure to this so I can get along with my life.[46]

Surprisingly, it seemed to be assumed without argument in *NXB* that *MC v Bulgaria* provides authority for such a case to engage Article 3 of the ECHR. But the

[42] ibid, [150].
[43] We may recall the observations of Lady Hale above (text accompanying n 23).
[44] See *MC v Bulgaria*, (n 41), [89].
[45] [2015] EWHC 631 QB.
[46] ibid, [6].

ready acceptance that a positive obligation arises on such facts might give us confidence that at least Article 8 would be held properly to be engaged on the very similar facts as suggested above.

The second element, whether the time limit *does* create a substantial barrier to justice, seems relatively easily satisfied, as the law is presently understood. It might, however, be necessary for the evidence of the alleged abuse to be *prima facie* sufficiently plausible that the allegation might otherwise have been prosecuted, else the time bar might not be thought to be such an 'effective' barrier in the applicant's case. It might also be important that the defendant is not also charged with even more serious offences (such as rape) against the same complainant. If he does face such other charges, it might then be thought that the complainant could still have 'effective' justice through prosecution for the alleged rape, especially since evidence of the underage seduction would likely be regarded as background evidence to the alleged rape and to some extent a conviction of rape might be seen as recognition of the fact of the other abuse too. This would not be 'perfect' justice, but a distinction may be thought to exist between 'perfect' justice and the 'effective' justice which Member States are required to seek by virtue of the doctrine of positive obligations.

The third element, whether the State might justify the time limit, is perhaps the simplest. We should not worry that time limits for offences may be relatively common on the continent. It is more to the point that time limits for indictable offences in England are not part of our culture, that this one is exceptional, and that it seems especially inapt for this offence to have been almost singled out in this way. Besides, by this stage of the analysis the applicant may also claim a violation of Article 8 alongside Article 14 of the ECHR (prohibition on discrimination). Article 14 provides:

> The enjoyment of the rights and freedoms set forth in this Convention shall be secured without discrimination on any ground such as sex, race, colour, language ....

The effect of this is that even if the State can justify *in itself* neglecting cases of historic underage sexual intercourse against girls today, it cannot simultaneously (without showing good reason for the difference) continue to prosecute the same allegations against boys. Yet not only are there no time limits for *any* historic sexual offences against young boys,[47] but such cases are actively pursued, at least where there is evidence of exploitation or grooming.[48] It is hard to see how this discrimination could be defended. So either a court, faced with appropriate facts, should hold that the time limit in Schedule 2 to the SOA 1956 violates Article 8 by itself or, more conservatively, that it violates Article 8 together with Article 14. The difference is immaterial to complainants.

[47] Indeed, in the SOA 1967, s 7, the legislature enacted a 1 year time limit for buggery but specifically made an exception for an 'offence by a man with a boy under the age of sixteen', which remained subject to no time limit.

[48] See, eg, the case of *Chapman*, reported in *Silverwood* [2015] EWCA Crim 2401, [17].

Finally, if the time limit in section 6 of the SOA 1956 (and following *J*) *is* thought to violate the complainant's right to effective prosecution of 'her' case under Article 8 of the ECHR, either by itself or when read with Article 14 of the ECHR, then section 3 of the Human Rights Act 1998 applies. It is submitted with some confidence that it is 'possible', even if it is otherwise not the preferred interpretation, to interpret Schedule 6 to the SOA 2003 so that it removes the time limit for all proceedings for the offence under section 6 of the SOA 1956 when commenced from 1 May 2004. Alternatively, one could reach a similar result by saying that it is 'possible' to construe the SOA 1956 so that the time limit attached to section 6 of the SOA 1956 does not have to be read into any charges under section 14 of the SOA 1956.[49]

When we consider the plausibility of the argument that the time limit has already been removed, either by ordinary canons of interpretation or by invoking the Human Rights Act 1998, it may seem odd that no case has yet been brought. In theory at least, domestic law does permit a complainant to challenge the time limit. On being told by the CPS that 'her' case cannot be prosecuted under either section 6 or section 14 of the SOA 1956, she could first challenge the decision under the Victims' Right to Review, and outline the legal arguments that may be made against the application of the time limit. If unsuccessful, she might seek judicial review of that decision on the basis that it is legally flawed because the time limit does not apply.

But such an applicant must move quickly to meet the three-month time limit for commencing judicial review.[50] Many victims take years to summon up the courage to revisit this aspect of their past, and are quite knocked back to square one when belatedly told of a hitherto unmentioned legal obstacle. Three months may quickly pass in such circumstances. Further, if she wishes to avail herself of the human rights argument (and she might be advised that this would be her best chance of success) then the particular alleged facts of her case would become important. On the above account, she might need to be alleging underage sexual intercourse with some element of grooming or manipulation, and the encounters might need to have persisted with sufficient regularity and long lasting effects for it to be accepted that Article 8 is engaged. It might also be necessary that she was 13 years old at the time of the offence, as opposed to 15 years old, at the time, and that underage sexual intercourse would have been by far the most appropriate charge that could properly be brought. Finally, there may need to be some *prima facie* plausibility to the allegation, such that one might expect the case 'otherwise' to be prosecuted.

In other words, even using human rights law has its limitations as a means of procuring reform by judicial means. It may be in fact for the better that no complainant has yet put the matter to the legal test, if otherwise a test case did

[49] Far from being 'impossible', this interpretation did find favour with the dissenting Lady Hale in *J*, without any discussion of the applicability of the Human Rights Act 1998.

[50] *Civil Procedure Rules*, Part 54, rule 54.5.

not disclose an ideal set of facts as set out above, and then failed accordingly. Presumably, neither the CPS nor the Secretary of State for Justice would much relish spending thousands of pounds on legal fees to defend the application of such an anachronistic time limit, but they would be expected to take the legal points available to them; and were a case to be successfully defended, it might then be harder to gather momentum for reforming a time limit which had seemingly been tested and declared compatible with human rights law. From that perspective, everyone should prefer legislative reform instead.

III. The Case for Legislative Reform

Legislative reform could be effectuated in one provision. For example, it might be provided that 'proceedings for the offence under section 6 of the Sexual Offences Act 1956 ("intercourse with a girl between thirteen and sixteen") shall not be barred only by virtue of the passage of time'.[51] Such a provision could be included in legislation on a miscellany of other criminal justice matters. There should be no difficulty in the relevant Secretary of State declaring that he or she believes the provision to be compatible with the Human Rights Act 1998. As it is a purely procedural matter, there is nothing in principle to suggest that such reform would violate any rights of prospective defendants. Compliance with Article 7 of the ECHR would only require that trial judges apply the substantive law as it was at the time and observe maximum sentence of two-year imprisonment when sentencing convicted defendants; and in the latter respect, defendants charged and convicted under section 6 of the SOA 1956 would still be considerably better off than they would have been if it were possible to charge them under the modern section 9 of the SOA 2003.

Further consequential rules could be enacted if thought appropriate, but from the legal perspective, none seems to be essential. The CPS would apply its own contemporary public interest test to the alleged facts of each case, which ought to rule out most proceedings where there was no grooming or exploitation of the girl.[52] If necessary, however, it could be provided that prosecutions enabled by the new provision should require the consent of the Director of Public Prosecutions, a device which pre-empts private prosecutions from being instituted and which

[51] Some might wish to be more explicit, and to add something like 'and paragraph 11 in Schedule 6 to the Sexual Offences Act 2003 shall be read accordingly'.

[52] See CPS Legal Guidance, *Rape and Sexual Offences – Chapter 2: Sexual Offences Act 2003 – Principal Offences, and Sexual Offences Act 1956 – Most commonly charged offences* (CPS Website, 2017). It states: 'where a defendant, for example, is exploitative, or coercive, or much older than the victim, the balance may be in favour of prosecution, whereas if the sexual activity is truly of the victim's own free will the balance may not be in the public interest to prosecute. … In addition, it is not in the public interest to prosecute children who are of the same or similar age and understanding that engage in sexual activity, where the activity is truly consensual for both parties and there are no aggravating features, such as coercion or corruption …'.

often seems to reassure Parliamentarians. At common law, prosecutors would probably not be held to any earlier assurances of non-prosecution which had been made on account of the time limit, and indeed any confessions made to the offence on that basis should be admissible.[53] There might be more disquiet over prosecuting offenders who have already been sentenced to prison (and since released) for other sexual activities with the same girl. But even here, no fault for the problem would normally be attributable to the prosecutor or police,[54] and it might be thought that, if it were decided that a prosecution for underage sexual intercourse might still be in the public interest, such cases could ultimately be dealt with fairly at sentencing.[55] At any rate, it is not obvious that any extra statutory provisions are needed to address these broadly familiar problems in criminal procedure.

There are several reasons to think that such a proposal, if properly understood, would be of interest to many MPs. There is today a wider acceptance that many complainants giving torrid accounts of sexual abuse in the late twentieth century, even against well-known figures and within public institutions, may have been telling the truth and that their cases should still be heard.[56] It is relevant too that, following various well publicised scandals including the prolonged sexual abuse of young teenage girls in Rotherham,[57] the political community is likely to regard grooming of young girls for sex as to be treated with comparable seriousness as rape. Indeed, it is very easy for non-lawyers to think that underage sexual intercourse following grooming *is* 'non-consensual' and must therefore constitute the offence of rape itself. By analogy, the Criminal Injuries Compensation Authority (CICA) has long been prepared to accept underage sexual intercourse following grooming as a 'crime of violence', on the questionable basis that there was no 'factual consent' from the girl.[58]

Caution is needed at this point; for although it is important that the gravity of many such offences is recognised, campaigners should be careful to explain that in law, there is a difference between rape and underage sexual intercourse. Both before and after the SOA 2003, an underage girl between 13 and 15 years old who

[53] In *Dunlop* [2006] EWCA Crim 1354 the Court of Appeal held that it was fair to admit at retrial a person's confession to a murder of which he had already been acquitted, which he had made at an earlier time when it was not yet possible for him to be retried.

[54] In *Connelly v DPP* [1964] AC 1254, it was held not to be an abuse of process to lay a belated charge arising out of the same facts from a previous trial if at the time of the first trial it was thought that the law did not permit that additional charge to be laid.

[55] Courts need only 'take account' of current sentencing guidelines in relation to offences committed before 6 April 2010.

[56] Theresa May, when she was Home Secretary, said 'Perpetrators must never be allowed to think that their horrific acts will go overlooked or go unpunished ... Victims and survivors ... deserve to be heard now, just as they should have been years ago, and they deserve justice, just as they did then': S Laville, 'Police expect 30,000 new child abuse reports from Goddard inquiry' *Guardian Online* (19 May 2016).

[57] See, eg, J Halliday, 'Rotherham: eight men jailed for sexually exploiting teenage girls' *Guardian Online* (4 November 2016).

[58] See J Halliday, 'Compensation body told Rotherham abuse victim she 'consented'' Guardian Online (11 September 2017).

agrees to sex, understanding its mechanics and feeling that she is free to make up her own mind whether to agree, gives valid consent to defeat a rape charge, just as any adult woman would.[59] The fact that many underage girls who are victims of sophisticated grooming techniques might be in denial about their own exploitation, and might wrongly consider that they take such decisions in their own interests, is precisely why offences relating to underage sexual intercourse have existed independently.[60] It is as well to explain that these cases cannot necessarily be prosecuted as rape, in order to emphasise the impact of the time limit problem. Finally, it might be urged that these cases are not necessarily of 'historic' importance only. Recalling the long delay in complaining that may be associated with reporting this offence,[61] it is surely just as likely that we need to prosecute some predatory offenders who have continued offending since 2004 but against whom only a victim from before 1 May 2004 is now ready to testify.[62]

One might imagine some disquiet from those who worry in general terms about fair trials for sexual offences after so many years.[63] But they would surely accept too that there is neither rhyme nor reason in leaving underage sexual intercourse as the one sexual offence which cannot be prosecuted today, and would have to concede that the current time limit is discriminatory against girls, as noted in Part II, and as such is indefensible.

So why have there been no MPs calling for such a simple reform? The most likely answer, to the author's mind, is that no one has alerted any MP to the problem; at any rate, the author knows of nothing which suggests otherwise. Today, it is the media and special interest groups who play the biggest role in alerting MPs to possible causes of law reform. But the problem is very hard to explain briefly and precisely, and even intelligent and earnest journalists have struggled to run an accessible story on it. The author has some experience here, having been contacted by Radio 4[64] and by a journalist for a national newspaper in consequence of a short article[65] that he once wrote on the subject. First, one explains that the problem 'only' arises in cases involving conduct up until 30 April 2004, and that it 'only' affects underage sexual intercourse with girls (why, they ask?). Usually it is

[59] *Olugboja* [1982] QB 320.

[60] Prosecutors and the Court of Appeal alike seem to have lost sight of this in *Ali* [2015] EWCA Crim 1328, when applying the SOA 2003. On the problem of arguably overcharging rape in relation to young complainants who appeared to agree to sex following grooming, see E Freer, 'Yes, no, maybe – recent cases on consent and freedom to choose' [2016] 1 *Archbold Review* 6.

[61] See n 24 and accompanying text.

[62] One victim, who contacted the author after her case was discontinued, explained her lengthy delay by the fact that the abuser had subsequently married her and fathered a child with her, and that she was for a long time anxious to cover up his offences. But she belatedly accepted that she was one of a string of victims of sexual offences committed by the abuser, and also became concerned for their daughter.

[63] It was concerns over miscarriages of justice which initially prompted the Home Affairs Committee Report in 2002 (n 24). In the event the Committee decided against recommending any time limit after hearing evidence.

[64] A programme mainly on the problem was then aired in *The Report* in June 2013.

[65] J Rogers, 'Fundamentally Objectionable?' (2007) *New Law Journal* 1252.

necessary to explain the difference between rape and underage sexual intercourse (a matter which many find difficult, as alluded to above). It is then necessary to explain why it is only recently that the time limit is such a problem, ie, because before *J* it used to be thought acceptable to charge under section 14 of the SOA 1956 instead (why did the House of Lords suddenly decide otherwise, some might interject?). When one is asked why the time limit was not abolished altogether in SOA 2003, the answer, as related in Part II, is that it quite possibly *was*; but, the CPS has not properly argued the point – for reasons unknown (anticipating thereby other questions[66]). For those who want to write short, but also accurate, summaries of the law for lay readers, the 'accessibility problem' that arises from these qualifications and uncertainties is considerable. The author is not aware of any mainstream newspaper which has as much as adverted to the problem, while countless newspaper articles have featured discussions of historic sex cases in clear ignorance of it.[67]

But there are two further reasons why interest from the media has been muted; and these bring us to our final section.

IV. Two Obstacles to Media Interest

In explaining the lack of media interest, there is more than the accessibility problem in play. Just as one photograph might be thought to be worth one thousand words of text, a single statistic proclaiming a high figure of prosecutions that would have been brought, but for the time limit, would likely substitute for a detailed explanation of the legal obstacle. But this brings us to our first obstacle in this Part: it is very hard to estimate how many prosecutions have been disabled by the time limit, let alone to guess how many might now be enabled by abolishing it. Alternatively, a quote from the CPS bemoaning the time limit, or at least acknowledging that the problem may merit some attention, might serve to give the story some perceived media impact. But (the second obstacle), the CPS has shown apparent indifference to it. These problems merit special attention, not least because of their potential role in obstructing other valuable reforms.

A. Difficulties in Estimating the Number of Affected Cases

The would-be reformer should expect to be asked how many allegations of underage sexual intercourse have already been abandoned on account of the time limit.

[66] But see Part IV for observations on the level of CPS engagement with the time limit problem.

[67] For example, see the continuing tabloid interest in the encounters said to have taken place between rock star Bill Wyman and his underage girlfriend in the 1980s: D Pilditch, 'I went to police over my dates with Mandy at 14 says Rolling Stone Mandy Smith' *Express Online* (1 April 2013). Among the speculation, there is no hint that any charges for underage sexual intercourse would today be time barred.

The sheer frequency of underage sexual intercourse[68] suggests that the number of cases that could otherwise have been prosecuted in the public interest since the decision in *J* in 2004 ought to be substantial. One journalist for a national newspaper, who contacted the author about this problem in 2014, was sufficiently interested as to send Freedom of Information requests to all police forces, hoping in this way also to catch recorded offences which might not have been communicated to the CPS. But he found it impossible to interpret the results. Variations in data between different police areas were immense, and widespread ignorance of the time limit was evident, even though the FOI request itself identified the problem. South Wales Police reported that some 59 offenders had, between the years 2007 and 2014, been charged with the offence under section 6 of the SOA 1956. It was not always clear in some such cases whether the recording was wrong, or whether it was right and that several time-barred charges had thus been identified. It was further pointed out by Kent Police that, in April 2009, the Home Office asked police forces to record all allegations of the offence under the broad category '22B – Sexual activity involving a child under 16' regardless of when the offence was alleged to have occurred. Doubtless this change served some administrative purpose but it makes it quite impossible to identify whether allegations relate to 'SOA 1956' offences or to 'SOA 2003' offences when they have been recorded from April 2009 onwards.

The journalist did not make a separate FOI request to the CPS. But there is little reason to think that the CPS would be able to assist more than the police on the matter of estimating numbers of affected cases. Whereas the police would at least record the alleged offence under the relevant code, time limit or not, the trail at the CPS, should the time problem be spotted, is apt to run off into a number of different directions. A range of alternative charges might conceivably have been brought by a prosecutor frustrated by the time limit. Thus, whenever a charge of rape against an underage girl has been preferred in relation to an incident before 1 May 2004, there is the possibility it was laid in circumstances when the case would, but for the time limit, normally have been charged as underage sexual intercourse.[69] The next place to look is the record of charges under section 14 of the SOA 1956, where defendants might have been wrongly prosecuted in ignorance of the ruling in *J*, or might instead (if *J* was observed) have been prosecuted for other indecent acts

[68] In 2001 it was estimated that between one quarter and one third of young people had their first heterosexual intercourse under the age of 16. K Welling et al, 'Sexual Behaviour in Britain; Early Heterosexual Experience' (2001) *Lancet* 1843.

[69] This almost certainly happened in *Kirk* [2008] EWCA Crim 434. Indeed, there is every temptation to bring a rape charge because, if put to the jury, they (if at least satisfied that sexual intercourse took place) are then entitled to convict of indecent assault as an alternative verdict, notwithstanding the lapse in time. This was acknowledged to be a further anomaly in *Cottrell* [2007] EWCA Crim 2016. For criticism, see J Rogers, 'Fundamentally Objectionable?' (2007) 157 *New Law Journal* 1252. To charge rape as a mere device for getting a case of time barred underage sexual intercourse to trial would be an abuse of process, *Timmins* [2006] 1 Cr App R 18; but that is not to say that it has not happened. One rather suspects that it has.

with the underage girl, which were not part and parcel of the sexual intercourse itself. Otherwise, the defendant who could not be charged with underage sexual intercourse may have been charged with inciting the underage girl to perform oral sexual intercourse.[70] Or, if, having seduced the girl, the defendant then persuaded her to have sex with others, he could have been prosecuted for procuring a third party to have sexual intercourse with a woman under 21,[71] or causing prostitution of a woman (of any age).[72] Further possibilities are easily imagined.

So, identifying cases where the time limit prevented a charge which would or might otherwise have been brought under section 6 of the SOA 1956 is an undertaking of such proportions that few would expect the CPS to do it; for to do it properly would require revisiting the full accounts of complainants in the files of almost everyone charged with, or who could have been charged with, *any* sexual offence against any underage girl committed up until 30 April 2004.

But that is not to say that the CPS cannot have been expected to have done more in other respects, which brings us to our second obstacle.

B. Lack of Engagement from the CPS

Ideally, the human rights argument as outlined in Part II would have been made by the CPS at the time in *J*, since it was (and is) possible to interpret the time limit in Schedule 2 to the SOA 1956 as applicable only to charges under section 6 of the SOA 1956. But, as a new argument, it might have been made at any time since. Today, the CPS should argue that Schedule 6 to the SOA 2003 abolishes the time limit for all trials commencing after the Act came into force, and use the human rights argument in reserve. To do this, it needs only to bring a charge under section 6 of the SOA 1956 and then take an interlocutory appeal to the Court of Appeal[73] if or when a trial judge follows the decision in *J* and rules the charge to be time barred.

But it would seem that no such strategy has ever been formulated. Only in *Boyes*,[74] when the decision in *J* was belatedly (in the Court of Appeal) brought to the attention of the Crown (none of the participants at the Crown Court having apparently noticed it[75]) did counsel for the Crown reportedly ask for permission to draft a question for consideration by the Supreme Court. But he later declined to do so, for reasons unexplained. The chaotic background to the case, however, hardly suggests that a well thought out submission had ever been planned.

[70] Contrary to the Indecency with Children Act 1960, s 1(1) and charged separately in *J*, (n 6).

[71] Contrary to SOA 1956, s 23.

[72] Contrary to SOA 1956, s 22. Both these latter offences were charged in relation to underage sexual activity in *Ali* [2017] EWCA Crim 1211.

[73] Under the provisions of the Criminal Justice Act 2003, ss 58–61.

[74] *Boyes* [2012] EWCA 1174.

[75] It was only the single judge, who was asked to give leave to appeal on sentence for a number of sexual offences, who noticed the problem.

Indeed, it is more likely that the chaos that plagues the underfunded CPS results in charges relating to underage sexual intercourse continuing to be made under section 14 of the SOA 1956, on account of a simple oversight of *J* and its implications. The author has seen many reports of trials where defendants are charged under section 14 and where it is only the alleged fact of underage sexual intercourse which is mentioned in the report: and it is usually not easy to credit that the prosecution must instead have been leading evidence of a separate, unmentioned, indecent assault.[76] It is on account of this uninspiring pattern that when some police forces purport to have records of offenders being tried and even convicted out of time (as the law is currently understood), one wonders whether some of these records may indeed be right. It is true that the decision in *J* is noted on the CPS website,[77] but only the bare reference is given, and with little indication of its importance. It is easy to imagine that some busy prosecutors who are not already *au fait* with the problem might overlook it when affected cases happen to come their way,[78] especially since more of their caseload falls under the SOA 2003 where there are no time limits of which to be wary. We might note that the Court of Appeal has itself complained that the analogous time limit for historic cases of gross indecency between men has been overlooked on several occasions.[79]

The picture which then emerges is one of a lottery where sometimes offenders are wrongly prosecuted despite the time limit, but no one knows how often it has happened. But journalists (and perhaps MPs) who may seek views or insight relating to the time limit are likely to turn to the CPS, and it is a significant frustration that the latter might be unable to provide much of either. Some criticism must be made of apparent indifference here. Even if it is too much to expect the CPS to compile statistics, it could at least form an impression of the problem and its working implications by surveying police investigators, its case workers, and trial lawyers.

Thus, specialist police officers who interview complainants could usefully be asked whether they feel obliged, perhaps awkwardly, to ask whether any separate (ie non-time barred) indecent activity also took place and then to focus their questioning on any such incidents, albeit no doubt to the consternation of the complainant. CPS case workers could be asked how often they have considered alternative charges on account of the time bar, and whether they have seemed

[76] This is so both in the law reports (eg *Ali* [2017] EWCA Crim 1211) and in media reports, even where celebrities are tried: see eg D Sapsted, 'Chris Langham 'abused girl over three years'' *Telegraph Online* (12 July 2007).

[77] CPS Legal Guidance, 'Rape and Sexual Offences – Chapter 2: Sexual Offences Act 2003 – Principal Offences, and Sexual Offences Act 1956 – Most commonly charged offences' (CPS Website, 2017).

[78] Or at least, the problem might not be noted until a rather late stage. See the elliptic passage in *NXB v CPS*, (n 45), [21].

[79] *Silverwood* (n 28); *Forbes* [2016] EWCA Crim 1388; *Coatman* [2017] EWCA Crim 392. A longer list can be found on Westlaw. In *Silverwood*, Lady Hallett concluded 'Problems of this kind are becoming increasingly common … Particular care should be taken in cases involving allegations of historic sexual abuse …'.

appropriate to reflect the apparent level of offending. Trial prosecutors might be asked for their impressions of such cases, where the jury hears of the sexual intercourse and yet is not asked to consider any count relating to it. It is surely possible that some juries wrongly speculate that the CPS itself does not believe the complainant on the matter of the sexual intercourse, thus causing them wrongly to doubt the complainant's evidence about other allegations. Ideally, affected past complainants should also be consulted. It would be invaluable to know whether *they* feel that their cases are ineffectively prosecuted on account of the time limit. One imagines that many might feel this way, even if other indecent activities, which they may remember less well, were prosecuted instead of the vaginal sexual intercourse. For many, the vaginal intercourse may well be the most regretted incident of all (eg if it necessitated an abortion). This author recently put this point to a former Crown prosecutor who was used to applying the time limit and charging other offences instead. Did complainants have a problem with this? 'I wouldn't know', came back the answer, and then, after a moment's thought, 'but quite possibly so'.

Some senior prosecutors have said to this author that they had not even heard of the time limit, as though to suggest that, if it is a problem, indeed it cannot be a serious one. But the fact that they have not heard of the time limit is as much a symptom of the problems within the CPS as a possible indication of their absence. It is impossible, to the author's mind, to credit such bland assurances when not even the most basic research seems to have been carried out within the CPS. But journalists and MPs may yet be inclined to give them credit.

V. Conclusion

It is arguable that the limit for the offence in section 6 of the SOA 1956 has already been abolished in respect of proceedings commenced since 1 May 2004 by virtue of Schedule 6 to the SOA 2003. For those complainants with suitable facts, an additional argument may be made that Schedule 6 must be so interpreted by virtue of the Human Rights Act 1998. But either way, it will be a courageous complainant who wishes to argue the point through the courts. An unambiguous legislative reform would be better.

So far, however, the indications are that starting a campaign for reform through the media is difficult. The difficulties should cause us to reflect that the police and CPS are predominantly concerned with law enforcement and not with law reform. It should not surprise us if they record offences and decisions in ways which assist them but might quite frustrate researchers who expect to find reasonably reliable statistics. The reform as proposed here would have had a better audience had the media been apprised of it shortly after the decision in *J*: for the media might then have been interested to run a story about its very potential to ruin a high number of very serious cases, and the CPS might then have obliged with a warning about the potential problems. But over ten years later, the evidence of the number of cases affected is missing and the CPS has altogether lost sight of the matter.

Admittedly, by no means all avenues of reform have been exhausted. The determined complainant with a suitable case might yet start judicial review of a decision not to prosecute on account of the time limit; or, perhaps the author, or an influential reader of this article, will prove able to bring the problem to the attention of appropriate MPs or the Ministry of Justice. Even now, it need not be too late for reform.

Comment on Chapter 7

Removing the Time Limit on Prosecutions for Underage Sexual Intercourse in the Sexual Offences Act 1956 – Some Comments and Concerns

HANNAH QUIRK

Jonathan Rogers makes a compelling case in his chapter for remedying what is presumably an unintended lacuna in the law, whereby an offence of 'unlawful sexual intercourse with a girl not under the age of thirteen but under the age of sixteen'[1] can no longer be prosecuted.[2] The offence (now abolished) had to be charged within one year of the incident and the common law 'work around' of charging indecent assault as an alternative was held to be unlawful in 2004.[3] As all sexual offences were reformed by the Sexual Offences Act 2003, this issue relates to only the unknowable number of offences that occurred before that date. Rogers makes a cogent, although not unproblematic, case for remedial action. He attacks the decision to uphold the time limit on the grounds of statutory interpretation and as a failure to protect the human rights of complainants. Whilst he acknowledges the remote prospect of his proposal being effected, due in part to the difficulties in attracting media attention and engagement from the Crown Prosecution Service (CPS), his chapter raises many interesting questions.

There is, nevertheless, an attractive case for establishing a route to convicting those who might otherwise escape justice, it is important to consider the harms that such a change could cause to innocent suspects and to due process rights overall. This response challenges some of the implicit assumptions of guilt made by those who share Rogers' aim. Whilst acknowledging the shortcomings of the

[1] Sexual Offences Act 1956, s 6.

[2] J Rogers, 'The Time Limit on Prosecutions for Underage Sexual Intercourse in the Sexual Offences Act 1956: A Continuing Problem', ch 7 of this volume.

[3] *J* [2004] UKHL 42.

criminal justice system in convicting sex offenders, this reply strikes a cautionary note, raising the spectre of wrongful convictions and adding to Rogers' historical analysis by locating his proposal in the context of the other due process losses that defendants have experienced. There has been a steady attrition of the rights of suspects and defendants over the last 25 years – much of it in the name of improving victims' rights – and, however tempting a simple reform might appear, it should be remembered that hard cases can make bad law.

I. Statutory Interpretation

There are valid reasons for setting the age of consent at 16, although the arbitrariness of this is underlined by divergence across the world, over time, and between heterosexual and homosexual acts. The age of consent ranges between 11 in Nigeria and 21 in Bahrain.[4] It was raised to 16 for heterosexuals in England in 1885,[5] but was set higher for homosexuals after homosexuality was decriminalised[6] until 2000.[7] Governments have repeatedly resisted suggestions to lower the age of consent, largely on child protection grounds.[8] The offence of unlawful sexual activity under section 6 (the subject of Rogers' critique) covered situations in which a male had sex with a teenage girl under 16 which, although consensual in fact, could not be so in law due to the legal presumption that a girl could not give her consent. (Non-consensual sex was prosecuted as rape.) Charges had to be brought within six months of the alleged incident.

The lack of a reason for the prosecution time limit within section 6 makes both attacking and defending it more difficult. The Sexual Offences Act 1956 was a consolidating statute but 'a complete coherence is not necessarily to be found among all its provisions'.[9] It is generally only the less serious, summary-only offences that have time bars.[10] At common law, there is no time limit for commencing a prosecution so, absent a statutory limitation, a prosecution may be brought at any time after the offence, unless the delay in proceedings amounts to an abuse of process.[11] Parliament specified that there should be a time limit for section 6, but

[4] 'From 11 to 21: Ages of Consent Around the World' *The Week* (6 March 2018).

[5] Criminal Law Amendment Act 1885, s 5.

[6] Sexual Offences Act 1967, s 1.

[7] Sexual Offences (Amendment) Act 2000, s 1; Criminal Justice and Public Order Act 1994, s 145.

[8] A Home Office Report recommended lowering the age to 14 (R Walmsley and K White, *Sexual Offences, Consent and Sentencing* (Home Office, 1979) cited in R Booth 'Whitehall Study Wanted Age of Consent Lowered to 14 and Sentences for Sex Cut' *The Guardian* (8 July 2014)). See also the Policy Advisory Committee on Sexual Offences, *Report on the Age of Consent in relation to Sexual Offences* (Cmnd 8216, 1981). The leaders of all the main political parties dismissed such a call from Professor John Ashton, the Faculty of Public Health President (see 'PM Rejects Call to Lower Age of Consent to 15' *BBC News* (17 November 2013)).

[9] *J* [2004] UKHL 42 [48] per Lord Clyde.

[10] Magistrates' Courts Act 1980, s 127.

[11] Archbold, *Criminal Pleading Evidence and Practice* (Sweet & Maxwell, 2017 Ed) 1–313.

gave no explanation as to why. The Criminal Law Revision Committee (CLRC)[12] subsequently endorsed the time bar as it 'ensures that a prosecution may not be brought in respect of events that have become stale'. This is undoubtedly a valid concern but does not apply solely to this offence – and the passage of time may not be an insuperable obstacle to a fair trial. The CLRC continued, however, that '[n]o limitation period applies to [the offence of unlawful sexual intercourse with a girl under 13]; nor, in view of its gravity, is it appropriate that one should'.[13] This might suggest that the limit is due to seriousness rather than evidential concerns – reinforcing the notion that no great harm was done through a quasi-consensual relationship. It should be noted, however, that the section 6 offence was triable on indictment, and had the same maximum penalty (two years) as indecent assault, which had no time limit.

Baroness Hale dismissed attempts at ex post facto rationalisation of the time limit:

> In short, the 1956 Act was a mess when it was enacted and became an ever greater mess with later amendments. It is not possible to discern within it such a coherent Parliamentary intention as to require it to be construed so as to forbid prosecution for a 'mere' act of sexual intercourse after 12 months where that act properly falls within the definition of an indecent assault. Although we do have to try to make sense of the words Parliament has used, we do not have to supply Parliament with the thinking that it never did and words that it never used.[14]

As the sole dissenting opinion in *J*,[15] she dismissed arguments that the prosecution was an abuse of process. She stated that the offender knew that he was committing a criminal offence at the time, and that the time limit is neither an essential ingredient of the substantive offence nor a substantive defence. The other four Lords, however, were firmly of the view that it was improper for the CPS to have charged the defendant with indecent assault rather than unlawful sexual intercourse in an attempt to circumvent the time limit on the latter offence. Lord Steyn was clear that 'the legislative adjuration is explicit and strong'[16] and that the intention of Parliament could not be evaded lawfully:

> Although it is not easily accommodated under any of the traditional categories of abuse of process … this is pre-eminently a corner of the law which must be considered from the point of view of legal principle … The judiciary may not render a statutory provision, such as a time limit, nugatory on the ground that it disagrees with the reason underlying it.

He concluded that, whilst the CPS had acted in good faith in charging the offence in this way, its actions were nevertheless ultra vires. Lord Clyde agreed that

[12] Criminal Law Revision Committee, *Fifteenth Report: Sexual Offences* (Cmnd 9213, 1984) [522].
[13] ibid, [523].
[14] *J* [2004] UKHL 42 [80].
[15] ibid.
[16] ibid, [37].

'[t]he essence of the wrong is an illegality which in turn is based upon a misconstruction of the Act. While the label of abuse [of process] may not be appropriate for such a situation the illegality of the course would justify the intervention of the court'.[17] Lord Bingham added that 'the deficiencies of the Act cannot absolve the court from its duty to give effect to clear and unambiguous provisions'.[18] Lord Rodger added that to construe the Act to evade the time bar would amount to a 'fraud upon an Act'.[19]

The Court of Appeal has subsequently indicated its 'evident sympathy with the vigorous dissenting speech of Baroness Hale of Richmond'.[20] Nevertheless, despite the inconsistencies in *J* and the need to protect the Article 3 and Article 8 rights of the complainant by providing a system of effective prosecution, the Supreme Court seems unlikely to revisit the issue.[21]

II. The 'Mischief' Addressed by the Time Limit

Much of the commentary that accords with Rogers' criticism of the time bar refers to a changed understanding of the harms that can result from quasi-consensual sexual relationships with underage girls. Specific offences have been created to prevent relationships between those in positions of authority and those under 18 years of age.[22] Most of the concern relates to cases with a significant age gap between the parties and the current anxieties around girls being 'groomed' and subsequently sexually exploited. It might be that such behaviour was insufficiently recognised, or happened less, before, but it is important to consider those who have behaved in a less reprehensible manner – or may even be innocent – who may be swept up in changes designed to catch the worst conduct.

The age gap between the parties is not necessarily a reliable indicator of whether the relationship is manipulative, coercive, or abusive. For the avoidance of doubt, 35 year olds should not be having sex with 15 year olds, but it could be in the context of a loving relationship that endures. Again, the purpose behind the Sexual Offences Act 1956 is difficult to deduce. Section 6 included a defence if the man was under the age of 24 and had reasonable cause to believe the girl was over 16, (the so-called 'young man's defence'). This would presumably have only applied to brief encounters where he did not know her age, rather than providing a, perhaps more defensible, 'Romeo and Juliet' defence of the kind that operates

[17] ibid, [49].
[18] ibid, [15].
[19] ibid, [64].
[20] P Mirfield, 'A Challenge to the Declaratory Theory of Law' (2008) 124 *LQR* 190, 190; *Cottrell (Steven)* [2007] EWCA Crim 2016; [2017] 1WLR 3262 (CA Crim Div).
[21] D Ormerod, 'Appeal: Change in Law Since Conviction – Court of Appeal's Approach to Conviction Under Previous Law' [2008] *Crim LR* 50, 52.
[22] Sexual Offences Act 2003, ss 16–21.

in some American States. (Such defences reduce the penalty or provide a defence where the couple are close in age and the sexual contact was factually consensual.)[23] Whilst the law has been held not to be discriminatory per se even though there is no comparable offence for a woman having sex with an underage boy (or indeed girl), it is arguably paternalistic, chauvinistic and illogical to suggest that where a boy and girl who may be in the same class at school have sex, he is old enough to be criminally responsible for his actions, whilst she is legally too immature to consent to sex.

In much of the criticism of the time limit there is an elision between quasi-consensual and more overtly abusive acts. Potter LJ[24] notes that it is often not until the victim is 'free of the influence of the defendant, [that she] is able to appreciate the degree to which their relationship was an abusive one'. Rogers refers to reports that suggest 'significant numbers of complainants are aged between 30 to 40 years when they report experiences of childhood *abuse*'.[25] He argues (without providing supporting evidence) that nowadays, since 'many offenders are much older than the underage girl, and might have trapped the girl into a longer term abusive relationship, or might have groomed girls from disadvantaged backgrounds (possibly also making them available to friends) we would describe the potential harms in much wider terms'.[26] This description alludes to the appalling cases of abuse networks that have been uncovered in places such as Rotherham and Oxford.[27] Convictions were, however, achieved in these cases under the more serious offences which they merited, such as rape and the 'sexual exploitation of children' offences.[28]

Baroness Hale's reasoning in *J* is also grounded in examples of sexual exploitation and abuse. She argued that the law was too slow to recognise that even consensual sexual activity with children 'was both harmful and abusive'.[29] She observed that it was not known why the complainant in that case said nothing until she was 17, but she noted that:

> … sexual abusers commonly groom their victims by making them believe that their behaviour is normal. They make their victims fall in love with them. They often threaten or cajole their victims into silence. Delayed reporting is then the result of the abuser's own actions and merits no special protection. It is only when the delay has prejudiced the chances of a fair trial that special protection is deserved. That is not this case.[30]

[23] See, eg, the Texas Penal Code, s 22.011(e).
[24] *J* [2002] EWCA Crim 2983; [2003] 1 WLR 1590, 1603, [39].
[25] See p 197 this volume, (emphasis added).
[26] See p 196 this volume.
[27] A Jay, *Independent Inquiry into Child Sexual Exploitation in Rotherham (1997–2013)* (Rotherham Met Borough Council, 2014).
[28] Sexual Offences Act 2003, ss 47–51.
[29] *J* [2004] UKHL 42, [74].
[30] ibid, [80].

III. Rights of the Defendant

It is unfair to defendants and appellants to assume a scenario which was not presented in evidence. Arguing, perhaps many years after an event, that consent was obtained as a result of manipulation or grooming, or even was injurious, is deeply problematic. It is possible to suggest reasons (based on real examples) as to why an allegation might be false or misdirected. Troubled adults, often having sought counselling, have made unfounded allegations about sexual abuse in their childhood that have led to miscarriages of justice.[31] False accusations can be made from jealousy, a desire for revenge, or attention-seeking. It must also be recognised that compensation is available to those reporting abuse under the Criminal Injuries Compensation Scheme, and civil actions for compensation against institutions may be possible if the allegations are made against, for example, a teacher or care worker. It does not diminish the experience of anyone who has been in an emotionally exploitative sexual relationship to caution that there is a risk of wrongful convictions for these offences.

Baroness Hale concluded in *J* that 'In my view, the appellant was guilty of conduct which constituted the offences with which he was charged at the time when he committed them; there is no good reason why he should not have been charged with and convicted of them …'[32] Her logic is, however, circular, as the prosecutor must necessarily take a decision regarding prosecution before guilt has been established. At times, Rogers also uses terminology suggestive of guilt (such as 'serious offences committed against them'[33] [the complainants]).

Baroness Hale acknowledged that a spectrum of behaviour is covered by this offence, from a teenage romance to prolonged and serious abuse of a position of trust by a person who would be free to do it again unless action was taken. She concluded '[i]t will all depend upon the circumstances, in which the interests of the accused, the victim and of society will all play their part. A just and humane prosecution policy should be capable of taking all these factors into account'.[34] This is not a sufficient safeguard. The interests of the accused, *complainant* and society are not equivalent. The burden of proof lies on the prosecution to establish guilt beyond reasonable doubt – this illustrates that priority should be given to avoiding wrongful convictions. This is a difficult political position at times, particularly when society might be demanding more prosecutions. John Smith, analysing the abuse of process argument in *J*,[35] considered that:

> The 'public conscience' is a somewhat vague concept but it is difficult to imagine that it would be affronted by the bringing of a prosecution in the circumstances of the

[31] R Burnett (ed) *Wrongful Allegations of Sexual and Child Abuse* (OUP, 2016).
[32] *J* [2004] UKHL 42 [69].
[33] See p 196 this volume.
[34] *J* [2004] UKHL 42 [90].
[35] C Barsby and JC Smith, 'Case Comment: Abuse of Process: Sexual Offences Act 1956 ss 6, 14 – Defendant Prosecuted for Offence of Indecent Assault' [2003] *Crim LR* 391.

present case. Indeed it is more likely that the public would be outraged to learn that a prosecution was not possible.

The criminal justice system obviously has to maintain public confidence but, particularly in such potentially emotive cases, it cannot be driven by public opinion. It is precisely with unpopular defendants that Parliament and the judiciary must hold fast to that golden thread 'that it is the duty of the prosecution to prove the prisoner's guilt'[36] and the 'maxim of English law that ten guilty men should escape rather than that one innocent man should suffer'.[37] Nor is it enough to vest the safeguard against overly broad legislation in prosecutorial discretion. The CPS in recent years has taken a very proactive approach to prosecuting allegations of sexual offences that previously would not have been charged, for which the Director of Public Prosecutions has faced both praise and criticism.

Rogers notes the benefits of a change in culture that recognises the difficulties which individuals may experience in reporting allegations of sexual assault. What is not addressed, however, is the extent to which this has arguably gone too far and, particularly regarding historical sexual accusations, the impossible position in which the suspect is now placed. The police operations and inquiries established following the allegations made against the late celebrity Sir Jimmy Savile, suggested startling levels of unacknowledged abuse. The subsequent ill-fated investigations into what appear to have been fanciful allegations against the late Sir Edward Heath, Field Marshall Bramall, Harvey Proctor and Paul Gambaccini show the importance of a disinterested police approach. Following criticism, the Metropolitan Police[38] has renounced its policy of 'believing victims'. Again, this policy was a well-intentioned attempt to correct previous failings in how complainants in cases of sexual violence were dealt with by the police and judicial system. It nevertheless, ran counter to years of attempts to counter the tendency for officers to assume they have identified the correct suspect and attempt to construct a case to support their belief. This was known to be a factor in miscarriages of justice leading to false confessions and failures to disclose material.

Lord Clyde noted the increase in recent years of historical or 'non-recent' cases involving sexual offences: '[s]uch prosecutions are not without their difficulties but, in general, the stance of the law is that time does not run against iniquity'.[39] Delay caused by the late reporting of a crime carries additional problems for defendants in sexual offence cases. Lord Steyn noted in *J* that the issue of whether there should be time limits for some sexual offences was an important one that he thought should be examined, perhaps by the Law Commission.[40] Whilst recognising the arbitrariness of any limit, he suggested that 'it may well be that the bringing

[36] *Woolmington* v *DPP* [1935] UKHL 1, 7.

[37] *Hobson* [1823] 1 Lew CC 261 Holroyd J.

[38] F Hamilton, 'Metropolitan police ditches practice of believing all victims' *The Times* (2 April 2018).

[39] *J* [2004] UKHL 42, [54].

[40] ibid, [20].

of truly stale charges, very many years after the events took place, are not in the interests of victims and society'.[41] He added, however, that this was a matter for Parliament, rather than the courts.

Rogers' worthy proposal should not be considered in isolation. It must be noted how many other procedural rights of defendants have been encroached upon. Somebody prosecuted for an offence committed in 1990 would now face a very different investigation and adjudication process with fewer safeguards and many additional hurdles in place. Adverse inferences could be drawn from his failure to mention when questioned by the police any fact relied upon at trial or from his failure or refusal to testify.[42] He would also be expected to submit a defence case statement in advance of trial,[43] and further particulars would be required in the Plea and Case Management Advocates' Questionnaire.[44] Similar fact, bad character and hearsay evidence are now easier for the prosecution to introduce,[45] the requirement for the court to warn the jury about convicting the accused on the uncorroborated evidence of the complainant has been abolished,[46] and the defendant would be less likely to qualify for legal aid.[47] The complainant would now give pre-recorded testimony, might appear behind a screen or by video link, and there would be restrictions on how she could be cross-examined. In addition, the Crown Prosecution Service now takes a much more proactive stance in pursuing prosecutions involving sexual offences. Indictments may now cover a range of dates rather than a specific incident, and conflicts in the complainant's testimony may be 'corrected' before trial – or attributed to the trauma that she experienced as a result of the crime.[48]

The Court of Appeal acted swiftly to limit the effect of the decision in *J* in the case of *Cottrell*,[49] limiting the basis on which those already convicted could appeal. This was a controversial decision[50] that sought to circumscribe the referral powers of the Criminal Cases Review Commission in dealing with suspected unsafe convictions, further reducing due process safeguards and making it harder for those who may have been wrongly convicted to have their convictions overturned.

[41] ibid, [29].
[42] Criminal Justice and Public Order Act 1994, ss 34–38.
[43] Criminal Procedure and Investigations Act 1996, s 5.
[44] Crown Court, *Plea and Case Management Hearing Advocates' Questionnaire* (Plea and Case Management Hearing, Criminal Procedure Rules 2011).
[45] Criminal Justice Act 2003.
[46] Criminal Justice and Public Order Act 1994, ss 33–34.
[47] The Fabian Society, *The Right to Justice: The Final Report of the Bach Commission* (September 2017).
[48] Consolidated Criminal Practice Direction, IV.34.12.
[49] [2007] EWCA Crim 2016.
[50] J Rogers, 'Fundamentally Objectionable?' (2007) 157 *New Law Journal* 1252; R Nobles and D Schiff 'Absurd Asymmetry – a Comment on R v Cottrell and Fletcher and BM, KK and DP (Petitioners) v Scottish Criminal Cases Review Commission' (2008) 71(3) *MLR* 464.

IV. Conclusion

Rogers' chapter is a thought-provoking one that illustrates the importance of statutory interpretation and the different approaches to it, ranging from the literal approach of the majority to the purposive approach of Baroness Hale. He makes a persuasive case. Even if the legislation were to be reformed, it would not remove rights that defendants had hitherto enjoyed (as when the right of silence was curtailed), it would merely deprive some defendants of an anomalous benefit. And yet … Repeated evidential changes have been introduced in recent years with the explicit intention of raising conviction rates generally as well as those trying to increase the number of prosecutions and convictions for sexual offences specifically. Particularly in historical cases, defendants face unique – almost insurmountable – obstacles in defending themselves. It is a desire to resist this ratcheting effect, rather than a particular objection to Rogers' proposal, that leads me to caution against a legislative change that might carry significant hidden costs to the fairness of the criminal justice system for limited benefit in terms of bringing small numbers of offenders to justice.

8

Safe and Effective Courtroom Participation for Domestic Violence Complainant-Witnesses

CHARLOTTE BISHOP

The serious and traumatic impact that ongoing, inescapable physical and psychological abuse has upon its victims still has not received adequate legal recognition, despite amendments to the non-statutory definition of domestic violence, and the introduction of the new criminal offence of 'controlling or coercive behaviour'.[1] Insufficient recognition of the traumatic nature of domestic violence has in turn led to insufficient support being given to traumatised victims within the criminal justice system, and insufficient guidance for criminal justice professionals and jury panels on the impact traumatic stress has on victims' interaction with, and participation in, the criminal justice process. As will be seen below, when domestic violence results in trauma for a victim – as is frequently the case – it has severe and ongoing implications for the individual which will affect their ability to participate in all stages of the criminal justice process. Research within the social sciences shows increasing recognition that the harm of domestic violence extends beyond the infliction of physical injuries to emotional distress and psychological trauma,[2] and States have been held to be under an obligation to

[1] The 2013 cross-government definition of domestic violence and abuse is: 'any incident or pattern of incidents of controlling, coercive, threatening behaviour, violence or abuse between those aged 16 or over who are, or have been, intimate partners or family members regardless of gender or sexuality. The abuse can encompass, but is not limited to: psychological; physical; sexual; financial and emotional': Home Office, 'Guidance: Domestic violence and abuse' (Gov.uk, updated 2016). Thus the non-physical aspects of domestic violence and/or abuse are now recognised. The new offence of controlling or coercive behaviour was introduced under the Serious Crime Act 2015, s 76.

[2] J Herman, *Trauma and Recovery: From Domestic Abuse to Political Terror* (Rivers Oram Press, 1992); V Tadros, 'The Distinctiveness of Domestic Abuse: A Freedom Based Account' (2004) 65(3) *Louisiana Law Review* 989; E Stark, *Coercive Control: How Men Entrap Women in Personal Life* (OUP, 2007); E Stark, 'Rethinking Coercive Control' (2009) 15 *Violence Against Women* 1509; E Williamson, 'Living in the World of the Domestic Violence Perpetrator: Negotiating the Unreality of Coercive Control' (2010) 16(2) *Violence Against Women* 1412; M Tagg, 'Psychological Impact on Those who Experience Domestic Abuse' in H Hughes (ed), *Domestic Abuse and Scots Law* (W Green, 2011) 169.

protect the psychological integrity of citizens by virtue of Articles 3 and 8 of the European Convention on Human Rights (ECHR).[3] However, because domestic violence has been constructed as a crime of physical violence rather than as an attack on the psychological integrity of the victim, the harm and impact upon the victim has frequently been misconstrued as being predominantly physical.[4] This has meant that human rights implications based upon the need to protect citizens' psychological integrity are not always recognised.

Inadequate recognition of trauma prevents appropriate protections being provided which in turn leads to various problems, including barriers when prosecuting domestic violence offences. Although these obstacles are complex, it is clear that victim reluctance to report and/or be a witness in criminal proceedings plays a significant part in the consistently high attrition rate for domestic violence-related offences.[5] Whilst prosecution might not always be the safest or most desirable option for a victim, and whether a case should be taken forward against the victim's wishes is a highly contentious issue, there are public interest considerations and human rights obligations that must be taken into account alongside the wishes of the victim, and it is important to avoid giving the message that perpetrators are able to act with impunity, because the criminal law is not adequately upheld.[6] It is also suggested that some of the reasons victims do not wish their partner or former partner to be prosecuted result from a lack of understanding among criminal justice professionals about the nature of the abuse they have suffered and the ways in which it may impact upon them when they attempt to participate in the criminal justice process.[7] Some of these barriers may be

[3] See *Eremia v Moldova* [2013] ECHR 3564/11 where the European Court reiterated that ill-treatment must attain a minimum level of severity if it is to fall within the scope of Art 3, the assessment of which is relative and contextual. Thus, for someone who is vulnerable because they are in an abusive relationship, the level of threat required to meet the threshold is lower than for a person who is not. Moreover, the Court deemed the risk to the applicant's physical and, importantly, *psychological* well-being imminent and serious enough as to require the authorities to act swiftly. With regard to Art 8, it was held in *X and Y v The Netherlands* (1985) 8 EHRR 235, that the right to private life encompasses the right to be protected from attacks upon physical and psychological integrity.

[4] C Bishop, 'The Limitations of a Legal Response' in V Bettinson and S Hilder (eds), *Domestic Violence: Interdisciplinary Perspectives on Protection, Prevention and Intervention* (Palgrave Macmillan, 2016).

[5] A Cretney and G Davis, 'Prosecuting Domestic Assault: Victims Failing Courts, or Courts Failing Victims?' (1997) 36 *The Howard Journal of Criminal Justice* 146; L Bennett, L Goodman and MA Dutton, 'Systemic obstacles to the Criminal Prosecution of a Battering Partner: A Victim Perspective (1999) 14(7) *Journal of Interpersonal Violence* 761; P Anderson, K Boyle, D Cook, G Hartley and M Roberts, *All Saints and Blakenhall Community District: Domestic violence Research Project* (Regional Research Institute, University of Wolverhampton, 2001); M Hester, 'Making it Through the Criminal Justice System: Attrition and Domestic Violence' (2006) 5(1) *Social Policy and Society* 79; A Robinson and D Cook, 'Understanding Victim Retraction in Cases of Domestic Violence: Specialist Courts, Government Policy, and Victim-Centred Justice' (2006) 9(2) *Contemporary Justice Review* 189.

[6] States are under a positive obligation to respond adequately when they become aware that an individual is experiencing domestic violence (*Kontrova v Slovakia* 31 May 2007, Application no.7510/04; *Opuz v Turkey* (2010) 50 EHRR 28).

[7] M Hester, 'Making it Through the Criminal Justice System: Attrition and Domestic Violence' (2006) 5(1) *Social Policy and Society* 1. A Robinson and D Cook 'Understanding Victim Retraction in Cases of Domestic Violence: Specialist Courts, Government Policy, and Victim-Centred Justice' (2006) 9(2) *Contemporary Justice Review* 189.

objective, lying in the ways in which complainants are in fact treated, while others may be subjective, lying in the expectations and fears of victims about how they will be treated, and it is likely that a combination of the two are often in operation. Therefore, increasing victim confidence by improving police and CPS responses is of paramount importance if the high social and economic costs associated with domestic violence are to be reduced and the physical and psychological integrity of those affected is to be better protected during the prosecution process.[8]

Underlying the recommendations outlined in Part II of this chapter lies the assertion that increased recognition of the traumatic nature of much domestic violence and abuse needs to be carried through into reforms of law and procedure. Part I of this chapter will therefore provide the background to this claim by considering various aspects of the historic and current legal and social understandings pertaining to domestic violence and trauma that contribute to the difficulties in prosecuting domestic violence. There will be a particular focus on the court process, as I have written elsewhere on the ways trauma may impact upon police and CPS decisions and evidence-gathering prior to trial.[9] It is acknowledged that the need to understand and accommodate trauma permeates the criminal justice system, since victims of all crimes may be experiencing its after-effects. Therefore, whilst the focus here is on domestic violence and abuse, the recommendations contained within could also be utilised in other contexts and, as Ellison and Munro suggest, ideally a 'trauma lens' would be applied throughout the criminal justice process.[10] However, it is also important to acknowledge that domestic violence is different from many other crimes because the abuse is perpetrated by an intimate partner or former-partner who exploits their knowledge of the victim, and the victim's trust, in order to carry out the abuse. This is known to make the impact of the resulting trauma more complex in nature and also to make automatic defence strategies such as dissociation, denial, minimisation and self-blame much more likely.[11] This in turn justifies the need for a specialist approach to the prosecution of cases of this kind and makes this an appropriate area in which to start developing the law to accommodate the additional difficulties which may be experienced by witnesses who have experienced trauma. It is also acknowledged that the recommendations contained in this chapter are likely to lead to additional costs and therefore, while it might be ideal for the whole system to take this approach, it is realistic to acknowledge that they are likely to only be taken

[8] Home Office statistics in 2010 estimate the costs of domestic violence to be at least £23 billion per annum, although the actual costs far exceed this figure because so much of the harm is unquantifiable (S Walby, *The Cost of Domestic Violence* (Women and Equality Unit, 2004)).

[9] C Bishop and V Bettinson, 'Evidencing Domestic Violence, including Behaviour that Falls under the New Offence of 'Controlling or Coercive Behaviour' (2018) 22(1) *International Journal of Evidence and Proof* 3.

[10] L Ellison and V Munro, 'Taking Trauma Seriously: Critical Reflections on the Criminal Justice Process' (2017) 21(3) *International Journal of Evidence and Proof* 183.

[11] A DePrince and J Freyd, 'Trauma-induced Dissociation' in M Friedman et al (eds), *Handbook of PTSD: Science & Practice* (Guildford Press, 2014). These phenomena, and their implications for prosecution, will be discussed in Pt II.

up in distinct areas. As the effects of domestic violence and abuse share sufficient similarities with sexual offences, the extension of the protections provided in this context to domestic violence cases can be well supported.

I. Obstacles in the Prosecution of Domestic Violence

There are many well-documented problems with the prosecution of domestic violence cases, but chief within these is an apparent unwillingness on the part of victims to come forward and high numbers of reported cases being 'lost' from the criminal justice system at various stages.[12] As previously stated, the reasons victims may choose not to report, or may report and later retract their complaint, are complex, but include a lack of awareness that they are the victim of a crime, fear that they will not be believed or taken seriously if they report the abuse, fear of reprisals or other negative consequences from the perpetrator, and fear about the court process. If a victim does report, the response received from the police will be a key determinant in whether they choose to support a prosecution.[13] The historic legal focus on physical injury as the central and most serious harm of domestic violence has certainly created obstacles in this regard, as many of the behaviours typical of an abusive relationship lay outside of the law's protection until very recently.[14] The inadequacy of the police response, and the resultant victim dissatisfaction, can in part be explained by this as the police were unable to charge perpetrators for abuse that was non-physical in nature.[15]

Substantive law reform has started to redress the primary focus on physical violence in recent years, and the last two years have seen high levels of government, academic and media attention being given to the non-physical aspects of domestic violence, with a new offence of 'controlling or coercive behaviour in an intimate or family relationship' recently introduced under the Serious Crime Act 2015, and new training being implemented to help police identify and secure evidence to enable prosecution of a pattern of coercive control.[16] Given the documented difficulties with providing protection and achieving justice for victims via

[12] There is around a 5% conviction rate for domestic violence related offences, see M Hester, 'Making it Through the Criminal Justice System: Attrition and Domestic Violence' (2006) 5(1) *Social Policy and Society* 1. For other difficulties with prosecution see, eg, Bishop, (n 4), and M Burton, *Legal Responses to Domestic Violence* (Routledge-Cavendish, 2008).

[13] A Cretney and G Davis, 'Prosecuting Domestic Assault: Victims Failing Courts, or Courts Failing Victims?' (1997) 36(2) *Howard Journal of Criminal Justice* 146; L Ellison, 'Prosecuting Domestic Violence without Victim Participation' (2002) 56 *MLR* 834; A Robinson and D Cook, 'Understanding Victim Retraction in Cases of Domestic Violence: Specialist Courts, Government Policy, and Victim-Centred Justice' (2006) 9(2) *Contemporary Justice Review* 189.

[14] V Bettinson and C Bishop, 'Is the Creation of a Discrete Offence of Coercive Control Necessary to Combat Domestic Violence?' (2015) 66(2) *NILQ* 179; Bishop, (n 4).

[15] See HMIC, *Everyone's Business: Improving the Police Response to Domestic Abuse* (HMIC, 2014).

[16] College of Policing, *New Training to Investigate Coercive Control* (Online publication, 2016).

the criminal justice system in the absence of serious physical violence, the new legislation and related training was definitely needed.[17] However, the legacy of the historical response to domestic violence no doubt continues to shape and distort perceptions of perpetrator and victim behaviour in this context.[18] Whilst the Statutory Guidance on the new offence draws attention to the need to consider 'the wider context and the potential evidence for these patterns of controlling or coercive behaviour' and that 'where a physical assault has occurred controlling or coercive behaviour may also be present',[19] there remains an underlying assumption that coercive control is different from, and therefore less serious than, physical violence. In reality, coercive control is no less serious than physical violence and, in fact, domestic violence may be best seen as a programme of coercive and controlling behaviours of which physical violence is just one of the tools used by the perpetrator to maintain power and control.[20] This distinction is important because when domestic violence is understood as a pattern of ongoing behaviours aimed at disempowering and controlling the victim, rather than isolated incidents of predominantly physical violence, the apparent 'space' between incidents, during which the victim could exercise her autonomy and leave the relationship, is understood not to be present. This has important implications in terms of witness testimony as it should prevent credibility being undermined when the victim remained in the relationship, or made attempts to leave but kept returning to the abuser.[21]

A. Trauma and Credibility

As highlighted above, the particular effects of trauma in this area have not been given recognition in the courts; rape and other sexual offences are increasingly recognised to be traumatic for the victim, whereas the likelihood of trauma resulting from domestic violence-related crimes is not yet widely appreciated.[22]

[17] For a full discussion of these difficulties, see V Bettinson and C Bishop, 'Is the Creation of a Discrete Offence of Coercive Control Necessary to Combat Domestic Violence?' (2015) 66(2) *NILQ* 179; Bishop, (n 4).

[18] Research by Robinson et al found that physical violence remains at the forefront of many police officers' expectations about domestic abuse and their response is less proactive in the absence of physical violence (A Robinson et al, 'Under the Radar: Policing Non-violent Domestic Abuse in the US and UK' (2016) 40(3) *International Journal of Comparative and Applied Criminal Justice* 1.

[19] Home Office, *Controlling or Coercive Behaviour in an Intimate or Family Relationship: Statutory Guidance Framework,* (December 2015) 12.

[20] Bishop, (n 4); Herman, (n 2); E Stark, *Coercive Control: How Men Entrap Women in Personal Life* (OUP, 2007); E Pence and M Paymar, *Education Groups for Men who Batter: The Duluth Model* (Springer, 1993).

[21] A victim's account of the abuse and the evidence provided by others may not be believed, since questions may be raised over why the victim 'stayed' if the abuse was that bad.

[22] Victims of sexual offences are automatically entitled to apply for 'special measures' under YJCEA 1999, s 17(4). The Judicial College recognises that the trauma associated with rape can have an impact upon victim memory and recall (Judicial Studies Board, *Crown Court Bench Book, Directing the Jury* (Judicial Studies Board, 2010)) and the CPS recognises that rape can inflict long-lasting trauma on

Even under the Istanbul Convention, which places a strong emphasis on 'psychological' factors,'[23] the term 'trauma' is mentioned explicitly only in the context of sexual offences.[24] This may in part be due to the association of domestic violence with physical violence, and the association of trauma with objectively life-threatening experiences such as war, terrorist attacks and natural disasters meaning that, in the absence of serious and life-threatening physical violence, domestic violence is not seen to be traumatic. However, a substantial body of research now links the psychological, emotional and physical abuse characteristic of domestic violence with psychological trauma or post-traumatic stress.[25] Physical violence and bodily injury are not prerequisites for trauma; the brain responds in the same way to verbal, emotional or psychological threats as it does to those which are physical.[26] Traumatic events produce 'profound and lasting changes in physiological arousal, emotion, cognition and memory',[27] all of which may manifest in survivor's interactions with the criminal justice process.[28]

The process of giving evidence itself may trigger a traumatic flashback, panic attack or episode of dissociation (where the brain becomes foggy and perceptions become distorted and unreal, causing the individual to become confused or disorientated), and the witness may become anxious, or forget momentarily where they are, or be unable to grasp and/or answer the questions.[29] If these reactions are not recognised and understood by those involved in all stages of the trial process, perceptions of the witness as reliable, credible and truthful may be seriously undermined. In addition, despite psychological research showing that in individuals with PTSD memory is usually disorganised and vague, with variability

victims (Crown Prosecution Service, *Policy for Prosecuting Cases of Rape* (CPS, 2010) 2). Also see G Smith and S Heke, 'From Report to Court: Psychology, Trauma and the Law' (Online Report, 2010). This is not to suggest the criminal justice system's approach to investigating and prosecuting sexual offences is unproblematic, but that there is recognition of the traumatic nature of rape and sexual violence is clear. However, whilst The CPS Guidance on the new offence of 'controlling or coercive behaviour' (Serious Crime Act 2015, s 76) does refer to the impact that 'recalling a traumatic event' may have in terms of the presentation in court of someone who has experienced this type of behaviour, it does not go into detail about the specific effects it may have (Crown Prosecution Service, *Legal Guidance: Controlling or Coercive Behaviour in an Intimate or Family Relationship* (CPS Website, 2016)).

[23] Istanbul Convention, Arts 3(a), 3(b), 33 and 46(h).

[24] ibid, Art 25.

[25] L Jones, M Hughes and U Unterstaller, 'Posttraumatic Stress Disorder (PTSD) in Victims of Domestic Violence: A Review of the Research' (2001) 2(2) *Trauma, Violence and Abuse* 99; M A Pico-Alfonso, 'Psychological Intimate Partner Violence: The Major Predictor of Posttraumatic Stress Disorder in Abused Women' (2005) 29 *Neuroscience and Biobehavioral Reviews* 181; MA Dutton, 'Pathways Linking Intimate Partner Violence and Posttraumatic Disorder' (2009) 10(3) *Trauma, Violence and Abuse* 211. See also Bishop and Bettinson, (n 9).

[26] Jon Allen, *Coping with Trauma: A Guide to Self-Understanding* (American Psychiatric Press, 1995) 14.

[27] Herman, (n 2), 93.

[28] This will be further explored in Pt II where there will be consideration of the ways in which trauma affects memory recall and witness demeanour and the influence this may have on perceptions of witness credibility and reliability.

[29] See Ellison and Munro, (n 10), for a further discussion.

and errors in recall across time and a tendency to overlook peripheral details, great importance is still placed on the internal consistency of the witness' account and the amount of minute, often insignificant and peripheral, detail that is recalled.[30] These are key criteria used by the police and prosecution to assess the veracity of a complaint and its potential credibility in court before deciding whether to take a case forward, and research with mock juries indicates that, when assessing evidence, witness testimony is perceived as more credible if it contains vivid detail, however insignificant, peripheral or irrelevant it is to the case.[31] Similarly, credibility tends to be undermined if a witness has to admit that they had not noticed or could not remember a particular detail, however insignificant.[32] In addition, if details of the witness' testimony, however small, are found to be inaccurate, it discredits the witness and their entire testimony and makes the opposing party's account more credible.[33]

It is due to the automatic defence mechanisms adopted by the brain during times of overwhelming stress and threat (ie, trauma) that a traumatic experience typically cannot be recalled as a cohesive and whole memory by the person who survived it. One such defence mechanism is dissociation, which is a common aspect of trauma that is frequently overlooked but which may have a particularly strong bearing on the ability of a witness to give evidence in court. During an inescapable traumatic experience, instead of the fight or flight mechanisms being activated, the brain adopts the freeze response – 'playing dead' in an attempt to protect the body from injury. Part of this involves switching off the parts of the brain associated with self-awareness, so that even if physical injury and strong emotional reactions such as fear, despair and helplessness occur, the individual will not be fully aware of them.[34] This is dissociation, in which aspects of the experience, such as consciousness, memory, emotions and bodily sensations, thoughts and sensory perceptions, are split off (or dissociated) from one another, thus

[30] AE Van Giezen et al 'Consistency of Memory for Emotionally Arousing Events: A Review of Prospective and Experimental Studies' (2005) 25(7) *Clinical Psychology Review* 935; C Brewin, 'Remembering and Forgetting' in M Friedman et al (eds), *Handbook of PTSD: Science and Practice* (Guildford University Press, 2014).

[31] R Fisher, N Brewer and G Mitchell, 'The Relation between Consistency and Accuracy of Eyewitness Testimony: Legal versus Cognitive Explanations' in R Bull, T Valentine and T Williamson (eds), *Handbook of Psychology of Investigative Interviewing: Current Developments and Future Directions* (Wiley, 2009). P Roberts and C Saunders, 'Piloting PTWI: A Socio-Legal Window on Prosecutors' Assessments of Evidence and Witness Credibility' (2010) 30(1) *OJLS* 101; J Brockhardt, E Sprohge and M Ash, 'Effects of the Inclusion and Refutation of Peripheral details on Eyewitness Credibility' (2003) 33 *Journal of Applied Social Psychology* 2187.

[32] B Bell and E Loftus, 'Trivial Persuasion in the Courtroom: The Power of (a few) Minor Details' (1989) 56(5) *Journal of Personality and Social Psychology* 669.

[33] J Brockhardt, E Sprohge and M Ash, 'Effects of the Inclusion and Refutation of Peripheral Details on Eyewitness Credibility' (2003) 33(10) *Journal of Applied Social Psychology* 2187.

[34] P Frewin and R Lanius, *Healing the Traumatised Self: Consciousness, Neuroscience and Treatment* (W Norton and Company Ltd, 2015).

preventing a cohesive and whole memory being formed.[35] This explains how a victim may be able to describe an event with little evidence of distress or emotion, and may have trouble explaining how she felt (for example frightened) at the time of the attack; the emotions may be stored separately from the details, with no thoughts or cognitions attached to them.[36] The significance of dissociation and amnesia in the context of domestic violence and abuse should not be underestimated, especially as research indicates these are far more likely following repetitive traumas with a deliberate human cause, rather than when there is a single traumatic event with a natural or accidental cause.[37]

The ways that trauma manifests may lead the police, Crown Prosecutors, magistrates, judges and jury members to conclude, based upon demeanour, that a witness is not telling the truth because they cannot talk convincingly and coherently about their experience. A commonly held misconception among those not informed about the effects of trauma is that if an event actually happened, the witness would be able to remember the details and would not hesitate before answering the questions.[38] Without sufficient information and guidance on the ways in which traumatic symptoms caused by ongoing abuse may impact upon a victim's ability to give a coherent and consistent narrative of the abuse in court, the veracity of a witness' account may be doubted and a perpetrator of domestic violence may not be convicted, or a sentence may be imposed that does not reflect the severity of the harm.

II. Recommendations for Reform

Having outlined some of the obstacles to prosecuting domestic violence, Part II will outline a series of recommendations for reforms to the law, policy and practice in this area, all of which would help to ameliorate these difficulties and enable safer and more effective participation for complainant-witnesses in domestic violence proceedings. They are all premised upon recognition of the need for the criminal justice system to take a 'trauma-informed approach' throughout its policy and practice in responding to domestic violence, both to protect complainant-witnesses from being re-traumatised by the court process, and to enable them to participate effectively without trauma undermining their credibility and reliability as witnesses. A trauma-informed approach is one that takes into account the

[35] J Chu, *Rebuilding Shattered Lives: The Responsible Treatment of Complex Post-Traumatic Stress and Dissociative Disorders* (Guildford Press, 1998); American Psychiatric Association, *Diagnostic and Statistical Manual of Mental Disorders: DSM-IV-TR* (American Psychiatric Association, 1994) 477.

[36] Herman, (n 2).

[37] The Sidran Traumatic Stress Foundation, 'What is Psychological Trauma?' (Sidran Institute Website, 1999); Sarah Cole, 'Virtual Friend Fires Employee' (Naked Law, 1 May 2009).

[38] M Conway, L Justice and C Morrison, 'Beliefs about Autobiographical Memory' (2014) 27(7) *The Psychologist* 502.

impact trauma has on an individual, and requires that professionals are trained to look for and identify the signs of trauma and how best to support individuals who are experiencing its ongoing effects.

A. Recommendation One: Pre-Trial Witness Interviews

One approach which adequately takes into account the significance and impact of traumatic dissociation is for there to be increased use of pre-trial witness interview (PTWI), which is a revolutionary development in English criminal procedure 'enabling prosecutors to interview key witnesses at an early stage in the process for the purposes of improving their decision-making in relation to charge selection, discontinuance and case preparation for trial'.[39] Pre-trial contact between prosecutors and witnesses was forbidden in criminal proceedings in England and Wales until very recently when this prohibition increasingly came to be viewed as contrary to the interests of justice.

PTWI has been possible since 2008, when the CPS Code of Practice for Pre-Trial Witness Interviews was introduced, and yet, despite the fact that they proved useful in improving Crown Prosecutors' perceptions of credibility and reliability ahead of trial, they are insufficiently used in domestic violence cases.[40] Due to the likelihood of errors and variability in recall over time, PTWIs are especially useful in the context of post-traumatic symptoms, since they give witnesses the opportunity to account for any apparent discrepancies or inconsistencies in their account prior to trial, and ensure that new evidence does not come out for the first time whilst the witness is giving evidence in court.[41] Furthermore, as the court process itself may trigger post-traumatic symptoms such as flashbacks, PTWIs can give witnesses the chance to prepare for the impact that giving evidence and telling their story in court may have upon them, emotionally and psychologically, but also physically. As will be explored further below, defence advocates have a tendency to portray common trauma reactions such as shaking and disorientation as suspicious, and so PTWIs could be one way of helping to reduce the ways in which trauma may undermine perceptions of witness credibility. Currently, PTWIs may actually be avoided when witnesses are 'vulnerable' to 'prevent trauma from repetition of the account',[42] and yet, given the impact that trauma is likely to have on a victim in court, it is arguably less traumatic for the witness to recount evidence and be questioned about her story prior to trial so that they are better-prepared for the court process. Therefore, the use of PTWI should be *considered* in all domestic

[39] 'Piloting Pre-Trial Witness Interviews (PTWI) by Crown Prosecutors – Facilitating the Practical Implementation of Criminal Justice Policy' (Impact Case Study, 2014, University of Nottingham).

[40] Roberts and Saunders, (n 31).

[41] ibid.

[42] Crown Prosecution Service, *Code of Practice for Pre-Trial Witness Interviews* (Ministry of Justice 2008) 5.

violence cases where the victim shows signs of trauma and dissociation, prior to a decision being made about her ability to come across well in court. It is important to note that there are objections to the use of PTWIs on the grounds that they may be used by the CPS to 'coach' witnesses; however, provided they are conducted in accordance with guidelines, then they are now an acceptable part of CPS practice in both indictable and summary-only offences.[43]

B. Recommendation Two: Review and Extension of 'Special Measures'

This recommendation involves extending and clarifying the use of 'Special Measures', such as screens and the use of live links, under the Youth Justice and Criminal Evidence Act 1999 (YJCEA) so that domestic violence complainants are automatically entitled to apply for them on appropriate grounds. This would assist in achieving the already-identified aim of these special measures; enabling witnesses to give their 'best evidence' by alleviating some of the stress associated with the giving of evidence in court.[44] Currently, witnesses are eligible to apply for 'Special Measures' if they meet the criteria specified in sections 16 and 17. Domestic violence complainant-witnesses are automatically eligible to apply for these under section 17(1), because they are 'victims of the most serious crime' (as defined by the CPS[45]), and their application will be granted if the court is satisfied that 'the quality of evidence given by the witness is likely to be diminished by reason of fear or distress on the part of the witness in connection with testifying in the proceedings'.[46] This category of witness is referred to as 'intimidated' in the CPS guidance. Domestic violence complainant-witnesses may also be eligible to apply under section 16, which provides for assistance by reason of 'age or incapacity'. Witnesses who fall into this category are often referred to as 'vulnerable', and, unless under the age of 17, must be suffering from a physical disability, a mental disorder under the Mental Health Act 1983 (MHA), or have a 'significant impairment of intelligence and social functioning'.[47] Post-traumatic stress disorder (PTSD) falls under the MHA, so a complainant-witness in a domestic violence case who meets the diagnostic criteria for this condition will be eligible to apply for Special Measures as a vulnerable witness. However, oftentimes PTSD is not

[43] Although the CPS PTWI Guidance for Prosecutors does state that interviews will normally be of most value in serious indictable-only cases, it also states that nothing precludes the holding of an interview in either-way or summary only cases (CPS, *Pre-Trial Witness Interviews – Guidance for Prosecutors* (CPS Website, updated 2018)).

[44] Ministry of Justice, *Achieving Best Evidence in Criminal Proceedings: Guidance on Interviewing Victims and Witnesses, and Guidance on using Special Measures* (Ministry of Justice, 2011).

[45] Crown Prosecution Service, *Code of Practice for Victims of Crime* (Ministry of Justice, 2015).

[46] YJCEA, s 17(1).

[47] ibid, s 16(2)(a).

diagnosed, or an individual may not meet the narrow diagnostic criteria despite experiencing significant post-traumatic symptoms,[48] and therefore this vulnerability may not be picked up by police at interview.

Evidence indicates that not enough applications are being made,[49] even though the Victim's Code requires prosecutors to give early consideration to making a Special Measures application to the court, taking into account any views expressed by the victim.[50] In part this could be because applications must be made by either police or Crown Prosecutors, who may not have enough training about mental health issues, and may not realise the likelihood that domestic violence complainants are experiencing ongoing effects from trauma.[51] Indeed, research by Burton et al suggests that the police find identifying vulnerable witnesses particularly difficult, and a recent HMIC Thematic Report investigating the extent to which police forces identify, protect and support those who are vulnerable exposed significant areas of concern.[52] The picture becomes more complicated because different criminal justice agencies use different definitions of vulnerability, with some being broader than others. Under the YJCEA, vulnerability is narrowly defined, and although the CPS guidance on the use of special measures imports these criteria, its toolkit for prosecutors involved in cases with a vulnerable victim takes a much wider view of 'vulnerability'.[53] Police guidance uses the statutory definition, but elaborates by providing prompts that may assist in the identification of vulnerable witnesses (although, as noted above, there are serious difficulties with this identification at present).[54] Therefore, it is unclear whether domestic violence complainant-witnesses will be eligible for special measures as vulnerable witnesses, rather than as intimidated witnesses, a distinction that is significant because of the emerging duties placed on judges, and the guidance provided for barristers on how vulnerable witnesses should be treated, discussed below.[55]

The above analysis indicates that the existing special measures under the YJCEA are in need of extension and clarification so domestic violence complainants continue to be automatically entitled to apply for them, as they are under

[48] S Mol, A Arntz, J Metsemakers, G Dinant, P Vilters-van Montfort and J Knottnerus, 'Symptoms of Post-Traumatic Stress Disorder after Non-Traumatic Events' (2005) 186(6) *British Journal of Psychiatry* 494.

[49] Ellison and Munro, (n 10). This is despite the fact that CPS research findings indicate that most applications for special measures are granted by the court.

[50] Crown Prosecution Service, *Code of Practice for Victims of Crime* (Ministry of Justice, 2015).

[51] Ellison and Munro, (n 10).

[52] M Burton, R Evans and A Sanders, 'Vulnerable and Intimidated Witnesses and the Adversarial Process in England and Wales' (2007) 11 *International Journal of Evidence and Proof* 1; HMIC, *Police Effectiveness, Efficiency and Legitimacy (PEEL): Police Effectiveness 2015 (Vulnerability): A National Overview* (HMIC, 2015).

[53] Crown Prosecution Service, *Toolkit for Prosecutors on Violence Against Women and Girls Cases Involving a Vulnerable Victim* (CPS Website, 2016).

[54] Ministry of Justice, *Vulnerable and Intimidated Witnesses: A Police Service Guide* (Ministry of Justice, 2011).

[55] Advocacy Training Council, *Raising the Bar: The Handling of Vulnerable Victims, Witnesses and Defendants in Court* (Advocacy Training Council, 2011).

section 17(1), but on appropriate grounds. Victims of domestic violence may be intimidated, may be vulnerable according to the criteria under section 16 of the YJCEA, or may be both. They are also likely to be have experienced *trauma*. It is suggested that either a new category should be added to the YJCEA based upon acknowledgement that there is a category of witnesses who may not meet the criteria to be considered 'vulnerable', but who are in need of special measures and protections due to trauma, or that the existing category of 'vulnerable' witnesses should be widened to automatically include victims of domestic violence in the same way as they are automatically included in the category of 'intimidated'.[56]

C. Recommendation Three: Limitations on Cross Examination

This recommendation involves extending the limitations placed upon cross-examination of child witnesses and witnesses in cases of alleged sexual offences to domestic violence hearings. Reform is needed here to prevent juries being unfairly biased by the presentation of evidence, which can easily happen when cross-examination is aggressive and aims at undermining witness credibility. The recommendation is also aimed at reducing possible attrition with victims deciding not to participate in the court process so as to avoid treatment of this kind. This recommendation would also prevent further attacks on the psychological integrity of domestic violence complainant-witnesses, in line with the human rights obligations referred to above.

At the heart of our adversarial system of dispute resolution lies the privileging of oral testimony and the right of the defence to cross-examine witnesses. At the same time, it is widely assumed that the amount of minute, often insignificant and peripheral, detail a witness can remember is a solid indicator of witness credibility, and that internal inconsistencies in a witness' account, particularly over time, are indicative of lying or fabrication. These beliefs form the foundation of the practice of cross-examination, and are known to be widely exploited by defence barristers who frequently engage in aggressive cross-examination, the strategies of which are intended to intimidate witnesses and undermine their credibility.[57] A range of cross-examination techniques are used to expose memory gaps, inaccuracies and inconsistencies, by homing in on minutiae and peripheral details, making it easy to achieve the aim of inducing errors.[58] The detrimental effect of

[56] This would not mean that all domestic violence complainants would be granted Special Measures, but all would be eligible to apply.

[57] L Ellison, *The Adversarial Process and the Vulnerable Witness* (OUP, 2001).

[58] M Kebbell, C O'Kelly and E Gilchrist, 'Rape Victims' Experiences of giving Evidence in English Courts: A Survey, Psychiatry (2007) 14(1) *Psychology and Law* 111; C Taylor, *Court Licensed Abuse* (Peter Lang, 2004).

such cross-examination techniques has been noted in sexual offences trials,[59] and this approach to cross-examination may further undermine the credibility of traumatised witnesses based not on the falsity of their account, but on the impact of trauma on a victim's ability to give a coherent narrative of her experiences. As outlined in Part I, any inconsistencies in testimony over time, and any failure to give a sufficiently detailed account of events, are likely to be seized upon by the defence to undermine credibility and by the jury to indicate the witness is not credible.

It has been suggested that there is now acceptance that testing a *vulnerable* witness's evidence using 'undiluted conventional cross-examination techniques does not produce reliable evidence' and can 'quite easily create a misleading impression of a vulnerable witness's competence and credibility', with a resultant negative effect upon jury assessment of the substance of the evidence given.[60] This has led to developments in the practice of cross-examination of vulnerable witnesses and the expectation, following the Court of Appeal's statement in *Lubemba*,[61] that it is appropriate for a Ground Rules Hearing to be held 'in every case involving a vulnerable witness, save in very exceptional circumstances'.[62] To date, the developments have predominantly occurred in the context of trials involving child witnesses and alleged victims of serious sexual offences, but due to the traumatic and psychologically harmful nature of much domestic violence and abuse, it is suggested that these protections should be extended to trials involving allegations of this kind where, despite a move in favour of other forms of evidence in the context of domestic violence cases, the focus on oral testimony persists.[63]

Any measures to protect vulnerable witnesses clearly need to be balanced against the defendant's fair trial rights.[64] However, humane treatment is one of the foundational principles of the law of evidence, and this extends to witnesses as well as the defendant. As 'confrontation is a right grounded in the personal dignity of the accused then it must make space for the dignity rights of others within the trial process'.[65] This can be achieved by putting in place safeguards that protect the overall fairness of the trial, but at the same time protect the victim from further attacks on their psychological integrity. Pre-trial cross-examination is now being

[59] L Ellison, 'Closing the Credibility Gap: the Prosecutorial use of Expert Witness Testimony in Sexual Assault Cases' (2005) 9 *International Journal of Evidence & Proof* 239; C Taylor, *Court Licensed Abuse* (Peter Lang, 2004); J Temkin, 'Prosecuting and Defending Rape: Perspectives from the Bar' (2000) 27(2) *Journal of Law and Society* 219; J Temkin, *Rape and the Legal Process* (OUP, 2002). J Temkin and B Krahé, *Sexual Assault and the Justice Gap: A Question of Attitude* (Hart, 2008).

[60] E Henderson, 'Bigger Fish to Fry: Should the Reform of Cross-Examination be Expanded Beyond Vulnerable Witnesses?' (2015) 19(2) *International Journal of Evidence & Proof* 83.

[61] *Lubemba (Cokesix); JP* [2014] EWCA Crim 2064.

[62] ibid [42].

[63] The need for 'creative' evidence-gathering is discussed in detail in Bishop and Bettinson, (n 9).

[64] Enshrined in ECHR, Art 6.

[65] L Heffernan, 'Calibrating the Right to Confrontation' (2016) 8(2) *International Journal of Evidence and Proof* 107. Also see M Redmayne, 'Confronting Confrontation' in P Roberts and J Hunter (eds), *Criminal Evidence and Human Rights: Reimagining the Common Law Procedural Traditions* (Hart, 2012).

rolled out nationally, following a successful pilot which saw an increase in early guilty pleas.[66] However, given that the defence's ability to cross-examine witnesses is essential to ensuring that the defendant's fair trial rights are protected, allowing cross-examination to be conducted and videoed beforehand is likely to be limited to trials of offences where the vulnerable position of the witness is already accepted (ie, child witnesses and victims of alleged serious sex offences). Therefore, limitations on the manner and content of cross-examination appear to be the best option moving forward, in order to achieve a fair balance between the defendant's rights and the rights of witnesses under Articles 3 and 8 of the ECHR. Judicial management of cross-examination can be achieved via the use of Ground Rules Hearings to determine the manner and content of questioning during cross-examination,[67] and judicial intervention when these rules are not adhered to by advocates.

In a line of recent cases, starting with *Barker* in 2010, the Court of Appeal set out a series of changes to questioning practice as regards vulnerable witnesses.[68] The cases 'underline the simple proposition that the objective of cross-examination is to investigate the truth by questions which must be clearly understood by the witness',[69] thus emphasising that cross examination is not just conducted for the purpose of protecting the defendant's fair trial rights. Also, significantly, in *Lubemba* it was made clear that the duty now placed upon a trial judge to control the questioning of a vulnerable witness is not a violation of the defendant's fair trial right per se.[70] However, successful reforms depend upon judges to implement and enforce them, and thus in *Wills* the Court of Appeal declared that '[i]n cases where it is necessary and appropriate to have limitations on the way in which the advocate conducts cross-examination, there is a duty on the judge to ensure that those limitations are complied with',[71] something which Henderson submits can be achieved through pre-trial directions, thus implying that the Court of Appeal envisages trial judges taking control of cross-examination 'behind the scenes as well as on centre stage'.[72] Again, this duty is predominantly recognised within trials for serious sex offences,[73] but the acceptance of its existence does provide for the possibility of it being extended to other contexts.

[66] Joint Statement by the Lord Chancellor, the Lord Chief Justice and the Senior President of Tribunals, *Transforming our Justice System* (September 2016); Ministry of Justice, *Process Evaluation of Pre-recorded Cross-Examination Pilot (Section 28)* (September 2016).

[67] The 2010 Criminal Procedure Rules made Ground Rules Hearings mandatory for intermediary trials and recommended them to be used for other trials where vulnerable people were involved.

[68] As well as *Barker, E* [2011] EWCA Crim 3028; *W* [2010] EWCA Crim 1926; *Wills [2011]* EWCA Crim 1938. Henderson notes that the initial series has been joined by many others including *Farooqi* [2013] EWCA Crim 1649 and *Lubemba* [2014] EWCA Crim 2064.

[69] The Rt Hon The Lord Judge, *The Evidence of Child Victims: the Next Stage* (Bar Council Annual Law Reform Lecture, November 2013).

[70] *Lubemba (Cokesix); JP* [2014] EWCA Crim 2064.

[71] [2011] EWCA Crim 1938 [16].

[72] E Henderson, 'Taking Control of Cross-Examination: Judges, Advocates and Intermediaries discuss Judicial Management of the Cross-Examination of Vulnerable People' (2016) *Crim LR* 181.

[73] Following *Wills*, the Judicial College began to teach this new direction in its accreditation courses for judges hearing cases of this kind, a message that was emphasised in Plotnikoff and Woolfson's Gateway 'toolkits' and in the 2013 Criminal Practice Directions and the Equal Treatment Benchbook.

Henderson points out that the Court of Appeal has been encouraging a more interventionist approach to cross-examination generally for more than a decade, yet it remains the case that judges do not intervene in the examination of vulnerable witnesses often enough.[74] This is despite the powerful impact that judicial intervention is known to have on the practice of advocates. Henderson considers the possibility that judges do not intervene because they use Ground Rules Hearings and other pre-trial conferences to set clear rules regarding the conduct for cross-examination beforehand, which advocates are complying with. However, whilst it is clear that setting ground rules is an extremely effective strategy which is being successfully used by some judges, her findings indicate that the overall picture within the criminal justice system with regard to interventions in cross-examination is more complicated. This could in part be due to judicial awareness of the potential for intervention to create the appearance of prejudice or partiality in front of the jury and the defendant. For this reason, around half the judges in Henderson's study 'stressed that interventions should be as minimal as possible'.[75] With reference to the balancing act needed to reconcile the defendant's right to test the evidence with the witness's need to be protected and enabled to understand the questioning, Henderson further found that some judges remain unsure that non-traditional methods of cross-examination test evidence adequately and so were not prepared to stop advocates using traditional methods.[76]

Evidence also suggests that Ground Rules Hearings, which can determine the sorts of questions and topics that can be examined and whether time limits are appropriate, are not being utilised as effectively as they could be, with some judges and advocates not even knowing of the requirement that they be used in all trials involving vulnerable witnesses. This is despite the fact that they are seen by many as key to the smooth running of trials involving vulnerable witnesses because they make intervention easy.[77] It is now considered best practice for the questions to be released to the court in advance,[78] but this obviously prevents advocates from changing their questions in response to answers to other questions, and thus could effectively be violating an aspect of the defendant's fundamental right to cross-examine witnesses. Ultimately, this could end up with reluctance to categorise witnesses in domestic violence cases as vulnerable, to limit the number of trials requiring these protections to be put in place. It seems that, following *Barker*, judges accept the need for greater management of cross-examination and yet, as indicated by Henderson's study, actual interventions remain few, with many judges preferring not to intervene.[79] Whilst there is clearly precedent for the

[74] J Plotnikoff and R Woolfson, 'Kicking and Screaming: The Slow Road to Best Evidence' in J Spencer and M Lamb (eds), *Children and Cross-Examination: Time to Change the Rules?* (Hart, 2012) 35.

[75] Henderson, (n 72), 186; 190.

[76] E Henderson, 'Communicative Competence? Judges, Advocates and Intermediaries Discuss Communication Issues in the Cross-examination of Vulnerable Witnesses' [2015] *Crim LR* 657.

[77] Henderson, (n 72), 195.

[78] Criminal Procedure Rules (2015) SI 2015/1490 and *Lubemba (Cokesix); JP* [2014] EWCA Crim 2064.

[79] Henderson, (n 72).

recommended reforms, successful implementation in domestic violence trials requires two things: recognition that these protections are needed and justified in this context, and judicial and advocate willingness to reform their practice. However, there is no doubt that these developments are capable of providing inroads into reforms that could be effectively utilised in the context of cases of alleged domestic violence offences.

D. Recommendation Four: Jury Information Regarding Trauma

This recommendation involves the provision of information to the jury on the dynamics of domestic violence and the impact trauma may have on witness testimony, with the aim of preventing verdicts from being influenced by erroneous preconceptions. It is contended that this could either take the form of a judicial direction or expert witness testimony, both of which would provide the jury with the information needed to determine the facts at issue. Of course, any provisions in this area must not prejudice the defendant's fair trial rights but, because there is still insufficient recognition of the non-physical aspects of domestic violence and its traumatic nature both legally and socially, expert testimony is necessary in certain cases: not to bolster the prosecution's case, but to contextualise and normalise the victim's response to abuse.[80] Expert testimony could help to prevent the victim being seen as lacking in credibility as a result of her demeanour or inability to give a coherent and consistent account, and could prevent evidence being assessed in light of erroneous assumptions about the impact of domestic violence.[81] In the context of sexual offence trials it is recognised that false or misguided beliefs concerning trauma may distort juror decision-making, and thus, as Ellison and Munro highlight, this provides precedent for the provision of information about aspects of trauma to the jury.[82] Research with mock-juries found that provision of information to the mock-jury to redress popular misconceptions had an impact on assessments of rape complainant credibility and the veracity of the account; jurors exposed to educational guidance were more willing to accept the feasibility

[80] M Dempsey, *The Use of Expert Witness Testimony in the Prosecution of Domestic Violence* (CPS, 2004).

[81] Due to the continued misplaced focus on incidents of physical violence as the defining characteristics of an abusive relationship, questions continue to be asked about why a victim did not leave if the abuse was that bad. Therefore, the account of a victim who 'stays' despite serious violence and abuse may not be viewed as truthful. Expert testimony could be used to dispel commonly held myths and explain the programmatic nature of domestic violence as being an attack on a victim's autonomy and liberty (see Bishop, (n 4), and Dempsey, (n 80)).

[82] See *Doody* [2008] EWCA 2394. Ellison and Munro, (n 10). See also L Ellison and V Munro, 'Reacting to Rape: Exploring Mock Jurors' Assessments of Complainant Credibility' (2009) 49(2) *British Journal of Criminology* 202 and L Ellison and V Munro, 'Turning Mirrors into Windows?: Assessing the Impact of (Mock) Juror Education in Rape Trials' (2009) 49(3) *British Journal of Criminology* 363 on the impact that provision of information on trauma reactions had on (mock) juror deliberations.

of a wide range of victim responses and were less influenced by a witness demeanour when assessing a complainant's credibility and the veracity of her account.[83] Again, given the similarities between domestic and sexual violence offences, it is contended that provision of information to the jury in cases of the former is both needed and likely to have a significant impact on juror decision making.

Just over a decade ago, acknowledgment of the important role of expert witness testimony in the prosecution of domestic violence was emerging within the CPS, based upon recognition of the myths surrounding domestic violence and the ways in which erroneous assumptions may lead factfinders to misunderstand the behaviour of the victim. In a 2004 CPS report on the use of expert testimony in domestic violence hearings, then Director of Public Prosecutions Ken McDonald QC highlighted that the 'average person' may be 'unfamiliar with the complex dynamics of domestic violence'.[84] The report proposed the use of expert testimony in domestic violence cases for a number of purposes, including to inform fact finders of commonly known characteristics of abuse victims so that they can compare the behaviour of the victim with that profile; reduce the likelihood of jury bias against the victim based on myths and misunderstandings; explain victim-retraction and assist the fact finder to evaluate – not enhance – the credibility of the victim. The aim is to 'level the playing field' so that the fact finder can properly evaluate the evidence and credibility of the victim, rather than reaching a conclusion based on erroneous assumptions.[85]

This report did not lead to a change in CPS practice but expert witnesses are commonly called upon in other contexts where an issue that needs to be decided in court calls for special skill or knowledge which a judge or jury do not possess. Whilst the *Turner* rule[86] makes expert evidence inadmissible if it expresses an opinion on matters which are within the competence of the jury, given that societal and legal myths and misunderstandings persist, and that the new offence of controlling or coercive behaviour has the potential to further complicate understandings of domestic violence, it is contended that there is a clear need for expert evidence here.[87] Whilst many jury members may *think* that they understand domestic violence, in reality they may have an understanding that is biased and erroneous; the exploitation of gender-role expectations in the commission of much domestic violence and abuse, particularly that which would fall under the new offence, means that the dynamics and behaviour may not be within the contemplation of many fact-finders.[88] In the context of cases of controlling or coercive behaviour, it

[83] L Ellison and V Munro, 'Turning Mirrors into Windows?: Assessing the Impact of (Mock) Juror Education in Rape Trials' (2009) 49(3) *British Journal of Criminology* 363, 374.

[84] Dempsey, (n 80), 1 (foreword by DPP Ken MacDonald QC).

[85] ibid, 2.

[86] *Turner* [1975] 1 All ER 70.

[87] See Bishop, (n 4). It is recognised that this need ought to subside with increased public education about coercive control.

[88] See Bishop, (n 4), and Bishop and Bettinson, (n 9).

is not just the behaviour of the complainant and the impact of the abuse upon her that needs to be understood, the behaviour of the defendant is also central to the successful prosecution of this offence.[89] Without an understanding of the dynamics of relationships characterised by coercive control, it may not be understandable how the behaviour could have a 'serious effect' on the victim, as required by the new offence.[90]

When it comes to the provision of information about trauma, and the effect it may have on a witness's demeanour and narrative, particular care is needed to avoid expert opinion as to the credibility, reliability or truthfulness of a witness. When an expert witness needs to express 'an opinion about whether, for instance, an individual suffered from a particular condition or vulnerability … [they] should be careful to recognise … the need to avoid supplanting the court's role as the ultimate decision-maker on matters that are central to the outcome of the case'.[91] This means that the expert cannot say that the complainant-witness *is* traumatised and therefore was a victim of domestic violence, but they can give evidence pertaining to the ways in which trauma manifests and say that, in light of this, the witness in question appears to have experienced trauma. Evidence is not generally admissible when it is adduced for the sole purpose of bolstering or increasing witness credibility (known as 'oath helping') unless it is considered relevant and necessary to assist the court to resolve the proceedings. It is suggested that expert evidence in these cases could meet both these criteria because credibility is particularly important in cases where the witness has experienced trauma. Some cases in the context of alleged sexual offences have held evidence which served to bolster the complainant's credibility where it went to the central issue rather than merely to credit.[92] In *Chandu Nagrecha*, Rose LJ held that because the outcome of the case turned upon the word of the complainant and the appellant, the issue essentially was one of credibility, and therefore evidence about the appellant's character should have been admitted.[93] It is suggested that because of the parallels that can be drawn between domestic violence and sexual offences, and the fact that in these cases the complainant's testimony may likewise be the sole or central piece of evidence, the same principles apply and therefore evidence about a complainant's background and characteristics should not be inevitably excluded.

Given the danger that jurors may regard expert testimony as affirmative evidence that the alleged offences took place because the complainant fits the profile of someone who had experienced domestic violence and trauma, it may be that an extended judicial direction would be an appropriate and less problematic

[89] See Bishop and Bettinson, (n 9).

[90] Serious Crime Act 2015, s 76(1)(c).

[91] *Pora v The Queen* [2015] UKPC 9, Lord Kerr [24]. See also *H* [2014] EWCA Crim 1555.

[92] *Funderburk* [1990] 1 WLR 587; *Chandu Nagrecha* [1997] Cr App R 401; *Amado-Taylor* [2001] EWCA Crim 1898; *The Queen v Tobin* [2002] EWCA Crim 190.

[93] [1997] Cr App R 401 [405].

way of providing additional guidance to jurors on the matters at issue in cases of this kind.[94] Some precedent and recent scholarship exists with regard to provision of information of this kind to the jury. For example, Durston notes that in sexual offence trials 'there has been some growth in judicial comment on evidence in recent years, as judges try to dispel stereotypical notions as to the behaviour of "typical" rape complainants'.[95] There is the concern that judicial directions may come too late, because jurors 'actively process evidence as it emerges'[96] and may make assessments about credibility throughout the trial which remain unchanged by the judicial direction. Whilst research by Ellison and Munro indicates that whether information was provided via expert testimony or a judicial direction appeared to make little difference (mock-jurors responded in broadly similar ways regardless of whether the educational guidance was presented by an expert near the beginning of the mock-trial or by the judge towards the end[97]), they also acknowledge that the significance of this finding is unclear in light of other research which found that mock-jurors made more use of expert testimony when it was presented at the beginning of the prosecution case before the complainant testified.[98] In addition, later cases[99] have imposed clear limitations on the growth of judicial comment in sexual offences trials and, despite arguments that the judiciary should be authorised to make comments about credibility in the context of cases like this, the line between the giving of evidence by a judge and the provision of directions based on judicial experience remains unclear.[100] Although the implementation of a judicial direction would be relatively straightforward and more cost effective for the CPS, the use of expert witness testimony is therefore favoured for the reasons explored above.

III. Conclusion

It is anticipated that the reforms and measures proposed in this chapter would make proving domestic violence in court less problematic, by increasing the likelihood

[94] This was suggested by the Criminal Bar Association in 2006 and Wolchever and Heaton-Armstrong in 2008 in the context of sexual offence cases (Criminal Bar Association, *Response to Consultation Paper 'Convicting Rapists and Protecting Victims'* (London, 2006); D Wolchover and A Heaton-Armstrong, 'Debunking Rape Myths' (2008) 158 *New Law Journal* 117)).

[95] G Durston, *Evidence: Text and Materials* (OUP, 2011) 8. And see *Doody* [2008] EWCA 2394.

[96] Young et al, *Juries in Criminal Trials: A Summary of the Research Findings* (Preliminary Paper 37, Vol 2, 1999) (Wellington, New Zealand Law Commission).

[97] See Ellison and Munro (n 83) at 363, 377.

[98] N Brekke and E Borgida, 'Expert Psychological Testimony in Rape Trials: A Social Cognitive Analysis' (1989) 55(3) *Journal of Personality and Social Psychology* 372; R Schuller and J Cripps, 'Expert Evidence Pertaining to Battered Women: The Impact of Gender of Expert and Timing of Testimony (1998) 22(1) *Law and Human Behaviour* 17.

[99] *JD* [2008] EWCA Crim 2557; *Breeze* [2009] EWCA Crim 255.

[100] G Durston, *Evidence: Text and Materials* (OUP, 2011) 8, 9.

that a victim will participate in the process, and by helping to increase awareness of the harmful impact abusive behaviour has upon the victim. Enhancing recognition of the traumatic nature of domestic violence and shifting the focus away from physical injury as domestic violence's most serious harm will assist all those involved in the criminal justice process – police officers, the CPS, magistrates, the judiciary, members of the public serving on jury panels and victims themselves – to identify abusive behaviour. Alleviating some of the stress associated with the giving of evidence, and enhancing the credibility of witness-complainant testimony in court, would encourage more victims both to report abuse and to participate in the criminal justice process through to prosecution, without having their safety and physical and psychological integrity compromised.

Comment on Chapter 8

Domestic Violence, Trauma and Vulnerability

VANESSA MUNRO

There have been repeated initiatives in England and Wales over recent decades, which have been designed with the express ambition to put the needs and concerns of victims at the heart of the criminal justice system.[1] Despite this, I have previously argued that there is an ongoing failure on the part of many policy-makers and practitioners to engage with the scale of trauma reactions amongst victims, witnesses and – indeed – defendants. Consequently, the ways in which trauma can mitigate against establishing credibility and produce barriers to effective participation in the criminal justice process, including in the courtroom, have been overlooked.[2]

Dr Bishop's excellent chapter in this collection provides a vivid illustration of the difficulties in this regard that are currently faced by complainant-witnesses in the context of domestic abuse.[3] Though there is still a great deal more to be done to improve criminal justice responses, the propensity to experience post-traumatic symptoms in the context of sexual assault is increasingly widely acknowledged and, to some extent at least, accommodated within existing special measures protections for testifying witnesses. By contrast, Bishop notes the relative lack of engagement with the preponderance of trauma reactions amongst those who have experienced non-sexual manifestations of domestic abuse, particularly where perpetrators' primary *modus operandi* has involved psychologically and emotionally damaging routines of coercive and controlling behaviour rather than acts of physical force.

Bishop's chapter can be read, then, as a call to broaden out the 'trauma lens' to domestic abuse. Of course, it is also important to bear in mind that trauma may be

[1] See, eg, Ministry of Justice, *Getting it Right for Victims and Witnesses* (MoJ, 2012); Home Office, *Justice for All* (Cm 5566, London, 2002).

[2] L Ellison and V Munro, 'Taking Trauma Seriously: Critical Reflections on the Criminal Justice Process' (2017) 21(3) *International Journal of Evidence and Proof* 183.

[3] C Bishop, 'Safe and Effective Courtroom Participation for Domestic Violence Complainant – Witnesses', ch 8 of this volume.

experienced by victims of a broad range of other criminal offences. It is incumbent on policy-makers and practitioners within the criminal justice system to engage more seriously with such reactions and their potentially debilitating impact upon the prospects for justice. That said, the specific context of domestic abuse certainly provides a compelling point for interjection, and with its parallels in many respects to the sexual violence context, the case for reform is, *prima facie*, a strong one. In her chapter, Dr Bishop highlights four key areas in which reform would be both feasible within current procedural protocols and desirable – in terms of increasing effective participation by complainant-witnesses in the trial process and promoting fairer outcomes therefrom. In this response, I will explore each in turn to reflect on the challenges and opportunities they offer.

I. Pre-Trial Witness Interviews

First, Bishop advocates the routine consideration by the Crown Prosecution Service (CPS) of a pre-trial witness interview in all domestic abuse cases in which the complainant-witness displays symptoms – for example of disassociation – that are indicative of experiencing post-traumatic stress. The aim here is to better inform assessments of a complainant-witness' credibility and ability to withstand the trial process upon which decisions about case progression are often made. Aside from the routine concerns about resource implications raised by pre-trial witness interviews, and the need to avoid any suggestion of 'coaching', which have been shown not to be insurmountable in the sexual offences context,[4] this suggestion could be relatively easily implemented – although to the extent that it would require CPS personnel to take responsibility for identifying trauma amongst witnesses, it may have underwhelming effects without significant investments in awareness-raising and training.

Perhaps more problematically, this move also quickly raises a question about the trial conditions under which the traumatised complainant-witness should be expected to give her account; and this speaks to the second of the proposals that Dr Bishop puts forward in respect of reviewing and extending the use of 'special measures'.

II. Review and Extension of 'Special Measures'

Special measures protections afforded under the Youth Justice and Criminal Evidence Act 1999 are designed to ameliorate the stresses associated with giving

[4] P Roberts and C Saunders, 'Piloting PTWI: A Socio-Legal Window on Prosecutors' Assessments of Evidence and Witness Credibility' (2010) 30 (1) *OJLS* 101.

testimony in the criminal courtroom and to ensure that witnesses are enabled to give their best evidence. Research in this area suggests that when they are operationalised effectively – and this is by no means universally the case – they are received positively by witnesses and can play a productive role in enabling participation in the trial process.[5] But access to such protections is restricted, and Bishop expresses clearly the concern that some complainants, particularly – but not exclusively – in the context of domestic abuse, will 'fall through the cracks' of this system, since despite suffering psychological symptoms that may undermine their ability to give testimony in the courtroom or make that process re-traumatising, they would not meet the existing criteria for a 'vulnerable' or 'intimidated' witness. To redress this, Bishop proposes that we must either extend the category of 'vulnerable' witness, or create an additional category to cover those who fall short of existing protections but are nonetheless in need of special measures due to their exhibiting symptoms associated with trauma that can act as a barrier to participation.

It is hard to fault the impulse to strive for greater inclusivity in respect of special measures protections so that opportunity is more appropriately matched to need. This is surely in the service both of the well-being of the witness and of the pursuit of justice through best evidence. But at the same time, the implementation of either of the proposals put forward poses some difficult dilemmas. On the one hand, fashioning a third gateway for entitlement that captures 'traumatised' witnesses who fall outside existing definitions of 'vulnerable' or 'intimidated' may require complicated engagement with shifting symptomatic criteria and thresholds. Psychological reactions to stressful events will vary greatly between individuals, and will be affected by a range of experiential, personal, and circumstantial factors. While feelings of emotional numbness, confusion, shock, shame, anger, acute anxiety or flashbacks are not uncommon, the precise ways in which a person may manifest trauma in the wake of criminal victimisation will be highly individual, with symptomology varying over time and context.[6] To act as a threshold for special measures entitlement, 'trauma' may require a level of definitional clarity in law that will be difficult to achieve.

Perhaps one obvious way of navigating this challenge would be to focus on witnesses who have been diagnosed with post-traumatic stress disorder (PTSD). This would certainly – through verification by a psychiatric diagnosis – create a clearer boundary, but it is important to bear in mind the constructed and shifting nature of that clinical labelling. This presents difficulties both through its medicalisation of what might well be better understood as 'normal' reactions to triggering events, and its failure to provide protection to complainant-witnesses who suffer

[5] B Hamlyn, A Phelps, J Turtle and G Sattar, 'Are Special Measures Working? Evidence from Surveys of Vulnerable and Intimidated Witnesses' (Home Office, 2004); M Burton, R Evans and A Sanders, 'Are Special Measures Working for Vulnerable and Intimidated Witnesses? Evidence From Criminal Justice Agencies' (Home Office, 2006).

[6] B Van der Kolk, A McFarlane and L Weisaeth, *Traumatic Stress: The Effects of Overwhelming Experience of Mind, Body and Society* (Guilford Press, 1996).

significant emotional distress that militates against courtroom participation but nonetheless fails to meet the criteria for a PTSD diagnosis.[7]

At the same time, bringing the traumatised witness more fully under the banner of vulnerability presents its own distinct challenges. As I have argued elsewhere, the operation of 'vulnerable' as a label and lever for State protection has legitimated both progressive and regressive interventions in individuals' daily lives, especially so in the gendered context of regulating women's bodies and behaviour.[8] It has opened the door to paternalistic and protectionist impulses that have, at times, significantly reduced individual women's potential for agency; and it has legitimated increased levels of State intervention as well as more dispersed and subtle strategies of surveillance and disciplining of the intimate lives of many women. What is often left unstated in the paradigm of vulnerability, moreover, are the questions of vulnerable *to what* and *why*. The failure to expose and interrogate those questions may prove particularly damaging in the current context because it risks allowing the criminal justice system to absolve itself of *its* responsibility for creating the complainant-witness' condition of vulnerability, albeit in conjunction with the actions of the alleged perpetrator and other potential stressors.

In some recent work that I have conducted with REFUGE, we have explored the scale of, and mediating and mitigating factors associated with, suicidal ideation and suicidal behaviour among survivors of domestic abuse in England and Wales. Our findings unquestionably support the concern raised by Dr Bishop in this chapter about the damaging impacts of domestic abuse – in physical, sexual and psychological forms – upon survivors' mental well-being. But they also demonstrate the extent to which engagement with the criminal justice system is itself often a primary trigger for the vulnerabilities for which special measures are then afforded;[9] and this realisation highlights the extent to which, for all the benefits that provision of such protections might offer to individual complainant-witnesses in giving testimony, the broader structural and cultural dynamics of the criminal justice process can help to create the very barriers that special measures are then imposed as a 'sticking plaster' to ameliorate.

Of course, what Dr Bishop proposes here is a programme of inter-linked reforms, and in her third proposal, it can be argued that she moves to address these concerns by embarking on a far more thorough-going challenge to some of

[7] G Eagle and D Kaminer, 'Traumatic Stress: Established Knowledge, Current Debates and New Horizons' (2015) 45 *South African Journal of Psychology* 22.

[8] V Munro, 'Shifting Sands? Consent, Context and Vulnerability in Contemporary Sexual Offences Policy in England and Wales' (2017) 26(4) *Social and Legal Studies* 417; V Munro and J Scoular, 'Abusing Vulnerability? Contemporary Law and Policy Responses to Sex Work and Sex Trafficking in the UK' (2012) 20(3) *Feminist Legal Studies* 189.

[9] V Munro and R Aitken, 'From Hoping to Help: Indentifying and Responding to Suicidality Amongst Victims of Domestic Abuse in England and Wales' (forthcoming, 2018); R Aitken and V Munro, *Domestic Abuse and Suicide: Exploring the Links With Refuge's Client Base and Work Force* (London, REFUGE, 2018).

the cornerstones of the adversarial process, which itself triggers anxiety, depression, and suicidality for many domestic abuse survivors.

III. Limitations on Cross Examination

In conjunction with the increased availability of special measures protections and improved case preparation through pre-trial witness interviews, Dr Bishop advocates an increased emphasis on judicial management of the manner and content of questioning during cross-examination. In the context of sexual offences, the Court of Appeal has insisted that, in every case involving a vulnerable witness, there should be a 'ground rules' hearing held ahead of trial at which the questions to be asked of complainant-witnesses, as well as the broader arrangements for cross-examination in terms of timings, breaks, and so on, should be presented by counsel for discussion and judicial approval.[10] Though distinct from the decision to roll out in England and Wales the use of pre-recorded cross-examination of vulnerable and intimidated witnesses, as provided for under section 28 of the Youth Justice and Criminal Evidence Act 1999, the move to institute ground rules hearings in relevant cases is clearly complementary to the feasibility of such initiatives. More broadly, it is also becoming common in discussions about best practice in relation to vulnerable witnesses in sexual offences trials for judges to be mandated to undertake a more interventionist role than might otherwise have been thought to be the adversarial norm, in order to ensure that these 'ground rules' – and the associated protections and provisions regarding cross-examination – are properly complied with in court.[11]

As the discussion in Dr Bishop's chapter makes clear, however, this is a significant shift in the way in which we have conventionally conceived of the function and operation of the criminal trial, and one that may not come easily to judges who have understood their role to be that of a primarily non-interventionist arbiter of competing, vigorously presented accounts provided by counsel. In the sexual assault context, moreover, this is further complicated by the fact that it is far from clear that all judges acknowledge the need for, and appropriateness of, existing restrictions and protections in respect of the types of question that can be put to complainant-witnesses, often interpreting the boundaries of evidential relevance disconcertingly loosely or allowing evidence to be sought and admitted from complainant-witnesses without adequate scrutiny.[12] It is not unreasonable to

[10] *Lubemba (Cokesix); JP* [2014] EWCA Crim 2064.

[11] See, eg, The Advocate's Gateway, *Working with Traumatised Witnesses, Defendants and Parties* (Toolkit 18, 2015) www.theadvocatesgateway.org; Advocacy Training Council, *Raising the Bar: The Handling of Vulnerable Victims, Witnesses and Defendants in Court* (Advocacy Training Council, 2011).

[12] For recent discussion of some issues arising in this context, see C McGlynn, 'Rape Trials and Sexual History Evidence: Reforming the Law on Third-Party Evidence' (2017) 81(5) *Journal of Criminal Law* 367.

hypothesise, based on the wealth of evidence regarding the existence of tenacious misconceptions and misunderstandings of the dynamics of, and victims' 'normal' reactions to, domestic abuse amongst criminal justice practitioners (and indeed society in general),[13] that similar difficulties may be experienced in transitioning towards a comparable model of case management, ground rules discussions and judicial intervention in this context. Indeed, particularly in respect of non-physical and/or non-sexual forms of coercive and controlling behaviour, the challenges faced may be acute.

Though the legislation criminalising coercive and controlling behaviour in England and Wales remains in its infancy, concerns have been expressed regarding the feasibility of securing convictions under it in a context in which psychological and emotional abuse continues to be perceived as less serious (and indeed less traumatic for victims), and more difficult to evidence in a way that sufficiently justifies marking the defendant's behaviour as meriting criminal sanction.[14] Where the judiciary may already feel a sense of disquiet with their newly assumed role within a case management model, their anxieties about ensuring fairness to the defendant by enabling a robust cross-examination of the complainant may be attenuated by the allegations at issue being somewhat less 'usual' and less 'tangible' than the impositions of bodily and psychiatric injury with which the criminal law is predominantly engaged. This will probably make the road to securing Bishop's third proposal a challenging and arduous one, notwithstanding the compelling arguments in its favour in terms of the better handling of vulnerable witnesses.

IV. Jury Information Regarding Trauma

Even where judges are receptive to embracing this cultural and logistical shift in their conventional *modus operandi*, moreover, this is not the end of the matter. For all the protections that can be put in place to support complainant-witnesses' trial participation and to encourage judges to temper the tone of cross-examination so that the prospects of re-traumatisation are reduced without imperilling the opportunity for a robust exploration of the truth, it is jurors – as ultimate arbiters of fact – who will evaluate credibility and attribute responsibility. In the sexual offences context, there is now a substantial evidence base that highlights the intractability of a number of statistically unfounded 'common sense' assumptions, which can have a tangible impact upon the ways in which complainants' testimony

[13] HMIC, *Everyone's Business: Improving the Police Response to Domestic Abuse* (HMIC, 2014); A Robinson et al, 'Under the Radar: Policing Non-Violent Domestic Abuse in the US and UK' (2016) 40(3) *International Journal of Comparative and Applied Criminal Justice* 1.

[14] C Bishop and V Bettison, 'Evidencing Domestic Violence, including Behaviour that falls under the new Offence of "Controlling or Coercive Behaviour"' (2017) 22(1) *International Journal of Evidence and Proof* 3.

is assessed by jurors.[15] Following the Court of Appeal's approval of jury instructions intended by the trial judge to redress this potentially prejudicial impact in the case of *Doody*, the Judicial Studies Board have now provided suggested directions that can (though need not) be utilised by judges in sexual offences cases where the matters arising are not deemed to be within the normal knowledge and experience of lay people and may be susceptible to bias or misinformation.[16]

In Bishop's chapter, she advocates the extended use of such jury education – not only via judicial instruction but also through the introduction of expert testimony – in domestic abuse cases, in order to address jurors' potentially 'biased and erroneous' assumptions regarding the dynamics of abusive relationships, the reactions of victims and the impact of abuse thereon, and the behavioural patterns of perpetrators that can cumulate to create conditions of coercion and control. On the one hand, this extension to domestic abuse seems entirely appropriate, for as Bishop has ably demonstrated, this is an area – akin to sexual violence – in which there is a high potentiality for trauma reactions during and in the aftermath of victimisation, including whilst giving testimony in the courtroom, which may be at odds with what a less informed juror might presume to be 'normal'. At the same time, however, there are two important expansions to the current state of play in respect of sexual assault trials that Bishop makes in her proposal, and both pose some potential difficulties in practice.

First, the matters upon which educational guidance can be provided to the jury seem potentially broader in Dr Bishop's proposals than has been permitted to date in the sexual offences context. It is one thing to provide jurors with robust psychological research that illustrates the ways in which a complainant-witness who is suffering, as a result of whatever cause, from PTSD (or perhaps trauma symptoms more broadly) might experience difficulties in linear and complete recall, or undergo episodes of disassociation that impact upon the quality of testimony; or indeed to marshal incontrovertible social science research in order to remind jurors that there may be a number of different types of post-assault reaction exhibited by victims of rape, which will be reflected in choices regarding when and to whom to report. Arguably it is another to seek to explain the substance and dynamics of domestic abuse, as Bishop proposes, since this goes to a contested area of definition and experience in which the boundaries that are at issue lie at the

[15] For further discussion, see L Ellison and V Munro, 'Better the Devil You Know? "Real Rape" Stereotypes and The Relevance of a Previous Relationship in (Mock) Juror Deliberation' (2013) 17(4) *International Journal of Evidence and Proof* 299; L Ellison and V Munro, 'A Stranger in the Bushes or an Elephant in the Room? Critical Reflections on Received Rape Myth Wisdom in the Context of a Mock Jury Study' (2010) 13(4) *New Criminal Law Review* 781; L Ellison and V Munro, 'Of Normal Sex and "Real Rape": Exploring the Use of Socio-Sexual Scripts in (Mock) Jury Deliberation' (2009) 18(3) *Social and Legal Studies* 1.

[16] *Doody* [2008] EWCA Crim 2394; Judicial Studies Board, *Crown Court Bench Book, Directing the Jury* (Judicial Studies Board, 2010).

heart of whether the defendant's behaviour is marked as criminal. Though carefully crafted guidance *may* be able to avoid it, there is certainly an increased risk here that evidence will be perceived to over-step the mark. And the risk of this is perhaps increased further in the context of Bishop's second extension, where she advocates the provision of this guidance not by the judge in the form of a judicial direction but by experts during the trial proceedings. When educational guidance was introduced in the sexual offences context, the proposal by the Office for Criminal Justice Reform to do so via general expert evidence proved controversial, with concern about the prospect of trials turning into a 'battle of experts'. Within the relatively tight parameters that were initially proposed for that sexual offences testimony, it might be thought that this was unduly cautious, but with the broader mandate that Bishop advocates for explaining the dynamics of domestic abuse and coercive control, there is perhaps greater scope for such battle lines to be drawn. Typically, this will do little to benefit the outcome of the complainant's case from their perspective but may do a great deal to increase the trial's proclivity to re-traumatise, re-stigmatise and re-disempower. Whether it provides the optimal source and time-frame for impact on jurors remains unclear, but drawing on the experience of initiating a comparable mechanism in rape trials, there is little doubt that guidance as part of the judge's final summing up will be perceived by many practitioners as more manageable and less controversial than expert testimony (or testimonies).

What this discussion also leaves unexplored is the impact of trauma on jurors. Our impulse to disabuse jurors of misconceptions and misunderstandings, including through the provision of information about how trauma can impact on a survivor of domestic abuse, may skip too lightly over the empirical likelihood that many jurors will themselves have been subjected to, witnessed or otherwise had close personal contact with situations of, domestic abuse. In a context in which such experiences may have had traumatic impacts upon them, whether in the far past or more recently, this can have unpredictable effects on their ability and willingness to engage with the narratives of abuse provided by others. A self-protecting impulse might 'kick in' which prevents jurors from listening openly to the accounts provided, blame may be ascribed to the complainant for having failed to leave an abusive relationship as the juror may have done, or conversely the account may incite greater sympathy from those who understand how difficult it is to find and remain in a place of safety. However this plays out, the complicating – but rarely acknowledged – factor that I want to draw attention to here is that jurors are also at risk of re-traumatisation on account of their role within the criminal trial: hearing traumatic narratives, seeing graphic evidence, watching upset trial parties, being asked to make a decision of such magnitude, and then being told not to talk about it to family or friends, requires a considerable amount of emotional labour, which is apt to cause some level of vicarious trauma for all jurors, and which is likely to be amplified in cases of jurors who have experienced domestic abuse. Indeed, previous research has shown that jury service can engender moderate to severe clinical levels of stress in some participants, and may lead in the longer term to symptoms associated with PTSD.[17] We have barely considered the implications of this in terms of how juror education is provided or received, let alone in terms of the broader outcomes and ethical standards of our criminal justice process.

V. Conclusion

Many complainant-witnesses in the domestic abuse context approach their engagement(s) with the criminal justice system painfully aware of its limitations and mechanisms for exclusion; they often do not have high hopes that it will work for them or with them.[18] At the heart of the proposals that Dr Bishop puts forward is a commitment to redress this by placing the complainant at the centre of the criminal justice process, developing mechanisms that will support her engagement with the investigation and prosecution process, offering protections that will enable her to participate effectively and give her best evidence at the trial, and ensuring that the account she gives is heard and evaluated in a fair and open-minded way. There is little in this to object to, or at least little that I would want to object to, albeit that there may be a few further discussions to be had around definitional boundaries and strategic implementation. But, to my mind, the question that Bishop's chapter highlights most starkly – a question whose bounds stretch far beyond the remit of domestic or sexual abuse – is how we can best negotiate the tension that emerges once the criminal justice system acknowledges the consequences of its own adversarial excesses in the context of traumatised trial participants, and what shadow this might cast on our broader conceptions of what securing 'best' evidence and pursuing 'truth' actually does, can or should entail within the criminal justice process. At the same time, of course, perspective matters; and we should be careful not to presume to colonise the survivors' processes for recognising truth, attributing blame and securing closure to the legal arena. Even with the best, most victim-centred processes and trial outcomes, the complex burdens associated with trauma that are experienced by survivors of domestic abuse cannot be easily redressed; the criminal justice system can and should play its part in enabling participation, affording recognition, and creating conditions of safety, but without a wider commitment amongst statutory agencies and society in general to respond with care and concern to the precariousness and complexity of survivors' lives, we will remain a long way from justice.

[17] B Bornstein, M Miller, R Nemeth, G Page and S Musil, 'Juror Reactions to Juror Duty; Perceptions of the System and Potential Stressors' (2005) 23 *Behavioural Sciences and the Law* 321; N Robertson, G Davies and A Nettleingham, 'Vicarious Traumatisation as a Consequence of Jury Service' (2009) 48 *Howard Journal of Criminal Justice* 1.

[18] R Aitken and V Munro, 'Adding Insult to Injury? The Criminal Law's Response to Domestic Abuse-Related Suicide in England and Wales' [2018] *Criminal Law Review* 732.

9

The Case for Restoring the Right of Silence

HANNAH QUIRK*

This chapter proposes repealing sections 34–38 of the Criminal Justice and Public Order Act 1994 (CJPOA), which curtailed the right of silence in police interview and at trial. This was a highly controversial measure; at the time there were public as well as Parliamentary protests against several of the provisions in the legislation.[1] Supporters of the CJPOA argued that the protection had become redundant with the rights bestowed upon suspects by the Police and Criminal Evidence Act 1984 (PACE), in particular, the right to legal advice at the police station. As a consequence, it was claimed – contrary to most academic research findings[2] – that 'criminals' were exploiting the right of silence in order to evade justice by 'ambushing' the prosecution with a defence produced for the first time at trial. Defenders of the right of silence argued that it was of both practical and symbolic importance: it protected the vulnerable against making false confessions and it emphasised the presumption of innocence and that the burden of proof lies on the prosecution. Once the CJPOA came into effect, however, neither the promised increased detection of crime, nor the threatened miscarriages of justice materialised, and there was little further discussion about revisiting the changes.

Almost 25 years on from the CJPOA, there has been a revival of academic interest in the topic,[3] and the toxicity of crime as a political issue has dissipated;

* I would like to thank Abenaa Owusu-Bempah for her response to this paper.

[1] Other controversial measures included restrictions on protests against fox-hunting, unauthorised raves and Travellers' settlements. See, R Card and R Ward, *Criminal Justice and Public Order Act: A Practitioner's Guide* (Jordan Publishing, 1994).

[2] Discussed below.

[3] A Owusu-Bempah, 'Judging the desirability of a defendant's evidence: an unfortunate approach to s 35(1)(b) of the Criminal Justice and Public Order Act 1994' (2011) *Crim LR* 15, 691; ALT Choo, *The Privilege Against Self-Incrimination* (Hart, 2013); S Easton, *Silence and Confessions: The Suspect as the Source of Evidence* (Palgrave Macmillan, 2014); A Marks, 'Expert evidence of drug traces: relevance, reliability and the right to silence' [2013] *Crim LR* 10, 16; A Owusu-Bempah, 'Silence in suspicious circumstances' [2014] *Crim LR* 2, 10; H Quirk, 'Twenty years on, the right of silence and legal advice: the spiralling costs of an unfair exchange' (2013) 4(4) *NILQ* 465–83; FMW Billing, *The Right to Silence*

it was barely mentioned in the last two general election campaigns, having been one of the most significant election issues for the previous two decades. Across the world, the right of silence has increasingly become part of 'international standards and recognized good practices'.[4] The European Union (EU) has adopted a series of directives requiring that suspects be given information on their procedural rights, including the right of silence.[5] The EU Referendum vote of June 2016 means that the UK will be unlikely to implement these measures. The White Paper, 'Legislating for the United Kingdom's withdrawal from the European Union', confirmed that the UK would be withdrawing from the EU's Charter of Fundamental Rights.[6] This means that, as the government seeks to determine what the 'post-Brexit' landscape might look like, criminal justice policy is one of the many issues that requires wide-ranging consideration. As a contribution to this debate, this therefore seems an opportune moment to examine the case for reinstating the right of silence.

Despite the right of silence having been described as 'a "bench mark" of British justice',[7] parliamentary sovereignty meant that the legislature could curtail it without impediment. This chapter does not seek to re-argue the abstract case against curtailing the right of silence as that was rehearsed extensively and unsuccessfully at the time. Rather, this is more akin to an application for leave to appeal against conviction – new evidence has become available that means the original decision may be unsafe.[8] This chapter first examines how the courts have interpreted the provisions broadly, with consequences that go far beyond those envisaged by Parliament in 1994. The judicial directions regarding adverse inferences from silence are unduly complex, and new evidence has emerged that casts doubt on whether lay magistrates and juries can be expected to understand them, explored in Part II. Part III examines how the value of legal representation at the police station has been undermined in ways that were not anticipated when the CJPOA was enacted because of the expansive interpretation of the legislation by the courts. The increase in unrepresented defendants at court has made the effects of the CJPOA more acute – a problem that seems likely to worsen with the reduced eligibility for legal aid.[9] Part IV explores how the legislation is being operated in a manner that appears unfair and discriminatory, which was not the expressed will

in Transnational Criminal Proceedings: Comparative Law Perspectives (Springer, 2016); H Quirk *The Rise and Fall of the Right of Silence* (Routledge, 2016).

[4] UN General Assembly, Res/67/187 [6].

[5] Directive 2012/13/EU of the European Parliament and of the Council of 22 May 2012 on the Right to Information in Criminal Proceedings, OJ L 142/1 (1 June 2012).

[6] Department for Exiting the European Union, *Legislating for the United Kingdom's Withdrawal from the European Union* (Policy Paper, 2017) [2.23].

[7] J Jackson, 'Curtailing the Right of Silence: Lessons from Northern Ireland' [1991] *Crim LR* 404.

[8] Criminal Appeal Act 1968, s 2 (as amended).

[9] An estimated 28% of defendants at the magistrates' court are unrepresented (Ministry of Justice, *Virtual Courts Pilot: Outcome Evaluation Report* (20 December 2010) 11). Latest figures show that in 2016, 7% of defendants at the Crown Court were not legally represented, an increase of 2% since 2010 (Ministry of Justice, *Criminal Court Statistics Quarterly, England and Wales, January to March 2017* (29 June 2017) 15).

of Parliament, and in possible contravention of human rights provisions. Part V contends that the legislation has changed the adversarial climate in which defendants are investigated and tried. Suspects are now expected to cooperate with the police investigation and trial process from the earliest opportunity in a way that, it is argued, undermines the presumption of innocence. The chapter concludes by making the case for reinstating an enhanced common law right of silence.

I. Judicial Extension of the CJPOA

The CJPOA provisions permit comment upon, and the drawing of inferences at trial from, the failure of suspects to:

- mention when questioned or charged any feature of their defence that could reasonably have been mentioned at that stage (section 34);
- answer questions relating to the presence of any substance, object or mark about their person (section 36);
- answer questions relating to their presence at the scene of an offence (section 37); and
- testify or, having been sworn, their refusal to answer questions without good cause (section 35).

There was much speculation when the CJPOA was passed as to how the courts might interpret it. As in Northern Ireland, the case law was relatively cautious at first, then developed rapidly.[10] Despite Lord Bingham's assertion that, since the CJPOA provisions 'restrict rights recognised at common law as appropriate to protect defendants against the risk of injustice they should not be construed more widely than the statutory language requires',[11] the opposite has occurred. The Court of Appeal made clear from the start that it would not permit a 'coach and horses'[12] to be driven through the provisions. Instead it has developed a 'normative expectation'[13] that defendants should cooperate fully in the criminal process, and an assumption that those who do not assist have something to hide.[14] Whilst the court has the right 'to exclude evidence (whether by preventing questions being put or otherwise) at its discretion',[15] it will allow this only in 'the most exceptional case'.[16] The court has shown itself 'so committed to crime control that

[10] J Jackson, M Wolfe and K Quinn, *Legislating against Silence: The Northern Ireland Experience* (Northern Ireland Statistics and Research Agency, 2000).

[11] *Bowden* [1999] 1 WLR 823; 2 Cr App R 176 [181].

[12] *Cowan, Gayle, and Ricciardi* [1995] 3 WLR 818; [1995] 4 All ER 939 at 380.

[13] R Leng, 'Silence Pre-trial, Reasonable Expectations and the Normative Distortion of Fact Finding' (2001) 5(4) *E&P* 240, 246.

[14] *Howell* [2003] EWCA Crim 1.

[15] CJPOA, s 38(6).

[16] *Condron (Karen) and Condron (William)* [1997] 1 Cr App R 185, 196.

at almost every turn – even when an interpretation favourable to the defence is plausible – the legislation has been construed in the prosecution's favour'.[17] This has gone far beyond anything predicted when the CJPOA was enacted. Failures to observe the checks that exist within the legislation have been tolerated, and adverse inferences have been permitted in circumstances when previously the interview might have been excluded entirely.[18] Whilst it is 'essential to a fair trial'[19] that the judge should direct the jury carefully regarding inferences from a suspect's silence, the Court of Appeal has held that convictions will not necessarily be rendered unsafe by defective directions relating to this.[20] It has also been held that failure to give the jury a specific direction that no adverse inference is open to them will not necessarily lead to an unsafe conviction.[21] This means that suspects have not received the protections that Parliament intended, and that some of the protections of PACE have been weakened without direct legislative authority.

Section 34 gives no guidance as to what inferences from silence may be 'proper'. In *Averill v UK* it was said that the extent to which adverse inferences may be drawn from an accused's failure to respond to police questioning must be 'necessarily limited'.[22] In *Argent*, Lord Bingham CJ indicated that there were six formal conditions that had to be met before section 34 could operate. These added little to the legislation and have been qualified subsequently.[23] The Court of Appeal rejected the argument that a proper inference is one that is relevant in determining whether the accused is guilty, as such a limited construction would thwart the intention of the Act.[24] There is now a presumption that any inference drawn will be adverse.[25] The Crown Court Compendium,[26] a reference source for judges preparing summings-up for juries, explains that the object of section 34 is 'to deter late fabrication of defences and to encourage early disclosure of genuine defences'. In an earlier edition, it stated that the basis of section 34

[17] R Pattenden, 'Silence: Lord Taylor's Legacy' (1998) 2 *E&P* 141 and 164.

[18] For example, allowing inferences from a 'no comment' interview that had taken place after the custody limit had expired. When questioning a suspect about issues covered under ss 36 and 37 of the CJPOA, the police should give a special warning using 'ordinary language,' that the suspect is capable of understanding of the consequences of failure to provide a satisfactory answer (PACE Code C, 10.11 and Note 10D). Inferences have been allowed when the police had issued a special warning in relation to the wrong offence, *Collins* [2014] EWCA Crim 773.

[19] *Condron v UK* (2001) 31 EHHR 1. See also, *Webber* [2004] UKHL 1; [2004] 1 WLR 404 [34].

[20] *Adetoro v UK* (46834/ 06) Unreported April 20, 2010; *Chivers* [2011] EWCA Crim 1212.

[21] *McGarry* [1999] 1 Cr App R. 377; *Francom* [2001] 1 Cr App R. 17.

[22] *Averill v UK* (2001) 31 EHRR 839, [47].

[23] (1) there must be proceedings against a person for an offence; (2) the alleged failure must occur before a defendant is charged; (3) the alleged failure must occur during questioning under caution by a constable or other person within s 34(4); (4) the questioning must be directed to trying to discover whether or by whom the alleged offence had been committed; (5) the alleged failure had to be to mention any fact relied on in the person's defence in those proceedings; and (6) the alleged failure must be in relation to a fact which in the circumstances existing at the time the accused could reasonably have been expected to mention (*Argent* [1997] 2 Cr App R 27, 32–33).

[24] *Beckles and Montague* [1999] Crim LR 148.

[25] *Condron (Karen) and Condron (William)* [1997] 1 Cr App R 185; *Napper* [1996] Crim LR 591.

[26] The Crown Court Compendium, Judicial College (May 2016), 1, [2].

'is an assumption that an innocent defendant – as distinct from one who is entitled to require the prosecution to prove its case – would give an early explanation to demonstrate his innocence'.[27] This shows a startling disregard for the presumption of innocence and, despite the Court's assertions to the contrary, makes it easier in some cases for the prosecution to discharge the burden of proof (discussed below.) The Compendium identifies permissible inferences, or 'conclusions' as it now describes them, as: that the fact now relied on is true but the defendant chose not to reveal it earlier; the fact is irrelevant; the fact is of more recent invention; the fact is fabricated; or that the defendant is guilty.[28] This offers no option for the jury just not knowing why the fact was not mentioned earlier and it conflates the evaluation of the evidence with the determination of facts in a way that is unlikely to be favourable to defendants.

The submission that 's 35 is so at variance with established principle that its use should be reduced and marginalised as far as possible', was rejected in the first appeal to test the provisions.[29] As section 35 contains no scope for limiting its interpretation other than 'where the mental or physical condition of the accused makes it undesirable for him to give evidence',[30] it was held that the provisions should be of otherwise general application. It is insufficient that the defendant merely suffers from some physical or mental condition, or that the condition may cause some difficulty in giving evidence. It was held that '[e]xtreme difficulty in giving evidence is quite common among defendants and other witnesses who give evidence in criminal trials. That does not in itself make it "undesirable" that that person should give evidence'.[31] The examples given initially where inferences should not be drawn, such as triggering an epileptic fit or a florid episode of schizophrenia,[32] consider the effects of testifying on the defendant's wellbeing rather than on the fairness of the trial. In practice, the bar has been set to an almost insurmountable level, as discussed below.

At the close of the prosecution's case, the court must satisfy itself, in the presence of the jury, that defendants who have not indicated that they intend to give evidence understand the consequences of such a 'failure'.[33] (The language used in many of the judgments is similarly freighted). The judicially devised warning that is used for unrepresented defendants goes further than is required by statute. It is more than twice as long and is in more coercive terms than for those who are represented.[34] The judge or magistrate may remind the accused of his or her 'duty'

[27] *Crown Court Bench Book* (2010) 258.

[28] *Crown Court Compendium* (2016) 17-4. See also *Argent* [1997] 2 Cr App R 27; *Daniel (Anthony Junior)* (1998) 2 Cr App R 373; *Milford* [2002] EWCA Crim 1528 [33]; approved in *Webber* [2004] UKHL 1; [2004] 1 WLR 404 [30].

[29] *Cowan, Gayle, and Ricciardi* [1995] 3 WLR 818; [1995] 4 All ER 939, 943. See also *Becourarn* 2005, 2597.

[30] CJPOA, s 35(1)(b).

[31] *Ensor* (2009) EWCA Crim 2519, 262.

[32] *Friend* (1997) 2 Cr App R 231.

[33] CJPOA, s 35(2); *Criminal Practice Direction* (2015) 26P.2.

[34] *Criminal Practice Direction* (2015) 26P.5.

to answer all proper questions and the risk of the drawing of inferences, although this should not be done in an oppressive manner.[35] The cumulative effect of the case law has been to create a far more coercive situation than it was clear that Parliament intended.

II. Lay Decision Makers

The House of Lords held that 'the object of section 34 is to bring the law back into line with common sense,'[36] but common sense and criminal evidence do not always cohere. As Easton[37] notes, '[c]ommon sense may be unreliable, impressionistic and unsystematic. It is because of the weaknesses of common-sense thinking that clear judicial guidance is so important'. Magistrates now have to give reasons for their verdicts in order to comply with the Human Rights Act 1998, but there has been no study of their decision making in relation to the right of silence. There is evidence that suggests magistrates never liked defendants not giving evidence and that they drew inferences prior to the CJPOA anyway.[38] Inferences from silence is one of the few types of evidence to require specific judicial directions. Section 34 has been condemned as 'a headache for the conscientious jury, and a tool with which the slapdash, incompetent jury may wreak injustice'.[39] As juries give their verdicts without explanation, and research into their decision making is prohibited,[40] it is not known to what extent jurors are drawing inferences, nor indeed, to what extent they did before the CJPOA. No empirical research has been conducted into jurors' interpretation of the CJPOA directions,[41] but two significant studies have been undertaken since the CJPOA was enacted that raise concern as to how jurors process judicial directions.[42] Cheryl Thomas's research has revealed worryingly low levels of comprehension.[43] She found that less than a third of jurors understood the – much more straightforward – judicial direction on self-defence. In a real trial, jurors may receive lengthy directions on multiple issues, which is likely to reduce their levels of understanding. As this confusion cannot be established in an individual case, there is no way of raising

[35] *Ackinclose* [1996] Crim LR 747.

[36] *Webber* [2004] UKHL 1; [2004] 1 WLR 404 [33].

[37] S Easton, 'Legal advice, common sense and the right to silence' (1998) 2 *E&P* 109, 114.

[38] See H Quirk, *The Rise and Fall of the Right of Silence* (Routledge, 2016) ch 5 and T Bucke, R Street and D Brown, 'Right of Silence: The Impact of the Criminal Justice and Public Order Act 1994' (Home Office Research Study, 2000).

[39] D Birch, 'Suffering in Silence: A Cost-Benefit Analysis of Section 34 of the Criminal Justice and Public Order Act 1994' [1999] *Crim LR* 769, 772.

[40] Contempt of Court Act 1981, s 8, now replaced by Criminal Justice and Courts Act 2015, s 74.

[41] T Bucke, R Street and D Brown, *Right of Silence: The Impact of the Criminal Justice and Public Order Act 1994* (HMSO, 2000) 66 and 110.

[42] C Thomas, *Diversity and Fairness in the Jury System in England and Wales* (Ministry of Justice Research Series, 2007); C Thomas, *Are Juries Fair?* (Ministry of Justice Research Series, 2010).

[43] C Thomas, *Are Juries Fair?* (Ministry of Justice Research Series, 2010) 35.

this as a ground of appeal. Appellate judges have professed their confidence in the ability of 'a fair-minded jury' to take account of a defendant's physical and learning difficulties,[44] without any evidence as to whether juries are in fact fair-minded. A report by Scope[45] found that jurors may misinterpret the demeanour of a defendant with a disability – assuming slurred speech is a result of intoxication rather than tiredness for example. Nor have they considered how juries might respond to explanations advanced by the defence as to why inferences should not be drawn. Some explanations for not testifying may risk further discrediting the defendant, such as memory loss being due to drug taking and head injuries.[46] As Leng concludes: 'The English approach abdicates the protection of procedural rights to untrained, ad hoc and unaccountable triers of fact (magistrates or jury) and turns reliance on the right to silence into a gamble.'[47]

III. Undermining of Legal Advice

The right to legal representation is enshrined in Article 6 of the European Convention on Human Rights (ECHR) as an essential component of the right to a fair trial. It has been described domestically as a 'fundamental right of a citizen'.[48] It is still only a minority of suspects that is legally represented at the police station, however.[49] Parliament has provided that the role of the legal representative at the police station is 'solely to protect and advance the suspect's legal rights'.[50] The way in which the Court of Appeal has interpreted the CJPOA has undermined the protective benefit of legal advice. Contrary to the expectation of some commentators, the Court of Appeal held that reliance on legal advice, of itself, would not avert inferences as this 'would render section 34 wholly nugatory'.[51] Whilst legal advice is 'a very relevant' circumstance to be taken into account, the Court considered that it is 'not so much the advice given by the solicitor, as the reason why the defendant chose not to answer questions that is important'.[52] A reliance on legal advice 'does not give a licence to a guilty person to shield behind the advice of his solicitor'.[53] The jury should 'consider whether or not he was able to decide for himself what he should do, or having got a solicitor to advise him he would not challenge that

[44] *Dixon* [2013] EWCA Crim 465; [2014] 1 WLR 525 [55]; *Charisma* [2009] EWCA Crim 2345.

[45] Scope, *Current Attitudes Towards Disabled People* (Milton Keynes: Scope, 2014, 9).

[46] *Charisma* [2009] EWCA Crim 2345.

[47] R Leng, 'Silence in Court: From Common Sense to Common Law: Azzopardi' (2002) 6 *International Journal of Evidence & Proof* 62, 68.

[48] *Samuel* [1988] 2 All ER 135, 144.

[49] P Pleasence, V Kemp and NJ Balmer, 'The Justice Lottery? Police Station Advice 25 Years on from PACE' (2011) *Crim LR* 3.

[50] PACE Code C, Notes 6D.

[51] *Condron (Karen) and Condron (William)* [1997] 1 Cr App R 185, 191.

[52] ibid, 192.

[53] *Betts; Hall* [2001] 2 Cr App R 257 [54].

advice in the light of the specific warning in the caution'.[54] The domestic court has essentially disregarded the European Court of Human Rights (ECtHR) ruling that it is essential to a fair trial for the judge to direct the jury not to draw an inference if satisfied that the defendant remained silent on legal advice.[55] Legal representatives now have to assess whether the risk of providing the police with information that may be used to charge or convict their client is outweighed by the potential risk of inferences being drawn from a no comment interview, should the case be brought to trial. The provisions have also removed one of the few bargaining chips that legal representatives had to gain disclosure of the police case before interview (they would sometimes recommend a 'no comment' interview until the police revealed their case).

By making custodial legal advice of potential evidential significance, perhaps requiring representatives to testify why they gave such advice, the CJPOA has compromised the lawyer-client relationship. Despite early protestations that the, almost sacrosanct, principle of legal professional privilege was not affected by the CJPOA,[56] in the court's desire to ensure that suspects do not evade inferences, another principle of a fair trial has been undermined.[57] The ECtHR held that requiring suspects either to have an unexplained silence from which inferences may be drawn, or to call the solicitor in an attempt to explain this silence, does not contravene Article 6 of the ECHR as the suspect experiences only the 'indirect compulsion' to waive privilege.[58] It might be argued that in practice this amounts to little more than Hobson's choice. So long as suspects are not exposed to a degree of compulsion which is sufficient to 'destroy the essence of the right',[59] no explanation was given as to why it should be 'obvious' that:

> These immunities cannot and should not prevent that the accused's silence, in situations which clearly call for an explanation from him, be taken into account in assessing the persuasiveness of the evidence adduced by the prosecution.[60]

The provisions make the testing of the prosecution case at trial more difficult as section 34 can be triggered even if no evidence is given or called,[61] for example if a fact not mentioned in interview is referred to in a defence case statement or in cross-examining a witness.[62] Cape's warning of the consequences was stark:

> The value of legal advice is thus diminished. If defendants can never be sure that they are acting reasonably in relying on the advice of their lawyer, then they can never be

[54] *Howell* [2002] EWCA Crim 1 [10].

[55] *Condron v United Kingdom* (2001) 31 EHHR 1 [62]; Lord Phillips of Worth Matravers 'Trusting the Jury' – The Criminal Bar Association Kalisher Lecture, 23 October 2007.

[56] *Bowden* [1999] 1 WLR 823; 2 Cr App R 176, 827; *Webber* [2004] UKHL 1 [27].

[57] *Seaton* [2010] EWCA 1980; H Quirk, 'Twenty years on, the right of silence and legal advice: the spiralling costs of an unfair exchange' (2013) 64(4) *NILQ* 465–83.

[58] *Murray v United Kingdom* (1996) 22 EHHR 29, 65.

[59] *Funke v France* (1993) 16 EHRR 297.

[60] *Murray v United Kingdom* (1996) 22 EHHR 29, 60.

[61] *Bowers, Taylor and Millan* [1998] Crim LR 817.

[62] *Webber* [2004] UKHL 1.

sure that they should accept their lawyer's advice. If they cannot be sure about that, then it raises the fundamental question of the utility of legal advice at the police station. Custodial legal advice may be guaranteed by the European Convention on Human Rights, but its value as such is in danger of being seriously eroded.[63]

IV. The Potentially Discriminatory Impact of the Legislation

The CJPOA was introduced on the premise that hardened criminals and terrorists were exploiting the provisions, but the legislation applies to all, and its effects have not been felt equally. At first the court appeared to make concessions for individual frailty and noted that:

> When reference is made to 'the accused' attention is directed not to some hypothetical, reasonable accused of ordinary phlegm and fortitude but to the actual accused with such qualities, apprehensions, knowledge and advice as he is shown to have had at the time.[64]

In practice, few allowances have been made. One third of suspects in police custody are 'mentally disadvantaged,' with an IQ of below 75. The average IQ score for detainees is 82, compared with a population average of 100. One-third of suspects experience extreme distress or mental disorder at being detained. The Psychiatric Morbidity of Offenders Study survey found that 70 per cent of prisoners had a mental disorder.[65] Young *et al.*[66] found that 6.7 per cent of suspects at a large London police station had intellectual disabilities, 23.5 per cent had Attention Deficit Hyperactivity Disorder, and 76.3 per cent had conduct disorder. The increased complexity of the decision making necessitated by the CJPOA is likely to affect these suspects disproportionately.

The PACE Codes of Practice identify 'special groups' of defendants who have additional protections in police custody, such as those with hearing and speech difficulties, limited ability to speak English, and juveniles.[67] Section 77 of PACE provides that special care must be exercised in relation to the mentally handicapped or mentally disordered, and the jury should be warned in these cases 'that there is special need for caution before convicting the accused in reliance on the confession'. The obverse is not true, however, and caution is not required before

[63] E Cape, 'Sidelining Defence Lawyers: Police Station Advice after *Condron*' (1997) 1 *E&P* 386–402.

[64] *Argent* [1997] 2 Cr App R 27, 33.

[65] Office for National Statistics, 'ONS Survey of Psychiatric Morbidity among Prisoners in England and Wales, 1997' (*UK Data Archive*, 2010).

[66] S Young, EJ Goodwin, O Sedgwick and GH Gudjonsson, 'The Effectiveness of Police Custody Assessments in Identifying Suspects with Intellectual Disabilities and Attention Deficit Hyperactivity Disorder' (2013) 11 *BMC Medicine* 248.

[67] Code of Practice C 3.12. 3.13 and 3.15.

drawing adverse inferences from a no comment interview or failure to testify. Surprisingly the ability of suspects to understand the caution or special warnings has not been considered by the English courts even though research has found very limited understanding of the caution among police station suspects and individuals attending a job centre.[68] Clare *et al.* reported limited understanding of the caution not only among the general population but also a sample of A-level students.[69]

Whilst the past two decades have been marked by the increased support given to vulnerable witnesses, the provision to give evidence by live link is the only special measure to which defendants are statutorily entitled.[70] The legislation has also been interpreted in a way that has a disproportionate effect on those with disabilities that make it difficult for them to give evidence. Inferences from failure to testify have been permitted in cases such as where the defendant was arguing diminished responsibility and claimed to have no recollection of the crime due to his (undisputed) alcohol dependency syndrome;[71] another in which the defendant was sufficiently unwell that he had to be sentenced under the Mental Health Act 1983;[72] and a murder on the basis of joint enterprise where the teenage defendant had profound intellectual disabilities including the language levels of an eight-year-old, high levels of suggestibility and compliance, and a severe stammer that could render him unable to speak when under stress.[73] In each case, the Court of Appeal has held that it does not require any concession for the increased challenges faced by the defendants with disabilities before drawing adverse inferences.

When the legislation was introduced in the House of Lords, Lord Taylor CJ said that the position of the very young and the vulnerable would have to be 'very specially considered',[74] but this has not been the case. Since the CJPOA was enacted, the European Court of Human Rights has made clear that special measures must be taken to ensure that young defendants receive a fair trial, including steps to assist their understanding and ability to participate in proceedings, and to prevent their avoidable intimidation, humiliation or distress.[75] This does not seem

[68] S Fenner, GH Gudjonsson and ICH Clare 'Understanding of the Current Police Caution (England and Wales) among Suspects in Police Detention' (2002) *Journal of Community & Applied Social Psychology 12/2.*

[69] ICH Clare, GH Gudjonsson and PM Harari 'Understanding of the Current Police Caution (England and Wales)' (1998) *Journal of Community & Applied Social Psychology* 8/5. An earlier Northern Ireland case under the equivalent provisions held that if a judge felt that a defendant had not understood the caution or had some doubts about it, section 34 should not be activated, *Martin* [1992] 5 NIJB 1 at 41, NICA *Archbold* 15-484.

[70] Youth Justice and Criminal Evidence Act 1999, s 33A. See also S Fairclough '"It Doesn't Happen … and I've Never Thought it was Necessary for It to Happen": Barriers to Vulnerable Defendants Giving Evidence by Live Link in Crown Court Trials' (2017) 21(3) *E&P* 209–29.

[71] *Barry (Adrian)* [2010] 1 Cr App R 32.

[72] *Charisma* [2009] EWCA Crim 2345.

[73] *Dixon* [2013] EWCA Crim 465.

[74] Hansard, HL, Vol. 555, col. 520.

[75] *V and T v United Kingdom* (1999) 30 EHRR 121. See also *SC v United Kingdom* [2005] 40 EHRR 10 and *C v Sevenoaks Youth Court* [2009] EWHC 3088 (Admin) regarding effective participation.

to have been applied in any meaningful way regarding section 35.[76] It has been held that youth, of itself, is an insufficient reason for withdrawing inferences from the jury; there needs to be either some additional evidence or exceptional factors to justify so doing.[77] Over 60 per cent of children who offend have communication difficulties, and of this group about half have poor or very poor communication skills; around a quarter of children who offend have IQs of less than 70 and an additional 30 per cent have borderline learning difficulties.[78] Baroness Hale noted that many child defendants have serious communication difficulties and that:

> … child defendants appearing [in the youth court] are often amongst the most disadvantaged and the least able to give a good account of themselves. They lack the support and guidance of responsible parents. They lack the support of the local social services authority. They lack basic educational and literacy skills. They lack emotional and social maturity. They often have the experience of violence or other abuse within the home. Increasing numbers are being committed for trial in the Crown Court where these disadvantages will be even more disabling.[79]

Other vulnerable defendants have also been disadvantaged by the legislation. In *Gledhill*,[80] the defendant, who was suffering from Battered Women's Syndrome, did not give evidence, as this would inculpate her abusive co-accused. She had told the police that she was frightened that her partner would kill her if she spoke to them. Had she testified and her fears been realised, it is arguable that the State's obligations under Article 2 (the right to life) of the ECHR might have been engaged. The Recorder concluded:

> … one returns to the position time and time again that her position is a difficult one, not an impossible one … One has a degree of personal sympathy with anybody in those circumstances, but the fact that she would find it undesirable, it seems to me, is not the test at all and I have to take a much more objective view. The Act is designed to prevent those who, by reason of their physical or mental condition, would not do themselves justice from going into the witness box. It does not extend, in my judgment, to excuse those who would find it difficult and would rather not face cross-examination and the ordeal of giving evidence.

The only 'before and after' study of the CJPOA[81] showed that the greatest effect of the CJPOA was on black suspects. There was a 66.7 per cent drop in the

[76] A Owusu-Bempah, 'Judging the Desirability of a Defendant's Evidence: An Unfortunate Approach to s 35(1)(b) of the Criminal Justice and Public Order Act 1994' (2011) *Crim LR* 1597; Practice Direction 2000.

[77] *Friend* [1997] 2 Cr App R 231; *AC* [2001] EWCA Crim 713 [40–41]; *Dixon* [2013] EWCA Crim 465 [57].

[78] R Harrington and S Bailey, *Mental Health Needs and Effectiveness of Provision for Young Offenders in Custody and in the Community* (Youth Justice Board, 2005); *Child and Adolescent Mental Health Services Interdepartmental Project Board Report* (2005), cited in J McEwan 'Vulnerable defendants and the fairness of trials' *Crim LR* [2013] 100, 103.

[79] *R (on the application of D) v Camberwell Green Youth Court* [2005] UKHL 4; [2005] 1 All ER 999, 1017.

[80] *Gledhill* [2007] EWCA Crim 1183.

[81] T Bucke, R Street and D Brown, 'Right of Silence: The Impact of the Criminal Justice and Public Order Act 1994' (Home Office Research Study, 2000).

proportion of black suspects making complete no comment interviews compared to 54.8 per cent for Asian and 37.5 per cent for white. Some of the judgments in this area give the sense of unfairness if not of outright discrimination. Muslim women who refuse to remove their niqabs are not *allowed* to give evidence, and adverse inferences may be drawn from this.[82] Inferences have been allowed from the silence of a suspect who was advised to make no comment as his solicitor was unclear what his instructions were and considered his understanding of English to be insufficient to deal with difficult legal concepts.[83] Presumably Parliament did not intend the CJPOA to have a discriminatory effect. Since it was enacted, the Human Rights Act 1998 has come into force, which places a duty on public bodies (such as the courts) not to discriminate on the grounds of *inter alia* sex, race, colour, language or religion. It is far from clear that the CJPOA would survive a challenge on the basis of these differential effects (although the courts' lack of sympathy for defendants not answering police questions or testifying means they may find the legislation to be compliant as the jury is not obliged to draw inferences). Parliament should consider an equality assessment of the existing legislation and any proposed reforms.

V. The Changed Trial Culture

The CJPOA was introduced as the first of a series of measures based on the assumption that '[t]he balance in the criminal justice system is tilted too far in favour of the criminal and against protecting the public'.[84] This ignored the careful balancing already undertaken by the Royal Commission on Criminal Procedure which had laid the basis for PACE. The Royal Commission on Criminal Justice did not find a disparity either. Nevertheless the idea of 'Exchange Abolitionism' – a trade-off between the right of silence and improved protections – took hold,[85] 'but … such an exchange was not fair and has cost suspects far more than was envisaged at the time'.[86]

The vocabulary used by the Court of Appeal in CJPOA cases suggests that judges 'have imported to the courtroom the traditional police suspicion of defendants and their legal representatives'.[87] The language used by the Court of

[82] *D (R)* (2013), unreported, 16 September Crown Court (at Blackfriars); *The Crown Court Compendium* Judicial College (May 2016) 17-5, 10.

[83] *Roble* [1997] Crim LR 449, 7.

[84] Michael Howard, HC Deb 11 January 1994, vol 235, col 25.

[85] S Greer, 'The Right to Silence: A Review of the Current Debate' (1990) 53 *MLR* 709, 730.

[86] H Quirk 'Twenty Years On, the Right of Silence and Legal Advice: The Spiralling Costs of an Unfair Exchange' (2013) 64(4) *NILQ* 465, 466.

[87] ibid, 468.

Appeal demonstrates its suspicion of defendants who seek to '*shelter behind*'[88] their lawyers, exploiting loopholes[89] rather than '*flushing out innocence* at an early stage'.[90] The Court of Appeal and the ECtHR have referred repeatedly to *bona fide* advice by lawyers; a dangerous insinuation that lawyers may advise in bad faith; that contravenes the principle that lawyers 'should never be identified with their clients or their clients' causes as a result of discharging their functions'.[91]

The judgment in *Howell*[92] undermines the adversarial system and appears to suggest a shift from the presumption of innocence to an assumption that the innocent have nothing to hide. The Court held that, rather than a suspect or defendant being entitled to say nothing and require the accuser to establish guilt, an innocent person will generally be expected to seize the chance of denying the allegations. The only 'good' reasons for remaining silent will be those approved of by the Court. It considered the purpose behind the legislation, finding that:

> [Section 34] … is one of several enacted in recent years which has served to counteract a culture, or belief, which had been long established in the practice of criminal cases, namely that in principle a defendant may without criticism withhold any disclosure of his defence until the trial. Now the police interview and the trial are to be seen as part of a continuous process in which the suspect is engaged from the beginning … This benign *continuum* from interview to trial, the public interest that inheres in reasonable disclosure by a suspected person of what he has to say when faced with a set of facts which accuse him, is thwarted if currency is given to the belief that if a suspect remains silent on legal advice he may systematically avoid adverse comment at his trial. And it may encourage solicitors to advise silence for other than good objective reasons.

This was an extraordinary change in judicial thought. It was taken further by the Criminal Procedure Rules 2005[93] which have effected a 'sea change' in the way in which criminal cases should be conducted.[94] Judges are now under a duty to manage cases actively and to ensure that evidence is presented in the shortest and clearest way. Managerialism appears to have taken priority over adversarialism. The strength of the presumption that defendants will now testify is exemplified by the refusal to withdraw inferences from the jury in *Cameron*.[95] After the complainant in this rape case refused to answer further questions from defence counsel, rather than stopping the case, the judge took the unprecedented measure of cross-examining her in a 'non-adversarial and non-searching' manner. This tipped the balance even further towards the prosecution as its witness had refused to

[88] *Becouarn* [2005] UKHL 55, [2005] 1 WLR 2589 [24], emphasis added.
[89] *Lee (John)* Crown Court (Harrow) [1998] CLY 906; *Kavanagh* (1997), unreported.
[90] *Hoare and Pierce* [2004] EWCA Crim 784; [2005] 1 Cr App R 22 [53–54], emphasis added.
[91] Principle 18 of the United Nations, Basic Principles on the Role of Lawyers.
[92] *Howell* [2002] EWCA Crim 1.
[93] SI 2005/384.
[94] *DPP v Chorley Magistrates' Court* [2006] EWHC 1795 (Admin) [24]; M McConville and L Marsh 'Adversarialism goes West: Case Management in Criminal Courts' (2015) 19(3) *E&P* 172–89.
[95] *Cameron* [2001] Crim LR 587.

testify without negative effects but the defendant was penalised for so doing. In *Tabbakh*,[96] the Court balanced the wellbeing of the defendant (a self-harming asylum seeker with an unchallenged diagnosis of post-traumatic stress disorder following torture) against the importance of establishing whether he had been involved in the preparation of terrorist acts. The Court of Appeal accepted the trial judge's view, that:

> … in an ideal world, with no other factors to be considered, one would want to avoid a situation arising where anyone was put under stress to self-harm. But his own health and welfare is not the only issue, in my judgment, which I should take into account in reaching a judgment as to whether it is undesirable for him to give evidence …

The CJPOA provisions have been used to create an expectation that suspects should cooperate with their investigation and trial, and that failure to do so is indicative of guilt. Appellate decisions affect the climate in which defendants are tried, and what happens earlier in the criminal justice process.[97] This has effectively made the police interview a part of the trial, but without the benefit of the safeguards or the rules of natural justice that attend a fair trial.[98] The interpretation by the courts of the CJPOA provisions hinders the adversarial preparation of the defence and is part of the armoury of increasingly inquisitorial powers given to the police, evidence from which may then be deployed in an adversarial context.[99] The right of silence is bound up with the foundational principles of the criminal justice system. As Leigh writes:

> The notion of fair trial in its application to criminal law incorporates three closely related, albeit distinct, principles. These are: that the accused be presumed innocent until proven guilty, that the State bear the burden of proof on the issue of guilt and innocence, and that the accused be not obliged to incriminate himself.[100]

The changes to the right of silence sit uneasily with the presumption of innocence, in some cases making it easier for the Crown to discharge the burden of proof. Other changes that have been introduced after the CJPOA such as the disclosure regime,[101] the credit given for early guilty pleas and case management procedures, have intensified the effects of the CJPOA (and probably could not have been given effect without the CJPOA provisions). Cumulatively, therefore, the investigation and trial process is now a very different one to that which Parliament considered in 1994 when it decided to curtail the right of silence.

[96] *Tabbakh* [2009] EWCA Crim 464 [8].

[97] *Howell* [2002] EWCA Crim 1.

[98] J Jackson, 'Silence and Proof: Extending the Boundaries of Criminal Proceedings in the United Kingdom' (2001) 5 *E&P* 145 and 147.

[99] E Cape 'The Revised PACE Codes of Practice: A Further Step towards Inquisitorialism' [2003] *Crim LR* 355, 369.

[100] LH Leigh, 'The Right to a Fair Trial and the European Convention on Human Rights' in D Weissbrodt and R Wolfrüm (eds) *The Right to a Fair Trial* (Springer-Verlag, 1997) 645–68, 658.

[101] Criminal Procedure and Investigations Act 1996, part II.

VI. Options for Reinstatement

Each time curtailing the right of silence was considered previously, it was by a Royal Commission or by the Criminal Law Revision Committee (CLRC) as part of a systemic review.[102] The CLRC has fallen into desuetude, there seems little prospect of another Royal Commission and the Law Commission has indicated that it is unwilling to review this area.[103] This means that the discussions around Britain's departure from the European Union offer a rare opportunity to consider holistically what protections suspects should receive and what expectations should govern a fair trial. A review of the right of silence provisions is integral to such an appraisal. These proposals focus on the general right of silence rather than examining all the broader, statutory exceptions to the right, such as for serious financial misconduct,[104] terrorism,[105] and certain road traffic offences.[106] Evidential provisions such as the requirement for alibi notices[107] and expert evidence[108] to be served in advance of trial and 'reverse onus' provisions[109] could be brought into a full review, but are not considered here for reasons of space.

If the focus is maintained on the CJPOA, simple repeal would be easy to achieve but would be problematic in practice, as the extant common law on what comment could be made from failure to answer police questions or to testify was conflicting.[110] The common law position was that judges could not direct the jury that the accused's silence was evidence of guilt[111] or detract from the proper direction by saying that an innocent man was likely to answer questions.[112] The Court of Appeal took the view that it was contrary to common sense to forbid juries and magistrates to draw inferences, and gave an unnecessary advantage to the guilty without helping the innocent.[113]

[102] *Report of the Royal Commission on Police Powers and Procedure*, Cmnd 3297 (London, HMSO, 1929); *Report of the Royal Commission on Criminal Procedure*, Cmnd 8092 (London, HMSO, 1981); *Report of the Royal Commission on Criminal Justice*, Cmnd 2263 (London, HMSO, 1993); Criminal Law Revision Committee, *Eleventh Report: Evidence (General)*, Cmnd 4991 (London, HMSO, 1972).

[103] Letter from the Law Commission, on file with the author.

[104] See, inter alia, the Companies Act 1985 s 447, the Insolvency Act 1986 s 219, the Financial Services Act 1986 s 105, the Banking Act 1987 s 41 and the Criminal Justice Act 1987 s 2.

[105] See the requirements to answer police questions relating to others under the Official Secrets Act 1911 s 7; The Defence of the Realm Regulation No 53, passed during World War I and every iteration of the Emergency Provisions Act 1973 (CP Walker, *The Anti-Terrorism Legislation*, 3rd edn (OUP, 2014)).

[106] Road Traffic Act 1988, s 172(2)(a).

[107] Criminal Justice Act 1967, s 11.

[108] Police and Criminal Evidence Act 1984, s 81.

[109] Magistrates' Courts Act 1980, s 101. See also M Blake and A Ashworth, 'The Presumption of Innocence in English Criminal Law' (1996) *Crim LR* 306.

[110] *Gilbert* (1977) 66 Cr App R 237, 244.

[111] *Leckey* (Dennis Edmund) [1944] KB 80.

[112] *Sullivan* (1966) 51 Cr App R 102.

[113] *Gilbert* (1977) 66 Cr App R 237, 245, per Viscount Dilhorne. See also *Sparrow* [1973] 1 WLR 488; *Mutch* [1973] 1 All ER 178; *Alladice* (1988) 87 Cr App R 380, 385; D Birch, 'Case Comment, Confession: Denial of Access to a Solicitor' [1988] *Crim LR* 449, 452.

Judicial comment was a common law development. The Criminal Evidence Act 1898, which first allowed defendants to testify, prohibited prosecutorial comment on a defendant's failure to testify.[114] Judges made it clear almost immediately, that the prohibition did not extend to the bench.[115] The most far reaching model would be to prohibit judicial as well as prosecutorial comment on a suspect's failure to answer questions or to testify. This would be consistent with the presumption of innocence and would be straightforward to implement.

Juries would need to be given some form of direction about silence – as discussed above, the 'common sense' view is that silence, or late mention of a fact is indicative of guilt so merely ignoring the issue would be of little protective benefit. Many practitioners were of the view that juries took silence into account before the CJPOA and this may still be a risk if juries were directed not to draw adverse inferences. The more attention a subject is given, perversely the more it may weigh in the minds of jurors. Without more research, this is unknowable, but this position is, theoretically at least, the most consistent with the presumption of innocence.

A complete 'no comment' at interview and trial is difficult to argue against in principled terms. The onus is on the prosecution to prove guilt and the privilege against self-incrimination is mentioned in almost every international human rights instrument. To draw inferences from this can only really be punitive. The evidential weight of the late mention of a fact when a story appears tailored to the evidence, however, is more difficult to resist. A compromise option would be to give a direction akin to the *Lucas* direction that must be given if a defendant has told lies. The jury should be directed to consider reasons why the defendant may have lied [or made no comment], such as to bolster a true defence, to protect someone else, or through embarrassment, panic or confusion. The jury may draw an adverse conclusion only if they are sure that a lie [or failure to answer questions] was due to a non-innocent reason.[116] Such a measure might be more politically and judicially acceptable, but lacks coherence in terms of the presumption of innocence. This would need careful consideration as the more caveats that are allowed, the more judges are likely to expand the provisions. The value of legal representation could be bolstered by a direction that inferences must not be drawn from silence if this was advised by a legal representative. Contrary to the political and judicial myth, there was little evidence of solicitors routinely advising 'no comment' interviews before the CJPOA.

In 1994, the Third Optional Protocol to the ICCPR was drafted, with the aim of guaranteeing under all circumstances the right to fair trial. It sets out that 'silence by the accused may not be used as evidence to prove guilt and no adverse consequences may be drawn from the exercise of the right to remain silent'.

[114] *Rhodes* (1899) 1 QB 77, 80.
[115] *Rhodes* (1899) 1 QB 77, 83.
[116] *Burge and Pegg* [1996] 1 Cr App R 163; *Randall* [1998] 6 Archbold News 1.

The United Nations General Assembly passed a weaker resolution[117] calling upon States to introduce measures to 'promptly inform every person detained, arrested, suspected or accused of, or charged with a criminal offence of his or her right to remain silent'.[118] The person should be advised of his or her 'rights and the implications of waiving them in a clear and plain manner'.[119]

Thus the trajectory in this country appears anomalous, but what happens here is of disproportionate global significance: 'The right of silence in England and Wales has never been a purely domestic issue'.[120] The right of silence was exported from this country to most of the common law world and the position taken by England and Wales on the right of silence has caused 'tremors' across the common law world.[121] After the curtailment of the right of silence was first raised seriously in 1972,[122] the right was abolished in Malaysia and Singapore as a result and other jurisdictions debated the issue. Since the CJPOA, the right has been reconsidered in India, several States in Australia, and it has been curtailed in New South Wales. What is concerning is that some jurisdictions have interpreted it as a measure that can only be introduced when a legal system reaches a certain level – 'Somehow, subtly, curtailing the right of silence had shifted from erroneous to aspirational – the mark of an advanced criminal justice system – a view enhanced by the lack of objection in England and Strasbourg'.[123] The detriment to suspects caused by the CJPOA has spread far beyond these shores. A principled reassessment of the measures would send a clear message across the common law world that the right of silence still matters.

VII. Conclusion

In sum, the current law is causing substantial unfairness (or certainly a perception of unfairness) and it appears to be operating in a discriminatory manner. It makes giving legal advice at the police station unnecessarily complex and requires directions that it appears are incomprehensible to the majority of jurors. In addition to these practical considerations, the right of silence has a particular symbolic value. Reinstating the right of silence would send an important message at home and abroad about the value of the presumption of innocence and the right to a fair trial.

[117] *United Nations Principles and Guidelines on Access to Legal Aid in Criminal Justice Systems* (Res/67/187, 2012) [6].

[118] Under Guideline 3, [43(a)].

[119] At [43(i)].

[120] H Quirk, 'The Right of Silence in England and Wales: Sacred Cow, Sacrificial Lamb or Trojan Horse?' in J Jackson and S Summers (eds) *Obstacles to Fairness in Criminal Proceedings* (Hart, 2018), 75.

[121] See H Quirk, *The Rise and Fall of the Right of Silence* (Routledge, 2016) ch 6.

[122] Criminal Law Revision Committee, *Eleventh Report: Evidence (General)* (Cmnd 4991, 1972).

[123] H Quirk, *The Rise and Fall of the Right of Silence* (Routledge, 2016), 170.

Comment on Chapter 9

How to Reinstate the Right of Silence

ABENAA OWUSU-BEMPAH

Dr Hannah Quirk has put forward a case for repealing sections 34–38 of the Criminal Justice and Public Order Act 1994 (CJPOA) and reinstating the right of silence.[1] Quirk presents several options for reinstatement of the right of silence, arguing in favour of an 'enhanced common law right of silence' (p 255). In support of Quirk's position to repeal the silence provisions, this response will elaborate on some of the more problematic aspects of the CJPOA before assessing the options for reform. An alternative reform option will then be proposed. This option goes beyond what is envisaged by Quirk, but could address her concerns about the CJPOA, including its inconsistency with the presumption of innocence.

I. Are the Silence Provisions Fit For Purpose?

Understandably, Quirk does not find it necessary to engage with the arguments for and against curtailing the right of silence that were rehearsed extensively prior to the enactment of the CJPOA.[2] Instead, Quirk focuses on the expansive and problematic ways in which the CJPOA provisions have been interpreted by the appellate courts. Nonetheless, the case for repeal can be strengthened by briefly considering whether the provisions have had their intended effect. As well as preventing guilty people from hiding behind silence, the provisions were intended to discourage 'ambush defences' (ie, intentional non-disclosure of potentially exculpatory information before trial, preventing advance scrutiny and investigation). The CJPOA has proven to be an ineffective and unnecessary means of achieving these ends. Empirical research conducted shortly after the provisions came into force found that the CJPOA had no noticeable impact on confessions, guilty pleas or

[1] H Quirk, 'The Case for Restoring the Right of Silence', ch 9 of this volume.

[2] Quirk examines the background and development of the CJPOA in H Quirk, *The Rise and Fall of the Right of Silence* (Abingdon, Routledge, 2017).

conviction rates.[3] This is not surprising given that research conducted prior to the enactment of the CJPOA found that only a minority of suspects exercised the right of silence and that silence did not increase the prospect of an acquittal.[4] The research also suggested that ambush defences were not a significant problem.[5] Even if legislation became necessary to prevent ambush defences, the CJPOA has been overtaken by the disclosure obligations in the Criminal Procedure and Investigations Act 1996 and the Criminal Procedure Rules 2015. If the silence provisions in the CJPOA do not meet any pressing or demonstrable need, on what basis can they be maintained?

One possible answer to the question posed above is that the CJPOA allows silence to serve a legitimate evidential function in so far as failure to answer questions or late mention of a fact is suspicious and indicative of guilt.[6] However, it is far from clear that silence is a reliable indicator of guilt, as there are various and wide-ranging reasons why an innocent suspect or defendant might remain silent in the police station or in court.[7] Even if guilt, nonetheless, remains a possible explanation for silence, the fact-finder might struggle to distinguish between innocent and guilty silence, and the courts have allowed inferences of guilt to be drawn in circumstances where the connection between silence and guilt is, at best, extremely weak. For example, inferences have been permitted where the defendant was advised by a solicitor to remain silent,[8] where the defendant was impeded by significant communication problems,[9] and where the defendant was simply putting the prosecution to proof rather than putting forward a positive defence.[10] The evidential function of silence is also curtailed by the conditions that must be met before inferences can be drawn. In accordance with Strasbourg jurisprudence, to maintain fairness, silence cannot be the main basis for conviction and the case against the accused must be so strong that it clearly calls for an explanation.[11] This means that it will usually be unnecessary to take account of silence in determining

[3] See T Bucke, R Street and D Brown, *Right of Silence: The Impact of the Criminal Justice and Public Order Act 1994* (London, HMSO, 2000).

[4] Royal Commission on Criminal Justice, *Report* (Cm 2263) (London, HMSO, 1993) 53–54.

[5] See R Leng, *The Right to Silence in Police Interrogation: A Study of Some of the Issues Underlying the Debate*, Royal Commission on Criminal Justice Research Study No 10 (London, HMSO, 1993); M Zander and P Henderson, *The Crown Court Study*, Royal Commission on Criminal Justice Research Study No 19 (London, HMSO, 1993).

[6] See M Redmayne, 'English Warnings' (2008) 30 *Cardozo Law Review* 1047.

[7] These reasons range from police non-disclosure to defendants being inarticulate, anxious, or protecting a loved one. See Quirk, above n 1, 18–19.

[8] As discussed by Quirk. See also, H Quirk, 'Twenty Years on, the Right of Silence and Legal Advice: The Spiralling Costs of an Unfair Exchange' (2013) 64 *NILQ* 465.

[9] See, eg, *Dixon* [2013] EWCA Crim 465. This issue is discussed further below.

[10] See, eg, *Whitehead* [2006] EWCA Crim 1486. Inferences cannot be drawn under s 34 unless the defence is relying on a previously unmentioned fact at trial, but ss 35–37 can apply regardless of the defence case at trial.

[11] *Murray v UK* (1996) 22 EHRR 29. See also the relevant directions set out in *The Crown Court Compendium Part I: Jury and Trial Management and Summing Up* (Judicial College, 2017) 17-1 and 17-5.

guilt; there will be other evidence on which to base a conviction. Thus, silence should ordinarily be afforded little, if any, evidential value.[12]

Since the evidential function of silence is both weak and problematic, we are left with what Redmayne describes as the 'incentivising' function of the CJPOA.[13] The threat of adverse inferences provides suspects in the police station and defendants in court with an incentive to speak. This may reveal the true purpose of the legislation: to incentivise (or coerce) accused persons to respond to the accusations against them. As Quirk notes, 'the CJPOA provisions have been used to create an expectation that suspects should cooperate with their investigation and trial' (p 266).[14] Indeed, research indicates that fewer suspects and defendants remained silent in the police station or in court following enactment of the CJPOA.[15] If suspects and defendants speak, they will provide information for investigation and/or assessment by the fact-finder, and early disclosure of information can help the prosecution prepare for trial. Cooperation can, therefore, assist with efficient fact-finding. However, using the threat of adverse inferences to coerce suspects and defendants to cooperate is not a legitimate or rational function of the legislation; drawing inferences from silence amounts to penalising defendants for their failure to actively cooperate with their own prosecution. Penalising non-cooperation in this way is not consistent with the presumption of innocence. Not only does the CJPOA effectively place a burden (or expectation) on suspects and defendants to explain why they are innocent, but allowing their silence to be associated with guilt, as Quirk points out, eases the prosecution's burden of proof.

If the only real function of the provisions is to coerce (or 'incentivise') cooperation and penalise non-cooperation, and if this is not a legitimate function, then, even without in-depth analysis of how the CJPOA has been interpreted, it is difficult to conceive of an argument against Quirk's proposition that the provisions should be repealed.

II. Interpretation of the Silence Provisions

Quirk's case for reform focusses on the expansive and objectionable way in which the silence provisions have been interpreted by the courts. This, she argues, provides 'new evidence' that the original decision to curtail the right of silence may be 'unsafe'. By presenting the argument in this way, Quirk makes a novel contribution to the silence debate. There is little point in simply repeating Quirk's

[12] R Leng, 'The Right to Silence Reformed: A Re-appraisal of the Royal Commission's Influence' (2001) 6 *Journal of Civil Liberties* 107, 110.

[13] Redmayne, (n 6), 1051.

[14] See also R Leng, 'Silence Pre-trial, Reasonable Expectations and the Normative Distortion of Fact Finding' 5 *E&P* (2001) 240.

[15] See T Bucke, R Street and D Brown, *Right of Silence: The Impact of the Criminal Justice and Public Order Act 1994* (London, HMSO, 2000).

observations on the interpretation of the provisions. However, there are two areas that warrant further consideration and provide additional evidence that the decision to enact sections 34–38 was unsafe. The first relates to silence as a response to police questioning. Quirk's examination of silence in the police station focuses on section 34. In particular, she demonstrates the way in which the interpretation of section 34 has undermined the right to legal advice. Little attention is paid to sections 36 and 37, which allow inferences to be drawn where an arrested person failed or refused to account to the police for the presence of suspicious objects, substances or marks, or their presence at or near the scene of a crime. Like section 34, these provisions have been applied far more expansively than is necessary. For example, it is not only silence that can result in an inference being drawn under sections 36 or 37, but also unsatisfactory explanations of the circumstances.[16] The implication is that the accused must not only cooperate with the police by offering a possible explanation, but must do so in a specific and detailed way. Also, unlike section 34, the defence case at trial is not relevant to whether inferences can be drawn under sections 36 and 37,[17] and the provisions do not include a reasonableness requirement.[18] The way in which sections 36 and 37 have been drafted and interpreted is problematic given that there will be situations where it is completely unreasonable to expect a suspect to provide a full account of a specific set of facts to the police, yet it may be open to the fact-finder to link the failure to account directly to guilt.[19]

The second point relates to the discriminatory effect of the CJPOA. Quirk notes various ways in which the CJPOA applies unequally, including the disproportionate impact it has had on black suspects. She also points to the case law on vulnerable defendants in the light of research on the prevalence of mental health problems and intellectual disabilities among suspects and defendants. In support of the case to repeal the silence provisions, more can be said about the application of the CJPOA to vulnerable defendants and defendants with health conditions or disabilities. Section 35(1)(b) provides an exception to drawing inferences from a defendant's silence in court if 'it appears to the court that the physical or mental condition of the accused makes it undesirable for him to give evidence'. Understandably, defendants with a physical or mental condition might not want to testify if testifying could be detrimental to their health, or if the quality of their evidence could be diminished by their condition. They might, for example, give confusing or inconsistent evidence or generally make a bad impression through no fault of their own. In sum, section 35(1)(b) has the potential to act as a safeguard for defendants who clearly have a reason, aside from guilt, to remain silent.

[16] *Compton* [2002] EWCA Crim 2835.

[17] ibid [32].

[18] Confirmed in *Roble* [1997] Crim LR 449 (CA).

[19] For further analysis of ss 36 and 37, see A Marks, 'Expert Evidence of Drug Traces: Relevance, Reliability and the Right to Silence' [2013] *Crim LR* 10; A Owusu-Bempah, 'Silence in Suspicious Circumstances' [2014] *Crim LR* 2.

However, as Quirk explains in Part I of her chapter, the bar for what constitutes 'undesirable' has been set 'to an almost insurmountable level' (p 257).

In creating an 'almost insurmountable' test for what constitutes 'undesirable', the courts have focussed on: the risk of testifying to the defendant's wellbeing;[20] the importance of the defendant's evidence, such that risk to health may be outweighed by the perceived importance of the defendant's testimony;[21] and the availability of special measures to assist the defendant to give evidence.[22] In respect of the last factor, eligibility for special measures should signal that a defendant will have particular difficulty in giving evidence. In practice, however, the availability of special measures has contributed to finding that defendants *should* testify, or else face the possibility of adverse inferences being drawn against them. As the case law has continued to develop, the courts have continued to raise the bar. In *Friend*, the first case in which the Court of Appeal examined section 35(1)(b), the Court noted that a mental condition might include 'schizophrenia where the experience of giving evidence might trigger a florid state'.[23] In *Mulindwa*,[24] the most recent reported case on the provision, the appellant had paranoid schizophrenia. A clinical psychologist took the view that Mulindwa's evidence might be unreliable as a result of his mental illness and psychological impairment. It was possible that Mulindwa would have delusions and respond to voices while giving evidence, and some of his answers might have resulted from symptoms of his psychosis. Yet, the trial judge directed the jury that they may draw an inference from Mulindwa's silence, and the ruling was upheld by the Court of Appeal. This decision was reached largely because the psychologist could have given evidence before the defendant testified, explaining to the jury the effect of Mulindwa's condition on his likely presentation when giving evidence. The Court rejected the defence submission that if the only way in which the defendant could fairly give evidence would be by the introduction of expert evidence to explain to the jury why some of his evidence might be unreliable, then it could not be other than 'undesirable' for him to give evidence.[25]

The question of whether to draw an inference against a silent defendant who has a mental or physical condition has effectively been transferred to the jury, with the jury being trusted to take account of the defendant's difficulties. In Part II of her chapter, Quirk notes the lack of evidence as to whether jurors are 'fair-minded' when it comes to drawing inferences from silence (p 259). Even if jurors are fair-minded, it is not clear why we must rely on their fair-minded nature in place of the law being fair. In any event, if jurors take account of a defendant's mental or physical condition and find that there is a sensible reason for silence, then no adverse

[20] See, eg, *Friend* [1997] 2 Cr App R 231 (CA); *Ensor* [2009] EWCA Crim 2519.

[21] *Tabbakh* [2009] EWCA Crim 464.

[22] *Dixon* [2013] EWCA Crim 465.

[23] *Friend* (1997) 2 Cr App R 231 (CA), 242.

[24] *Mulindwa* [2017] EWCA Crim 416.

[25] ibid [28].

inference should be drawn.[26] If the courts are satisfied that this is the approach the jurors will take, there seems little point in allowing jurors to consider the possibility of drawing an inference from the defendant's silence in the first place. Directing juries that they may hold silence against a defendant, despite there being a clear explanation for silence, reinforces Quirk's proposition that the Court of Appeal has 'developed a "normative expectation" that defendants should cooperate fully in the criminal process' (p 255).[27]

III. Reform Options

Quirk considers three options for reform or 'reinstatement' of the right of silence in Part VI. The first option is to simply repeal the silence provisions in the CJPOA and return to the common law position on the right of silence. This option, as Quirk demonstrates, is not ideal. The cases on the common law right of silence are conflicting and unclear. Quirk also rejects the second option, which is to prohibit all comment on failure to answer police questions or testify in court, including judicial comment. This option, although 'consistent with the presumption of innocence and … straightforward to implement' (p 268), is also unattractive. It would leave jurors to draw their own inferences from a defendant's silence. We would, therefore, be unable to protect defendants from 'unreliable, impressionistic and unsystematic' common sense inferences.[28]

The third option considered by Quirk is to adopt a *Lucas*-type direction, whereby the judge would alert the jury to possible innocent reasons for failure to mention a fact or answer questions, and direct the jury that they may draw an adverse conclusion only if they are sure that the failure was due to a non-innocent reason. This is a 'compromise option'. It recognises that the inference can be difficult to resist, but it reduces the risk of an erroneous inference being drawn. As it stands, jurors can only be directed to consider an innocent explanation for silence if there is evidence to support the explanation.[29] Thus, if the defendant fails to meet the expectation to speak, they bear the burden of justifying silence. In the absence of evidence to support a reason for silence, jurors are effectively left to speculate guilt.

Maintaining some scope for adverse inferences could make the compromise option politically viable. But it is not clear that it would be judicially acceptable. Back in 2005, the House of Lords rejected the argument for a *Lucas*-type direction

[26] *The Crown Court Compendium Part I: Jury and Trial Management and Summing Up* (Judicial College, 2017) 17-5.

[27] See also Leng, (n 14), 246.

[28] S Easton, 'Legal Advice, Common Sense and the Right to Silence' (1998) 2 *E&P* 109, 114.

[29] *Cowan, Gayle, and Ricciardi* [1996] QB 373 (CA), 386.

on the basis that it might mislead the jury as to the reason for silence, and result in unfounded speculation.[30] However, as Quirk notes, the climate has recently changed: 'the discussions around Britain's departure from the European Union offer a rare opportunity to consider what protections suspects should receive and what expectations should govern a fair trial' (p 267). Quirk also notes the revival of academic interest in the right of silence, as well as international developments. A recently adopted EU Directive on the presumption of innocence states that exercise of the right to remain silent shall not be used against accused persons or considered to be evidence that they have committed the criminal offence concerned.[31] It is possible that these developments, coupled with the fact that the CJPOA continues to be interpreted far more expansively than necessary, could convince the legislature and judiciary to revisit inferences from silence.

Quirk's compromise option, while potentially viable, is not without fault. This may explain why Quirk does not appear to have committed herself to the proposal or explained precisely what it should entail. It is not clear how far the compromise option ventures from the current law. At present, juries must be directed that they may only draw an inference against a defendant if 'there is no sensible explanation' for the defendant's failure to mention a fact, provide an account or give evidence, other than that they had no answer or none that would stand up to scrutiny or cross-examination.[32] A problem with the present position (which could be rectified by the compromise option) is that jurors may be unaware of the possibility of a sensible explanation for silence. Thus, where it applies, the compromise option may simply enable jurors to more accurately make the assessment which they are already supposed to make.

Quirk notes that the current judicial direction to juries on silence is complicated, not even-handed, and of unknown effect (Part II in particular), but does not specify how much, if any, of the direction should be maintained under the compromise option. It is also not clear how jurors' understanding of the direction could be improved, if aspects of it were to be maintained. Perhaps written directions could help. Even so, a fundamental problem with the compromise option, as Quirk acknowledges in Part VI, is that it 'lacks coherence in terms of the presumption of innocence' (p 268). As explained above, drawing adverse inferences from silence undermines the presumption of innocence, or, as Quirk puts it, sits 'uneasily with the presumption of innocence' (p 266). The current law is based on the assumption that an innocent suspect or defendant would give an explanation of their innocence.[33] The compromise option, while reducing the risk of erroneous

[30] *Becouarn* [2005] UKHL 55; [2005] 1 WLR 2589 [24].

[31] Directive 2016/343 of the European Parliament and of the Council of 9 March 2016 on the strengthening of certain aspects of the presumption of innocence and of the right to be present at the trial in criminal proceedings, Art 7(5). The Directive does not apply to the UK.

[32] *The Crown Court Compendium Part I: Jury and Trial Management and Summing Up* (Judicial College, 2017) 17-1, 17-2 and 17-5. See also, *Cowan, Gayle, and Ricciardi* [1996] QB 373 (CA), 381.

[33] *Hoare and Pierce* [2004] EWCA Crim 784; [2005] 1 WLR 1804 [53].

inferences, would still allow this assumption to be made, and would not sufficiently remedy the existing expectation that defendants should actively cooperate and explain themselves.

To fully reinstate the right of silence, reform must go further than a modified *Lucas* direction. It is, therefore, proposed that, as well as prosecution comment, adverse judicial comment on silence should be prohibited. This does not mean that judges should stay silent on the matter of silence. But, instead of merely alerting jurors to potential innocent reasons for silence, judges should also direct jurors not to draw inferences from silence. Quirk rightly points out that, despite being told not to, jurors may nevertheless draw inferences: as she observes, 'the more attention a subject is given, perversely the more it may weigh in the minds of jurors' (p 268). Perhaps this could be avoided if judges explained to jurors why they should not draw inferences from silence, namely because: (1) there are many innocent reasons for silence, such that any perceived link between silence and guilt is necessarily speculative (unless other evidence proves that silence stems from guilt, in which case it is unnecessary to draw an inference); and (2) it is the prosecution's job to prove guilt, and not the defendant's job to speak and explain their innocence, or to account for the accusations against them. A direction along these lines could act as a warning or caution as to the potential risks of drawing inferences from silence while reminding the jury of the respective roles of prosecution and defence.

IV. Conclusion

In the event that repeal of sections 34–38 of the CJPOA and reinstatement of the right of silence proves politically unviable, steps should be taken to lessen the unfairness of the existing law. Such steps could be taken by the legislature or the judiciary. For example, jurors should be directed not to draw inferences where a defendant was advised to remain silent by a legal representative (Quirk suggests that juries be directed along these lines as part of the 'compromise option'); sections 36 and 37 should not be applied where the accused offered an account falling short of a full account of a specific set of facts, or where the failure or refusal to account was reasonable; a much more cautious and sympathetic approach should be taken to the question of whether it is 'undesirable' for a defendant with a physical or mental condition to give evidence. Quirk's analysis also shows a need for the appellate courts to take more seriously errors at the trial stage, including where defective directions are given to the jury.

Quirk notes that 'the cumulative effect of the case law has been to create a far more coercive situation than it was clear that Parliament intended' (p 258), but also that the CJPOA is just one factor that has contributed to a change in trial culture. Other factors include the introduction of disclosure obligations on the defence and the Criminal Procedure Rules. Within the new culture, or style, of criminal procedure, defendants are required to actively cooperate in pursuit of efficient fact-finding, often at the expense of due process and fair trial rights.[34] Quirk presents a strong case to reinstate the right of silence. If successful, it could signal another shift in the nature of criminal procedure, this time towards a system in which fairness is taken seriously and the defendant's autonomy is respected by according them the freedom to choose whether and how to respond to accusations against them.

[34] See A Owusu-Bempah, *Defendant Participation in the Criminal Process* (Abingdon, Routledge, 2017).

10A

'Lawyers' Law' and the Limitations and Flaws of the Role of Reform Bodies in Criminal Law

PETER ALLDRIDGE

The aim of this chapter is to reflect on the history of the involvement of law reform bodies (predominantly but not only the Law Commission), and then to draw attention to some issues to do with the failure of law reform. It should be said at the outset that I am not in a position to judge the effect of the financial position of reform bodies such as the Law Commission upon their choices of subject matter, so this chapter will not deal with resources and resource implications. We should admit frankly that to the extent that these matters are between the Ministry of Justice and the Commission, there is little to be said from the outside, save that it would be tragic were the Commission's funding to be so reduced, or be so closely linked to specific projects, as to make it no longer worthwhile.

Beyond these immediate considerations, the search for the limits upon law reform bodies depends upon a range of considerations, and this is where we begin.

The chapter will then turn to the types of indicators that might suggest an area either to be good or bad for law reform efforts, and explore the deep-seated antipathy towards letting go of the 'flexibility' of the common law offences, and the incremental extension of criminal law it enables. This will introduce a wider discussion of a particular way of reasoning that typifies many of the Law Commission's ventures in the area of criminal law, which, it will be argued, has the tendency to generate reasons for unjustified expansion of the criminal law. The chapter will finish with a plea for a return to the roots of the Law Commission's involvement in criminal law – to decriminalisation.

I. 'Lawyers' Law'

Opening the House of Lords' debate on the first report of the Law Commission, which repays rereading, (Professor) Lord Lloyd of Hampstead spoke of the 'old fallacy' that there was a discrete category of 'lawyers' law' separate from another implied category – probably 'politician's law'.[1] He drew an immediate response from Lord Reid, defending the distinction.[2] Lord Gardiner, chairing the debate,[3] did not express a view on this point. The idea criticised by Lord Lloyd, that there is a sustainable distinction between 'lawyer's law' and some 'other', crops up in various areas of legal discourse. It is sometimes used by judges to circumscribe the appropriate areas of judicial activism.[4] This chapter will suggest that the 'fallacy' is still with us and that this might not be a bad thing. 'Lawyer's law' has a particular meaning in the American realist schools and Roscoe Pound, meaning a very goal-oriented notion of law.[5] The earliest mention of the expression 'lawyers' law', in the English (academic) legal literature, was in an article in the *Law Quarterly Review* in 1911, by the Bridgend polymath Harry Randall, as it happens calling upon the then Lord Chancellor, Lord Loreburn, to codify the criminal law.[6] The idea in the English discourse is more of 'law of interest only to lawyers'. If the analogy is something like a car, the idea is that lawyers will need to know mechanical and electrical information about what makes it go, and the driver (any non-lawyers – lay observers or politicians) will only need to know how to operate it safely.

One of the ideas underlying 'lawyers' law' is that of an *élite* – that lawyers need to know more about an area of law than the people to whom it applies. There was a move in the 1960s and early 1970s towards the 'everyday word' style of drafting and interpreting criminal statutes.[7] It was said,[8] not unreasonably, that if people

[1] HL Debates, Nov 16 1966, vol 277, cc1266-343.

[2] See n 6.

[3] Gardiner was the father of the Commission. See (eds) G Gardiner and A Martin, *Law Reform Now*, 2nd edn (Victor Gollancz, 1963) and his speech introducing the Law Commissions Bill, HL Deb 1 April 1965 vol 264 cc1140-223. R Stevens, *The English Judges: Their Role in the Changing Constitution* (Bloomsbury Publishing, 2002) 41 argues that Gardiner was (professionally) conservative and that his view of the aims of the Law Commission was 'to reform and restate black letter rules'.

[4] Notably by Lord Reid and Lord Diplock in *Pettitt v Pettitt* [1970] AC 777. Lord Reid said at 794–95: 'We must first have in mind or decide how far it is proper for the courts to go in adapting or adding to existing law. Whatever views may have prevailed in the last century, I think that it is now widely recognised that it is proper for the courts in appropriate cases to develop or adapt existing rules of the common law to meet new conditions. I say in appropriate cases because I think we ought to recognise a difference between cases where we are dealing with "lawyer's law" and cases where we are dealing with matters which directly affect the lives and interest of large sections of the community and which raise issues which are the subject of public controversy and on which laymen are as well able to decide as are lawyers. On such matters it is not for the courts to proceed on their view of public policy for that would be to encroach on the province of Parliament.' See also AA Paterson, 'Lord Reid's Unnoticed Legacy – a Jurisprudence of Overruling' (1981) 1 *OJLS* 375–90, and now *Jogee* [2016] UKSC 8 (where common law goes wrong it is open to judges to sort things out, but there is no such scope with bad statutes).

[5] U Moore and G Sussmann, 'The Lawyer's Law' (1931) 41 *Yale LJ* 566, and P Selznick, '"Law in Context" revisited' (2003) 30 *Journal of Law and Society* 177–86.

[6] HJ Randall, 'Resurrection of Our Criminal Code' (1911) 27 *LQR* 209.

[7] *Brutus v Cozens* [1973] AC 854. See DW Elliot, 'Brutus v Cozens – Decline and Fall' [1989] *Crim LR* 323.

[8] An aspiration frequently expressed, *though* seldom so *elegantly* – and not in the context of criminal law – as the Bishop of Southwark's speech on the Unemployment Insurance Bill, HL Deb 15 December 1927 vol 69 cc1014 et seq: '[H]ere is a Bill of the greatest interest to something like 12,000,000 people,

were to be sent to prison by applying criminal statutes, then they should be able to understand them. This doctrine had a lingering effect on the draft Code of 1985,[9] but really it had run into the buffers when the House of Lords split 3–2 on the meaning of the word 'threat'.[10]

The notion of 'lawyers' law' and its opposite(s) has a functional significance to the Law Commission. It is very helpful to have Bills classified as consolidating and 'non-contentious'[11] for the purposes of their Parliamentary passage.[12] It implies a depoliticization of law, or, at least, of that part of it under scrutiny – depoliticisation of criminal law for reform purposes, if you will. Exclusion of the 'political' element from criminal law reform means that law reformers, including the Law Commission and the Criminal Law Revision Committee, have never dealt head-on with the major recurrent themes (drugs, organised crime, terrorism, the prison population, sentencing differentials, the proceeds of crime, police and other investigatory powers, the death penalty[13]) that have contributed so significantly to the alteration of criminal justice over the past 50 years. Tony Smith's assertion that the criminal law is 'in an immeasurably[14] better condition than it was in 1965'[15] is therefore redolent of Mary Lincoln and *My American Friend*. Apart from the prison population, drugs, the attrition of defence rights,[16] and a number of other things, the criminal law may well be neater, but that is a fairly limited achievement. More positively, exclusion of the political element implies that the Law Commission's ambitions must be limited and realistic.

There are, of course, alternatives to the use of the Law Commission (or the Criminal Law Revision Committee (CLRC)) as law reform bodies. There are the traditional departmental white papers, (maybe still) Royal Commissions,[17]

and it is cast in a form which will be quite unintelligible to the vast majority of them. Cross-word puzzles are all very well in their place. I have always regarded them as a harmless but irritating form of amusement, but they become perfectly objectionable when they are taken as a model for an Act of Parliament.'

[9] Law Commission, *Codification of the Criminal Law* (Law Com No 143, 1985).

[10] *Treacy v DPP* [1972] AC 537.

[11] Criminal Law Revision Committee, *Second Report: Suicide* (Cmnd 1187, 1960); Suicide Act 1961.

[12] Standing Orders 59 (House of Commons) and 51 (House of Lords) make Law Commission Bills eligible for the consolidating Bills fast-track procedure. (HC Debates, 1 March 1999: vol 326 cc736–7 (John Bercow et al). See now the 2010 Protocol with the LC (LC321); G Hammond, 'The Legislative Implementation of Law Reform Proposals' in M Dyson, J Lee, S Wilson-Stark (eds), *Fifty Years of the Law Commissions* (Bloomsbury, 2017) 175 et seq.

[13] The last three were subjects of noteworthy Royal Commissions.

[14] I am assuming the word was not used literally.

[15] ATH Smith, 'Criminal Law and the Law Commission 1965–2015' [2016] *Crim LR* 381, 392.

[16] A Ashworth, 'Is the Criminal Law a Lost Cause?' (2000) 116 *LQR* 225–56.

[17] F Herschell, *Royal Commission on the Metropolitan Board of Works* (1888–89) – Public Bodies Corrupt Practices Act 1889; E Gowers, *Royal Commission on Capital Punishment* (Cm 8932, 1953) – Homicide Act 1957; C Philips, *Royal Commission on Criminal Procedure* (Cmnd 8092, 1981) – Police and Criminal Evidence Act 1984, Prosecution of Offences Act 1985; Runciman, *Royal Commission on Criminal Justice* (Cm 2263, 1993) – Criminal Appeal Act 1995. The last Royal Commission was that on Long Term Care for the Elderly (Cm 4192, 1998–9), so it may be that the genre is obsolete or obsolescent. If so, this is to be regretted.

a Committee chaired by a judge[18] or otherwise, a private members' Bill,[19] or doing nothing in the hope that judges will sort the matter out.[20] This chapter will try to identify some criteria by reference to which we might be able to identify in advance what might and might not be a successful law reform project.

Reformers have become less ambitious, more constraints, financial and political, have been imposed upon them over time, and neither of those is necessarily a bad thing. The Commission should be most comfortable, and its proposals should be most easily received and implemented, in the area of 'lawyers' law'. In the search for the limits of the area that can be given to law reform bodies, and looking back over both the Law Commission's and the CLRC's involvement[21] in criminal law, as it seems to me, the areas in criminal law in which the Law Commission has been most successful are criminal damage,[22] character evidence,[23] the year and a day rule in homicide,[24] corroboration,[25] criminal jurisdiction,[26] poison pen letters[27] and counterfeiting and forgery.[28] Not so successful where legislation has been forthcoming are attempts,[29] hearsay,[30] and bribery (two goes).[31] Unsuccessful

[18] Roskill, *Committee on Fraud Trials* (1986) – Criminal Justice Act 1987; Auld, *Review of the Criminal Courts* (2001) – Criminal Justice Act 2003.

[19] Abortion Act 1967.

[20] *Bourne* [1939] 1 KB 687; *R* [1991] UKHL 12.

[21] In the days of the CLRC, there does not appear to have been any distinction of principle as to which issues got referred to the Law Commission and which to the CLRC. The Criminal Law Act 1967 contained elements from the CLRC, *7th Report: Felonies and Misdemeanours* (Cmnd 2659, 1967) and the Law Commission (Law Com 3 and Law Com 7) (n 73).

[22] Criminal Damage Act 1971, based on Law Commission, *Criminal Law: Offences of Damage to Property* (Law Com No 29, 1970), except for the omission of a definition of 'recklessly'.

[23] Criminal Justice Act 2003, Pt 11 Ch 1, based on Law Commission, *Evidence of Bad Character in Criminal Proceedings* (Law Com No 273, 2001).

[24] Law Reform (Year and a Day Rule) Act 1996, based on Law Commission, *Legislating the Criminal Code: the Year and a Day Rule in Homicide* (Law Com No 230, 1995).

[25] Criminal Justice and Public Order Act 1994, ss 32–33, based upon Law Commission, *Corroboration of Evidence in Criminal Trials* (Law Com No 202, 1991).

[26] Territorial Sea Act 1987, based upon Law Commission, *Report on the Territorial and Extra-Territorial Extent of the Criminal Law* (Law Com No 91, 1978). Criminal Justice Act 1993, based upon Law Commission, *Jurisdiction over Offences of Fraud or dishonesty with a Foreign Element* (Law Com No 180, 1989).

[27] Malicious Communications Act 1985, based on Law Commission, *Poison Pen Letters* (Law Com No 147, 1985).

[28] Forgery and Counterfeiting Act 1981, based upon Law Commission, *Criminal Law: Report on Forgery and Counterfeit Currency* (Law Com No 55, 1973).

[29] Law Commission, *Attempt and Impossibility in Relation to Attempt, Conspiracy and Incitement* (Law Com No 102, 1980), intended to deal with *Haughton v Smith* [1975] AC 476, but which led to the Criminal Attempts Act 1981, and *Shivpuri* [1987] AC 1 overruling *Anderton v Ryan* [1985] AC 560.

[30] Criminal Justice Act 2003, Part 11 Chapter 2, based on Law Commission, *Legislating the Criminal Code: Evidence in Criminal Proceedings: Hearsay Report* (Law Com No 245, 1997), intended to deal with *Kearley* [1992] 2 AC 228, but which required *Twist* [2011] EWCA Crim 114 finally to put it out of its misery.

[31] Law Commission, *Corruption* (Law Com No 248, 1998); *Legislating the Criminal Code: Bribery* (Law Com No 313, 2008) – Bribery Act 2010.

because unimplemented are the mental element in crime,[32] general defences,[33] codification,[34] and offences against the person.[35]

II. Case Studies

This chapter will consider three cases – the Suicide Act 1961, the abolition of the marital rape exception, and the attenuation of the right to silence. In none of these was there a direct party political divide, as providing indications as to what might and might not be good areas for law reformers. The studies have been selected as ones which probe the limits of lawyers' law, and which have at sometimes been regarded as appropriate matters for law reformers and at others for politicians.

The Suicide Act 1961, rendering suicide no longer a crime, was a CLRC Bill.[36] The debates[37] seem to have been informed more by Glanville Williams, Malcolm Bradbury and Norman St John-Stevas than by the CLRC under Sellers LJ. It is unlikely that the same kind of issue would be regarded as one for a Law Reform body today. It is simple, accessible, and not one on which any legal expertise is required. Leo Abse said:

> I want more than a lawyers' Bill. [...] I want this to be a genuine piece of social legislation which will make some contribution, albeit a small one, towards trying to deal with this grave and grim problem which belongs to the whole nation.[38]

The Act has been considered by the courts from time to time,[39] but not in such a way as to raise doubts as to its drafting or sense. That is to say, as an exercise in law reform it appears to have been successful and was thought an appropriate matter for law reformers at the time, but in an area that would not now be sent to law reformers.

[32] Law Commission, *The Mental Element in Crime* (Law Com No 89, 1978).

[33] Law Commission, *Criminal Law: Report on Defences of General Application* (Law Com No 83, 1977).

[34] Law Commission, *Codification of the Criminal Law* (LC No 143, 1985); *Criminal Law: A Criminal Code* (Law Com No 177, 1989); *Legislating the Criminal Code: Offences against the Person and General Principles* (Law Com No 218, 1993).

[35] CLRC, *14th Report: Offences Against the Person* (Cmnd 7844, 1980), Law Commission, *Legislating the Criminal Code: Offences against the Person and General Principles* (Law Com No 218, 1993); *Reform of Offences Against the Person: A Scoping Consultation Paper* (CP No 217, 2014).

[36] CLRC, *Second Report: Suicide* (Cmnd 1187, 1960).

[37] HC Debates, 19 July 1961 vol 644 cc1407-26.

[38] Leo Abse at col 1415.

[39] Most notably in *Attorney General v Able* [1984] QB 795; *R (on the application of Pretty) v DPP* [2001] UKHL 61; *R (on the application of Purdy) v DPP* [2009] UKHL 45; *R (on the application of Nicklinson) v Ministry of Justice* [2014] UKSC 38; and *R (on the application of Conway) v Secretary of State for Justice* [2017] EWCA Civ 275.

The move towards abolition of the marital rape exception was confused by the involvement of Law Reform bodies, legislators and then the courts, all trying to achieve the same end.[40] Too many cooks were involved. The CLRC recommended retention of the exception.[41] This recommendation was criticised heavily.[42] Under Item 5 of its Fourth Programme the Law Commission produced a Working Paper[43] and a Report[44] deploying the sorts of arguments the Commission deploys – measured, exhaustive, analytical, and comparative. Legislation was planned.[45] Meanwhile, the courts got involved, and by going beyond what would normally be expected of judicial activity, changed the law themselves.[46] The lasting legacy of the disparate efforts to deal with the marital rape exception are looseness in judicial law-making and a decision of the ECHR undermining Article 7.[47] None of this was the fault of law reform bodies. As an exercise in law reform, the abolition of the marital rape exemption was probably one that could have been achieved by law reformers, courts or legislators, but not all three.

The right to silence debate was triggered by the CLRC Report on Criminal Evidence.[48] At that time, the right to silence was thought such a politically sensitive issue as to require the entire report, most of which was very sensible and non-controversial, to be rejected. Consideration of the right to silence was then made a part of the terms of reference of the Philips[49] and Runciman[50] Royal Commissions, being one of very few areas of the terms of reference considered by the Commission that did not arise directly from the precipitating case (the Birmingham Six[51]). Attenuation of the right to silence was then a preoccupation of Michael Howard,[52] and had been trialled in Northern Ireland.[53]

With these examples in mind, can we say anything about the sorts of issues on which Law Reform bodies should not be consulted as being too sensitive/divisive or otherwise inappropriate? Consider some issues bearing upon the success of law reform efforts, all of which arise on continua and none of which should be thought to be dispositive.

[40] See A Williamson, 'The Law and Politics of Marital Rape in England, 1945–1994' (2017) 26 *Women's History Review* 382–413.

[41] *Fifteenth Report: Sexual Offences* (Cmnd 9213, 1984).

[42] C Wells, 'Law reform, Rape and Ideology' (1985) 12 *Journal of Law and Society* 63–75.

[43] Law Commission, *Rape Within Marriage* (WP 116, 1990).

[44] Law Commission, *Rape within Marriage* (Law Com No 205, 1992).

[45] Implementation by Criminal Justice Public Order Act 1994 Part XI. See now Sexual Offences Act 2003, s 1.

[46] *R* [1992] 1 AC 599.

[47] *CR v UK* (1995) 21 EHRR 363.

[48] CLRC, *Eleventh Report: Evidence* (Cmnd 4991, 1972).

[49] C Philips (Chair), *Royal Commission on Criminal Procedure* (Cmnd 8092, 1981).

[50] W Runciman (Chair), *Royal Commission on Criminal Justice* (Cm 2263, 1993).

[51] *McIlkenny et al* (1991) 93 CAR 287.

[52] See H Quirk, *The Rise and Fall of the Right to Silence* (Routledge, 2017) ch 4.

[53] The Criminal Evidence (NI) Order 1988 (1988 No 1987 (NI 20)).

A. Politics

The ghost of the Law Reform Commission of Canada, which produced excellent reports few of which were implemented, and was then abolished, alarms any other Law Reform body. The degree of autonomy allowed to the Law Commission has varied over time, but it must always maintain a sufficiently high implementation rate to avoid threats to its existence. This means that proposals for reform of criminal law need to appeal to the current government, and may frequently be commissioned by it. Communications between the Ministry of Justice and the Commission will be critical to what is and is not appropriate to the Commission.

Politics should mean that some areas are always out of bounds to law reform bodies. For years, until 1997[54] for example, efforts by the Commission, or the CLRC, to do anything about the state of the law of offences against the person were met by shrugs. The relevant people would say that while the Home Office was, in principle, in favour[55] of whatever the latest reform proposal was,[56] since any attempt to encapsulate the definition of murder in a statute would involve a two-day set piece debate on the death penalty before any of the substantive law provisions had been considered, they did not have the Parliamentary time. (This hardly explains, of course, why both the CLRC and Law Commission were asked to consider the area during this period).[57]

B. Time and Historical Specificity

The boundaries of 'lawyers' law' are not fixed but change with time. One would not now expect assisted dying (for example) to be referred to the Law Commission. The end of Butskellite consensus, from 1979 forwards, probably gave rise to greater fragmentation of political opinion and a consequential reduction in the range of issues upon which there is or might be the sort of consensus that might underpin the handing over of issues to technocrats.

C. Legal Complexity

Simple issues can be overthought. Marital rape probably was both too accessible and too (legally) simple to be an appropriate area for a law reform body.

[54] Ultimately when the Human Rights Act 1998, s 21(5) came into force on 9 November 1998. On 10 October 2003, with effect from 1 February 2004, the UK acceded to the 13th Protocol to the ECHR, which prohibits the death penalty in all circumstances.

[55] Apparently not every Home Secretary was as receptive to the views of the Commission. See Smith, (n 15), at fn 28 (Soskice).

[56] CLRC, *Fourteenth Report: Offences Against the Person* (1980); Law Commission, *Legislating the Criminal Code: General Principles and Offences Against the Person* (Law Com No 218, 1993).

[57] See n 35.

Clever lawyers are wasted if they are not given difficult legal problems. The 'year and a day rule' was probably as simple as the marital rape issue, but was a better choice for law reform because it was almost certain not to attract the noises off, either in the courts or in Parliament, which complicated the marital rape issue.

D. Parliamentary Procedure

The 'Draft Bill' procedure was introduced in the late 1990s, to allow Parliamentary discussion on a Bill otherwise than by means of a second reading vote or textual amendment.[58] The Corruption Bill 2003 and Bribery Bill 2009, both Law Commission Bills, were both subject to the Draft Bill procedure. It seems to me that Bills ought not to be subject to both, and that these procedures should be regarded as alternatives. In the areas served by the Law Commission, what the Law Commission can do – discussions, legal analysis – is probably a better way to examine an area than by a Parliamentary Committee. The fair wind given to uncontentious Law Commission Bills by Parliamentary Standing Orders, is, however, a boon of which full advantage should be taken.

E. Susceptibility to Empirical Evidence

Commissioning of empirical research studies is more of what might be expected of Royal Commissions. The 1981[59] and 1993[60] Commissions both had empirical research done on the right to silence, and then both decided, in effect, that the evidence did not help it to reach conclusions on the right to silence. Leaving aside the wrangles over money implicit in any attempts to conduct significant empirical research, the skill set in social sciences to establish and supervise may not necessarily be found in the Law Commission.

F. Interaction with Existing Law

The less interaction with other areas of law, particularly case law, the better for the reformer. *Tabula rasa* can be good. Hence the success of Law Commission reports on criminal damage and forgery, and not so much, perhaps, hearsay, where although the common law of hearsay was abolished,[61] some common law rules were retained[62] and it was not clear exactly what that meant, and how the

[58] And see SW Stark, 'Promoting Law Reform: By Means of Draft Bills or Otherwise' in Dyson et al, (n 12).

[59] C Philips (Chair), *Royal Commission on Criminal Procedure* (Cmnd 8092, 1981).

[60] W Runciman (Chair), *Royal Commission on Criminal Justice* (Cm 2263, 1993).

[61] Criminal Justice Act 2003, s 118(2).

[62] Criminal Justice Act 2003, s 118(1).

boundaries of relevance and hearsay were to be drawn. There are cases where it might be appropriate to retain common law rules as a part of a statutory scheme, but there should be a presumption against retaining common law rules as part of a new scheme.

G. Consultees

It is a matter of concern if the only consultees in a given area of criminal law are the police, the CPS and victims. In many areas the structure of the questions and the identity of the consultees determines the answers. The Law Commission is not equipped to engage in democratic consultations, and should at least be aware that consultation may have the effect of creating pressure for extending the criminal law.

H. Noises off

The greater the chance of legislators or courts dealing with a particular area, the stronger the argument against law reform bodies becoming involved. This was the problem with marital rape.

III. Common Law Offences – The Best as Enemy of the Good

Codification of criminal law was (and some argue, remains)[63] part of the Law Commission's agenda, but even if we cannot have codification, it would be good for all criminal offences to have statutory definitions. The law reform process in England and Wales has failed to dispense with common law offences of conspiracy to defraud, cheat,[64] murder, corrupting public morals,[65] outraging public decency[66] and public nuisance.[67] Partly, no doubt, for the reason given above,[68] homicide still has no statutory definition, and Coke's definition is still rehearsed. It is striking that a nation that prosecuted a civil war to place taxation on a statutory basis[69] has on numerous occasions fought shy of putting the definitions of two of the main crimes of tax evasion on a similar footing, and, instead, retains the

[63] See ATH Smith, 'Criminal law and the Law Commission 1965-2015' [2016] *Crim LR* 381, 388–9.
[64] Alldridge, *Taxation and Criminal Justice* (OUP, 2017) ch 4.
[65] *Gangar* [2012] EWCA Crim 1378.
[66] *Hamilton* [2007] EWCA Crim 2062.
[67] *Rimmington* [2005] UKHL 63.
[68] See discussion in Pt I.
[69] Bill of Rights 1689 (1 W & M c 2) Art 4.

common law offences of cheat and conspiracy to defraud. On the occasions when it has been reviewed, conspiracy to defraud survived. Despite various proposals,[70] (in particular, the attempt during the enactment of the Fraud Act 2006,[71] to abolish conspiracy to defraud,[72] and the restrictions placed by the Theft Act 1968 upon cheat),[73] fear of the unforeseen dishonest act has led to the retention of the common law offences of conspiracy to defraud and cheat. Notwithstanding the view, expressed by the Law Commission and others, that the offence has 'no place in a coherent criminal law',[74] and Lord Lloyd of Berwick's '... instinctive dislike, [...] of these catch-all offences such as conspiracy to defraud ...',[75] Parliament has repeatedly refused to take the plunge and place the matter entirely on a statutory footing.[76]

IV. Analogy – Lists, Wedges, Slopes and Incrementalism

A repeated argument in Law Commission documents proceeds along the lines 'the criminal offence in question (φ ing) extends to case x_1, x_2, and x_3 but not case x_n: case x_n is, in relevant respects, like cases x_1, x_2, and x_3: therefore the offence should extend to case x_n'. The alternative argument: 'φ ing extends to cases x_1, x_2, and x_3 but not to case x_n: case x_n is, in relevant respects, like cases x_1, x_2, and x_3: therefore the offence should not extend to cases x_1, x_2, and x_3' is seldom heard.

Over the 50 years of its existence the Law Commission has, in a number of areas, provided arguments for the extension of the criminal law, and in very few to its diminution. One of the principal sorts of argument for such extensions comes in the analogical extension of laws. If, for example, it is a crime to threaten to kill, why should it not be a crime to threaten harm less than that?[77] Notice how this approach restricts the sphere of discussion. Instead of the more general question 'what should be done about area of law x?' the question is 'given that a particular set of legal provisions obtains in respect of categories a and b, should they also

[70] Law Commission, *Conspiracy to Defraud* (WP 56, 1974); *Conspiracy to Defraud* (Law Com No 228, 1994); *Legislating the Criminal Code: Fraud and Deception* (CP No 155, 1999); *Fraud* (Law Com No 276, 2002).

[71] HC Debates, 12 Jun 2006: Col 543 (Vera Baird QC, S-G).

[72] And see Fraud Act 2006 explanatory notes, stating that conspiracy to defraud retained 'for the time being' [6].

[73] Theft Act 1968, Sch 2.

[74] Law Commission, *Fraud* (Law Com No 276, 2002).

[75] HL Debates, 22 June 2005: col 1665. Conspiracy to defraud also survived the Post-Legislative Assessment of the Fraud Act 2006 carried out by the Ministry of Justice, *Memorandum to the Justice Select Committee* (Cm 8372, 2012).

[76] 'Whether the Law Commission or academics like it or not, the broad umbrella offence of conspiracy to defraud is and has been for a long time part of our law.' *Norris v Government of the United States of America and others* [2007] EWHC 71 (Admin); [2007] 2 All ER 29, [98] (Auld LJ).

[77] Law Commission, *Criminal Law: Legislating the Criminal Code, Offences Against the Person* (Law Com No 218, 1993), [23.1] and Draft *Criminal Law Bill* cl 9, repeating Law Commission, *Legislating the Criminal Code: Offences Against the Person and General Principles* (CP No 122, 1992), [11.1].

apply to c and to d?' This invites consideration of the relevant features of a and b and assessing whether they might also be present in c and d, and, perhaps to add a view as to whether, were the law consistent, it might also apply to e and f. It might eventuate in the provision applying to a, b, c and d without consideration ever having been given at one and the same time, to whether there should be such a provision applying to a, b, c and d.

It is perfectly understandable that law reform bodies will not want to begin any consideration of any given area of law with a general enquiry into the justifications for punishment and criminal proscriptions, but references structured like this make assumptions (it is justifiable that the criminal provision exist, and it exists as the result of some perfectly rational and ahistoric consideration). The objection is that the original prohibition was generally put in place in response to some specific historical occurrences, and that it is wrong to exclude from the process of reconsideration those same matters.[78]

Incrementalism as a response to individual instances is a bugbear for the law reform process. The racist killing of Stephen Lawrence, which gave rise to the MacPherson Enquiry and Report and the claim that the Metropolitan Police was 'institutionally racist', was shocking, and legislators did in response to it what legislators do: they legislated. The vice exposed by the Lawrence killing (racist youths protected by incompetent or corrupt police officers) did not really call for either of the two reforms to the criminal justice system that flowed from it, aggravated sentencing and attenuation of the double jeopardy rule. Since the crime involved was murder, no provision for aggravation was required. Convictions were finally obtained in the individual case, but legality should require us not to change criminal procedure retrospectively to secure convictions.[79] The other major reform to which the Lawrence enquiry gave rise was the abrogation of the double jeopardy rule so far as concerns defendants against whom there is 'new and compelling' evidence. Although this reform had been given the Law Commission treatment already,[80] it was by no means uncontroversial. On this analogical line of reasoning, the question that may now be addressed is: 'Given that the double jeopardy rule has been abolished so far as concerns those cases to which Part 10 of the Criminal Justice Act 2003 applies, should it be extended?' Legislation passed in response to shocking events ought to be reconsidered in calmer light before it is extended by analogy. The fact that we legislate for aggravated sentencing for racial motives arising from a particular historical conjuncture around the Lawrence enquiry,[81]

[78] 'So Walpole enacted, as part of his terror, brutal legislation … criminalising some, but not all, threats against property. Two-and-a-half centuries later, along came the Law Commission and instead of asking why he did it at all wondered why he did not go the whole hog.' Alldridge, 'Threats Offences – a Case for Reform' [1994] *Crim LR* 176, 186.

[79] *Dobson*, Treacy J, Central Criminal Court, 4 January 2012.

[80] Law Commission, *Double Jeopardy* (CP No 156, 1999); *Double Jeopardy and Prosecution Appeals* (Law Com No 267, 2001). The cases to which the exception was to apply were extended from a small group of very serious crimes to more general application as a result of the Auld Report, *Review of the Criminal Courts of England and Wales* (2001) ch 12, [61–62].

[81] Macpherson of Cluny, *The Stephen Lawrence Inquiry* (Cm 4262, 1999).

does not commit us to universalise and recognise a further series of groups having similar characteristics – or if it does, that should be part of the equation at the time of the original legislation. And this was what was wrong with the aggravated sentencing provisions of Part 12 of the Criminal Justice Act 2003.[82]

At the heart of these responses – the disinclination of those involved in criminal law (not, or not only the Commission) to scrap common law offences, the propensity of the Commission and others to extend the criminal law incrementally and the disinclination (again of the Commission and of others) to decriminalise, is an irrational fear of the consequences of one person devising a new way of behaving such that, with the benefit of hindsight, it might have been good that it be criminal. As with other irrational fears, it is best confronted.

Where the issue is the criminal standard of proof, we talk about the number of guilty people we would want to see acquitted rather than see one innocent person convicted.[83] Those kinds of claims can be seen as allocations of the risk of error. The same kind of approach seems to me appropriate for extensions to the criminal law. When was that time that something bad happened because something had been decriminalised, or not criminalised that should have been, and what was lost? Do we really need to be so scared?

V. Decriminalisation

Everyone seems to agree that we have too many criminal offences, and that too much conduct is criminal. There are periodic Statute Law (Repeals) Acts,[84] directed against obsolete or obsolescent legislation. Decriminalisation in general was never explicitly part of the Commission's remit.[85] Nonetheless, its earliest ventures in the area did include decriminalisation.[86] Perhaps because that was never really part of any electoral mandate, perhaps because it was never a political priority, perhaps because there are few votes in decriminalisation, and (again perhaps) because any serious attempts to decriminalise must fall into the 'political' category, there has never been a strong decriminalisation movement. If the argument for decriminalisation is about the boundaries of individual liberty – most obviously in the cases

[82] Legal Aid, Sentencing and Punishment of Offenders Act 2012, s 65.

[83] A Volokh, '*N* guilty men' (1997) 146 *University of Pennsylvania Law Review* 173–216.

[84] The most recent, the Statute Law (Repeals) Act 2013 Schedule 1 Part 2 Group 4 repeals the Forgery of Foreign Bills Act 1803 43 Geo 3 c139, which was probably overlooked when the Forgery and Counterfeiting Act 1981, based upon Law Commission, *Criminal Law: Report on Forgery and Counterfeit Currency* (Law Com No 55, 1973) was prepared, and Group 7 repeals the Sale of Offices Acts 1551 and 1809 which, (perhaps together with the Honours (Prevention of Abuses) Act 1925) should have been dealt with by the Bribery Act 2010.

[85] ie, under Law Commissions Act 1965, s 3.

[86] The Law Commission started its activity in the area of criminal law with *Proposals to abolish Certain Ancient Offences* (LC No 3, 1966) – Criminal Law Act 1967, s 13; *Proposals for Reform of the Law relating to Maintenance and Champerty* (Law Com No 7, 1966) – Criminal Law Act 1967, s 13.

of personal autonomy, drugs and so forth – or free speech it might not have great purchase, but the argument for reducing the discretionary powers of the State whenever possible is always a strong one.

VI. Conclusion

It would be good to formulate, as part of this exercise, an account of what might and might not be good as law reform projects. Whether that means retaining the phrase 'lawyers' law' does not matter much, but whether we can identify the characteristics of appropriate law reform projects does. I have suggested some. On criminalisation, it is too easy, and too well received, to recommend criminalisation of something, and too difficult, and not well received, to recommend decriminalisation. That (largely political) consideration has been compounded over years by the practice of the Law Commission in recommending, almost as a default position, incremental extension of criminal law, and also by the appropriation of the law reform process to answer particular precipitating events.

10B

Criminal Law Reform: A View from Across the Border

PAMELA R. FERGUSON*

This chapter offers some reflections on the process of reforming criminal law and procedure from a Scottish perspective. It considers four potential reform avenues: judicial decisions, legislation emanating from the Scottish Parliament (including potential codification), the Scottish Law Commission, and judge-led reform projects. It assesses the achievements of each of these in recent years and argues that while the reconvening of the Parliament has resulted in a great deal of legislation which impacts on criminal law and procedure, it has failed to deliver systematic reform.

I. Judicial Decisions

Peter Alldridge's plea[1] for all criminal offences in England and Wales to have statutory definitions is one which may be echoed – and indeed amplified – for Scotland, where the majority of core crimes remain creatures of the common law. Certain 'institutional writings' of the eighteenth and nineteenth centuries are treated as primary sources of law and remain the starting point for those in search of the definitions of murder, assault, fraud, theft, robbery, reset,[2] extortion,[3] wilful fire-raising[4] and breach of the peace. The leading institutional work relating to criminal law is Baron David Hume's *Commentaries on the Law*

* My thanks are due to Professors Colin Reid and Alan Page for helpful comments on earlier drafts of this chapter.

[1] P Alldridge, '"Lawyers' Law" and the Limitations and Flaws of the Role of Reform Bodies in Criminal Law', ch 10A of this volume.

[2] 'Reset' is similar to the English crime of handling stolen goods, as defined by the Theft Act 1968, s 22(1).

[3] 'Extortion' is similar to the English crime of blackmail, as defined ibid, s 21(1).

[4] 'Wilful fire-raising' is similar to the English crime of arson, as defined by the Criminal Damage Act 1971, s 1(3).

of Scotland, Respecting Crimes,[5] and there are numerous cases in which the High Court of Justiciary, sitting as a court of appeal, has refined or redefined Hume's definitions.[6]

The sequence of events leading to the modernisation of sexual offences tells us much about the mechanics of criminal law reform. Throughout the twentieth century, rape continued to be defined according to Hume, that is, as requiring forced penile penetration of the vagina and the overcoming of the complainer's will.[7] There was a public outcry in 2001 in the case of *HM Advocate v Watt*[8] when the trial judge withdrew a charge of rape from consideration by the jury on the basis that there was no evidence that the accused had 'overcome the will' of the complainer, since she had offered no resistance. On appeal by the Crown, the court held that an error had been made in a case decided 144 years previously; the correct definition of rape was sexual intercourse without the complainer's consent.[9] This decision also drew attention to the fact that the law was not in keeping with modern thinking: the requirement for vaginal penetration meant that 'male rape' was a misnomer and non-consensual penile penetration of the mouth or anus (and indeed vaginal penetration by anything other than the penis), was common law sexual assault rather than 'rape'. The Scottish Law Commission (SLC) was invited by the Government to examine the law on sexual offences,[10] culminating in the enactment of the Sexual Offences (Scotland) Act 2009,[11] but in the meantime trenchant criticism had followed the court's redefinition, primarily on the basis that the Scottish Parliament, rather than the appeal court, should be the provenance of major criminal law reform.[12]

Some appeal court judges have been less willing to tinker with the common law than others. In *Drury v HM Advocate*[13] in 2001, a murder case concerning provocation based on sexual infidelity, Lord Mackay stated:

> If there is to be any major reconsideration of the doctrine of provocation … then such reconsideration requires to be undertaken by the Scottish Parliament and not by this court. I would take such a view whether the proposals for change were designed to extend or designed to restrict, to any material extent, the range of factual circumstances

[5] 4th edn (Bell & Bradfute, 1844).

[6] For the appeal court's influence on common law crimes in recent years, see *Petto v HM Advocate* [2011] HCJAC 78 (murder); *Tomney v HM Advocate* [2012] HCJAC 138 (involuntary culpable homicide); *Stewart v Nisbet* [2012] HCJAC 167 (assault).

[7] Hume's, *Commentaries on the Law of Scotland, Respecting Crimes*, 4th edn (1844), vol i, 301, 302. 'Complainer' is the Scottish term equivalent to a complainant in English law.

[8] March 2001, High Court of Justiciary (unreported). Further public concern followed the case of *McKearney v HM Advocate* [2004] HCJAC 3.

[9] *Lord Advocate's Reference (No 1 of 2001)* 2002 SLT 466.

[10] Scottish Law Commission, *Report on Rape and Other Sexual Offences* (SLC No 209, 2007).

[11] Section 1 of the 2009 Act now defines rape in a gender neutral way so far as the complainer is concerned, and expands the definition to include penile penetration of the anus or mouth. The common law crime of sodomy has been abolished (2009 Act, s 52(a)(iv)).

[12] See J Chalmers, 'How (Not) to Reform the Law of Rape' (2002) 6 *Edinburgh Law Review* 388, 388.

[13] 2001 SLT 1013.

> to which the doctrine of provocation may be applied. Changes of that nature involve issues of considerable sensitivity. They are for politicians to decide upon, not judges.[14]

In 2003 in *Webster v Dominick*,[15] the appeal court's decision to abolish the common law crime of 'shameless indecency' and replace it with 'public indecency' led to renewed criticism, again on the basis that such reforms ought to be left to Parliament.[16] By 2011, however, when a five-bench appeal court called for further reform of the definition of murder, in *Petto v HM Advocate*,[17] and stated that comprehensive re-examination of the mens rea of homicide was 'long overdue',[18] the court was equally clear that this was 'not the sort of exercise that should be done by *ad hoc* decisions of this court in fact-specific appeals'.[19]

It is not clear why the court felt able to reshape the common law in *Webster* but unable to undertake a similar exercise in *Petto*. This may have been due to the fact that the issues in *Petto* were of greater complexity; it may be that the academic disapproval described above caused it to draw back from radical reformulations of common law crimes; or it may have been simply due to the different compositions of the court.[20] Another, equally plausible, explanation has been suggested, namely that the court was acknowledging that by the end of its first decade the Scottish Parliament had 'found its voice in criminal law'.[21] Whether this 'voice' is 'pitched' appropriately is considered further, below.

In assessing the courts as a law reform mechanism, it must be borne in mind that incorporation of the provisions of the European Convention on Human Rights (ECHR) into domestic law made Scottish criminal law and procedure subject to further review, initially by the Judicial Committee of the Privy Council and now by the Supreme Court.[22] The Convention has had little effect on substantive criminal law: the common law crimes of shameless indecency and breach of the peace were attacked for being ill-defined and too vague to satisfy the requirements of Article 7, but these challenges were side-stepped[23] or rejected[24] by the appeal court. In respect of criminal procedure, however, the Supreme Court's ruling in 2010 in *Cadder v HM Advocate*[25] – that confessions were inadmissible if made by

[14] ibid, [3]. See also Lord Nimmo Smith [9].

[15] 2005 JC 65; 2003 SLT 975.

[16] See J Burchell and C Gane, 'Shamelessness scotched: the domain of decency after *Dominick*' (2004) 8 *Edinburgh Law Review* 231, 247, arguing that it should be left 'to the elected representatives of the people to draft legislative changes where necessary'.

[17] [2011] HCJAC80.

[18] ibid, [22].

[19] ibid.

[20] *Drury* was decide by the Lord Justice General (Rodger), and Lords Cameron, Johnston, Nimmo Smith and Mackay. In *Petto* the court comprised the Lord Justice Clerk (Gill) and Lords Osborne, Kingrath, Eassie and Carloway.

[21] J Chalmers, 'Developing Scots criminal law: a shift in responsibility?' (2017) 1 *Juridical Review* 33, 34.

[22] From 1 October 2009.

[23] *Webster v Dominick* (n 15).

[24] *Smith v Donnelly* 2002 JC 65; 2001 SLT 1007.

[25] [2010] UKSC 43; 2011 SC (UKSC) 13.

detained suspects who had not been offered legal advice – followed the decision of the Strasburg Court in *Salduz v Turkey*,[26] overruling the approach which had been taken by the High Court. *Cadder* was a highly controversial case,[27] with the then Justice Minister criticising the Supreme Court for 'undermining' the Scottish court's authority, and calling for restoration of 'the centuries-old supremacy of the High Court as the final court of appeal in criminal matters'.[28] More than 850 cases had to be abandoned by the Scottish prosecution service, due to a lack of corroborated evidence resulting from the inadmissibility of confessions obtained without a prior offer of legal assistance.[29] The *Cadder* case also led to emergency legislation.[30] In a small jurisdiction such as Scotland, however, too few cases come before the courts to allow the law to be developed in a methodical fashion – and this is exacerbated by the continuing prevalence of common law crimes.

II. The Scottish Parliament

The Westminster Parliament had frequently been criticised for its neglect of Scottish criminal law, and devolution offered the hope that a more holistic approach would be taken to reform.[31] Although Holyrood has shown little interest in criminal law codification (discussed further, below), an assessment I conducted in 2010 found that more than a third of the 147 statutes enacted in the Parliament's first decade affected criminal law or procedure.[32] This included more than 400 offence provisions.[33] The impression gained was of a legislature

[26] (2009) 49 EHRR 19.

[27] For an analysis of *Cadder* and its aftermath see P R Ferguson, 'Repercussions of the *Cadder* case: The ECHR's Fair Trial Provisions and Scottish Criminal Procedure' [2011] *Crim LR* 743; Lord McCluskey, 'Supreme Error' (2011) 15 *Edinburgh Law Review* 276; F Leverick, 'The Supreme Court Strikes Back' (2011) 15 *Edinburgh Law Review* 287; F Stark, 'The Consequences of *Cadder*' (2011) 15 *Edinburgh Law Review* 293; R White and PR Ferguson, 'Sins of the Father? The "Sons of *Cadder*"' [2012] *Crim LR* 357.

[28] See, 'Cadder statement' *BBC News Online* (23 February 2011).

[29] 'Rape allegations among cases affected by Cadder ruling' *BBC News Online* (9 February 2011).

[30] Criminal Procedure (Legal Assistance, Detention and Appeals) (Scotland) Act 2010, s 1 which inserted s 15A(3) in to the Criminal Procedure (Scotland) Act 1995. This has now been replaced by s 32 of the Criminal Justice (Scotland) Act 2016 (in force from 25 January 2018).

[31] Writing in 1993, Styles noted that Scotland was 'a country whose legislature is composed of members with little interest in Scottish matters of any sort'. SC Styles, 'Something to declare: a defence of the declaratory power of the High Court of Justiciary' in RF Hunter (ed) *Justice ad Crime: Essays in Honour of the Right Honourable the Lord Emslie* (T&T Clark, 1993) 211, 220. In relation to Scottish criminal law in particular, Westminster's approach has been described as one of benign neglect: PR Ferguson and C McDiarmid, *Scots Criminal Law: A Critical Analysis*, 2nd edn (Edinburgh University Press, 2014), [22.5.1]. See also TM Jones, 'Common Law and Criminal Law: The Scottish Example' [1990] *Crim LR* 292, 301: 'the United Kingdom Parliament has never shown much interest in the substantive criminal law of Scotland'.

[32] PR Ferguson, 'Criminal Law and Criminal Justice: An exercise in ad hocery' in EE Sutherland *et al* (eds) *Law Making in the Scottish Parliament: The Early Years* (Edinburgh University Press, 2011) 208. The review covered the period from 1999 to 2009, inclusive.

[33] ibid, 216.

concerned about peripheral matters such as alcohol misuse,[34] animal welfare[35] and sentencing for weapons offences,[36] rather than about modernising core criminal offences. As described above, its greatest achievement was the reform of sexual offences,[37] but MSPs seemed generally unaware of the backward state of Scotland's sexual offence laws, and the definition of rape in particular, until this was brought to their attention by the media following the *Watt* case.[38] Updating my assessment for the purposes of this chapter, 37 of the 120 statutes passed between 2010 and 2017 contain offence provisions, with at least 212 new offences.[39] These range from misuse of an owner-occupied croft[40] to being involved in serious organised crime,[41] both criminalised in 2010, and include the more recently created offences of selling nicotine vapour products to children,[42] and carrying out a burial without prior authorisation.[43] Alcohol,[44] animal welfare,[45] and weapons[46] continue to feature, as do yet more sexual offences.[47] There has been a further increase in aggravations based on some particular feature of the complainer: those based on sexual orientation and disability were introduced

[34] See, in particular, the Licensing (Scotland) Act 2005.

[35] Protection of Wild Mammals (Scotland) Act 2002; Fur Farming (Prohibition) (Scotland) Act 2002; Animal Health and Welfare (Scotland) Act 2006.

[36] Custodial Sentences and Weapons (Scotland) Act 2007.

[37] This is also discussed further, below.

[38] See discussion in Pt I above. One MSP stated during a Parliamentary debate: 'I still remember all too clearly the shock and disbelief that I felt when I first heard … that a judge in a Scottish court had ruled that sex without a woman's consent is not rape unless the attacker uses force or the threat of force. I still cannot comprehend that we have in place a law that offers so little protection to women.' Although rape was a common law crime at the time of the decision in *Watt*, the motion which led to this debate stated: 'That the Parliament notes with grave concern the recent ruling by Lord Abernethy that sex without a woman's consent is not rape unless the attacker used force or the threat of force … [and] urges the Minister for Justice … to review *the legislation* on sexual assault and rape …'. (The Scottish Parliament, *Official Report: Plenary* (25 April 2001) (emphasis added).

[39] The review searched for the phrases 'commits an offence', 'is an offence' and 'is guilty of an offence' within the legislation and then checked that sections containing these words did indeed create an offence. The estimated number of new offences is a conservative one since it does not include offences created by statutory instruments, nor those created for Scotland by the Westminster Parliament.

[40] Crofting Reform (Scotland) Act 2010, s 34, inserting s 19C in to the Crofters (Scotland) Act 1993.

[41] Criminal Justice and Licensing (Scotland) Act 2010, s 28.

[42] Health (Tobacco, Nicotine etc. and Care) (Scotland) Act 2016, s 2.

[43] Burial and Cremation (Scotland) Act 2016, s 9(1).

[44] Criminal Justice and Licensing (Scotland) Act 2010, ss 184, 192, 196. See also s 26 which provides that a court must not treat an accused person's intoxicated state at the time of the offence as a mitigating factor in determining sentence.

[45] Marine (Scotland) Act 2010, s 107 (prohibition on killing or injuring seals); Wildlife and Natural Environment (Scotland) Act 2011, s 6 (prohibition on killing or injuring certain wild animals). See also ss 8, 13, 14, 21, 30, 34.

[46] Air Weapons and Licensing (Scotland) Act 2015; Criminal Justice and Licensing (Scotland) Act 2010, s 34. The Criminal Justice (Scotland) Act 2016, s 84 increases the maximum penalty for possessing an offensive weapon or bladed article in a public place from 4 to 5 years' imprisonment.

[47] Criminal Justice and Licensing (Scotland) Act 2010, s 42 (offence to possess extreme pornography) and s 43 (additional offences of voyeurism); Abusive Behaviour and Sexual Harm (Scotland) Act 2016, s 2 (offence to disclose a photograph or film of a person in an intimate situation); Human Trafficking and Exploitation (Scotland) Act 2015, ss 1 and 32 (offences relating to human trafficking).

in 2009,[48] and a more recent provision specifies that an offence is aggravated if it involves abuse of the accused's partner or ex-partner.[49] As regards common law defences, those involving 'insanity' have been replaced by broadly similar statutory defences involving 'mental disorders',[50] but self-defence, coercion and necessity continue to be shaped by the courts. My 2010 assessment found only two examples of decriminalisation; these related to consensual homosexual acts and to common grazing regulations for crofts.[51] Two additional offences have been decriminalised since then, namely common law sedition,[52] and the little-known crime of leasing-making.[53]

The Scottish Parliament has also made many changes to criminal procedure. My 2010 assessment noted that district courts (administered by local authorities) had been replaced by justice of the peace courts (administered by the Scottish Courts and Tribunals Service)[54] and specialist domestic abuse,[55] youth offending,[56] and drug abuse[57] courts had been established. The maximum penalties in the sheriff courts had been increased,[58] and sentence discounts for guilty pleas had become a matter of statute.[59] Mandatory 'preliminary hearings' were introduced in solemn cases,[60] designed to encourage pre-trial agreement of

[48] Offences (Aggravation by Prejudice) (Scotland) Act 2009, ss 1 and 2. These provisions are discussed further, below.

[49] Abusive Behaviour and Sexual Harm (Scotland) Act 2016, s 1.

[50] Criminal Justice and Licensing (Scotland) Act 2010, ss 168–171, inserting ss 51A, 51B, 53E and 53F in to the Criminal Procedure (Scotland) Act 1995.

[51] Convention Rights (Compliance) (Scotland) Act 2001, s 10 (decriminalising consensual homosexual acts involving more than two people); Crofting Reform etc. Act 2007, s 28 (providing 'a new means of enforcing common grazing regulations' such that breach of the regulations is no longer a criminal offence (Scottish Government's *Explanatory Notes* on the Act)).

[52] Criminal Justice and Licensing (Scotland) Act 2010, s 51(a). Sedition seems to have involved writings of an inflammatory nature, designed to lead to subversion of established institutions by illegal means.

[53] ibid, s 51(b). Leasing-making comprised slandering the monarch or the monarch's family. The common law offence of bigamy has also been abolished, but this is not really a decriminalisation since it has been replaced by a statutory offence which includes purported marriages by those who are already in a civil partnership: see the Marriage and Civil Partnership (Scotland) Act 2014, s 28(3), which inserts s 24(A1) in to the Marriage (Scotland) Act 1977.

[54] Criminal Proceedings etc (Reform) (Scotland) Act 2007, Pt 4.

[55] See Scottish Executive, *Evaluation of the Pilot Domestic Abuse Court* (2007).

[56] See Scottish Executive, *Evaluation of the Airdrie and Hamilton Youth Court Pilots* (2006).

[57] See Scottish Executive, *Establishing Drug Courts in Scotland: Early Experiences of the Pilot Drug Courts in Glasgow and Fife* (2003).

[58] The maxima are now 12 months' imprisonment in summary procedure, and five years' imprisonment in solemn procedure (the latter are tried on indictment before a judge and jury). See the Criminal Proceedings etc (Reform) (Scotland) Act 2007, s 43(a) which amends the Criminal Procedure (Scotland) Act 1995, s 5(2)(d) (summary), and the Crime and Punishment (Scotland) Act 1997 s 13(1)(a) (solemn).

[59] Criminal Procedure (Amendment) (Scotland) Act 2004, s 20, which amends the Criminal Procedure (Scotland) Act 1995, s 196. The sentencing discount seems to be unpopular with Scottish judges: see G Brown, *Criminal Sentencing as Practical Wisdom* (Hart, 2017).

[60] See n 58.

uncontested evidence between the prosecution and the defence, and the maximum period during which an accused person may be imprisoned prior to trial on indictment was increased from 110 to 140 days.[61] Victims of certain crimes were given the right to make a statement to the court describing the impact of the crime, to receive information about the convicted person's release or transfer, and to make written representations to the Scottish Ministers concerning release.[62] Special measures were introduced to assist particularly 'vulnerable' witnesses in testifying.[63] Yet more changes have been made since the 2010 assessment. These include the setting up of a sentencing council to promote consistency in sentencing practice,[64] and the expansion of the definition of 'vulnerable witnesses' to include those aged 17 or under, and victims of alleged sexual offences, human trafficking, domestic abuse or stalking.[65]

Some procedural changes have followed English law, such as the introduction of a detailed pre-trial disclosure regime,[66] and the abrogation of double jeopardy restrictions.[67] The 2010 assessment noted that the plight of complainers in serious sexual offence trials had been recognised by prohibiting an accused from conducting his own defence.[68] More recent reforms provide that juries must now be given directions to counteract certain rape myths, such as that delay in reporting rape may be indicative of a false allegation,[69] or that failure to offer physical resistance to sexual advances means that there was consent.[70] Criminal procedure may undergo yet more changes in the near future if the recommendations of recent reviews, conducted by Lord Carloway and Lord Bonomy, are implemented. These are discussed further below.

[61] Criminal Procedure (Amendment) (Scotland) Act 2004, s 5, which amends s 65(4) of the Criminal Procedure (Scotland) Act 1995 (hereafter 'the 1995 Act').

[62] Criminal Justice (Scotland) Act 2003, Pt 2.

[63] Vulnerable Witnesses (Scotland) Act 2004, ss 1–3.

[64] Criminal Justice and Licensing (Scotland) Act 2010, ss 1 and 2. The Council was established in October 2015 and its first guidelines will be for wildlife and environmental offences, and for causing death by dangerous driving.

[65] See the Victims and Witnesses (Scotland) Act 2014, s 10, which amends the Criminal Procedure (Scotland) Act 1995.

[66] Criminal Justice and Licensing (Scotland) Act 2010, Pt 6.

[67] A second trial may now be held where the original acquittal was 'tainted' by an offence against the course of justice (by the accused or some other person); where the accused has subsequently admitted the offence; or on the basis of new evidence which was not available, and could not with reasonable diligence have made available, at the first trial. See the Double Jeopardy (Scotland) Act 2011, ss 2–4. For a discussion of cases which have been re-prosecuted under these provisions see P Duff, 'Scottish criminal evidence law adrift?' in P Duff and PR Ferguson (eds) *Scottish Criminal Evidence Law: Current Developments and Future Trends* (Edinburgh University Press, 2018).

[68] Criminal Justice and Licensing (Scotland) Act 2010, s 69(2)(a), which inserts a new version of s 288C in to the Criminal Procedure (Scotland) Act 1995.

[69] Abusive Behaviour and Sexual Harm (Scotland) Act 2016, s6, which inserts s 288DA in to the 1995 Act, ibid.

[70] ibid.

III. The Scottish Law Commission

In common with its counterparts in the rest of the UK, the Scottish Law Commission is under a duty, inter alia, to prepare 'comprehensive programmes of consolidation'.[71] Writing in 2003, Alex Samuels described English criminal procedure as 'scattered in a variety of statutes',[72] and 'distinctly user-unfriendly'.[73] North of the border, the main statute is the Criminal Procedure (Scotland) Act 1995, which Samuels termed 'a satisfactory consolidation and code'.[74] The 1995 Act is, however, less of a consolidating measure than it once was. It has been frequently amended, with many new sections added, such that between sections 52 and 53 we now find sections 52A to 52U,[75] and inserted between sections 227 and 228 are not only sections 227A to 227Z, but also sections 227ZA to 227ZN.[76] This is hardly 'user-friendly'. Additionally, important procedural changes have been introduced by several statutes which have not amended the 1995 Act. For example, the recent Criminal Justice (Scotland) Act 2016 made major reforms to the law governing police powers on detaining and questioning suspects – matters dealt with hitherto in the 1995 Act. For a proper understanding of criminal procedure, one must now be familiar with the 1995 Act, the 2016 Act, and several other key statutes.[77] Further consolidation is long overdue.

There is also a need for consolidation of the substantive law, for example, in relation to various statutory aggravations which are based on particular characteristics of the victim. We have a provision where the accused's offence was motivated by prejudice based on the victim's race,[78] and one based on the victim's religion.[79] Further provisions create similar offences where the prejudice stemmed from the victim's disability,[80] sexual orientation,[81] or transgender identity.[82] In each case, the initial offence is aggravated if 'at the time of committing the offence, or immediately before or after doing so, the offender evinces towards the victim … malice and ill-will' based on the victim's membership (or presumed membership) of a protected group, or in the case of disability, sexual orientation or transgender identity, based on one of those characteristics. It is also an offence where the

[71] Law Commissions Act 1965, s 3(1)(d).

[72] A Samuels, 'Why do we not have a criminal code?' (2003) 67 *Journal of Criminal Law* 214, 216.

[73] ibid.

[74] ibid.

[75] Sections 52D(6A), 52G(4A), 52H(1A) and 52R(1A) were brought into force on 30 September 2017.

[76] See also ss 271A to 271Z, and ss 288A, 288B, 288BA, 288BB, 288BC and ss 288C to 288G of the 1995 Act.

[77] See in particular the Victims and Witnesses (Scotland) Act 2014.

[78] Crime and Disorder Act 1998, s 96(2). See also the Criminal Law (Consolidation) (Scotland) Act 1995, s 50A ('racially aggravated harassment').

[79] Criminal Justice (Scotland) Act 2003, s 74(2).

[80] Offences (Aggravation by Prejudice) (Scotland) Act 2009, s 1(2).

[81] ibid, ss 2(2)(a)(i) and 2(2)(b)(i).

[82] ibid, ss 2(2)(a)(ii) and 2(2)(b)(ii).

accused acted from a motive of 'malice and ill-will' towards a person within a protected group or with a protected characteristic. These offences could readily be combined. A *Draft Criminal Code for Scotland with Commentary* was prepared in 2003 by a small group of Scottish academics, including the author of this Chapter.[83] The project was an unofficial one, and our Code has not been enacted, but the SLC published the draft in order to foster debate.[84] Section 7 of this Code offers a model for consolidation:

> (1) An offence may be aggravated by the intent or motivation with which it is committed, by the manner or circumstances in which it is committed, by the serious nature of the effects produced, by the special vulnerability of the victim; or by the abuse of a special relationship between the perpetrator and the victim, and may be charged and tried accordingly.
>
> (2) An offence under this Act may, in particular, be aggravated –
>
> (a) ...
>
> (b) if motivated by hatred or contempt for, or malice or ill-will towards, a group of persons defined by reference to race, colour, religion, gender, sexual orientation, nationality, citizenship or ethnic or national origins;
>
> (c) if accompanied by expressions of abuse or ill-will based on the victim's membership or supposed membership of any such group.

The reference in section 7(1) to 'the special vulnerability of the victim' would include disabled victims, but 'disability' could equally be added to the list of characteristics described in section 7(2)(a).

The UK Law Commissions are also under a duty to codify the law.[85] Lord Hope has suggested that 'a vast undertaking' such as codification of Scottish substantive criminal law 'will certainly need to be done through the Commission'.[86] Although the SLC has described the Draft Code as offering 'useful models' for its later work on sexual offences,[87] and other new offences bear the hallmark of some of the Code's innovative provisions,[88] the codification exercise generated judicial and

[83] *Draft Criminal Code for Scotland with Commentary* (Scottish Law Commission, 2003). The other members of the 'Draft Code' team were Eric Clive, Christopher Gane and Alexander McCall Smith.

[84] For a description of the project see E M Clive, 'Submission of a Draft Criminal Code for Scotland to the Minister for Justice' (2003) 7 *Edinburgh Law Review* 395. The Code is discussed further, below.

[85] Law Commissions Act 1965, s 3(1). The Commissions should also aim for 'the elimination of anomalies, the repeal of obsolete and unnecessary enactments, the reduction of the number of separate enactments and generally the simplification and modernisation of the law' (ibid). These are also the duties of the Northern Ireland Law Commission: see the Justice (Northern Ireland) Act 2002, s 51(1). For a detailed analysis of the UK Law Commissions see M Dyson, J Lee and SW Stark (eds), *Fifty Years of the Law Commissions: The Dynamics of Law Reform* (Bloomsbury, 2017).

[86] Lord Hope of Craighead, 'Do we still need a Scottish Law Commission?' (2006) 10 *Edinburgh Law Review* 10, 26.

[87] Scottish Law Commission, *Report on Rape and other Sexual Offences* (SLC No 209, 2007) [1.9].

[88] See, for example, the Criminal Justice and Licensing (Scotland) Act 2010, ss 38 and 39, which create the offences of 'threatening and abusive behaviour' and 'stalking', and compare s 48 of the *Draft Criminal Code* ('making unlawful threats'), s 49 ('violent and alarming behaviour') and s 50 ('intrusive and alarming behaviour', which is defined to include stalking).

academic hostility,[89] and the Commission has not sought to further advance the project.[90] This is largely due to the lack of appetite among Scottish politicians for comprehensive codification – an antipathy which continued even when the Scottish National Party became the largest party at Holyrood, following the 2007 general election.

Leaving aside codification, the Commission's major achievement in relation to the substantive law is its work on sexual offences,[91] as described previously. As also noted above, in 2001 the appeal court had called for reform of the law of provocation arising from sexual infidelity, and the SLC's Seventh Programme of Law Reform in 2005 included a project to review this.[92] Five years later, its Eighth Programme explained that it preferred to consider provocation as part of a general review of the law of homicide which would include self-defence, coercion and necessity as part of that project.[93] Review of homicide was not included in its Ninth Programme in 2015, however, the Tenth Programme, published in February 2018, states that the Commission intends 'to examine the law of homicide and to develop proposals for modernising the law in this important and sensitive area'.[94]

There are currently five commissioners, one of whom is part-time, aided by three legal assistants.[95] None of the current commissioners has a particular interest or expertise in criminal law. An agreement between the Committee of Heads of the Scottish Law Schools and the SLC, signed in September 2016, allows academics to be seconded to the Commission for particular projects,[96] and it is to be hoped that the Commission will use this to draw on the expertise of some of Scotland's criminal law academics to assist with the reform of homicide laws.

IV. Judge-Led Reviews

Following *Cadder*[97] the Scottish Government invited Lord Carloway, a High Court judge, to review 'key elements of Scottish criminal law and practice'.[98] The resulting *Carloway Review* in 2011 made many important recommendations regarding

[89] See T Jones, 'Towards a Good and Complete Criminal Code for Scotland' (2005) 68 *MLR* 448; L Farmer, 'Enigma: Unravelling the Draft Criminal Code' (2002) 7 *Scottish Law and Practice Quarterly* 68.

[90] For the argument that codification should not be a general priority for the Commissions, see SW Stark, *The Work of the British Law Commissions* (Hart, 2017) ch 5.

[91] Scottish Law Commission, *Report on Rape and Other Sexual Offences* (SLC No 209, 2007).

[92] Scottish Law Commission, *Seventh Programme of Law Reform*, (SLC No 198, 2005), [2.46].

[93] Scottish Law Commission, *Eighth Programme of Law Reform*, (SLC No 220, 2010), [2.13].

[94] Scottish Law Commission, *Tenth Programme of Law Reform*, (SLC No 250, 2018), [2.17].

[95] The Law Commissions Act 1965, s 2(1) prescribes that the Scottish Law Commission shall consist 'of a Chairman and not more than four other Commissioners'.

[96] SLC Press Release, 'Scottish Law Commission and Scottish Law Schools to work more closely together on law reform' (*SLC Website*, 15 September 2016).

[97] [2010] UKSC 43; 2011 SC (UKSC) 13.

[98] *The Carloway Review: Report and Recommendations* (2011) [1.0.1].

police powers of arrest, and the law and practice of questioning and detaining suspects,[99] many of which have since been enacted.[100] However, the nature of the process has been criticised:

> Never before in the history of Scottish – or English – criminal procedure has wide ranging law reform been potentially so dependent on the views of a single individual. The process has empowered Lord Carloway to frame the discussion in a manner which may, in practice, close down the consideration of alternatives.[101]

Lord Carloway's recommendation to abolish the requirement for corroborated evidence met with great hostility from the judiciary, legal profession and academia, and in 2014 the Government set up a further judge-led committee, chaired by Lord Bonomy. Its remit was to consider what further reforms might be required if the corroboration requirement were indeed abolished, and a preliminary analysis, commissioned from a small group of academics,[102] formed the focus of debate for the Committee and its subsequent report.[103] The *Bonomy Review* stressed that many of its recommendations would enhance the criminal process whether or not the corroboration requirement is retained,[104] and the Scottish Government has now stated that the future of corroboration requires further consideration.[105]

There followed in 2015 the *Evidence and Procedure Review*, an internal Scottish Court Service research project, once more led by Lord Carloway,[106] and a further report: *Evidence and Procedure Review – Next Steps*, in 2016.[107] One key recommendation was that an audio-visual recording be made in advance of the trial of the evidence in chief and cross-examination of children and other vulnerable witnesses, and that this recording should replace live testimony from the witness at trial.[108] By focussing on considerations of efficiency, and recommending greater use of technology to improve 'truth finding', these latest reports have arguably paid

[99] For the full terms of reference see ibid, 13–14. These are also listed in the Scottish Government Consultation Paper, *Reforming Scots Criminal Law and Practice: The Carloway Report* (Consultation Paper, 2012) 5. For a summary and critique see PR Ferguson and FE Raitt, 'A clear and coherent package of reforms? The Scottish Government Consultation Paper on the Carloway Report', (2012) *Crim LR* 909; J Chalmers and F Leverick, '"Substantial and Radical Change": A New Dawn for Scottish Criminal Procedure?' (2012) 75 *MLR* 837.

[100] See the Criminal Justice (Scotland) Act 2016.

[101] Chalmers and Leverick (n 99), 862.

[102] J Chalmers et al, *Post-Corroboration Safeguards Review: Report of the Academic Expert Group* (August 2014).

[103] I Bonomy, *Post-Corroboration Safeguards Review* (Final Report, April 2015), also known as the 'Bonomy Review'.

[104] ibid, [1.6].

[105] 'Plans to abolish corroboration put on hold by Scottish Government' *BBC News Online* (23 April 2015).

[106] Scottish Court Service, *Evidence and Procedure Review Report* (March 2015). The other members of the Review team were High Court Judge Lady Dorrian, Sheriff Principal Craig Scott and Eric McQueen, Chief Executive of the Scottish Court Service.

[107] Scottish Courts and Tribunals Service, *Evidence and Procedure Review – Next Steps* (February 2016).

[108] ibid, [74].

insufficient attention to the importance of the accused being able to challenge the evidence at trial. The proposals may well be beneficial, but should not be enacted without a more thorough assessment of their implications.[109] Given the enormous controversy that surrounded Lord Carloway's proposals concerning the abolition of corroboration, judge-led reform may be the least desirable of the potential law reform mechanisms.

V. Conclusion

Changes to Scottish criminal law and procedure have become more frequent in the last 18 years, in large measure due to the re-establishment of the Scottish Parliament but also due to the need for Scotland to implement decisions of the ECtHR. However, the Parliament has largely responded to events, and to particular cases such as *Watt* and *Cadder*, rather than adopting a holistic approach to law reform.[110] While there has been no shortage of legislation, much of this has involved tinkering around the edges by invoking the criminal sanction to enforce regulatory schemes of one kind or another. Instead of curing the law reform deficit, this approach has increased the sense of a fragmented system which lacks cohesion. Reform and development of core crimes, and indeed defences, has been left to the appeal court, as and when suitable cases come before it. There remain too many areas of uncertainty: Is blasphemy still a crime?[111] Does child abduction require conduct to be committed against the child's will? Is robbery an appropriate charge where the accused has threatened something other than immediate personal violence? Is it aggravated theft if premises were entered via an unlocked window? What exactly is the mens rea of breach of the peace?[112] This lack of clarity is regrettable in a mature legal system, and could be said to breach the rule of law.

Judge-led law reform projects may produce recommendations more quickly than the SLC, but this may be at the expense of sufficiently detailed analysis. If this mechanism is to be employed, there is much to be said for the commissioning of a preliminary academic report which offers a detailed summary and critique of the current law, as well as drawing lessons from other jurisdictions, as was done in the Bonomy Review. However, future judge-led reviews may be unnecessary if one or more of the SLC's commissioners had an interests and expertise in criminal law and procedure. A suitable person should now be appointed, even if only on a part-time basis. Better still, the Scottish Parliament should establish a Criminal Law

[109] For a more detailed critique see PR Ferguson, 'Reforming Scottish Criminal Procedure: In Search of Process Values' (2017) 4 *Bergen Journal of Criminal Law and Criminal Justice* 167.

[110] See 'The future development of Scots criminal law', ch 22 in Ferguson and McDiarmid (n 31). See also Chalmers (n 21), 36: 'relatively absent from the development of criminal law and procedure in Scotland … is pro-active rather than reactive reform'.

[111] It was abolished for English law by the Criminal Justice and Immigration Act 2008, s 79(1).

[112] These and other uncertainties are described further in Ferguson and McDiarmid (n 31) [22.10].

Review Board, comprising representatives from the judiciary, the Crown Office and Procurator Fiscal Service, the defence bar, academia, victims' organisations, and the police.[113] The Board would be tasked with reporting to the Parliament on an annual basis, in order to develop a comprehensive criminal law, and to ensure that offence provisions accord with the principles of fair labelling. It could also recommend the repeal of redundant and overlapping offences.

In September 2015, Scottish academics who specialise in aspects of criminal law, evidence or procedure wrote to Michael Matheson, the Cabinet Secretary for Justice, expressing concern about the law's future development.[114] We noted that the reform of much of English criminal law was spearheaded for 27 years by the Criminal Law Revision Committee, a standing committee of legal experts, before being superseded by the Law Commission. We suggested that Scotland would benefit greatly from establishing a body with a similar remit, and offered to meet with Mr Matheson to discuss this proposal. In response to our letter, Mr Matheson's Private Secretary reminded us that the Scottish Government would soon begin a further criminal law reform project (a reference to the second Carloway Review, and the enactment of some of Lord Bonomy's recommendations). He conveyed Mr Matheson's regrets at being unable to meet with us and suggested that we instead meet with officials in the criminal justice division. Given this somewhat tepid response, we declined to take up this offer. It is clear, therefore, that a Criminal Law Review Board is unlikely to be established in the foreseeable future. In the meantime, those of us who signed the letter to Mr Mathieson might do well to put our energies into establishing a Scottish body, similar to the English *Criminal Law Reform Now Network*.[115]

[113] This was first suggested in PR Ferguson and C McDiarmid, *Scots Criminal Law: A Critical Analysis*, 1st edn (Edinburgh University Press, 2009), [22.7.1].

[114] I was the principal author of the letter, and its co-signatories were Derek Auchie, School of Law, University of Aberdeen; John Blackie, Professor Emeritus, School of Law, University of Strathclyde; Ilona Cairns, Lecturer, School of Law, University of Aberdeen; Liz Campbell, formerly Senior Lecturer, School of Law, University of Edinburgh (now a professor at the University of Durham); Sarah Christie, Reader in Law, Robert Gordon University; Sharon Cowan, Professor of Law, University of Edinburgh; Fraser Davidson, former Professor, Division of Law and Philosophy, University of Stirling; Antony Duff, Professor Emeritus, Division of Law and Philosophy, University of Stirling; Peter Duff, Professor of Criminal Justice, University of Aberdeen, and former member of the Scottish Criminal Cases Review Commission; Lyndsey Farmer, Professor of Law, University of Glasgow; Sir Gerald Gordon, formerly a sheriff, temporary High Court judge, and Professor of Law, University of Edinburgh; Genevieve Lennon, Lecturer, School of Law, University of Strathclyde; Gerard Maher, QC, Professor of Criminal Law, University of Edinburgh, and former member of the Scottish Law Commission; Claire McDiarmid, Reader in Law, University of Strathclyde; Donald Nicolson, OBE, Professor of Law, formerly University of Strathclyde (now at the University of Essex), and Maria O'Neill, Senior Lecturer, University of Abertay.

[115] For more information on the *Criminal Law Reform Now Network*, see JJ Childs and J Rogers, 'Criminal Law Reform Now: A New Reform Network' (2017) 81 *Journal of Criminal Law* 282, and the Network's website: www.clrnn.co.uk.

INDEX

A

abandonment *see* **wilful abandonment**
Abse, Leo 283
Adams, John Bodkin 146
Adams, R v 146
Adams (Terence George) 53–54
Adams v CPS 2, 2n, 21
adjectival law
  repeal 198
Adomako, R v 110, 113, 114, 116
adversarial system
  right of silence 265
  vulnerable witness 234–238, 247–248, 251
aid agencies
  combating corruption 1
Alldridge, Peter 98, 131
Alliston, Charlie 115n
Alverstone CJ 199
ambush defences 270, 271
Andrews v DPP 109–110, 130
Anti-Social Behaviour, Crime and Policing Act 2014 37n, 39
Anti-Social Behaviour Orders (ASBOs) 37, 37n
Argent, R v 256
arms trafficking
  Financial Reporting Orders 51n
Arnold, Thurman 86
Arthur, R 168, 169, 174
Ashworth, Andrew 101, 111, 121
Aslam, Sean 50
asset freezing 2, 13, 22
  see also proceeds of crime
Asset Recovery Incentivisation Scheme (ARIS) 30, 30n, 31–32
Asset Recovery Offices 3
Assets Recovery Agency 23, 23n
Assisted Dying Bill 2014 154
assisted voluntary dying (AVD)
  assisting journey to Dignitas 134–135, 135n, 137, 142–143, 148
  Australia 154
  autonomy, protection of 135, 136, 137n, 140–141, 141n, 143, 144, 145, 148–150, 151, 153, 160
  blanket criminalisation 140, 155
  Canada 154
  categories seeking euthanasia 136
  conscience clause 153
  continuous deep sedation 146
  CPS consultation 135, 139–141, 157
  CPS policy 133–139, 156–160
  criminal homicide 136, 144, 155, 157
  Daniel James case 134–135
  'dark figure' of illegal killing 145–147, 150–151, 153
  De Minimis principle 158–159, 160, 162
  disability-rights groups 151
  double effect doctrine 146–147, 148, 151
  DPP guidelines 134–136, 136n, 141–142, 156–160, 162
  effectiveness of policy 133, 145–147
  efficiency and economy of policy 133, 145–147
  euthanasia 134, 136–139, 143–144, 145–146, 153
  family or friends, assistance from 141, 145, 151, 156, 158
  freedom-based policy 133, 148–154
  generally 285
  human rights aspect 148, 154, 155–156, 160
  improper motive 135
  inhuman and degrading treatment 148
  justice generally 133, 142
  justice for perpetrators 143, 144, 148
  justice for victims 142–144, 148
  legality principle 160–161
  'locked-in' syndrome 137
  margin of appreciation 137
  medical endorsement 141, 148, 158
  medical euthanasia 145–147, 148, 156
  mischief addressed 159–163
  motivation of suspect 145
  necessity 137–138, 137n
  Netherlands 137n, 141, 150, 151, 152

- number of cases referred to CPS 145
- number of prosecutions 145, 148
- police investigations 145, 146
- pre-death regulation 151, 153
- professional assistance 141, 144, 145, 156, 158
- proposed public consultation 148, 153
- prospects for legislative reform 156
- providing specialist advice 142
- providing substantial assistance 143–144
- public interest/democracy 133, 139–141
- quantitative approach 140
- rationality of victim 144
- right to make an autonomous choice 135
- Scotland 155n
- self-starvation 137–138, 148, 153
- 'slippery slope' argument 144, 149, 152–153, 156
- social and palliative care 145–146, 149, 151, 154
- South Africa 154
- suicide 132, 134–136, 137–139, 142–143, 153
- suicide in an organised way 142–143
- suicide/euthanasia kits 143, 148
- suspect-oriented factors 139
- United States 154
- victim-oriented mitigating factor 139
- weighting factors 139–140

Atkin LJ 109–110, 112
attempt liability *see* **criminal attempt**
Australia
- assisted voluntary dying 154
- Unexplained Wealth Orders 16, 17–18

autonomy, principle of
- assisted dying 135, 136, 137n, 140–141, 141n, 143, 144, 145, 148–150, 151, 153, 160
- civil preventive orders 73–74

Averill v UK 256

B

Bagnall (Darren John) and another 56
Barker, R v 236, 237
Batchelor (Andrew John) 44
Bateman, R v 110
Baybasin and others 53, 55–56
Beijing Rules on Juvenile Justice 175, 177
Bingham LCJ 131, 255, 256
Bingham LJ 194, 217
Birmingham Six 284
blackmail
- Financial Reporting Orders 51n

Bolger, Peter 15n
Bonomy Review 299, 303–304, 305
Boyes, R v 210
Bradbury, Malcolm 283
bribery 11
- preparatory offences 96

Bribery Bill 2009 286
Bridges, Andrew 47
Brooks (John Alan) 46, 57
Bulger, James 166, 166–167n, 175
Bullock, K and Lister, S 26
burden of proof
- right of silence and 253

Burke, Ray 15n

C

Cadder v HM Advocate 295–296, 302, 304
Camden Asset Recovery Inter-Agency Network (CARIN) 3, 3n
Cameron, R v 265–266
Canada
- assisted voluntary dying 154
- Law Reform Commission of 285
- proceeds of crime 17

capacity
- manslaughter 108, 122

Cape, E 260–261
Carlile Report 169n
Carloway LJ 299, 302–303
Carloway Review 299, 302–303, 304, 305
Chalk, Alex 125–126
Chandra Dharma, R v 199, 200
Chandu Nagrecha, R v 240
child
- adolescents 187, 189–190
- age of consent 159, 177
- age of criminal responsibility 165, 166–168, 177–179, 184–192
- Beijing Rules on Juvenile Justice 175, 177
- causing or allowing death of 102
- Centre for Social Justice Report 173, 178
- criminal justice system generally 165–166
- cross-examination 234, 303
- Crown Courts 169, 169n, 181
- culpability 187–188
- current law 167–171
- developmental immaturity 178–179, 185
- developmental research 172, 173–174
- *doli incapax* presumption 165, 167–168, 171, 177–178

fair trial, right to 262–263
fitness to plead 166, 168–170, 179–180, 183, 192
ground rules hearing 235
international law 165, 174–176
legal aid cuts 169
leniency, principle of 184–185
local authority statutory duties 165
number in youth justice system 180–181
politically subordinate role 185–186, 187, 189–190
proposed no developmental immaturity defence 166, 167, 170–171, 186–187
reforming the criminal justice system 166, 177–183, 184–192
responsibility and agency 172–173
right to be heard in judicial proceedings 175
special status 165–167
UN Convention on the Rights of the Child 165, 174–175
Unfitness to Plead report 177
Youth Courts 168–169, 179–180, 179n, 181, 182, 183
youth offender institutions 166
Children Act 1989 169
Children and Young Persons Act 1933 167, 180
Children and Young Persons Act 1963 167, 167n
Children and Young Persons Act 1969 167n
Church, R v 108
civil preventive orders (CPOs)
see also individual orders
autonomy, principle of 73–74
duration 61–62, 67
efficacy 38
formal legal warnings 38
inconsistencies between 38–39
justification 38
legitimacy 38
necessity 56, 63, 64, 67, 68–69
negative obligations 62, 67–68
piecemeal development 67–68, 74
positive obligations 62, 67–68
prevention as aim 41, 70
proportionality 56, 64–65, 67, 68–70
proposed consolidating legislation 64–66, 67–69, 74
proposed reforms 37–39, 61–74
targeting criminal record holders 37–38, 68, 70–74
three-stage process 38
transfer of Parliamentary authority 38
Clare, ICH, *et al* 262
Clarke, Charles 47–48
Clarkson, CMV 77n, 107
Clegg, Private Lee 131
Clyde LJ 216–217, 220
coercive state institutions in liberal democracies 70–73
Coggan, J 150
Colombia
Unexplained Wealth Orders 17
common law
criminal law reform and 286–288, 290
incremental extension of criminal law 279, 289–290
right of silence 255, 267–268, 269, 275
Scotland 293
confiscation regime
see also proceeds of crime
allocation of confiscated funds 29–32
enforcement costs 1, 6, 7, 12, 21
incentivisation schemes 6, 11, 12–18, 27, 30–32
Law Commission review 27
piecemeal legislation 26–27, 33
proposed codification 1, 6, 12, 20–24, 27, 33–35
proposed specialist courts 6–7, 22, 27, 28–29
Working Group on Confiscation report 26
consolidating Bills 281
conspiracy
criminal attempt 77
Serious Crime Prevention Orders 43
Cook, Vanessa 138
Coroners and Justice Act 2009 101, 125, 126
Corporate Manslaughter and Corporate Homicide Act 2007 115, 117–118, 123
corruption
see also proceeds of crime
aid agencies 1–2
data protection legislation 14
Irish legislation 14–16, 15n
non-conviction based asset forfeiture 18
UNCAC 17
Unexplained Wealth Orders 16–18
Worldwide Freezing Orders 4
Corruption Bill 2003 286

Cottrell, R v 221
counterfeiting
Financial Reporting Orders 51n
courts
enforcement costs 1
proceeds of crime and courts system 6, 7, 10, 22, 27, 28–29
proposed specialist confiscation courts 6–7, 22, 27, 28–29
CR v UK 284n
Crime and Courts Act 2013 27, 128
criminal attempt
actus reus 92–93, 95
awareness 80
bespoke offences, creating 75, 83–88, 91, 92–95, 97, 99
clarity of prohibition 78–79, 78n, 83, 84, 86–88
conduct element 75, 76–77, 77n, 78, 81–82
consistency in application 94–95
conspiracy 77, 85
Conspiracy and Attempts 75, 75n, 76–77, 76n, 79–80, 88, 88n, 92
Consultation Paper, Conspiracy and Attempts 75n, 76–77, 76n, 77n, 87n, 92, 98
consummated offence and 78, 78n
definition 78–79
drug-related offences 79
factual element 81–82
fair labelling 78–79, 78n, 86–88
inchoate offences 81, 81n, 87, 93, 96–97
intent 76n, 80–82, 86
knowledge 76n, 80, 81–82
LC 143 75n
LC 177 75n
liability generally 76, 80–82
lower boundary of liability 75, 77–80, 81n, 83–84, 86–87
meaning of attempt 94
mens rea 75, 75n, 76–77, 76n, 80–82, 82–83n, 83, 92–95, 97
murder 77
murder by way of omission 79
negligence 80
offences covered 77–80
overcriminalisation 96, 98
physical element 75, 83
possession offences 85, 85n, 96
preparatory acts 75, 75n, 76–77, 77n, 78, 80n, 85, 85n, 86, 90, 92, 93, 98
preparatory acts, bespoke offences 95, 96–98, 99
previous attempts at reform 75, 75n, 76–77
recklessness 76n, 80, 81–82
severity of attempted crime 79–80, 79n
summary offences 85
terrorist activity 79
ulterior intent 86–87, 87n
ulterior mens rea 97
wilful abandonment defence 75–76, 88–90, 91, 93
Criminal Attempts Act 1981 75n, 76
Criminal Behaviour Orders (CBOs) 37, 37n, 61, 62
criminal and civil law, separation 38
Criminal Evidence Act 1898 268
Criminal Finances Act 2017 22, 24, 27, 33
Criminal Justice Act 1991 167n
Criminal Justice Act 1993 6
Criminal Justice Act 2003 105, 290–291
Criminal Justice and Immigration Act 2008 47, 128
Criminal Justice (International Co-operation) Act 1991 26
Criminal Justice and Police Act 2001 57
Criminal Justice and Public Order Act 1994
right of silence 253, 255–258, 264, 267, 270
Criminal Justice (Scotland) Act 2016 300
criminal law reform
case studies 283–284
codification 287, 296, 301–302
common law offences 286–288, 290
consolidating Bills 281
consultees 287
decriminalisation 279, 290–291
Draft Bill procedure 286
empirical evidence 286
extensions of criminal law 288–290
incremental extension 279, 289–290, 291
interaction with existing law 286–287
Law Commission Bills 286
Law Commission reports 282–285
lawyers' law 279–291
legal complexity 285–286
obsolete legislation 290
Parliamentary procedure 286
political considerations 285, 290–291
reform bodies 279–291
Scotland 293–305
statutory definitions 287, 293–294
time and historical specificity 285

Criminal Law Revision Committee (CLRC) 216, 267, 281, 282, 285, 305
Second Report: Suicide 283
Eleventh Report: Evidence 284
Fourteenth Report: Offences Against the Person 285
Fifteenth Report: Sexual Offences 284
Criminal Procedure Rules 2005 265
Criminal Procedure (Scotland) Act 1995 300
criminal responsibility, age of
Beijing Rules on Juvenile Justice 175, 177
Belgium 176
Centre for Social Justice Report 173, 178
children's politically subordinate role 185–186, 187, 189–190
cognitive element of responsibility 172
current law 167–171
developmental immaturity 178–179, 185
developmental immaturity defence 166, 167, 170–171, 186–187
developmental research 172, 173–174
doli incapax 165, 167–168, 171, 177–178
fitness to plead 166, 168–170, 179–180, 183, 192
generally 165, 166–168, 184–192
Germany 176
Ireland 175
Irish Republic 175
leniency, principle of 184–185
murder 166, 166–167n, 170–171, 175, 178, 187
Netherlands 176
Northern Ireland 175, 178
proposed reforms 177–183
responsibility and agency 172–173
Scotland 175, 176, 178, 179
Sweden 176
Unfitness to Plead report 177
volitional element of responsibility 172
Crook, Frances 49
Crown Prosecution Service
assisted voluntary dying 133–139
intimidated witnesses 232
pre-trial witness interviews 231, 244
special measures 231, 232, 233
victims of most serious crime 232
vulnerable witnesses 232, 233
culpability
wrongdoing distinguished 187–188
Cuthbertson, R v 25
cyber crime
money laundering offences 23
Serious Crime Prevention Orders 43

D
Dangerous Dogs Act 1991 131
data protection legislation 14
Davies (Jonathan Robert) 55
Davis, Hugh, QC
Civil Preventive Orders: Sexual Offences Act 2003 40
***De Minimis* principle**
assisted dying 158–159, 160, 162
democracy
coercive state institutions within 70–73
criminal liability and 188–190, 192
Dennis, Ian 22–23
deterrence
asset freezing or confiscation 1, 3, 5
causing death by dangerous driving 103–104
Dholakia, Lord 168, 172, 175, 178, 182
diminished responsibility
defendant pleading 262
fitness to plead 171
homicide 101, 125, 171, 178
manslaughter 139n
Diplock LJ 25, 166, 171, 280n
director, persistent insolvency 19–20
Dobby, R v 116n, 118n
***doli incapax*, presumption of** 165
abolition 167–168, 171, 177–178
Domestic Violence, Crime and Victims Act 2004 37n
domestic violence and abuse
controlling or coercive behaviour 223n, 226–227, 228n, 239–240
conviction rate 226, 226n
court process 225
courtroom participation 223–251
cross-examinations 234–238, 247–248, 251
defendant's fair trial rights 235–236, 238
definition 223n
dissociation as automatic defence mechanism 229–230, 231
evidence-gathering 225, 226–227, 228–230
expert testimony 238, 239–241
ground rules hearing 235, 236, 237, 247–248
human rights obligations 224, 224n, 234, 236

intimidated witnesses 232, 234–235, 244, 247
jury information regarding trauma 238–241, 248–251
non-physical 226–228, 242, 243
obstacles in prosecuting 225, 226–230
pre-trial witness interviews 231–232, 235–236, 244
proposed reforms 230–242
protection of victims 226
reasons for non-reporting 226
special measures, review and extension 232–234, 244–247
supporting victims 223
trauma affecting memory 228–230, 231, 234–235
traumatised victims 223–251
victim credibility 227–230, 231, 234–235, 238–241, 242, 243, 244
victim remaining in relationship 227
vulnerable defendants 263
vulnerable witnesses 231–234, 237, 243–247

Doody, R v 249

double effect doctrine
medical euthanasia 146–147, 148, 151

double jeopardy rule
attenuation 289, 299

Downes, Edward 152

downward policy transmission
proceeds of crime 10

DPP v Newbury 111–112

Draft Bill procedure 286

driving, causing death by
constructive manslaughter 109–110, 130
dangerous driving 103–104, 113, 116–123, 120n, 130
dangerous driving, meaning 117
drunk driving 112–113, 119, 122
gross negligence manslaughter 116n
intended to cause injury 130
intentional violation of Highway Code 120–121, 123, 130
intentionally killing 130
manslaughter 108, 109–113, 115–123, 115n, 130–132
maximum sentence 118, 118n
mobile phone used whilst driving 120n
murder 130
negligence 110, 122, 130
proposed reforms 116–117, 130–132
recklessness 130
retributive punishment 116
Sentencing Guidelines 118n
unlawful act manslaughter 116n, 130
whilst disqualified 112–113, 119n
whilst uninsured and unlicensed 112–113, 119n

Drug Trafficking Offences Act 1986 26

Drug Travel Restriction Orders (TROs) 39, 42, 57–58, 63, 67
duration 57–58, 61, 67
frequency of use 58
proposed reforms 61–74
purpose 57
reoffending, risk assessment 58
SCPO imposed alongside 57

drug-related offences
causing death while over drive limit 112–113
criminal attempt 79
Financial Reporting Orders 51–52n, 52
preparatory offences 96
Serious Crime Prevention Orders 43, 44, 46–47
Ten-Year Strategy for Tackling Drugs Misuse 57

Drury v HM Advocate 294–295

Duff, Antony 84, 87, 107

Dunlop, Frank 16

Durston, G 241

duty of care
corporate manslaughter 117
manslaughter 114–115, 119, 122–123

E

Easton, S 258

Elliott, Catherine 178

Ellison, L and Munro, V 225, 238, 241

endangerment
preparatory offences 96

environmental crime
financial investigation 7–8, 13–14

Eremia v Moldova 224n

European Convention on Human Rights
assisted dying 148, 154, 155–156, 160
fair trial 168, 235–236, 235n, 259, 262–263, 271, 296
psychological integrity, protection 224, 224n, 234
right to legal representation 259
SOA 1956 time limit for prosecutions 200–205, 217

European Union
Charter of Fundamental Rights 254
proceeds of crime measures 12, 23
right of silence 254, 276
euthanasia *see* **assisted voluntary dying**
exchange abolitionism 264

F
fair trial, right to
children 262–263
ECHR 168, 235–236, 235n, 259, 262–263, 271, 296
right of silence 271–272
false accounting
Financial Reporting Orders 51n
Faulks, Lord 182
Fazekas, M and Nanopoulos, E 12
Field, Frank 59
FIFA case 11
Financial Reporting Orders (FROs) 39, 51–57, 63, 67
abolition 53
aim 51
appeals 53–57
breach 52
duration 51–52, 67
frequency of use 52
necessity 54, 56
obligations under 52
proportionality 54, 56
proposed reforms 61–74
trigger offences 51, 51–52n
fitness to plead
children 166, 168–170, 179–180, 183, 192
Crown Court test 169
diminished responsibility 171
effective participation 170, 180
learning difficulties 170–171
legal aid cuts 169
Youth Courts 166, 168–170, 179–180, 183
Football Banning Orders 61
Forced Marriage (Civil Protection) Act 2007 37n
Forced Marriage Protection Orders 37n
Ford, David 175
France
proceeds of crime 17, 30–31
fraud
ancillary professionals 19
burden of proof test 13
Financial Reporting Orders 51–52n, 52
motivation for 4
preparatory offences 96
problems with system 6
proceeds of crime *see* proceeds of crime
Serious Crime Prevention Orders 43, 44–46, 47
Solicitors Disciplinary Tribunals 19
Fraud Act 2006 19, 288
free speech protections
age of criminal responsibility and 189–192
freedom model
assisted voluntary dying 133, 148–154
fruit of the poisoned tree doctrine 15

G
Gang-Related Violence Injunctions 37n
Gangmasters and Labour Abuse Authority 59
Gardiner LC 280
gemeinschaft **ideal** 103, 104, 117
George, K 149
gesellschaft **concept** 103, 117
Gilderdale, Kay 152
Gilligan, John 15n
Glazebrook, Peter 86, 87, 93
Gledhill, R v 263
GMC v Bawa-Garba 132
Grayling, Chris 128
Greasley, K 150, 151, 152, 154
grievous bodily harm
intention to cause 104, 125–126
ground rules hearing
vulnerable witnesses 235, 236, 237, 247–248
Guerin, Veronica 15n

H
Hale LJ 196, 216, 217, 219, 222, 263
Hanson, Damien 47
Haq (Mohammad Izhar-Ul) 47
Hart, HLA 172
hearsay, reform of rules 286–287
Heayns (Christopher Francis) 44–46
Henderson, E 236, 237
Herring, J 137–138, 149
HM Advocate v Watt 294, 297, 304
Hobbes, Thomas 71
Hollingsworth, K 172–173
Holmes, Oliver Wendell 79
homicide
see also manslaughter
advertent lethal risks 106

age of criminal responsibility 166, 166–167n, 170–171, 175, 178, 187
assisted dying *see* assisted voluntary dying
assisted suicide *see* assisted voluntary dying
attempted, by way of omission 79
attempted murder 77
attempts at reform 285
causing or allowing death of child or vulnerable adult 102
causing death by driving 103–104, 108, 109–113, 116
constructive 102
corporate manslaughter 102, 104, 117–118, 123
correspondence principle 104, 105, 106, 107–108, 113
deterrence 103–104
diminished responsibility 101, 125, 171
double effect doctrine, medical euthanasia 146–147, 148, 151
double jeopardy rule 289, 299
fault element 104
foreseen risk of death 105–106, 108, 122
intention to cause grievous bodily harm 104, 122, 125–127, 130
intention to kill 104, 105, 122, 126–127, 130, 132
joint enterprise 129
loss of control 101, 170–171, 178
malice aforethought 104
mandatory life sentence 105, 132
mens rea 104, 105–106, 295–296
murder 104–106
Murder, Manslaughter and Infanticide 101, 105, 125
need for law reform 101
new constructive offences 102
partial defences 101, 124–125, 170–171
Partial Defences to Murder 101, 124–125
political will for reform 102
proposed codification 102–116, 127–129
proposed degrees of murder 105, 122, 129–132
provocation 101, 125, 126, 294–295, 302
recklessness 105, 108
regulatory domain offences 116–123
retributive punishment 103–104, 116
risk of causing death 104, 105, 107, 122
technological change and 131
Horder, Jeremy 86, 87, 102, 129
accounts of law-making 103, 104, 127
Homicide and the Politics of Reform 127–128
on manslaughter 106–107, 108, 112–113, 116–117, 119n, 120–121
Howard, Michael 284
Howard League for Penal Reform 49
Howe (Kevin), R v 142
Howell, R v 265
human rights
assisted voluntary dying 148, 154, 155–156, 160
children in criminal justice system 165, 170, 174
domestic abuse victims 224, 224n, 234, 236
right to legal representation 259
SOA 1956 time limit for prosecutions 200–205, 210, 212, 217
Unexplained Wealth Orders 16
Human Rights Act 1998
assisted dying 155–156
discrimination by public body 264
magistrates 258
sexual offences 202, 204, 205
Human Trafficking and Exploitation Act (Northern Ireland) 2015 60
Human Trafficking and Exploitation (Scotland) Act 2015 60
Hume, David
Commentaries on the Law of Scotland... 293–294
Hungary
allocation of confiscated funds 31
Huxtable, R 146

I

immigration offences
Financial Reporting Orders 52
Serious Crime Prevention Orders 43
innocence, presumption of 253, 257, 265, 268, 269, 270, 275, 276
insolvency, persistent 19–20
intellectual property offences
Financial Reporting Orders 51n
intention
criminal attempt 76n, 80–82, 86
manslaughter 107, 111, 112, 120, 126–127, 129, 130, 132
mens rea 80–82
murder 105, 126–127, 130, 132
ulterior 86–87, 87n
International Covenant on Civil and Political Rights (ICCPR) 268–269
Interpretation Act 1978 198, 199–200

Irish Republic
age of criminal responsibility 175
allocation of confiscated funds 31
Criminal Assets Bureau (CAB) 15–16, 15n, 31
fruit of the poisoned tree doctrine 15
Proceeds of Crime (Amendment) Act 2005 14–16
Unexplained Wealth Orders 17
Istanbul Convention 228
Italy
resistance to UWOs 17

J
J*, *R v 194, 195, 197, 204, 208, 209, 210–211, 216–217, 219–220, 221
Jackson, Isabella 43
James, Daniel 134–135, 152
Jogee*, *R v 129, 132
joint enterprise, homicide 129
Judge LJ 114
jury
disabled defendants 259
information regarding trauma 238–241, 248–251
judicial directions, comprehension 258–259
right of silence, judicial guidance 256, 258, 260, 267–268, 275–277
Justice Act (Northern Ireland) 2015 49
juvenile court, establishment 165–166

K
Kamenka, E and Tay, A 103
Kant, Immanuel 71
Keating, H and Bridgeman, J 138
Keating, Michael 15n
Keown, J 150
kleptocracy
asset freezing or confiscation 4, 11
non-conviction based asset forfeiture 18
Kruisbergen, E, et al 9–10

L
Laird, K 27
Law Commission 279, 281, 282–283, 285, 286, 288, 291
Attempt and Impossibility in Relation to Attempt, Conspiracy and Incitement (Law Com No 102, 1980) 75, 282
Bills 286
Codification of the Criminal Law (Law Com No 143, 1985) 75, 281, 283
Conspiracy and Attempts (Law Com No 183, 2007) 76, 76n, 79–80, 88, 88n, 92
Conspiracy and Attempts (Law Com No 318, 2009) 75, 75n, 77, 79–80, 88, 88n, 92
Criminal Law: A Criminal Code (Law Com No 177, 1989) 75, 282, 283
extension of the law 288–290
Murder, Manslaughter and Infanticide (Law Com No 304, 2006) 101, 105, 125
Partial Defences to Murder (CP No 290, 2004) 101, 124–125
Rape Within Marriage 284
Scottish 300–302
Unfitness to Plead (Law Com No 364, 2016) 168, 177, 177n
law-making
bureaucratic-administrative model 103–104, 112, 117, 127
deterrence as aim 103–104
lawyers' law 279–291
reform as political process 1
retribution as aim 103–104
traditional-codificatory model 103–104, 121, 127
Law Reform Commission of Canada 285
Lawrence, Stephen 289
Lawrence (Stephen)*, *R v 114
Lawson, Sarah 138
lawyers' law 279–291
legal advice
at police station 253, 254, 259–261
ECHR right to 259
legal aid cuts 169, 221
unrepresented defendants 254, 257
legality principle
assisted dying 160–161
Leigh, LH 266
Leng, R 259
Leveson, Sir Brian 128
liability 188–190
Liberty 48
Lloyd LJ 288
Lloyd of Hampstead, Lord 279–280
Locke, John 71
Loder, Cari 143
Loreburn LC 280
loss of control defence
homicide 101, 170–171, 178
Lubemba (Cokesix)*, *R v 235, 236
Lund, Frank 138–139

M
McDiarmid, Claire 178–179
McDonald, Ken, QC 239
McDonald, Mark 176
McIntyre (Andrew James) 46–47
Mackay LJ 114, 115, 294–295
MacPherson Enquiry and Report 289
magistrate
as lay decision maker 254, 258–259
Magnusson, R 146–147
Malaysian 1MDB case 11
malice aforethought
murder 104
manslaughter
attack on physical integrity 107, 108
capacity and 108, 122
constructive 107, 107n, 109–110, 112, 130
corporate 102, 104, 117–118, 123
correspondence principle 104, 106, 107–108, 113
diminished responsibility 139n
drink/drug driving 112–113, 119, 122
duty of care 114–115, 115n, 117, 119, 122–123
endangerment 107
foreseeable risk of death 107–108, 111–112, 114–115, 122, 123
intention 107, 111, 112, 120, 122, 126–127, 129, 130, 132
involuntary 106
joint enterprise 129
Law Commission review 101
medical 115, 132
negligence 110, 111–112, 113–116, 116n, 122, 130, 132
omission, liability through 115n
one punch 106
proposed codification 115, 122–123, 127–128, 131
recklessness 108, 130
regulatory domain offences 116–123
regulatory offences and 109–113
retributive punishment 116
Sentencing Guidelines 105n, 118n
unlawful act 106–113, 115n, 116n, 130
vehicular 108, 108n, 109–113, 115–123, 115n, 127–128, 130–132
voluntary 106
Mareva injunction 4
Martin, Howard 146, 147
Mason, J and Laurie, T 146
Matheson, Michael 305
MC v Bulgaria 200–201, 202
medical practitioner
double effect doctrine 146–147, 148, 151
euthanasia and 141, 145–147, 148, 156, 158
manslaughter by 132
Meeking, R v 110–111
mens rea
awareness 80
criminal attempt 75, 75n, 76–77, 76n, 80–82, 82–83n, 92–95, 97
homicide 104, 105–106, 295–296
inchoate offences 81, 81n, 93
intent 80–82
knowledge 76n, 80, 81–82
negligence 80
recklessness 80, 81–82
ulterior 97
Mental Health Act 1983 262
post-traumatic stress disorder 232
Miah, Mohammed 130
Misra, R v 114
Misuse of Drugs Act 1971
forfeiture orders 25
Mitchell, Barry 101, 106, 119, 129
M (John), R v 169
Modern Slavery Act 2015 37n, 59
Modern Slavery Strategy 59
Monckton, John 47
money laundering
ancillary professionals 18–19
asset freezing or confiscation 2, 11
cyber crime 23
environmental crimes 13–14
expansion of measures against 5
Financial Reporting Orders 51n, 52
Irish legislation 15n
Serious Crime Prevention Orders 43
Solicitors Disciplinary Tribunals 19
Montgomery, J 136
Mulindwa, R v 274
Mullen, Davison, and Bingham 56–57
murder *see* **homicide**
Murphy, Baroness 125

N
National Crime Agency (NCA) 59
Register of ancillary orders 43
negligence
dangerous driving 110, 122
manslaughter 110, 111–112, 113–116, 116n, 130, 132

Netherlands
age of criminal responsibility 176
assisted voluntary dying 137n, 141, 150, 151, 152
confiscation system 9–10
Neuberger LJ 129
***New Powers Against Organised and Financial Crime* Green Paper** 40, 42
New Zealand
proceeds of crime 17
NHS Protect
price-fixing cases 13
Nicklinson, Tony 137–138, 142, 151, 152, 153, 154
niqab, defendant's refusal to remove 264
non-conviction based asset forfeiture (NCBAF) 18
Northern Ireland
age of criminal responsibility 175, 178
Serious Crime Prevention Orders (SCPOs) 41
Sexual Offences Prevention Orders (SOPOs) 39–40
Slavery and Trafficking Prevention Orders 60
Violent Offences Prevention Orders 49–51
NXB v CPS 202–203

O
obsolete legislation 290
offence
clarity of prohibition 78–79, 78n, 83, 84, 86–88
criminal attempt *see* criminal attempt
endangerment offences 96
possession offences 85, 85n, 96
preparatory acts 75, 75n, 76–77, 77n, 78, 80n, 85, 85n, 86, 90, 92, 93, 98
preparatory acts, bespoke offences 95, 96–98, 99
offences against the person
attempted reform of law 285
Offences Against the Person Act 1861 111–112
***One Step Ahead* White Paper** 51
Orentlichter, D 147
organised crime
Financial Reporting Orders 39, 51–57
One Step Ahead White Paper 51
scope 7
Serious Crime Prevention Orders 37n, 39, 40–47
Ormerod, David, QC 102
Osborn-Brooks, Richard 128
out-of court disposals 133
Owen, Tim, QC 28
Oxford, child sexual exploitation 218

P
parsimony, principle of 84
people trafficking
Financial Reporting Orders 51n
Gangmasters and Labour Abuse Authority 59
Modern Slavery Strategy 59
Serious Crime Prevention Orders 43
Slavery and Trafficking Prevention Orders 39, 41–42, 59–61
Slavery and Trafficking Risk Orders 37, 37n
Trafficking and Exploitation Prevention Orders 39, 41–42
Pettitt v Pettitt 280n
Petto v HM Advocate 295
Phillips, PC Dave 130
pimping
Financial Reporting Orders 51n
Police and Criminal Evidence Act 1984 253, 256, 264
police interview
right of silence 253, 255, 265–266, 273
right to legal advice 253, 254, 259–261
police investigation
costs 1
Policing and Crime Act 2009 37n
political process
law reform as 1
positive obligations doctrine 201–202
Potter LJ 218
Pound, Roscoe 280
pre-trial disclosure
Scotland 299
pre-trial witness interviews
domestic abuse cases 231–232, 235–236, 244
objections to 232
post-traumatic symptoms and 231–232
preparatory acts
bespoke preparatory offences 95, 96–98, 99
criminal attempt 75, 75n, 76–77, 77n, 78, 80n, 85, 85n, 86, 90, 92, 93, 98
Pretty, Diane 155n
Pritchard, R v 169
Proceeds of Crime: Fifth Report of session 3, 3n

proceeds of crime
allocation of confiscated funds 29–32
ancillary professionals 18–19
assessing realisable assets 7
asset recovery 1, 5
Asset Recovery Incentivisation Scheme (ARIS) 30, 30n, 31–32
assets discovered post-confiscation order 6
burden of proof tests 13
business targets 12–18
cash 5
civil recovery mechanisms 22, 23–24
complexity of legislation 21, 25–27, 28–29
confiscation 1–27
'confiscation problem' 26–27
core nominals 18
courts system and 6, 7, 10, 22, 27, 28–29
cyber crime 23
default sentences 21
downward policy transmission 10
drug trafficking offences 26
enforcement costs 6, 7, 12, 21
enforcement process 21
enforcement targets 18–20
environmental crimes 7–8, 13–14
EU measures 12, 23
Financial Reporting Orders 52n
forfeiture 1, 25
hidden assets 9
hired assets 2
hypothetical proceeds 10–11
ignoring expenditures and losses 10
incentivisation schemes 6, 11, 12–18, 27, 30–32
interest payments 21–22
international cases 3
investigation efficiency 22–23
Irish legislation 14–16, 15n
kleptocracies 4, 11, 14
living expenses, permitted expenditure 13
Mareva injunctions 4
mental attitude of investigators 10
money laundering 2, 11
Netherlands confiscation system 9–10
no apparent assets, where 5–6
overseas assets 3, 4, 6, 9–10, 11, 13, 18–19
overseas residents 4
past entertainment expenditures 5–6
percentage of confiscation orders collected 21
percentage rise in confiscation 5
persistent insolvents 19–20
piecemeal legislation 26–27, 33
post-conviction orders 4–5
pre-conviction asset restraint 5
price-fixing, NHS cases 13
private sector role in enforcement 12–18
problems with system 6–7, 21
proposed code for confiscation 1, 6, 12, 20–24, 27, 33–35
proposed specialist courts 6–7, 22, 27, 28–29
purpose of regime 21
Recovering the Proceeds of Crime (2000) 26
repeat trading standards complainees 19–20
Restraint Orders 22
sanctions for non-co-operation 6
scope of organised crime 7
Solicitors Disciplinary Tribunals 19
spending behaviour of criminals 4–5, 6, 9, 10
stage at which seized 4–5, 7
sufficient cause of action 13
system inefficiency and ineffectiveness 6–7
terrorism 2
transnational organised criminals 2
under-performance of measures 2, 3–8, 35
Unexplained Wealth Orders 16–18
US confiscation system 8–9, 11–12, 30–31
Worldwide Freezing Orders 4
Proceeds of Crime Act 1995 26
Proceeds of Crime Act 2002 20, 26–27
complexity 21
reform 27–28, 33–35
Proceeds of Crime Inquiry 2016 28
Proceeds of Crime (Scotland) Act 2002 8
Protection of Freedoms Act 2012 131
Protection from Harassment Act 1997 37n
Restraining Orders 37, 37n
provocation defence
homicide 101, 125, 126, 294–295, 302
replaced by loss of control 101
Psychiatric Morbidity of Offenders Study 261
punishment in liberal democracies 70–73
Purdy, Debbie 134–136, 154, 155n, 156

R
R (Collins) v The Secretary of State for Justice 128
R (Nicklinson) v Ministry of Justice 137–138, 142, 151, 152, 153, 154
R (Pretty) v DPP 155n

R (Purdy) v DPP 134–136, 154, 155n, 156
Randall, Harry 280
Rap, S 174
rape
see also sexual offences
law reform in Scotland 294, 297, 297n, 299
marital rape exception 283, 284, 285–286, 287
Rawls, John 71
Re A (Children) (Conjoined Twins: Surgical Separation) 137
Rebalancing the criminal justice system... 48
Redmayne, M 272
reform *see* **criminal law reform**
Reid LJ 280, 280n
Reid, John 48
Restraining Orders 37, 37n
retribution, public interest in securing 103–104, 116
right of silence
adverse inferences from silence 254, 255–257, 258, 259–264, 267–268, 271, 273–277
ambush defences 270, 271
Appeal Court 264–265, 267
comment on silence permitted 255
common law 255, 267–268, 269, 275
curtailment 253–254, 269, 283, 284
EU directives 254, 276
evidential value of silence 271–272
exchange abolitionism 264
impact of curtailment 270–272
international standards 254, 268–269, 276
judicial extension of CJPOA 254, 255–258
judicial guidance 256, 258, 260, 267–268, 275–277
lay decision makers 254, 258–259
magistrates 258–259
mental ability of suspects 261–263, 2745
normative expectation of cooperation 255, 272, 275
potentially discriminatory impact 254–255, 261–264, 269, 273
presumption of innocence 253, 257, 265, 268, 269, 270, 275, 276
purpose of curtailment 253, 256–257, 258, 264, 270, 273, 277
reinstatement, options for 267–269, 275–277
reinstatement, proposed 253–278
remaining silent on legal advice 259–260
right to legal advice 254, 259–261, 273
statutory exceptions 267
trial culture 164–166, 255
unrepresented defendants 254, 257
vulnerable defendants 257, 261–263, 273–274
Risk of Sexual Harm Orders 37, 37n
Road Traffic Act 1930 109
Road Traffic Act 1934 109
Road Traffic Act 1956 110
Road Traffic Act 1988 103, 110, 111, 112, 113, 117, 119, 121
Road Traffic Act 1991 110
Rodger LJ 195, 217
Rodway v The Queen 199
Rogers, Jonathan 77n
rogue states
asset freezing or confiscation 2
Rose, R v 113–115
Rose LJ 240
Ross v Lord Advocate 155n
Rotherham, child sexual exploitation 206, 218
Rousseau, Jean-Jacques 71
Royal Commissions 281–282, 284, 286
Rudling, R v 113–114

S
St John-Stevas, Norman 283
Salduz v Turkey 296
Samuels, Alex 300
Savile, Jimmy 220
Sayre, Francis 79
SC v UK 170, 179–180
Scofield, R v 83
Scotland
age of criminal responsibility 175, 176, 178, 179
assisted suicide 155n
Bonomy Review 299, 303–304, 305
Carloway Review 299, 302–303, 304, 305
Cashback for Communities 31
codification of criminal law 296, 301–302
common law 293
confessions 295–296
criminal law reform 293–305
cross-examination of children 303
Draft Criminal Code... 301
Evidence and Procedure Review 303–304
institutional writings 293–294
judge-led reviews 302–304
pre-trial disclosure 299

Proceeds of Crime (Scotland) Act 2002 8
rape, reform of law 294, 297, 297n, 299
Scottish Law Commission 300–302
Scottish Parliament 296–299
Serious Crime Prevention Orders (SCPOs) 41, 43
sexual offences, reform of law 294–295, 297, 302
Sexual Offences Prevention Orders (SOPOs) 39–40
special measures 299
Trafficking and Exploitation Orders (TEPOs) 60, 67
vulnerable witnesses 299, 303–304

Sellers LJ 283

Serious Crime Act 2007 27, 41, 42

Serious Crime Act 2015 20, 27, 37n, 41
ancillary professionals 19
domestic violence and abuse 223n, 226, 228n

Serious Crime Prevention Orders (SCPOs) 37n, 39, 40–47, 67
aim 41
appeals 44–47
cyber crime 43
duration 41–42, 43, 61–62, 67
enhanced 53
frequency of use 42–43
necessity 42, 69
offences for which imposed 43
organisations subject to 40, 41
other cpos imposed alongside 42, 57
penalty for breach 42
power to impose 42, 42n
proportionality 42, 44, 47, 67
proposed reforms 61–74
travel bans 40
TRO imposed alongside 57

Serious Fraud Office
allocation of confiscated funds 31

Serious Organised Crime and Police Act 2005 27, 51

Sexual Harm Prevention Orders (SHPOs) 39, 40, 41
duration 40, 61–62, 66, 67
power to impose 42
proposed reforms 61–74
SCPO imposed alongside 42
travel restrictions 40

sexual offences
accessibility problem 208
against young boys 198, 203, 218
age of consent 159, 177, 194, 195–196, 202, 215
age gap between parties 217–218
associated trauma 227–228, 227–228n, 235, 243
consent, generally 206–207, 218, 219
Criminal Injuries Compensation scheme 196n, 206, 219
cross-examination of witnesses 234–235
defendants in historical cases 215, 217, 220–222
delay in complaining 197, 207, 218
ground rules hearing 235
implicit assumptions of guilt 214–215
jury information regarding trauma 238–239, 248–249
law reform in Scotland 294–295, 297, 302
legal aid cuts 221
marital rape 283, 284, 285–286, 287
maximum penalty 197
no time bar under SOA 2003 197
positive obligations doctrine 201–202
pre-trial witness interviews 231, 244
public interest test 205, 205n
rape 203, 206–208, 209, 215, 218, 297, 297n, 299
rights of suspects and defendants 215, 219–222
sexual activity with a child 193, 197, 209
sexual exploitation of children 218
special measures under YJCEA 227–228n, 244–245
underage sexual intercourse 194–197, 194n
unfounded allegations 219, 220
victim credibility 235, 238–239

Sexual Offences Act 1956
accessibility problem 208
case for legislative reform 205–208
CPS response to time limit issue 210–212
earlier assurances of non-prosecution 206
gender-specific limitations 193, 203, 207
human rights argument against time limit 200–205, 210, 212, 217
indecent assault 194, 214
legal challenges to time limit 197–205
media interest in reform 208–212, 214
mischief addressed by time limit 217–218
number of affected cases 208–210
public interest test 205, 205n
reasons for time limit 195–197, 215–216
rights of suspects and defendants 215, 217, 219–222

statutory interpretation of time limit 197–200, 215–217
time limit for prosecutions 193–222
underage sexual intercourse 194, 194n
unlawful sexual intercourse 193, 214, 215
Victims' Right to Review 204
young man's defence 195, 217–218
Sexual Offences Act 1967 198
offences against young boys 198, 203
Sexual Offences Act 2003 39, 159, 193
SOA 1956 time limit for prosecutions 197–200
Sexual Offences Prevention Orders (SOPOs) 39–40, 41
duration 39, 61–62, 66, 67
effect 39
power to impose 42
proposed reforms 61–74
purpose 39
SCPO imposed alongside 42
Sexual Offences (Scotland) Act 2009 294
Sexual Risk Orders 37, 37n
Shipman, Harold 146
silence, right of *see* right of silence
Silverwood and Chapman, R v 198, 199
Simon, Ricky Michael 50
Singh, R v 114
Slavery and Trafficking Prevention Orders (STPOs) 39, 59–61
duration 41–42, 59, 61–62, 66, 67
frequency of use 60–61
penalty for breach 60
prohibitions 59
proposed reforms 61–74
purpose 59
Slavery and Trafficking Risk Orders 37, 37n
Smith LJ 169
Smith, John 219–220
Smith, S 144
Smith, Tony 281
Solicitors Disciplinary Tribunals 19
Soneji, R v 26–27
South Africa
proceeds of crime 17
special measures
intimidated witnesses 232, 245
proposed review and extension 232–234, 244–247
Scotland 299
sexual offences 227–228n, 244–245
Victim's Code 233
vulnerable witnesses 232, 245
Stantiford, Bradley 50
statutory definitions 287, 293–294
Steyn LJ 26–27, 166, 197, 216, 220
substantive law, repeal 198
suicide, assisted *see* assisted voluntary dying
Suicide Act 1961 137, 159n, 283
blanket criminalisation of assisted suicide 140, 155, 157

T
Tabbakh, R v 266
Tadros, V 105
tax credit fraud
Financial Reporting Orders 52n
tax evasion
Financial Reporting Orders 52n
Irish legislation 15n
Taylor LCJ 262
Taylor, Charlie 166, 169
Taylor, R 106
technological change
homicide law and 131
terrorism
asset freezing or confiscation 2
criminal attempt 79
Financial Reporting Orders 51–52n
Theft Act 1968 288
Thomas, Cheryl 258
Thomas LCJ 33, 131
Thompson, Robert 166–167n, 181
time limit for prosecution
see also Sexual Offences Act 1956
common law 215
indictable offences 203
trading standards
repeat complainees 19–20
Trafficking and Exploitation Prevention Orders (TEPOs) 39, 60, 67
duration 41–42, 61–62, 66, 67
proposed reforms 61–74
transnational organised crime
asset freezing or confiscation 2
Unexplained Wealth Orders 18
Transparency International 18
traumatised defendant 266
traumatised witnesses
domestic abuse *see* domestic violence and abuse
Mental Health Act 1983 232
sexual offences 227–228, 227–228n, 235, 243
trauma affecting memory 228–230, 231, 234–235

Turner, R v 239
Tutu, Bishop Desmond 152

U
Unexplained Wealth Orders (UWOs)
generally 16–18
interim freezing orders 16
United Nations Convention against Corruption (UNCAC) 17
United Nations Convention on the Rights of the Child (UNCRC) 165, 174–175
United States
administrative forfeiture 9n
criminal forfeiture 9n
criminal judicial forfeiture 9n
Englewood, Colorado, town statute 68
License to Steal 11
proceeds of crime confiscation 8–9, 11–12, 30–31
Racketeer Influenced and Corrupt Organizations Act (RICO) 11, 14

V
V and T v UK 170n, 181
value added tax
Financial Reporting Orders 52n
Van Duyne, PC, et al 10
Venables, Jon 166–167n, 181
venture capital firms
proceeds of crime measures 12, 14
Vere of Norbiton, Baroness 182
victim of crime
see also vulnerable witness
Justice for All 142
Right to Review, sexual offences 204
Victim's Code 233
Violent Offences Prevention Orders (VOPOs) 39, 49–51
duration 49, 61–62, 66, 67
examples 50–51
proposed reforms 61–74
qualifying offenders 49
restrictions/requirements 49
Violent Offender Orders (VOOs) 39, 47–51
aim 47–48
definition of serious violent harm 48–49
duration 49, 61–62, 66, 67
examples 49–50
necessity 48
number imposed 49
penalty for breach 49
proposed reforms 61–74
qualifying offenders 48, 49
restrictions 49
support for 49
vulnerable adult
causing or allowing death of 102
vulnerable defendant
post-traumatic stress disorder 266
right of silence and 257, 261–263, 273–274
vulnerable witness
CPS guidance 232, 233
credibility 227–230, 231, 234–235, 238–241, 242, 243, 244
cross-examination 234–238
domestic abuse victims 231–234, 237, 243–247
ground rules hearing 235, 236, 237, 247–248
jury information regarding trauma 238–241, 248–251
learning difficulties 170–171, 263
post-traumatic stress disorder 228–229, 232–233, 245–246, 249, 251
Scotland 299, 303–304
special measures under YJCEA 227–228n, 232–234, 244–247

W
Walford, B
'Homicide in Canada' 129
Waya, R v (Terry) 21
weapon
preparatory offences 96
Webb, George 138–139
Webster v Dominick 295
Wellman, Christopher Heath 71–72
Wells, C 109
White, Elliot 47
wilful abandonment
defence of 75–76, 88–90, 91, 93
preparatory acts 90
Williams, Glanville 283
Wills, R v 236
Woods, Gary 50–51
Worldwide Freezing Orders 4
Wright (Brian Brendon) 54–55
wrongdoing
culpability distinguished 187–188

X
X and Y v Netherlands 201, 224n

Y
Young, S, *et al* 261
Youth Court 181
fitness to plead 168–169, 179–180, 179n, 182, 183
Youth Justice and Criminal Evidence Act 1999
special measures 227–228n, 232–234, 244–247
vulnerable witnesses 232–234, 247–248